CLARK C. SPENCE is an Assistant
Professor of History at Pennsylvania
State University. Born in Great Falls,
Montana—located on the "Last
Frontier" of which he writes—he
studied at the University of Colo-
rado and received his Ph.D. at the
University of Minnesota.

BRITISH INVESTMENTS AND THE AMERICAN MINING FRONTIER 1860-1901

Published under the direction of the American Historical Association from the income of the Albert J. Beveridge Memorial Fund.

For their zeal and beneficence in creating this fund the Association is indebted to many citizens of Indiana who desired to honor in this way the memory of a statesman and a historian.

British Investments and the American Mining Frontier

1860-1901

BY CLARK C. SPENCE

Department of History
The Pennsylvania State University

PUBLISHED FOR THE

American Historical Association

CORNELL UNIVERSITY PRESS

ITHACA, NEW YORK

CORNELL UNIVERSITY PRESS

First published in 1958

For permission to quote sundry materials that appear in this book thanks are
due to: The Bancroft Library, University of California, for a pamphlet and
some verses about the Emma Silver Mining Company, Ltd.; Dodd, Mead &
Company, Inc., for verse from *Some Victorian Men* by Harry Furniss; *The
Economist* for the passage from its issue of June 6, 1885; McGraw-Hill Book
Company, Inc., for a passage from the *Engineering & Mining Journal;* Mining
World, Ltd., for the poem by "L. G. H." from *Mining World and Engineer-
ing Record;* and Random House, Inc., for W. S. Gilbert's lines from *Utopia,
Limited* as printed in *The Complete Plays of Gilbert and Sullivan.*

PRINTED IN THE UNITED STATES OF AMERICA BY THE
VAIL-BALLOU PRESS, INC., BINGHAMTON, NEW YORK

To ERNEST S. OSGOOD

Preface

THIS study is designed to investigate British capital investment and its impact on the "last" mining frontier of the American West between 1860 and 1901. The year 1860 provides a logical point of departure, coinciding with the opening of this particular mineral frontier in the days immediately prior to the Civil War. The area involved includes all those regions linked directly to the Rocky Mountains and in addition Nevada and Dakota on the fringe. Not being a geographical or chronological part of this broader whole, the Pacific Coast proper is not embraced, although certainly British interests in that region were not insignificant.

If the year 1860 is a sound beginning date, the death of Queen Victoria in 1901 is convenient in fixing the end of this period of financial speculation and investment so far as the British public was concerned. By that time the techniques and methods of company promotion and operation had become more restrained and more closely controlled as the heyday of uninhibited financial manipulation passed. With the twentieth century came new laws to curb statements made in prospectuses and to define more clearly the responsibilities of company officials. Underwriters assumed more of the task of distributing shares to the public, and the whole mechanism of company flotation and operation became more conservative.

Since most available source materials deal with British-registered joint-stock companies, this survey is of necessity concerned mainly with limited liability corporations, rather than with American companies with shares held in England. While some British firms undoubt-

Preface

edly have evaded the writer's detection, probably the great majority and certainly the most important have been unearthed.

In the general picture of British investment in western mining, promotional aspects are of especial importance and worth close consideration. Likewise, the problems of organization and operation loom large; consequently attention is devoted to capital structure, management, and the legal entanglements which beset most British concerns formed to operate west of the Mississippi. Treated first in broad terms, then through a single case study, these promotional and operational questions help explain why so many joint-stock enterprises came to a bad end. The relationship of the alien corporation to the federal government and its mineral land policy has also been considered. Finally, an effort has been made to ascertain the amount of capital involved and the relative degree of success or failure during the whole period.

This study has been made possible by the aid and encouragement of many people. The staffs of numerous libraries and archives have contributed much, and I am particularly grateful to Mr. John Corneby of the Companies Registration Offices, London, and to Mr. Robert E. Burke, formerly of the Bancroft Library, for making far easier the task before me. I am sincerely indebted to Mr. Robert G. Athearn, who first gave encouragement in his seminar on western history at the University of Colorado; to Mr. Ernest S. Osgood, who guided the study through as a doctoral dissertation at the University of Minnesota; and to Mr. Herbert Heaton, also of the University of Minnesota, who generously read the entire manuscript and offered many valuable and constructive criticisms.

I am deeply grateful to the Beveridge Award Committee of the American Historical Association for making publication possible. The suggestions of the Committee, under the chairmanship of Mr. Ralph Hidy, have been most helpful. Mr. John Hope Franklin, a member of the original Committee and later chairman, has done much to facilitate completion of the final draft. Financial aid has been given by the Central Fund for Research of the Pennsylvania State University. A basic debt of gratitude is owed to my wife, Mary Lee, for her heavy investment of time and enthusiasm. Responsibility for all errors is mine alone.

University Park, Pennsylvania   CLARK C. SPENCE
April 12, 1958

Contents

BRITISH INVESTMENTS AND THE AMERICAN MINING FRONTIER
1860-1901

: CHAPTER I :

The Background
of Investment

PROBABLY no American generation witnessed such a profound and far-reaching metamorphosis as did that which lived through the half-century following 1860. It survived a grave national crisis which threatened to split the Republic asunder, then plunged quickly into a new era whose keynotes were industrialism and expansion. As a predominantly rural and agrarian society gradually gave way to an urban one, it seemed as if many aspects of Hamiltonian dreams were being realized. Iron, then steel, rails tied together the four corners of the nation, linking raw materials and real or potential markets with the seats of manufacturing farther east. Those same rails slashed across the Great Plains, helped people the prairies and the mountains, and contributed to the final breaking of the red man's spirit as the American frontier movement drew to a close.

This Last Frontier, 1860–1890, was characterized by the rapid exploitation of the public domain; probably never before had such wild raids been made on the American soil and subsoil. If agriculture in this increasingly technological era required more capital, the mineral industry, by its very nature, came to demand even larger amounts.

Although the settlement of the frontier and the rise of an urban industrial society were in this instance both basically American achievements, contributions from foreign sources must not be overlooked.

1

Europe gave of her ideas, her manpower, and her capital, continuing to do so untrammeled until the outbreak of World War I. The migration of Europeans and the impact of their thought upon America have been closely studied; the capital movement to bridge the Atlantic has not been so thoroughly examined.

The total story of European investments in the United States is prodigious and wide-ranging. In varying amounts according to local and international conditions, European capital flowed into enterprises flung from Cape Cod to the Golden Gate and from Key West to Lake Superior. Investors from France, Germany, Holland, and Great Britain, all eager for profit, contributed funds to well-nigh every phase of the industrial and transportation revolution, subscribing to state and municipal bonds, supporting railroad issues, dabbling in banking, shipping, brewing, ranching, and a host of other activities.

Not the least of such investments in the period after 1860, although by no means the most successful from the European standpoint, were those in western mining. In any given period, particularly from 1860 to 1901, it was the British who dominated European investment in these mines. If we exclude California, Oregon, and Washington, leaving the mining regions commonly associated with the Last Frontier, English firms stand out prominently. To be sure, numerous examples of continental capital might be cited,[1] but they are insignificant alongside the

[1] Dutch capital dominated the Mining Company Nederland, which operated in Colorado in the 1870's, and the *Maatschappij tot Exploitatie van Zilvermijnen,* which was active in Utah in the same decade. See *Boulder County News,* May 2, 1873; Frank Fossett, *Colorado; Its Gold and Silver Mines* (New York, 1880), 262; H. W. B. Kantner, *A Hand Book on the Mines, Miners, and Minerals of Utah* (Salt Lake City, n.d.), 35, 241–242; C. Clark to registrar of companies (London, Aug. 24, 1878), Winamuck Silver Mining Co. of Utah, File No. 6744, Registrar of Companies Office, Bush House, London. (All files are hereafter cited as C.R.O. with number. Those preceded by the letter "B" are on microfilm at the Bancroft Library, University of California; those preceded by the letter "E" are in the offices of the Queen's remembrancer, Parliament Square, Edinburgh.) French capital controlled the Pandora and Oriental Mining Company (1880) in Colorado and the Société Anonyme des Mines de Lexington, which operated in both Utah and Montana. Robert A. Corregan and David F. Lingane (eds. and comps.), *Colorado Mining Directory* (Denver, 1883), 720; Kantner, *Hand Book on the Mines of Utah,* 41; *Engineering and Mining Journal* (New York), June 21, 1884, 457 (cited hereafter as *E. & M. Jour.*). Belgian capital dominated the Carr Mine and Colorado Co. in 1900, just as German did the Rocky Mountain Exploration Company, Ltd., in the same period. Summary of Capital and Shares to Dec. 19, 1900, Carr Mine and Colorado Co., C.R.O. B-66890; Summary of Capital and

2

efforts of the British, who in the forty-one years under consideration registered at least 518 joint-stock companies, including reorganizations, to exploit the mineral fields of the West, excluding the Pacific Coast.[2]

Even in the colonial period, the British had been interested in frontier mines. As early as 1770 London capitalists financed exploration of the southern shore of Lake Superior in search of copper and organized a company to distribute stock in England, although with scanty success.[3] A keen interest in the California gold boom evoked a brief flurry of London joint-stock company promotion for operation in Pacific Coast mines in the years 1850–1855.[4] Mismanagement and heavy losses, especially in the Grass Valley and Mariposa areas, soon served, however, to make foreign capitalists wary of such ventures.[5]

By the eve of the Civil War Englishmen were beginning to show a revived interest in American mining. Particularly in North Carolina were efforts made to entice British capital into the exploitation of precious metal resources.[6] The guns at Fort Sumter cut short these efforts, and domestic conflict retarded the development of investment from abroad until after Appomattox. That the American Civil War

Shares to Feb. 28, 1901, Rocky Mountain Exploration Co., C.R.O. B-52760. Even some Chinese capital was present in three firms operating in Colorado in the late 1880's and early 1890's. *Report of Annual General Meeting of Mendota Mining Company* (March 30, 1891); Report of meeting of the Sheridan Consolidated Mining and Milling Co. (Dec. 12, 1893), *Shanghai Mercury*, Dec. 13, 1893; J. A. Porter to Messrs. Drysdale, Ringer & Co. (Denver, Jan. 22, 1892). The last three items are located in the William A. Bell MSS, Colorado State Archives, Denver.

[2] Files of these companies are located at the offices of the registrar of companies, Board of Trade, London, and the Queen's remembrancer, Edinburgh. All were limited in liability, although for the sake of brevity, the term "limited" has been dropped throughout the notes of this study.

[3] Cleona Lewis and Karl T. Schlotterbeck, *America's Stake in International Investments* (Washington, 1938), 88–89.

[4] Between Oct., 1851, and Jan., 1853, thirty-two British mining concerns were formed to take up claims in the United States. A large number of these were to operate in California, and some were founded upon claims of uncertain validity transferred by John C. Frémont. Leland H. Jenks, *The Migration of British Capital to 1875* (New York, 1927), 383.

[5] Report of J. Ross Browne on the Mineral Resources of the States and Territories West of the Rocky Mountains, *Ho. Exec. Doc.* No. 202, 40 Cong., 2 Sess. (1867–1868), 20.

[6] *Mining Journal* (London), March 10, Nov. 17, 1860, 164, 782; Great Kanawha Co., *Prospectus* (1860). Unless otherwise noted, all prospectuses are located in the Reference Library, Share and Loan Department, Stock Exchange, London.

should have worked to postpone the introduction of British capital is understandable. A disruptive process, the struggle raised labor and transportation costs and generally hindered the growth of railroads into the territories. Since the territories were under federal control, neither the large British capitalist nor the petty investor felt secure in risking funds in the West so long as the outcome of the conflict remained uncertain. Some men of money still remembered the disastrous California ventures or had memories of catastrophic Mexican undertakings. Others looked askance at the depreciated greenback currency and feared to invest lest dividends be paid in that medium.[7]

At the same time there were factors in England that worked to slow down the flow of capital to all parts of the world during the middle sixties. The year 1864, says Sir John Clapham, was "a year of true cotton famine, the last year of a war of attrition in America, a year of war in Denmark, and a year of experimental and rather reckless applications of British capital overseas."[8] This combination brought a mild financial crisis in 1864. Two years later the failure of the "most trusted private firm in England," the fiscal house of Overend and Gurney, provoked a very severe panic.[9] Though both these panics were largely restricted to the British Isles and both ended rapidly, they undoubtedly helped to restrict the international capital movement from London.

The American Civil War, financial dislocations within England, and the fact that western mining in the 1860's was still mainly in the frontier stage help to explain why British investments were small during the sixties. Research unearths only sixteen joint-stock companies incorporated in London to operate in mines in the West during that decade. In contrast, the first few years of the seventies brought a veritable boom of investment in such companies. As a British traveler put it in 1871:

English capitalists have either become less circumspect and prudent, or else American owners of mining properties have grown more ingenious and plausible, for the eagerness of the former to purchase such properties is only equaled by the readiness of the latter to part with them.[10]

[7] *Mining Journal,* Jan. 14, 1865, 18.

[8] *The Bank of England* (New York, 1945), II, 259.

[9] Walter Bagehot, *Lombard Street* (14th ed.; London, 1915), 175.

[10] W. Frazer Rae, *Westward by Rail: A Journey to San Francisco and Back and a Visit to the Mormons* (2d ed.; London, 1871), xx.

4

The Background of Investment

In Great Britain at least sixty-seven companies were registered with the Board of Trade from 1870 through 1873 to carry on mining or milling in the trans-Mississippi West exclusive of the Pacific Coast. Five of them were reorganizations of earlier concerns and some of the others failed to raise adequate operating capital. Nevertheless, it is obvious that the early seventies brought a marked increase in attention from the British investor, and it is equally evident that the interest was especially concentrated on Nevada, Colorado, and Utah.

TABLE I

British Companies Incorporated to Operate
in Western Mines, 1864–1873 *

Area	1864	'65	'66	'67	'68	'69	'70	'71	'72	'73	Total
Arizona				1		1	1				3
Colorado		1					2	14	2	3	22
Idaho			1			1		2			4
Montana											0
Nevada	1	3	3	2		2	5	10	3	4	33
New Mexico											0
Utah								8	6	6	20
Wyoming							1				1
Total	1	4	4	3	0	4	9	34	11	13	83

* The writer found no companies registered in 1860–1863.

How can this upsurge of interest be explained? Was it mere coincidence that capital sought these special regions? To answer these questions it is necessary to consider conditions in the mineral industry in the West, as well as the general situation in both the United States and Great Britain.

Almost every mining frontier followed a course similar to that through which the American West was passing in the middle or late 1860's. In every new gold field, placer and gulch mining by individuals or small local combinations predominated for the first few years. Since the gold was usually found in sand or gravel on the bedrock, the comparatively simple processes of panning or sluicing could be readily and economically applied for its extraction. This surface mining soon played out, however, and as hard-rock mining below the surface was resorted to, new and expensive problems were encountered. Hoists, pumping equipment, and drilling and tunneling machinery called for a considerable capital outlay. Development or "dead work" might go on for months before the mine became a paying proposition, if ever.

Since gold in hard-rock veins was often found in combination with other metals, the relatively simple process of extraction by stamping,[11] heretofore used almost exclusively, now broke down completely. With new discoveries and the increased importance of silver during the mid-sixties, the problem of smelting and refining assumed new proportions. The stamp mill was useless for extracting silver from complex ores. Consequently the introduction of complicated concentrating and roasting processes brought incessant demands for more capital.[12]

In the early sixties eastern capitalists stepped boldly into the field. But gross inefficiency, mismanagement, overcapitalization, and excessive speculation combined to bring depression to the mining industry in many western regions and the subsequent failure of numerous eastern enterprises. One contemporary Colorado writer described this phase in the Central City region:

Over a hundred eastern companies were formed, and were instrumental in bringing to the country large sums of money, which was chiefly expended by men of no experience, in putting up ill-contrived mills, in all sorts of places, containing worthless machinery, instead of opening the mines as they should have done.[13]

Unwarranted experimentation with new expensive methods and equipment contributed to financial chaos, as "process mania" took com-

[11] In the stamping process ore was first pulverized in a stamp mill and then mixed with water, after which mercury was used to draw off the gold. Heating then drove off the more volatile mercury, leaving free gold. An estimated 50 to 60 per cent of all gold was lost through this process, however. The stamp mill, operated by steam or water power, had from 5 to 125 weights (stamps), each weighing from 600 to 900 pounds and striking downward from a camshaft arrangement as many as sixty times a minute. Ovando J. Hollister, *The Mines of Colorado* (Springfield, Mass., 1867), 338–339; G. Thomas Ingham, *Digging Gold among the Rockies* (Philadelphia, 1880), 122–123.

[12] Traveling in Colorado in June, 1866, Bayard Taylor saw many stamp mills, "all of primitive pattern, mostly idle," while their owners waited for new processes. *Colorado: A Summer Trip* (New York, 1867), 70.

[13] Ned E. Farrell, *Colorado, the Rocky Mountain Gem, as It Is in 1868* (Chicago, 1868), 18.

6

mand of many an eastern superintendent. Early in 1866 one mining expert reported to the British press that "the most ridiculous manipulations" had been tried, "with a view of stimulating amalgamation, the substances varying from coffee and urine to sulphate of copper and sodium." [14] Speaking of activities in the mining center of Empire, Colorado, the United States commissioner of mineral statistics later reported that "everything, from superheated steam to tobacco-juice, was tried on Empire ores." [15] Other contemporaries criticized such unscientific experiments [16] and referred disdainfully to technological "experts" from the East who introduced fantastic new methods at the mines. One writer commented upon the "Improved-back-action-lightning-gum-elastic-cylinder-and-Spanish-fly amalgamator," with which the "expert" could *draw* gold from a Rocky Mountain turnip." [17]

The host of spectacular failures tended to make outside capital not only shy, but decidedly cool toward western mines in the mid-sixties. They did, however, indicate that there was a very real need for capital and for reliable processes. The age of the individual entrepreneur, working with his hands on a small scale, was at an end in many of the older, established camps. Capital was now vital for continuing the mineral industries after the preliminary work had been accomplished.

With the need for capital recognized, there ensued a scramble to find it. When westerners turned to the eastern seaboard, they met with some success, but never enough. Besides, every mining man knew that New York "did not understand mining at all" and that San Francisco was "infested by a number of broken-down Washoeites and the agents of a few capitalists there to serve as middlemen." [18]

Financially the United States was still a young nation—a debtor nation with no surplus supply of capital. Her rapidly expanding economy offered opportunities more attractive and more certain than mining, and investments were channeled more and more into industry or

[14] W. T. Rickard to editor (Gold Hill, Nev., n.d.), *Mining Journal*, April 7, 1866, 210.

[15] Statistics of Mines and Mining in the States and Territories West of the Rocky Mountains, *Ho. Exec. Doc.* No. 210, 42 Cong., 3 Sess. (1872–1873), 279.

[16] See Browne, *Ho. Exec. Doc.* No. 202, 40 Cong., 2 Sess. (1867–1868), 401; Frank C. Young, *Echoes from Arcadia* (Denver, 1903), 56.

[17] *The Rocky Mountain Directory and Colorado Gazetteer, for 1871* (Denver, 1870), 245.

[18] *Mining Journal*, March 11, 1871, 210.

transportation. With a capital shortage, interest rates were much higher in America than in England and offered an extra inducement to investment from abroad. Interest rates in Idaho were represented to be from 30 to 40 per cent per annum in 1870,[19] and those in Colorado were calculated at from 2 to 3 per cent per month.[20] Contrast these figures with the 3 or 4 per cent per year paid in London.[21] Although some Americans took exception to the contention that there was not sufficient capital in the United States to develop the mines,[22] the fact remains that the scarcity of domestic capital pushed interest rates to high levels, which in turn helped draw investment from outside.

Another factor in the West contributing to increased interest from potential investors in Great Britain was the gradual increase in "civilization" as time went on. Whereas civilization had previously meant whisky to the British traveler,[23] now it came to mean the development of towns, the expansion of transportation and communication facilities, and the elimination of the Indian menace.

The completion of the first telegraph between East and West in 1861 reduced communications to a matter of minutes instead of weeks. In like fashion the successful laying of the transatlantic cable in 1867 linked England and America with a slim wire that helped materially to foster closer understanding and bring western potentialities before the public mind across the ocean.

Similarly the extension of the railroads broke down western isolation and gave encouragement to settlers and investors alike. Western promoters boosting mines abroad minimized the transportation problem, but few could deny that it existed. Colorado, "the most accessible, as it is the most prolific and abundant, gold field of the world," could be reached from England in less than three weeks, according to the London *Mining Journal* in early 1866.[24] Two years later a Nevada

[19] *Ibid.*, Dec. 17, 1870, 1057.

[20] Jesse Archibald to editor (Central City, Jan. 15, 1870), *ibid.*, Feb. 5, 1870, 113; William Cope to editor, *ibid.*, June 4, 1870), 480.

[21] Jesse Archibald to editor (Central City, Jan. 15, 1870), *ibid.*, Feb. 5, 1870, 113.

[22] "P" to editor (London, Jan. 9, 1869), *ibid.*, Feb. 13, 1869, 111.

[23] From Denver in 1866 a prominent Englishman could write: "Here we are, scalps and all. . . . Civilization means whisky! post-offices don't count." Charles Wentworth Dilke, *Greater Britain: A Record of Travel in English-speaking Countries during 1866 and 1867* (London, 1868), I, 109.

[24] Jan. 13, 1866, 19.

newspaper could point with pride to a manager who arrived in Reno to take charge of a mill owned by a British firm only twenty days and eighteen hours after leaving London.[25]

At the moment when such comments were being made, sweating, cursing Irish laborers were pushing the Union Pacific railroad across the plains to its junction with the coolie-built Central Pacific. Consequently after 1869 the gap in space and time between London and the West was even narrower. This first transcontinental railroad came within striking distance of the mineral fields in Colorado, Utah, and Nevada; other lines, such as the Kansas Pacific and the Denver Pacific into Denver, or the Virginia and Truckee in Nevada, brought these regions into sharper focus abroad. Since smelters were lacking in the early West, any improvement in freight facilities and any reduction in rates meant that ores which were not among the very richest could be hauled with profit from the mining camps to smelters in the eastern United States or in Europe.

It is noticeable that the surge in British capital investment in the seventies came in those mining regions served by rails. In Idaho, Montana, Arizona, and New Mexico, where travel still went over long laborious routes for almost another decade, English investors displayed but slight interest. These four territories accounted for only seven of the eighty-three western joint-stock companies formed in Great Britain between 1860 and 1873. Wyoming, which was indeed served by the Union Pacific, did not figure as a major area of investment simply because her mineral resources were limited.

That railroad development was an important consideration in paving the way for an influx of capital is illustrated by the constant emphasis westerners placed upon it in their promotional activity abroad. Coloradans boasted of cheap rail transportation before it ever became a reality.[26] New Mexicans in 1871 emphasized in London that the rich Burro silver mines were located on the proposed route of the Texas Pacific railroad.[27] Investors were solicited on behalf of certain projected lines on the ground that the lines would benefit English investments in the mines. One of the reasons given for the chartering of the

[25] *Humboldt Register,* Sept. 5, 1868, quoted in *Mining Journal,* Oct. 24, 1868, 755.

[26] Jesse Archibald to editor (Central City, April 19, 1870), *Mining Journal,* May 21, 1870, 436.

[27] *Ibid.,* Feb. 4, 1871, 91.

Colorado Mineral Railway in 1871 was that it would be to the advantage of British capitalists who had already "heavily invested in mines and reduction works" in the Rockies and who supported the enterprise in order to link their property to main routes.[28]

The railroad helped to narrow the gap between Europe and the American West and made it ever easier to follow local developments and to bring greater publicity to bear abroad. English company directors could follow the situation at the mine better and keep account of investments, though factors of time and distance continued to plague absentee owners throughout the half-century. It also became easier for the inveterate British traveler to penetrate the West and for mine owners to ship exceedingly rich, though hardly representative, ores to smelters in England and Wales. Thus important contacts were strengthened immeasurably.

How much the control of the red man meant to the British capitalist is difficult to say. But when Englishmen contemplating investment in the mid-sixties inquired uneasily about the "unknown and unquiet state of the country," western promoters went out of their way to inform them that the Indian menace no longer existed. The redskins, according to one such promoter in 1867, were no more annoying than "the buzzing of a fly around either yours or my head."[29] New Mexicans were quick to point out that the Indians were cleared away from their mines whether they actually were or not.[30]

Regardless of what was said, the fact remains that the areas first to receive substantial amounts of British capital were those in which the Indian problem had been controlled or minimized relatively early. In Nevada the Indian menace was never as great as it was in the mountain areas; in Utah and Colorado the struggle between whites and reds was never as bitter and protracted as in New Mexico, Arizona, and Montana, for example. The British investor demanded assurances that stable, effective government existed and that life and property were protected before he was willing to risk his money in western ventures. Thus both the extension of transportation and the control

[28] *Boulder County News*, Nov. 17, 1871; Jan. 19, 1872.
[29] Robert O. Old to editor (London, n.d.), *Rocky Mountain News* (Denver), May 13, 1867.
[30] *Mining Journal*, Feb. 25, 1871, 153.

of the Indians were linked with mining development and with capital investment.

In Utah there was an additional obstacle to be overcome before capital could flow. There the traditional opposition of the Mormon Church to exploitation of mineral resources served to hinder mining development until at least 1870. Brigham Young discouraged mining for many years for fear that it would detract from agriculture and bring into Utah a swarm of non-Mormons whose presence might mean a substantial diminution in control by the church fathers.[31] Late in the sixties William S. Godbe set in motion a movement to liberalize Mormon policy and to develop the mineral industries in the territory.[32] As a result of the Godbeite schism and increasing external pressure, the Mormon leaders bowed to the inevitable and begrudgingly threw the mineral fields open to exploitation by all comers, including the British.[33]

If western mining by 1870 showed a very real need for capital, if the coming of the railroad was helping to break down isolation, if the Indian threat was being relieved, and if local as well as national government was giving encouragement to the extractive industries in the West, conditions in Britain were also by that time conducive to investment in the intermountain regions. Capital was available in England. It is true, Victorian prosperity was occasionally disrupted by financial relapse as in 1873, 1882, and again in 1893, but in general the English investing public was quite willing to plunge funds into all types of enterprises in every part of the globe. Englishmen dabbled in canals in the Near East, railways in Russia or Argentina, cattle ranching in Texas, or silk culture in the Orient. Each new mining boom area received due attention—western America in the early seventies; India in the eighties; Canada, South Africa, and Australia in the nineties. British capital coming into American mines between 1860 and 1901 ebbed and swelled but was no isolated phenomenon. Rather it came as part of a larger whole which took the pound sterling to even the most isolated corners of the world, seeking, amoebalike, to reproduce itself with a minimum of effort.

[31] Report of Rossiter W. Raymond on the Mineral Resources of the States and Territories West of the Rockies, *Ho. Exec. Doc.* No. 54, 40 Cong., 3 Sess. (1869), 168; *Mining Magazine and Review* (London), I (Feb., 1872), 117.

[32] MS statement of William Samuel Godbe (Sept. 2, 1884), Bancroft Library.

[33] Raymond, *Ho. Exec. Doc.* No. 54, 40 Cong., 3 Sess. (1869), 168.

Such broad investment was made possible not only because capital was available in Great Britain, but also because the machinery of joint-stock investment had been worked out along lines which encouraged owners of small capital to combine to undertake projects calling for a massing of capital. The joint-stock company was no newcomer in England, but the Companies Act of 1862 simplified chartering and added the magic word "limited" at the end of the company's name, thus restricting the liability of any shareholder under normal conditions to the amount of share capital to which he had subscribed. With the capital of a corporation and also its funded debt divided into convenient shares and bonds, readily transferable, investment was popularized, while risk was somewhat diminished.

Few would argue, however, that mining is not, and was not even more so in the earlier period, a highly speculative venture. Although the element of risk may be reduced by shrewd valuation and efficient management, its hazards are still greater than those in practically any other industry. Moreover, a mine is a wasting asset: it is but a storehouse, producing nothing in the sense that a farm produces a crop; in time its capital value will be reduced to zero. Even plant and equipment may go on the scrap heap when that point is reached. Thus under these circumstances mining investors expected large profits, justifying the high expected rate of return by the high risks involved. An innate gambling spirit and the hope of striking the mineralogical jackpot prompted many an investor to plunge on the market, often with little distinction between undeveloped mines and those actually producing. As always, the mineral industry attracted risk capital from this kind of speculator.

It is not surprising that the infant mortality rate of foreign mining companies was extraordinarily high in the early period. Risk was great. Evaluation and management were made difficult by the distance factor. Yet in all fairness it should be pointed out that the mortality rate of British public companies in general was also high in the era under consideration and that the investor's judgment proved erroneous a remarkable share of the time.[34] But in mining, though the odds were long, the stakes were high and basic human nature changes slowly, if at all.

So by 1870 the stage was set on both sides of the Atlantic. Condi-

[34] See H. A. Shannon, "The Limited Companies of 1866–1883," *Economic History Review*, IV (Oct., 1933), 290–307.

tions were conducive to investment in both England and America. Among the first to move across the plains to the mountain gold fields were Englishmen, fully as interested in mineral wealth as their Yankee brethren. As the United States census returns showed mounting numbers of British-born residents in the West, such organizations as the Sons of Malta,[35] the Sons of St. George,[36] or the Albion Society might there be found celebrating "memorable days of England"[37] and bringing Englishmen together in their adopted land. By the early seventies cricket clubs, manned almost entirely by Englishmen connected with the mines, carried the British athletic tradition deep into the Rockies.[38] A few years later conscientious patriots saw fit to name a townsite high in the headwaters of Colorado's San Juan River after England's great Liberal prime minister, William E. Gladstone.[39]

Undoubtedly many of these migrants retained their ties with friends and business associates in England and played some role in calling attention to opportunities for immigration and investment in the great West. A high percentage of American mine promoters operating between the West and England through the period were of British birth and utilized family or personal connections wherever available.[40]

Of particular importance were the "robust, stout-chested, pink-cheeked lads from the tin mines of Cornwall," who swarmed into the Rockies from the Lake Superior region in the sixties and soon attracted others from their native land.[41] These "Cousin Jacks" or "Saffron cake eaters," as they were familiarly called, not only made direct contributions in the shape of mining or milling techniques, but they also formed a vital link between the American West and England. It was the Cornish "expert," self-trained and uninhibited, who formed the backbone of practical mine management during the entire period and was foremost in promoting, inspecting, and publicizing western mines through British periodicals.

[35] *Canon City* [Colo.] *Times,* Feb. 16, 1861.
[36] *Denver Republican* April 26, 1892.   [37] *Ibid.,* Oct. 22, 1882.
[38] *Daily Colorado Miner* (Georgetown), Oct. 1, 1873 (cited hereafter as Georgetown *Miner*).
[39] Unsigned letter to William E. Gladstone (London, March 23, 1878), Brit. Mus. Add. MS 4456, Gladstone Papers, CCCLXXI, f. 191.
[40] Below, 32–33.
[41] Young, *Echoes from Arcadia,* 87. For an excellent account of the Cornish movement in a particular locality, see Lynn Perrigo, "The Cornish Miners of Early Gilpin County," *Colorado Magazine,* XIV (May, 1937), 92–101.

TABLE II

British-born Residents of the West *

Area	1860	1870	1880	1890
Arizona	. . .	137	1,066	1,520
Colorado	510	1,524	11,672	20,828
Dakota	58	253	3,456	12,602
Idaho	. . .	880	2,497	4,551
Montana	. . .	889	2,021	8,788
Nevada	413	2,860	5,147	2,721
New Mexico	148	129	477	1,816
Utah	9,262	15,920	25,258	26,766
Wyoming	. . .	614	1,667	5,060
Total	10,391	23,206	53,251	84,652

* *Eighth Census of the Unted States* (1860), I, 549, 553, 565, 573, 578; *Ninth Census* (1870), I, 345, 347, 348, 351, 363, 364, 365, 373, 377; *Tenth Census* (1880), I, 492, 494; *Eleventh Census* (1890), II, 600–601. These figures show English, Welsh, Scots, and those classified as "Great Britain not specified," but do not include Irish or "British-Americans." The figure for Dakota in 1890 includes both North Dakota (5,217) and South Dakota (7,385). Utah's figures surpass all others because of the large number of Mormon converts recruited in England.

Another important contact with English mining and smelting interests was maintained through the shipment of American ores to Liverpool or Swansea for refining. Cheaper labor costs and superior processes made this a profitable enterprise for mining companies and smelters alike so long as there were few efficient refining plants in the West. During the Civil War ore from California and the Comstock Lode was shipped to England for smelting.[42] By 1872 the Marquess of Bute had conceived an elaborate plan of operating a line of steamers between Swansea and New York especially to haul ore and had dispatched an agent to negotiate for ores in Colorado, Utah, Nevada, and California.[43] The erection of smelters in the West eventually elim-

[42] *Mining Journal*, Feb. 11, 1860, 88; March 12, 1864, 189.
[43] *Daily Central City Register*, Dec. 12, 1871; *Colorado Miner* (Georgetown), Dec. 14, 1871 (cited hereafter as *Weekly Miner*). How far this plan progressed is impossible to say. The archives of the present Marquess of Bute contain no materials dealing with the project. Catherine Armet, archivist and librarian to the Marquess of Bute, to the writer (Rothesay, Isle of Bute, July 3, 1954).

inated this practice, but smelters did not come overnight. As late as 1873 federal sources showed $1,003,000 worth of matte shipped to Britain from Colorado alone.[44] From 1882 to 1884 the Anaconda Copper Company shipped 37,000 tons of ore from Montana to Swansea, and even after constructing its own smelter in the Deer Lodge Valley it continued to ship matte to Wales until 1892.[45]

The crying need for both more and effective smelters in western regions was in itself a factor tending both directly and indirectly to promote English investments: directly, because British-owned smelters were established in the West; indirectly, because ores sent to Britain for refining had to be extremely rich and, as such, proved to be good advertisements for the mineral resources of the trans-Mississippi regions.

Nor may the impact of the British traveler be overlooked as a bond between the Old World and the New. A recent study of his wanderings and writings in the Intermountain West cites 129 books and 13 articles written by Englishmen and Englishwomen who visited the region between 1865 and 1900.[46] Often he—or she—had something to say about the mines, sometimes unfavorable, but frequently laudatory,[47] and undoubtedly the traveler's words influenced investors. Some visitors took great pains to praise specific western mines to the English public.[48]

These more or less chance contacts between Englishmen and western mines were augmented by promoters on both sides of the Atlantic, with a flood of publicity constantly keeping American mining op-

[44] Statistics of Mines and Mining in the States and Territories West of the Rocky Mountains, *Ho. Exec. Doc.* No. 141, 43 Cong., 1 Sess. (1873–1874), 284. Matte is the term applied to a crude mixture of impure sulphides obtained from smelting sulphide ores.

[45] Thomas A. Rickard, *A History of American Mining* (New York and London, 1932), 353–354.

[46] Robert G. Athearn, *Westward the Briton* (New York, 1953), 187–202.

[47] See Maurice O'Connor Morris, *Rambles in the Rocky Mountains* (London, 1864); James Bonwick, *The Mormons and the Silver Mines* (London, 1872); A. B. Legard, *Colorado* (London, 1872); Henry Hussey Vivian, *Notes of a Tour in America* (London, 1878).

[48] *Silverland*, written by George A. Lawrence in 1873, is overly sympathetic to the Emma Silver Mining Co. in Utah. Lawrence had visited Utah at the expense of the company. *A Rapid Run to the Wild West*, "by an Edinburgh Lady," seems to have been written by a Mrs. Gordon who accompanied her husband west in 1883 on business for the Arizona Copper Co. Its view of mining is somewhat prejudiced.

portunities before the potential investor. A few American periodicals were available in London to impart information about the mines, but the supply was probably very limited. As early as 1862 the Denver *Rocky Mountain News* could boast an agent on the Strand;[49] twenty-five years later the influential *Engineering and Mining Journal* of New York announced that English interest in American mines and equipment warranted the opening of a London office.[50]

But it was the British periodical, rather than the American, which was the medium utilized consistently in spreading tidings—glad or sad—throughout the years. The London stalwarts, the *Times* and the *Standard,* could always be relied upon to discuss the latest mining news from America, presenting the bad along with the good.[51] Such sedate periodicals as the *Economist* and the *Statist* emphasized the financial side of mining in impartial fashion, and the West was duly covered in their columns. While a number of English mining periodicals might be cited,[52] only two stand out as having been of real importance in publicizing western America. Throughout the entire period the London *Mining Journal* could be depended upon to survey the world mining frontier in infinite detail. After 1871 it was joined by another responsible organ, the *Mining World,* and today the two continue to be England's leading mining periodicals. Through their columns were reported new discoveries, news of old regions, information on specific mines and companies, and a veritable wealth of material on all aspects of life on the mineral frontier. Through them also were reflected the hopes and aspirations of promoters, British and Americans alike. Letters and articles, sometimes signed, as often not, poured in extolling the virtues of western mines in general or in particular. Such interested bystanders as Robert Lease, former United States consul at Ostend, Belgium, or Charles S. Richardson, an exceedingly active Colorado engineer, contributed dozens of articles on mining and mining investment in the United States.[53] At times the *Mining*

[49] April 10, 1862.   [50] Feb. 26, 1887, 145.

[51] The *Times,* for example, might wax enthusiastic over the mines of Nevada and Idaho in the sixties or in 1874 devote half a column to the possibilities of gold in the Black Hills. April 4, Nov. 3, 1863; Sept. 14, 1874.

[52] Among others, *The Mining Magazine and Review, The Mining Review and Weekly Commercial Record,* and *The Mining and Smelting Magazine* contributed during their spotty careers.

[53] Between 1860 and 1881 Richardson wrote numerous letters to the *Mining Journal* dealing with the mineral resources of Virginia, Connecticut, Maine, New York, New Jersey, and New Mexico but concentrating primarily on Colorado;

Journal and the *Mining World* could be sharply critical of western ventures, but both also lent their columns to the worst fly-by-night schemes that promoters could offer.

In addition to these reputable general mining periodicals there were more specialized ones, devoted entirely or primarily to pushing western enterprises. J. P. Whitney, commissioner for Colorado at the Paris Exposition of 1867, announced in May of the following year that he had "got a mining paper started in London devoted to Colorado interest." [54] The widely known American promoter, Asbury Harpending, who was soon to be involved in the great diamond scandal of 1872, established the *Stock Exchange Review* during 1871 to "guide" the British investing public along "safe and sane" lines. In the following decade, the *Financial and Mining News,* "A Daily Journal Publishing the Latest News of Europe and America," gave sympathetic coverage to Anglo-American mining schemes.

Near the end of the century the *Anglo-Colorado Mining and Milling Guide* made its appearance in London, under the direction of one Edward Toye. Although this illustrated monthly proved to be neither objective nor trustworthy, it undoubtedly contributed something toward promoting investment. Its columns carried frequent advertising of Colorado property or engineering services, and it perpetuated many a rumor that might otherwise have died a natural death without crossing the Atlantic. Its degree of objectivity may be judged from one of its more "literary" endeavors acclaiming the merits of Colorado's most recent mineral boom.

> There was a young man in Klondyke
> Who said he would make a big strike;
> But he lives in a hovel with pick and his shovel,
> He's forgotten what money looks like.

On the other hand:

> A young man in the camp Cripple Creek,
> Went to work with his shovel and pick;
> Now he sits in his chair a big millionaire,
> In the country where money's made quick.[55]

Lease ran a series of twelve articles in the *Journal* in 1868 and 1869 pushing Colorado as an area for investment and immigration.

[54] *Central City Register,* May 2, 1868.

[55] I (June 25, 1898), 77.

British Investments and American Mines

Along with newspaper and periodical publicity went a varied array of pamphlets and books designed to portray the glories of western gold and silver to the less-favored English cousin. Many of these were published by individuals or small combinations attempting to dispose of mines abroad, but probably as many were of a general nature, not endorsing any particular lode or property. When the Scarff brothers set out to dispose of several Gilpin County mines in 1868, they planned to publish and circulate in London ten thousand pamphlets describing the territory of Colorado.[56] In addition to distributing sixteen thousand copies of Robert Old's *Colorado: United States, America* (1869) [57] and an unknown number of the revised edition printed in London three years later,[58] the British and Colorado Mining Bureau scattered some five hundred copies of Ned Farrell's little booklet, *Colorado, the Rocky Mountain Gem.*[59] Like others of his kind Farrell painted a glowing picture of Colorado's mineral resources but warned off "fast young men who are only useful in carrying a gold-headed cane." [60] Former Governor William Gilpin published in London in 1871 his *Notes on Colorado*, a glorification of the Rocky Mountain areas subtly couched in pseudo-scientific terms.[61]

Lincoln Vanderbilt, "the Great American Traveller," purported to give Englishmen a lucid insight into conditions in the great mining West in 1870. Colorado "is Heaven blessed in climate and all worldly goods," he wrote glibly.[62] As for Arizona, "nowhere in the world is there such a rich section of country for mining, and favourable facilities for working these wonderfully productive mines, as embraced in an area of 40 miles square, lying east and south of the town of Prescott." [63]

To these and many other pamphlets of a general nature [64] must be

[56] *Daily Colorado Herald* (Central City), March 7, 1868 (cited hereafter as Central City *Herald*).

[57] *Daily Denver Tribune*, July 17, 1869.

[58] *Mining Review* (Georgetown), III (Dec., 1873), 389.

[59] *Rocky Mt. News*, July 11, 1868.

[60] "Rogues and light-fingered gentry do not thrive," wrote Farrell. "They seem to become afflicted with a throat disease, caused by too close contact with a rope." *Colorado*, 59.

[61] Pp. 13, 15, 45–46.

[62] *The New and Wonderful Explorations of Professor Lincoln Vanderbilt* (London, 1870), 21.

[63] *Ibid.*, 32–33.

[64] For examples see S. J. Abington, *The "Great West"* (London, 1871); John R. Murphy, *The Mineral Resources of the Territory of Utah, with Mining Statistics*

added dozens of publications written and circulated by the thousands on both sides of the Atlantic at the authorization of territorial legislatures,[65] boards of trade or of immigration,[66] and other official or semi-official agencies soliciting both capital and population.

The influence of such writing in helping foster investment in mining is so nebulous as to be unmeasurable. Yet it is clear that both individuals and groups went out of their way to advertise western mines in Britain throughout the period from 1860 to 1901. It is clear also that much of this promotional literature was warped and far from honest, though it was not necessarily new. In much of the first half of the nineteenth century comparable propaganda had been used in efforts to draw British pounds into land, canal, banking, and other areas of endeavor in the Western Hemisphere.[67] But new or old, accurate or misleading, it was this publicity which was largely responsible for building up in the mind of the potential investor his picture of mining in the region beyond the Mississippi.

A recognition of these several factors, then, leads to the conclusion that the real beginnings of British investment in western mines did not come in the seventies by sheer coincidence. Rather it followed a dearth of investment in the previous decade because of changes on both sides of the ocean. By 1870 the negative effect of the Civil War was removed; America was entering a new era of industrial and transportation expansion which worked to tie together more closely the East and

---

and Maps (London, 1872); William Weston, *Descriptive Pamphlet of Some of the Principal Mines and Prospects of Ouray County, Colorado* (Denver, 1883); John R. Marsh, *Cripple Creek: The Richest Goldfields of the World* (London, 1896).

[65] See *The Territory of Arizona; a Brief History and Summary of the Territory's Acquisition, Organization, and Mineral, Agricultural and Grazing Resources* (Tucson, 1874). This was published by order of the Arizona Legislature to give "reliable information" on the territory.

[66] For examples see Colorado Territorial Board of Immigration, *Resources and Advantages of Colorado* (Denver, 1873); Denver Board of Trade, *Resources of Colorado* (Denver, 1868); Utah Board of Trade, *The Resources and Attractions of the Territory of Utah* (Omaha, 1879).

[67] See David Hoffman, *The Fremont Estate: An Address to the British Public* (London, 1851); Robert Allsop, *California and Its Gold Mines* (London, 1853); *A Statement of the Advantages to Be Derived from the Employment of £50,000 upon the Security of Lands in the Mexican Province of Texas* (n.p., n.d.); Charles G. Haines, *Considerations on the Great Western Canal, from the Hudson to Lake Erie; with a View of Its Expanse, Advantages and Progress* (n.p., 1818); *Practical Information respecting New Brunswick* (London, 1834); *The Illinois Central Railroad: A Historical Sketch of the Undertaking* (London, 1855).

the West, as well as the Old World and the New. The decline of the Indian menace lowered one barrier to investment, and capital scarcity and high interest rates acted as a positive inducement to English investors. These changes came at a time when capital was available in Britain and when joint-stock organization with limited liability contributed much to a boom era of English investment in all parts of the world. That there should have been contacts between western mines and the London money market was partially coincidental and partially the result of conscious, directed publicity efforts conducted on both sides of the sea.

: CHAPTER II :

Individual Promoters

ELEMENTS do not always combine spontaneously in nature. When mixed together at a given temperature, for example, oxygen and hydrogen produce no reaction. But when a catalyst in the form of platinum particles is added, the two unite to form water. The catalytic agent accelerates the desired action, yet remains itself unchanged.

It might be said that the same principle generally holds true for movements of capital. Capital for investment and natural resources for exploitation may both be available, yet without some sort of a catalyst the two elements may never come together with the hoped-for response. The catalyst in this instance is the promoter—the ambitious, energetic entrepreneur who seeks to effect a union between capital and resources.

So it was with British capital and the western mineral empire after 1860. Always present to encourage and to channel the flow of capital was the promotional agent—the "Scadder" so aptly described by Dickens—who worked his claims or those of someone else "with his jaw instead of his pick," according to the common expression used in early Washoe.[1] The importance of the promoter or the speculator cannot be overemphasized, and to comprehend the general movement of mining investment it becomes necessary to look at the man behind it and endeavor to answer certain relevant questions: Who was that man? How did he operate? What special problems did he encounter? And what, insofar as is ascertainable, was his exact relationship to the overall stream of capital during the period?

[1] Charles Howard Shinn, *The Story of the Mine* (New York, 1901), 137.

21

British Investments and American Mines

One of the easiest generalizations to be made about the promoter is that his was an exceedingly diverse breed. Poor indeed was the provident Yankee who could not scrape up something to offer on the British market, and many were those who made the effort. Nor did the American pre-empt this particular field: alongside him toiled dozens of English agents, equally aspiring and adroit in the promotional arts. But of whichever nationality, men of all types were involved, and it becomes well-nigh impossible to focus on the "typical" promoter, either British or American. Some were professionals of long experience; some were rank amateurs. Some were bona fide mine owners; many were merely agents acting as intermediaries. Some were upright and honest; others were rascals.

Whatever their differences, these "Scadders" of the mining world had much in common. Invariably and incurably optimistic, they brought together both the best and the worst of western America and Victorian England. Many were almost Barnumlike in their contempt for the average investor, British or otherwise. After all, was it not true that if there were no "flats" there would be no "sharps"? A great number of these agents were men with direct links to the British Isles. Some were native-born Englishmen, some became permanent residents of the West; some worked through family or friends, some exploited professional acquaintances.

At the Langham Hotel, located a few blocks from Oxford Circus in London, congregated a veritable Yankee colony during the decades between 1860 and 1901. Almost every conceivable type of American seems to have been present at one time or another and to have been engaged in mine promotion. Responsible Britons and Americans alike often viewed them with displeasure. Marmaduke Sampson, the city editor of the London *Times,* in 1872 warned his readers against them. "Nine times in ten," he said, "the promoters are mere western adventurers, with nothing to spare of either capital or character, who could not find a respectable banker in New York to co-operate with them." [2] The *Wall Street Journal* commented adversely upon the "Carpet Baggers from Nevada, each having on hand from one to a dozen 'excellent properties,'" who appeared in London to exploit the booming market of the early seventies.[3]

[2] June 14, 1872.
[3] Quoted in *Mining World, and Engineering & Commercial Record* (London), Sept. 9, 1871, 577 (cited hereafter as *Mining World*).

Individual Promoters

One evening late in the spring of 1872 Benjamin Moran, the secretary of the United States Legation, picked up his pen and described the day's many visitors:

I have observed that they are of a much lower class now than in any year heretofore in my time. There is seldom a gentleman among them. On the contrary the great majority are badly dressed and badly behaved, with rude manners and poor address. Nearly all are speculators and not a few have silver and gold mines to sell which are generally swindles. But the eagerness with which the English catch at these manifest frauds is remarkable. The result is that our credit is being damaged, and the popular idea that we are rascals—which was dying out—is rapidly being revived.[4]

Moran was undoubtedly prejudiced in his views, and his thinking may have been colored considerably by the London press. Not all American promoters and agents were of questionable character; in their ranks were men of all walks and stations of life—from legitimate miners, lawyers, and brokers to the dregs of human society, many engaging in mine promotion as a secondary or side-line activity.

Many were men well known in local or even national affairs within the United States. One of the first arrivals at the Langham Hotel in the sixties was the wild-eyed radical, William Cornell Jewett, more familiarly known in the West as William "Colorado" or William "Crazy" Jewett, because of his visionary efforts to bring a peaceful settlement of the Civil War through European intervention.[5] Jewett's attempts to promote the sale of Colorado mines in 1862 and 1863 seem to have been no more effective than his efforts to bring the war to a negotiated conclusion and served to earn him the distrust of his countrymen rather than their plaudits.[6] Asa P. Stanford, brother of the illustrious Leland, came to sell Nevada mines and remained to dabble in the shares of various companies.[7] A well-known businessman in the West, Samuel

---

[4] Journal of Benjamin Moran, XXXIII (June 15, 1872), 159–160, MSS, Library of Congress.

[5] Jewett held several meetings to promote peace during the war and in 1863 addressed circulars to the heads of various European governments urging mediation in American affairs. *Dictionary of American Biography*, X, 73; *Rocky Mt. News*, June 30, Aug. 24, 1863.

[6] Jewett organized the European and Colorado Gold Mining Company after jaunts to England and the Continent in 1862 and 1863. *DAB*, X, 73; *Rocky Mt. News*, Feb. 26, May 4, 1863.

[7] Memo. of Agreement (Oct. 1, 1870) between Asa P. Stanford, P. Patton Blyth, and Edward F. Satterthwaite; *Memorandum and Articles of Association*, 13 (cited hereafter as *Mem. & Art.*), South Aurora Silver Mining Co., C.R.O. B-5114.

Newhouse, of Denver and Salt Lake City, proved to be one of the most adept of all promoters on the Anglo-American mining scene.[8]

Even public officials were to be found assiduously pushing mining schemes under London's dreary skies. Senator William Stewart of Nevada was a key figure in the sale of the Emma mine in 1871.[9] Former Governor William Gilpin of the territory of Colorado gave his open support to the hawking of the San Luis and Sangre de Cristo Grant, which boasted mining as well as grazing lands in the Rockies.[10] Governor Edward M. McCook of the same territory was active in trying to interest the Marquess of Queensbury in several Gilpin County lodes in 1871 and 1872.[11] A decade later it was William Edward Dorsheimer, twice lieutenant governor of New York and soon to be elected to Congress, who concluded the transaction which placed Colorado property in the hands of Crooke's Mining and Smelting Company, Ltd., of London.[12]

Some promoters found themselves in business almost unintentionally. Louis T. Wigfall, fire-eating ex-senator from Texas, lined up on the wrong side during the Civil War and just "happened" to be in England for some years thereafter,[13] "loafing around on the mining tack," as a

[8] A Pennsylvania lawyer, Newhouse migrated to Leadville in 1879, built up a small reserve in the freighting business, and commenced to invest in mines. After 1896 he maintained offices in Salt Lake City, New York, and London. It was Newhouse who first introduced modern steel skyscraper construction into the Mormon capital. *DAB*, XIII, 461. Among the Anglo-American mining companies formed as a result of his work were the Denver Coal Co. (1890), the Utah Consolidated Gold Mines (1896), the Newhouse Tunnel Co. (1893), and the Boston Consolidated Gold Mines (1898), all operating in Utah or Colorado.

[9] Below, 142–144.

[10] *Notes on Colorado*, 45–46; Herbert O. Brayer. *William Blackmore* (Denver, 1949), I, 70–77.

[11] A former United States minister to Hawaii and a Civil War officer with a brilliant record, McCook was governor of Colorado from 1869 to 1873 and again in 1874–1875 but was not a popular official. *DAB*, XI, 602. For references to his efforts to sell the Kansas and other lodes in Colorado, see *E. & M. Jour.*, Nov. 21, 1871, 329; James Thomson, Diary of Business Done for the Champion Gold and Silver Company in Colorado, Nov. 1, 7, 1872, 82–83, 87, MS Don e. 47, Bodleian Library, Oxford University (cited hereafter as Thomson Business Diary).

[12] *DAB*, V, 387–388; Memo. of Agreement (April 17, 1882) between John J. Crooke (by William Dorsheimer) and the Crooke's Mining and Smelting Co., C.R.O. 16664; *Economist, Weekly Commercial Times, Bankers' Gazette, and Railway Monitor: A Political, Literary, and General Newspaper* (London), June 6, 1885, 693 (cited hereafter as *Economist*).

[13] Wigfall (1816–1874), a lawyer, was an extremist of the southern states' rights

contemporary expressed it in 1873.[14] In the middle sixties Dr. Curran L. Seaton of Idaho Springs, Colorado, had visited England in an effort to dispose of certain Clear Creek properties.[15] Failing in this, he returned home and sent one L. C. Duncan to London as an agent to form a company. Left two years without operating funds, Duncan ultimately turned up in Whitecross Prison,[16] and into his place stepped the self-exiled Wigfall. Wigfall took over the Seaton property for £5,000. "I shall have to sacrifice a considerable portion of the property however to secure the £5,000 working capital," he wrote his son in 1869. "How much I can save I do not know, but certainly enough to make us comfortable for the balance of our lives." [17] If he failed to achieve this goal, it was not for lack of effort.[18] As a result of what other promoters called his "insane attempts," [19] two British companies were incorporated to acquire part of the property, but neither proceeded beyond the preliminary stages.[20]

Others besides Wigfall took advantage of their stay in England to engage in more or less accidental promotional activity. Early in 1884 a London newspaper carried the following item: "Colonel Jack Haverly will sail from New York for London next month with the Mastodon Minstrels and a few Colorado mines." [21] It explained that Haverly's Minstrels were performing at the Drury Lane Theater while their sponsor was offering to the British public "some of the most promising

---

school and is probably best known for his visit to Fort Sumter during its bombardment in 1861 to demand its surrender. Briefly in command of the "Texas Brigade," he resigned to sit in the Confederate Senate and fled to England with the Union victory. *DAB*, XX, 187–188.

[14] George A. Lawrence, *Silverland* (London, 1873), 10.

[15] *Rocky Mt. News*, Oct. 22, 30, 1865.

[16] Louis T. Wigfall to Halsey Wigfall (London, June 15, 1869). Wigfall MSS, Family Correspondence, 1865–1871, Library of Congress.   [17] *Ibid.*

[18] Wigfall had difficulties with a Mancunian "scamp" named Clark who promised to purchase an interest, then refused. Jacobs, another Englishman, caused consternation when he temporarily tied up all papers pertaining to the property because of debts owed to him. Louise Wigfall to Halsey Wigfall (London, July 3, 1869); Charlotte Wigfall to [?] (London, Sept. 1, 1869); Louise Wigfall to Halsey Wigfall (London, July 28, 1869), *ibid.*

[19] Hiram A. Johnson to H. M. Teller (London, Sept. 10, 1872), Teller MSS.

[20] Memo. of Agreement (July 12, 1870) between Louis T. Wigfall, James Campbell Rowley, and the Colorado Mining and Land Co., C.R.O. 5003; *Mem. & Art.* (1871), 3, 5, Renishaw Silver Mining Co., C.R.O. 5656.

[21] *Financial & Mining News* (London), April 16, 1884.

mines of Colorado"—all personally selected.[22] Competition and a prolonged heat wave spelled financial disaster for the theatrical undertaking; [23] London's reaction to the mining property is not recorded.

Some promoters, like Erwin Davis, were "old hands" at the business. In September, 1869, Davis had failed in San Francisco and gone into bankruptcy for a half-million dollars when William Ralston and the Bank of California came into power on the Pacific Coast. He then went to Britain where he dabbled in American mines and sold Turkish bonds short on the London market.[24] Himself a "stock broker and manipulator of stocks," Davis regarded the English mode of operation as *decidedly old fogyish. They did not understand bulls and bears on the stock exchange,*" he concluded contemptuously.[25] Consequently, the California expert set out to teach the British a few of the tricks of promotion and speculation—at their expense. He was largely responsible for the formation of at least three English companies incorporated to acquire mines in Utah.[26] His wild manipulation of the shares of these concerns was halted only when the Utah courts stayed his hand.[27]

Another good example of the "professional" was Colonel William James Sutherland, an American who worked the British mining markets for nearly thirty years. Sutherland had received his military title as the result of having once been on the staff of a Cuban governor and is described as having had "most of the characteristics of the typical promoter of the nineteenth century: expansive and expensive, florid and flamboyant, persuasive and persistent." [28] With him, in almost every enterprise with which his name was associated, was a small handful of Englishmen, always the same closely knit group, who along with Sutherland, accepted large numbers of vendors' shares but who were

[22] *Ibid.,* June 10, 1884.

[23] Christopher ("Jack") Haverly organized the Mastodon Minstrels in 1878, and this was their second excursion to London. After this trip Haverly speculated in pork and lost his investment. The last three years of his life were spent in the West, where he was engaged in mining until his death in 1901. *DAB,* VIII, 410–411.

[24] *Mining Journal,* April 21, 1877, 435.

[25] Davis *v.* Flagstaff Silver Mining Company of Utah, Ltd., 2 *Utah Reports* (1877), 88.

[26] Included were the Flagstaff Silver Mining Co. of Utah (1871), the Last Chance Silver Mining Co. of Utah (1872), and the Tecoma Silver Mining Co. (1873). *Ibid.,* 87; *Mining World,* Feb. 7, March 7, 1874, 277, 455.

[27] Davis had loaned the Flagstaff company money to pay dividends in order to bull the market and sell out his own holdings. 2 *Utah Reports* (1877), 87–88.

[28] Rickard, *History of American Mining,* 68.

quick to dispose of them. Sometimes operations were carried on through the Doris Syndicate, Ltd., a promoting organization; [29] sometimes they were carried out independently. But through whatever medium, it was Sutherland who took the initiative and who was chiefly responsible for introducing mines located in Nevada, Colorado, and Alaska.[30]

Many American agents or vendors were, like Sutherland, trained in the legal profession. Another large group was made up of professional brokers. One of the most successful in this category in the 1890's was Verner Z. Reed of Colorado. As a young man Reed had done well erecting houses in Colorado Springs and selling them on the installment plan.[31] Branching out, he began to deal in Cripple Creek mining stocks and ultimately opened offices in London and Arbroath, Scotland. The author of several racy novels, this "prototype of Scott Fitzgerald" [32] made frequent journeys to the Continent and, despite a slow market as a result of Transvaal competition, succeeded in selling Cripple Creek interests in both France and Belgium.[33]

In England, Reed was responsible in 1898 for the sale of important

[29] *Mem. & Art.*, 8; Memo. of Agreement (Sept. 17, 1888) between William James Sutherland and the Doris Syndicate, C.R.O. 27338.

[30] For some of Sutherland's connections, see Memo. of Agreement (Jan. 19, 1885) between William James Sutherland and the Candelaria Waterworks and Milling Co., C.R.O. 20684; Memo. of Agreement (Feb. 22, 1887) between William James Sutherland and the Princess Mining Co. of London, C.R.O. B-23975; *Mem. & Art.*, 22, Cripple Creek Pioneers, C.R.O. B-46878; Summary of Capital and Shares to Jan. 12, 1888, Legal Tender Milling and Mining Co., C.R.O. B-24972; Walter R. Skinner (ed.), *The Mining Manual for 1897* (London, 1897), 1212. All of these companies were organized to operate either in Nevada or Colorado.

[31] Born in Ohio, Reed grew up in Iowa and came to Colorado at the age of twenty-two. Here he sold lots along the Fontaine-qui-Bouille and gradually expanded until he formed his own investment company. Frank Waters, *Midas of the Rockies* (Denver, 1949), 210–211.

[32] Marshall Sprague, *Money Mountain* (Boston, 1953), 211. The Library of Congress contains at least four works by Reed: *Lo-to-kah* (New York and Boston, 1897), *Tales of the Sun-Land* (New York and London, 1897), *Adobeland Stories* (Boston, 1899), and *The Soul of Paris and Other Essays* (New York and London, 1914).

[33] Reed sold stock in the C.O.D. Gold Mining Co., a Cripple Creek organization, to a French syndicate for $360,000. Sprague, *Money Mountain*, 211–212. He also helped sell the Ingham mine in Cripple Creek to a Belgian concern, the Ingham Consolidated Gold Mining Co., incorporated in Oct., 1895. Fred Hills, *The Official Manual of the Cripple Creek District, Colorado, U.S.A.* (Colorado Springs, 1900), 256.

Rocky Mountain properties to the Moon-Anchor Consolidated Gold Mines, Ltd.[34] Late the following year a partisan London publication heralded his impending return with the announcement that "Mr. V. Z. Reed is coming to town again shortly with some more of 'Colorado's good things' for the B. P." [35] And foremost among these "good things" Reed brought the famous Independence Mine, owned by Winfield Scott Stratton of Colorado Springs.[36]

Reed was well acquainted with Stratton and in addition enjoyed excellent contacts in London with the powerful Venture Corporation, Ltd. Beginning in 1898, he subtly commenced to "sell" the Independence to the chief engineer of the Venture Corporation, John Hays Hammond. Early in the following year Reed succeeded in reaching a tentative agreement for sale of the mine, and Stratton went to Europe to give his final seal of approval.[37] According to a story recounted by Hammond and others, Stratton proved to be most obdurate when haggling over price. As a last resort, so goes the story, the Venture Corporation honored him with a banquet, offering a flat $5,000,000 at the outset of the meal. When the mustachioed old sourdough refused, the offer was raised by half a million or so at each succeeding course until finally, as the group was settling down to its liqueurs, Stratton signed for $10,000,000.[38]

Since Stratton was recovering from a serious illness and in no condition for such a banquet, this account is probably only colorful fiction.[39] It is true, however, that Stratton did sell the mine for $10,000,000 to a newly formed British company, Stratton's Independence, Ltd., one of the largest English firms ever to operate in western mines.[40]

[34] Memo. of Agreement (Dec. 17, 1898) between the Moon-Anchor Gold Mining Co. (by Verner Z. Reed) and George Butcher, C.R.O. B-59975.

[35] *Anglo-Colorado Mining Guide,* II (Sept. 30, 1899), 136. "B. P." is the normal abbreviation for "British Public."

[36] The standard biography of Stratton is the very sympathetic *Midas of the Rockies,* by Frank Waters.

[37] *Ibid.,* 211–212.

[38] Hammond, who refers erroneously to "William Stratton," also errs in setting the final price at $7,500,000. *The Autobiography of John Hays Hammond* (New York, 1935), II, 491–492.

[39] Waters, *Midas of the Rockies,* 215.

[40] Capitalized at £1,100,000, it acquired the Independence and other Cripple Creek claims totaling nearly 111 acres in all. Memo. of Agreement (April 27, 1899) between Winfield Scott Stratton and George Butcher; Statement of Nominal Capital (April 29, 1899), Stratton's Independence, C.R.O. B-61817.

Verner Reed's commission of $1,000,000 on this deal enabled him to retire temporarily to Bohemian life in Paris before returning to the West to make a second fortune in oil and banking.[41] As for Winfield Scott Stratton, Colorado welcomed him and his $10,000,000 with open arms:

> You have made a bully deal,
>> Mr. Stratton;
> And we share the joy you feel,
>> Mr. Stratton;
> Few there were took thought or heed
> That so great a thing indeed
> Could be slung by one slim Reed,
>> Mr. Stratton.[42]

Reed's success was striking, but it must not be regarded as typical of American experience in England. For every Reed there were a hundred who failed or who reaped only limited benefits. Yet a few did manage to husband combinations of luck and hard work into modest fortunes by acting as links between the capital market of the Old World and the resources of the New.

These few representative samples serve to indicate that there was no typical American promoter. Men from all walks of life were involved, with varying degrees of success. The average American in London was undoubtedly far less fortunate than Sutherland or Reed. Once he arrived he usually found that numerous obstacles arose to block his path. Some of the trials and tribulations are set forth in the correspondence of Hiram A. Johnson, who spent nearly two years in England endeavoring without avail to sell Colorado mines.

The law partner of Henry M. Teller of Colorado, Johnson was "a breezy, rather boisterous type . . . an adventurous individual with more than a touch of the gambling spirit in his make-up." [43] As early as 1863 he had established an office in New York to deal in Rocky

---

[41] Reed lived in France for nearly thirteen years. Among other accomplishments he achieved renown by driving an underslung Panhard across the Sahara Desert. When he returned to America, he amassed an estimated $30,000,000 or $40,000,000 from banking and Wyoming oil. Waters, *Midas of the Rockies*, 228; Sprague, *Money Mountain*, 314.

[42] *Colorado Springs Gazette*, quoted in the *Anglo-Colorado Mining Guide*, II (May 27, 1899), 68.

[43] Elmer Ellis, *Henry Moore Teller* (Caldwell, 1941), 29.

Mountain mining properties.[44] In 1871 he appeared on the London scene.[45]

His first impression was that Englishmen were "exceedingly staid 'and long suffering.' . . . They need to be well assured, and act with caution and apparent distrust." [46] His second impression was less favorable. *"This flat footed degenerate people* require much time for deliberation," he complained. "The fact is they are decidedly slow." [47] Nevertheless he was determined to "wait out" his cautious quarry.

Attempting to dispose of the Illinois lode in Gilpin County, as well as some copper lands near Golden, Johnson found difficult going. "Old Halloway," with whom he was endeavoring to negotiate, proved a "very hard nut to crack." [48] His joy over the proposed sale of the Illinois quickly vanished when an adverse engineering report called the property overvalued.[49] He never seemed to appreciate the leisurely pace at which the British businessman moved. "All England is 'grouse shooting' in Scotland," he grumbled in August.[50] A bit later he complained that business was dull because so many Englishmen were vacationing north of the Tweed, sunning themselves on the seashore, or touring the Continent.[51]

Johnson could also point to more compelling reasons for his lack of success. "The continued agitation of the *Alabama* question is still destructive of all business of a speculative character here," he informed Teller early in 1872.[52] And when this particular obstacle was overcome,

[44] A popular and able lawyer at Morrison, Ill., Johnson in 1858 took young Henry M. Teller as his partner. Johnson was one of the town's important citizens and took an active part in the senatorial campaign of Stephen A. Douglas during the same year. In 1860 he was lured westward to the Colorado gold fields and prevailed upon Teller to join him at Central City. After opening offices in New York in 1863, Johnson never returned to his Colorado law practice. The Teller brothers purchased his property there, including his share in the law firm. *Ibid.*, 29–30, 54–55; William A. Davis, *History of Whiteside County, Illinois* (Chicago, 1908), I, 327.

[45] Johnson's first letter from England, written to Thomas L. Carpenter and dated Feb. 24, 1871, announced his arrival after a rough voyage. Hiram A. Johnson MSS, Bancroft Library.

[46] The same (London, March 14, 1871), *ibid.*

[47] The same (March 31, 1871), *ibid.*   [48] The same (May 6, 1871), *ibid.*

[49] The same (July 22, Aug. 12, 1871), *ibid.*

[50] To Teller (London, Aug. 26, 1871), Teller MSS.

[51] The same (Sept. 10, 1872), *ibid.*   [52] The same (Feb. 19, 1872), *ibid.*

he forecast, "the mines already on the market will have proved such unmitigated swindles that you cannot give away a mine." [53]

Johnson's difficulties were those of the vast majority of American promoters in the British Isles. Yet despite them, the Langham Hotel clique never diminished appreciably. And as might be expected, British agents refused to relax while the Yankees dominated the field. Some even carried the fight to the West and did their utmost to entice their countrymen to invest. To be sure, Englishmen in the West were hardly as numerous as Americans in London, but at least a few directed operations on the spot or scurried back and forth across the Atlantic. Information available on one such Englishman, Colonel George William Heaton of Brighton, provides an interesting insight into the problems and methods of the promoter on the American side.

A Cambridge graduate and a lawyer by profession, Heaton had crossed the plains to California as a tourist in 1858, and in the following year became high sheriff of Vancouver Island for a brief period.[54] An inveterate hunter, he was familiar with the West; a well-bred Briton, he might naturally have been expected to maintain proper contacts in England. Heaton visited Colorado in 1870 to investigate its resources and for the next half-dozen years was interested in promotional work there and in England.

Western editors were attracted to the romantic Heaton. One local newspaper described him as

an erect, spare, broad-shouldered man of about 40 years of age—looking 10 years younger—with a handsome, unflinching, mahogany-colored face and dark beard, close-cut hair slightly frosted above the temples; a keen, determined eye; a cool, courteous, impassive look of presence of mind, betoking [sic] a man who knows what he wants and means to have it.[55]

Equally impressive was Heaton's reputed command of six languages and the fact that he "wears a vast sombrero hat, rides a good horse, and holds that life is too short to smoke bad cigars in." [56]

[53] *Ibid.*
[54] Born in 1833, George William Heaton was the son of Rev. George Heaton of Cheltenham, Gloucester, and received the B.A. from Cambridge in 1856. He was admitted to Lincoln's Inn (1864) and was called to the bar in 1868. J. A. Venn (comp.), *Alumni Cantabrigienses* (Cambridge, 1947), III, pt. 2, 316–317; *Boulder County News,* June 20, 1873.
[55] *Denver Mirror,* June 29, 1873.   [56] *Ibid.*

The presence of the colorful colonel was soon noticed by others in the Rockies and beyond. Correspondence began to flow from Colorado, Utah, New Mexico, and California offering "exceptional" property at equally "exceptional" prices.[57] From Georgetown, Colorado, James W. Cummings volunteered his co-operation in August, 1870:

If you stile wish to get controle of a lode that is supposed to be equal or perhaps better than the Terrible, with a view of selling in England, I think if you were here within a few days, an arrangement could be made for a lode that I believe to be first class in every respect, with plenty of ore in sight that I think would please the most fastidious among your English friends.[58]

Heaton rejected most of the offers but did collaborate with Cummings to secure options on some "splendid property" in Colorado.[59] Cummings then set out late in 1870 for England to place these mines on the market,[60] after a ton of ore from the Mountain Ram lode had been dispatched to Swansea in order to "prove" the richness of that mine.[61] But after five months in London Cummings was in distress at his failure to make a sale. "It is possible I may get turned out-doors," he wrote Heaton. "If so, God only knows what I would do as I have not got a coper [*sic*] of money." [62] Although Heaton rushed to his aid, the combined efforts of both men failed, and the property remained unsold.

Heaton was also one of the backers of the National Tunnel Company, registered in Colorado in late 1869 to carry on work in Gilpin County.[63]

---

[57] "Now, Mr. Heaton," wrote Thomas Jennings from Utah, "if you has a Connection in London to bring out a mine or two I stand high here & can a Shure you that I can put many thousands of pounds in your pockets & the directors also in a Short time. . . ." Salt Lake City, Aug. 30, 1872. See also George T. Clark to Heaton (Denver, Sept. 6, 1871); John Dold to Heaton (Las Vegas, N. Mex., April 19, 1871), Teller MSS.

[58] To Heaton (Georgetown, Aug. 28, 1870), *ibid.*

[59] Included were the Glasgow and Sterling mines near Georgetown, 1,700 feet of the Mountain Ram, and 3,000 feet of the Hamiltonian, the latter in the same region. Cummings to Heaton (Georgetown, Nov. 6, 1870; Murrayville, Ill., Dec. 19, 1870); Cummings to [?] (London, March 16, 1871); Title Bond, filed Sept. 19, 1870, *ibid.*

[60] Cummings to Heaton (Georgetown, Oct. 18, 1870), *ibid.*

[61] The same (Murrayville, Ill., Dec. 19, 1870), *ibid.*

[62] The same (London, March 29, 1871), *ibid.*

[63] Peter C. Johnson to Heaton (Black Hawk, Sept. 12, 1871); National Tunnel Co., Certificate of Incorporation (Nov. 20, 1869), *ibid.;* Thomas B. Corbett, *The Colorado Directory of Mines* (Denver, 1879), 227.

Despite his repeated attempts to interest British capitalists in this enterprise,[64] his company was soon dissolved, having failed to comply with territorial law. On its ruins was constructed a new organization, the Sierra Madre Tunnel Company, with an ambitious, twelve-mile tunnel undertaking as its goal.[65] With Heaton at the helm, at least a small amount of British capital was invested, but by 1876 work had been discontinued.[66] George Heaton's experiences were hardly successful, but they paralleled those of a host of other operators, both British and American.

Other Englishmen continued to make similar attempts throughout the remainder of the nineteenth century. Perhaps because his enemies were more numerous or more vociferous than some, the Chelsea promoter, Herbert Charles Drinkwater, received more than his share of adverse publicity during the period. "This financial vampire," as a contemporary called him,[67] first appeared on the western scene in connection with an abortive venture called the Enterprise Syndicate, Ltd., in 1887.[68] He brought marvelous tales of richness back to Liverpool and Manchester and persuaded a "group of monied nincompoops"[69] to support his Old Guard Mining Company, Ltd., in developing mines in Arizona.[70] This undertaking was reported to have cost about $100,000 before it succumbed "owing to mismanagement by parties sent out from England."[71] Thrown under the sheriff's hammer at Tombstone, the Old Guard mine was purchased by the Star Syndicate, Ltd., another of Drinkwater's offspring.[72] When adverse publicity blocked this effort,[73] Drinkwater neatly substituted in its stead the Victorian Mines Syn-

[64] Peter C. Johnson to Heaton (Diamond Springs, Colo., Feb. 1, 1872), Teller MSS.

[65] Corbett, *Colorado Directory*, 235; *Boulder County News*, June 20, 1873.

[66] Below, 77–78; Samuel Cushman and J. P. Waterman, *The Gold Mines of Gilpin County* (n.p., 1876), 98.

[67] *Financial Observer and Mining Herald* (London), Oct. 11, 1890.

[68] *Ibid.; Mem. & Art.*, 1, Enterprise Syndicate, C.R.O. 24289.

[69] *Financial Observer*, Oct. 11, 1890.

[70] *Ibid.*, Nov. 1, 1890; Old Guard *Prospectus* (May 14, 1887).

[71] Report of the Committee on Mines and Mining on Mining Interests of Aliens in the Territories, *Senate Report* No. 2690, 50 Cong. 2 Sess. (1888–1889), 8–9. The company was wound up in 1888 on the petition of a creditor and dissolved in 1896. Court Order, High Court of Justice, Chancery Division (Feb. 17, 1896), Old Guard Mining Co., C.R.O. 24410.

[72] *Financial Observer*, Oct. 18, 1890; *Mem. & Art.*, 1–2, C.R.O. 30303.

[73] *Financial Observer*, Oct. 18, 1890.

dicate, Ltd.,[74] only to be checked again when the editor of the *Financial Observer and Mining Herald* recognized a picture accompanying the Victorian prospectus as being a retouched photograph of the Old Guard mine. "If anyone puts a brass farthing into this swindle," snapped the editor, "he deserves to lose it." [75] Apparently not much was lost, for the syndicate did not proceed.[76]

Granted that a variety of promotional agents were involved throughout the period, how did such men proceed? Did any set pattern of operation emerge? Or was it largely a matter of individual discretion as to technique and method? Again, hard and fast rules are difficult to draw, for company promotion and speculation of any kind was in the nineteenth century a rough-and-tumble business with few holds barred. Yet necessity forced Englishmen and Americans alike to follow well-beaten paths a good deal of the time.

Although some owners of western mining property carried on direct negotiations with the potential English investor or purchaser, most did not. Most assigned the task to an intermediary—a Verner Z. Reed, a William Sutherland, or a Hiram Johnson—who normally handled affairs from their inception to their completion. In a few instances the intermediary proceeded to an advanced stage; then the actual owner arrived to complete arrangements.[77] But it should be made clear that the promoter, the agent, the vendor—by whatever name he was known—generally operated for a share of the profits received from the sale. He was usually not particularly interested in the property at hand; his task was to effect a sale, with little or no regard for subsequent results.[78]

It was the standard practice for the promoter to take exclusive options

[74] *Ibid.; Mem. & Art.,* 1–2, C.R.O. 32232.

[75] *Financial Observer,* Oct. 18, 1890.

[76] The concern was dissolved in 1895, and its file indicates that subscriptions were never received. Dissolution Notice (June 11, 1895), C.R.O. 32232.

[77] Robert O. Old of the British and Colorado Mining Bureau carried on negotiations for the sale of the Terrible lode in 1869, then early in 1870 one of the co-owners, Frederick A. Clark, crossed the Atlantic to complete the transaction. *Rocky Mt. News,* Jan. 17, 1870. In like fashion Verner Reed laid the groundwork in 1898 and 1899 for the sale of the Independence; then owner Winfield Stratton arrived in London to handle the final arrangements. Waters, *Midas of the Rockies,* 211–212.

[78] A few promoters tried an alternate method under which the promoter actually purchased the property from its owner and worked it to prove its value before selling it. *Mining Industry and Tradesman,* VIII (Dec. 3, 1891), 233.

on promising lodes, giving him the right to sell for a specified period of time and ordinarily for a stated minimum price. Then, armed with a number of such bonds, as they were called, he hurried to England to palm off as many as possible.

Nothing begat success like success.

We are aware that at the present moment several parties, excited by the success with which some first-rate properties have been successfully negotiated in our market, have rushed to the "West," and come back with their pockets stuffed with "bonds" of all kinds of mining properties, obtained at nominal figures from "the boys," hoping to negotiate them also successfully.

So commented the London *Mining World* in 1871.[79] Sometimes it was necessary to "pay some earnest money down," as Colonel Heaton expressed it, in order to secure such options.[80] Occasionally agreements were flouted by one party and the courts were asked to intervene.[81] The time limitations on most options often meant that the promoter raced against the calendar—and frequently lost.

One example of the race against time will suffice. A small group of Coloradans headed by William Byers of Denver bonded property in Boulder County in 1870 and authorized representatives to dispose of it in London. Negotiations were still in progress when the option expired and the owners steadfastly refused to renew it again.[82] Moreover, shortly before the deadline date the group's London agent had written asking that a power of attorney be sent immediately. The bond itself did not convey title and no sane Englishman would have paid down money on its simple transfer since there would be no way of knowing what encumbrances had been placed on the property without re-examining the title and bringing it up to date.[83] Hence the use of the bonding arrangement had its shortcomings. And in this particular instance, because of

---

[79] *Mining World*, May 13, 1871, 134.

[80] MS Prospectus, n.d., signed by George Heaton, Teller MSS.

[81] David E. MacLean, an Englishman, brought suit against the owners of the Colonel Sellers mine, located near Leadville. He charged that he had been sent abroad to sell the mine and that the owners agreed to take $1,200,000 for it, allowing him anything over that amount. When MacLean secured a bid of $1,550,000, they refused to sell, believing they could get more. *E. & M. Jour.*, June 11, 1887, 425.

[82] William N. Byers to the London and Colorado Co. (Denver, Sept. 27, 1870); Byers to W. W. Ramage (Denver, Sept. 21, 1870), Byers Letterbook (1868–1871).

[83] Byers to Ramage (n.p., Nov. 8, 1870), *ibid.*

35

failure to supply the agent with a power of attorney, because of the influence of the Franco-Prussian War, and because of procrastination which allowed the option to expire before negotiations were finished, the entire effort collapsed.[84]

A few owners or intermediaries made efforts to attract British capital through the mails. Advertisements in London periodicals offered a multitude of investment opportunities in every part of the West. For example, a "Gold and Silver Miner" of Central City appealed in 1869 for "some influential Gentlemen to assist in Forming a Joint-Stock Company to Work some valuable Gold and Silver Mines in Colorado. A safe investment. Only a small capital required." [85] Nearly twenty years later, at the end of the period, a typical advertisement in the *Anglo-Colorado Mining and Milling Guide* followed the same general line: "£25,000 will purchase three-fifths interest in, and equip on large scale, an extremely valuable Placer Gold Mining Property in Western States of America. Over 900 acres will yield £1,000 per acre. Prompt action necessary. Address 'S.V.T.,' P.O. Box 1168, Salt Lake City, Utah." [86]

It is extremely doubtful, however, if such naïve mail-order approaches produced much result. The majority of sales were completed in London or Edinburgh through personal contacts, which meant that the seller or his agent must be on the spot. Yet undoubtedly some investment did come as a response to solicitations from friends or associates in America. Englishmen in the West were certainly not adverse to using personal influence to further their own ends where mine sales were concerned. Wrote an itinerant Briton in 1880: "The number of Englishmen who have become demoralized in Colorado, and deliberately put their best and oldest friends at home in for schemes that they have tried themselves and failed in—just to get out of loss themselves—is terrible to think of." [87]

An excellent example of this type of promotion—via letter and cable to overseas acquaintances—is provided by the efforts of J. Barr Robertson in the middle 1870's. In San Francisco as manager of an Anglo-

[84] Byers to A. E. Langford (n.p., Sept. 23, 1870); Byers to the London and Colorado Co. (Denver, Sept. 27, 1870); Byers to H. C. Justice (n.p., Oct. 17, 1870), *ibid.*

[85] *Mining Journal,* Dec. 11, 1869.

[86] *Anglo-Colorado Mining Guide,* I (June 25, 1898), 16.

[87] Samuel Nugent Townshend, *Our Indian Summer in the Far West* (London, 1880), 41.

California land company but personally interested in several mines on the Comstock lode, Robertson telegraphed an acquaintance in England late in 1875, asking if he or some of his friends "*might* wish to make a venture of about £2,000." "Your prompt reply 'No' set the matter at rest at once," wrote Robertson to the same person shortly thereafter.[88]

But Robertson did not despair. He continued to urge his correspondents across the Atlantic to "make a venture" in Nevada mines.[89] His persistence was rewarded in December, 1875, when he induced Eugene McLoughlin of London to invest £800 in two thoroughly speculative enterprises on the Comstock, the Atlantic Consolidated Mining Company and the Oregon Consolidated Gold and Silver Mining Company, both undertakings in which he was himself personally interested. Robertson guaranteed McLoughlin against loss and promised the transaction would be closed in six months with substantial profits.[90]

Returns did not, unfortunately, follow the prescribed schedule. Within four months the now skeptical McLoughlin was demanding the restitution of his money; [91] when the stipulated six-month term had expired, Robertson was forced to request an extension of time.[92] By the autumn of 1876 he admitted that for the time being at least the shares were worthless, but he assured McLoughlin his money was "perfectly safe in the Atlantic," [93] meaning the company, although he might as well have meant the ocean.[94]

Such long-range courtships as that carried on by Robertson produced doubtful results, if any at all. To be effective, a project had to be pushed in England, not from 5,000 miles away. Consequently, the promoting agent, representing himself, an individual owner, or even a combination

---

[88] To H. J. Trotter (n.p., Nov. 1, 1875), J. Barr Robertson Letterbook, Bancroft Library.

[89] To James MacDonald (n.p., Jan. 24, 1876), *ibid.*

[90] To Eugene McLoughlin (n.p., Dec. 13, 1875). Robertson bought shares at one dollar per share and planned to dispose of one-quarter of the stock when it had risen to four dollars. The same (San Francisco, Dec. 20, 1875), *ibid.*

[91] Peter Robertson to McLoughlin (San Francisco, April 19, 1876), *ibid.* Peter was J. Barr Robertson's brother.

[92] J. B. Robertson to McLoughlin (San Francisco, June 2, 1876), *ibid.*

[93] The same (San Francisco, Aug. 23, 1876), *ibid.*

[94] In September, Robertson admitted that he could not raise the £800 and asked McLoughlin to accept security in shares of the California Land Investment Company, Ltd. McLoughlin refused. San Francisco, Sept. 22, 1876; Oct. 30, 1876, *ibid.*

of owners,[95] journeyed to Mecca to make certain that his own or his client's interests were being solidly championed. When he arrived in London, he usually proclaimed his mission to the winds, although occasionally some promoters proceded in quasi-secretive fashion with contacts home through a special telegraphic code and an innocent-appearing "dummy" as a front for promotional activity carried on from the shadows. Sometimes internal dissension hindered operations. For example, in 1887, a group in London pushing Idaho mines developed a sudden internal split. One faction went its own way, printing thousands of prospectuses for a proposed new company, Wide West Gold, Ltd. Out of spite, the dissenting group registered a company under that very name,[96] thus compelling the first faction to reprint all its publicity materials, adding "Rocky Bar" to the name.[97]

If possible, the promoter dispatched selected ore specimens to Liverpool or Swansea for assaying and saw that favorable results were broadcast far and wide. Frequently, also, he might maintain samples of ore or bullion for display in some "City" office as an added attraction. Ores from Idaho, Nevada, and Colorado were shown at the Paris Exposition of 1867, then were brought to London for private exhibition by partisans interested in encouraging investment.[98] Individual promoters knew the value of such samples well [99] and occasionally even presented editors of mining periodicals with specimens from western mines soon to be introduced on the British market.[100] Two brothers promoting Colorado mines in the late sixties not only collected eight boxes of ore samples,

---

[95] Eight residents of Central City, Colo., in 1870 pooled their resources to send a man to England to offer their mines on the market. Thomas Jennings to George Heaton (Bald Mountain, Colo., Sept. 17, 1870), Teller MSS.

[96] *E. & M. Jour.*, Feb. 4, 1888, 89. This concern was registered without Articles of Association and with a broad scope of operations including any of the territories of the United States. *Memo. of Association*, 1, Wide West Gold, C.R.O. B-25600.

[97] *E. & M. Jour.*, Feb. 4, 1888, 89; Rocky Bar Wide West Gold, *Prospectus* (Jan. 7, 1888).

[98] Denver *Tribune*, Sept. 26, Oct. 8, 1867; *Rocky Mt. News*, Oct. 4, 1867; *Mining Journal*, June 8, 22, 1867, 381, 421; Jan. 18, 25, 1868.

[99] William A. Bell, an Englishman trying to dispose of the Ten-Forty silver mine near Jamestown, Colo., wrote his associates in 1869 stressing the need to send rich ore samples to him in London so that the mine's worth might be proved. To William J. Palmer (London, Oct. 16, 1869); David H. Moffat, Jr., to William J. Palmer (Denver, Feb. 17, 1870), Palmer MSS.

[100] *Mining Journal*, Feb. 19, 1870.

but also constructed a complete model of a working mine to take with them.[101] At the end of the century the great Venture Corporation, Ltd., held a gigantic mining exhibit at Earl's Court in London, at which for five months they displayed ores from all over the world. It was not by accident that Colorado's minerals were given special emphasis, for the Venture Corporation was at this time busily engaged in dumping one million shares of Stratton's Independence, Ltd., upon the market.[102]

Self-sufficing as he was, the average American promoter in England could not hope to handle all aspects of his work without local aid. The psychology of the British investor and the intricacies of company law prompted many a Yankee to work through or in conjunction with an English associate or firm. Louis T. Wigfall for a time endeavored to deal through one Jacobs, "a little beast," according to Wigfall's daughter.[103] Hiram Johnson began his activities in 1871 with the co-operation of an Englishman named Goldring, but within a few months it became clear that the two were in variance. Johnson found occasion to express his frank disgust toward his ex-colleague.

You cannot rely on his statements. I have caught him in several most flagrant lies. He misrepresented his own respectability and lied wilfully about his family connections and what he could do here in the way of selling properties. I waited nearly two months for him to make good one of his promises, but finding him utterly insufficient I went to work on my own hook. . . . He is in fact a downright Jew and that tells the whole story.[104]

After severing connections with Goldring, Johnson then endeavored to work through a Briton named Ettinger, who by late 1871 had "already made two *successful failures* to sell the Illinois" property.[105] Johnson's experiences did not foster in his mind an attitude of charity toward London's financial circles. "The fact is there is no place in the world where a man is so completely deceived as to his prospects as here," he

---

[101] Denver *Tribune,* April 24, 1868; Central City *Herald,* March 20, 1868.

[102] These were the shares originally accepted by the owner in exchange for the property. Waters, *Midas of the Rockies,* 222–223.

[103] She also referred to Jacobs as "a wretched little Jew." Louise Wigfall to Halsey Wigfall (London, July 3, 1869), Wigfall MSS.

[104] Johnson did relent momentarily: "But with all his shortcomings he is industrious and has some other good points which may prove available." Johnson to Carpenter (London, May 24, 1871), Johnson MSS.

[105] Johnson to Teller (London, Dec. 30, 1871), Teller MSS.

wrote. "The *middlemen* or *tauters* as they are called here promise everything and accomplish nothing."[106]

Despite his bitterness Johnson must have realized that the British
middleman did accomplish a great deal and, indeed, was indispensable
to the sale of western mines in London. Influential brokers, solicitors,
or financial agents provided contacts, made the arrangements for organizing and registering the necessary joint-stock companies, and led
the campaigns to dispose of the shares—even those paid to the vendor
as part of the purchase price. In this respect the English company promoters—those actually concerned with "bringing out" the formal organization—performed a task which few Americans were fitted to
undertake and in so doing provided the lubrication necessary to keep
the wheels of capital investment turning. It was to be expected that
the price exacted for such services would be a heavy one.

A number of British individuals and firms played leading roles as
middlemen between American vendors and the English public. The
partnership of Coates and Hankey handled several transactions of that
nature in the seventies, as did the powerful London manipulator, Baron
Albert Grant.[107] In the following decade Thomas and S. P. Gilbert were
responsible for the formation of half a dozen concerns to operate mines
in the West,[108] while much-maligned Harry Marks was likewise engaged.[109] Among the sixty companies of all types promoted by Harry
Seymour Foster prior to 1901 were a number of Anglo-American mining concerns with interests in the intermountain region.[110]

Mention might also be made of Jabez "Teddy" Balfour, M.P., the
promoter who customarily opened his company meetings with prayer
but who ultimately fell foul of the law and went to prison for his shady
manipulations.[111] Another, Whitaker Wright, was one of the most controversial financial figures after Baron Grant. English-born, a veteran of
the Leadville boom, a millionaire at the age of thirty-three, Wright

---

[106] The same (London, Sept. 10, 1872), *ibid.*   [107] Below, 143–144.
[108] *Financial Observer*, Aug. 23, 1890.
[109] One outspoken editor openly referred to Marks as a "thief" and challenged
Marks to bring suit for libel. *Ibid.*, Sept. 27, 1890.
[110] Henry Hess (ed.), *The Critic Blackbook* (London, 1901), I, 218–219.
[111] *Anglo-Colorado Mining Guide*, VII (Feb. 27, 1904), 27; Jabez Spencer
Balfour, *My Prison Life* (London, 1907), 7–10, 27. For another similar example,
see Harry Furniss, *Some Victorian Men* (London, 1924), 92.

was one of London's leading mining promoters from the early nineties until his arrest in 1903 on charges of swindling the public by means of fake companies.[112] Fleeing to America, he was apprehended, extradited, and returned to England,[113] where he stood trial but terminated the legal proceedings by swallowing a dose of potassium cyanide.[114]

This is not to infer that all English financiers who promoted Anglo-American mining companies were corrupt and were exposed as such. Some undoubtedly were dishonest and were never unmasked. The great majority, however, were probably as honest as might reasonably be expected and carried on their work silently but effectively behind the scenes. As additional middlemen they raised the price of mines offered in England and invoked the wrath of their American counterparts. But the Yankees recognized, much as they might wish to do otherwise, that the British promoter was there as a vital and unavoidable part of the system and could not be circumvented.

Thus it is seen that mine promotion in England was not a simple procedure. To the field was attracted a host of intermediaries of very diverse nature and background, ranging from drones and drifters to competent mining men and important political figures. In a final analysis, their degree of success was almost as varied. At the worst, there was the plaintive appeal of a James Cummings on the verge of starvation; at the best, there was the million-dollar experience of a Verner Reed. Somewhere in between the two extremes fell the remainder of the hundreds who tried their hand at mine promotion abroad.

The promoter soon learned that distance was both his friend and his enemy. The distance factor prevented too close a scrutiny of the merchandise in many cases and eased the task of minimizing disadvantages. Yet at the same time distance complicated negotiations and often dragged them out unnecessarily while conditions and sentiments changed from favorable to adverse.

The promoter soon learned, too, that the British investing public required special treatment that could best be obtained at the hands

[112] *Dictionary of National Biography,* Suppl. 2, III, 711–712.
[113] Wright *v.* Henkel, 190 *U.S. Reports* (1902), 40–41, 63.
[114] *DNB,* Suppl. 2, III, 713; Hammond, *Autobiography,* II, 446.

of British practitioners. Complex company laws called for specialists who knew the loopholes and the stresses and strains at all points. Thus it was that the Englishman was assigned an important role in promotional campaigns. The techniques of publicity remained largely British throughout the period, although the Langham Hotel set learned rapidly and soon felt at home in its new environment.

⁝ CHAPTER III ⁝

Co-operative Promotion

JUST as mining proved too great a task for the individual in many instances, so also did the work of disposing of mines on the English market sometimes lend itself more to co-operative than to single-handed endeavor. Throughout the forty years under consideration, various "agencies," "bureaus," and joint-stock companies cropped up on both sides of the Atlantic, specifically designed to facilitate the sale in Great Britain of western mining property. Some were established by Americans, some by Englishmen, but most slipped away into obscurity with departures as silent as their arrivals had been boisterous. Most were legitimate, but a few apparently operated as fraudulent organizations from the beginning.

Such co-operative groups were contemplated as early as 1866,[1] and examples are numerous. Customarily the "agency" or "bureau" maintained offices in England and in America. Engineers in the West were available to inspect property for prospective buyers; ore displays, literature, and high-pressure salesmen were "standard equipment" in the

---

[1] The American Bureau of Mines, established in New York in 1866 "to place the mining enterprises of this country on a sure and conservative basis," had a representative in Paris and was contemplating another in London in mid-1867. It was headed by a board of thirteen trustees, mostly financiers, and a twelve-man "Board of Experts," including a number of college professors. *Prospectus of the American Bureau of Mines* (New York, 1866), 4–5; *Mining Journal*, 15 June 1867, 400. The organization soon fell by the wayside, failing, according to one New York editor, primarily because capitalists were more interested in speculative ventures than in facts. *E. & M. Jour.*, May 7, 1872, 298.

London branches. Robert O. Old's[2] British and Colorado Mining Bureau, for example, was established in 1868, with offices in Georgetown, Colorado, and in Bartholomew House, directly behind the Bank of England.[3] On display to the English public were more than 560 specimens of ore, numerous Colorado newspapers, books, annual reports, prospectuses, photographs, and maps.[4] During its existence the Bureau published two pamphlets written by Old, praising the resources of the Rockies and urging investment therein.[5]

The British and Colorado Mining Bureau's activities encompassed a broader scope than most of the agencies of its kind. First of all, it was to act as a medium through which ores might be shipped to England for smelting, thus providing it with a profit as intermediary and at the same time proving the richness of Rocky Mountain ores abroad. After a concerted publicity campaign by Old, at least limited amounts of Colorado ore were freighted to Britain with profit.[6] "We don't propose to ship any ore to Liverpool just yet," commented the editor of the Central City *Register,* "but as the farther it is carried, the more it nets, we may send a lot to China round the Horn." [7]

[2] Born in Somersetshire, Old had emigrated to New York in 1847, then to Illinois and Nebraska before being attracted to Colorado in 1860. A merchant, he dabbled in mining, but soon devoted all his time to the latter, eventually becoming one of the most prominent mining men of the Georgetown region. For biographical sketches see Aaron Frost, "History of Clear Creek County," in *History of Clear Creek and Boulder Valleys, Colorado* (Chicago, 1880), 524; Henry Dudley Teeter, "Some of the Mines and Miners of Georgetown, Colorado," *Magazine of Western History,* XII (Sept. 3, 1890), 503.

[3] Originally Old announced that the Bureau would be organized as a joint-stock company in England. Central City *Herald,* 11 May 1868; *Colorado Transcript* (Golden), June 17, 1868. Indexes of the Companies Registration Offices, and of the registrar of friendly societies, 17 North Audley Street, London, disclose no registration of a concern by this name. This would infer that Old's Bureau was an association or partnership with unlimited liability.

[4] Old, *Colorado,* 38–57, 60–61.

[5] See his *Colorado: United States, America* (London, 1869) and his *Colorado: United States, America, Its Minerals and Other Resources* (London, 1872).

[6] *Rocky Mt. News,* Dec. 8, 13, 1869. Shipping cost estimates varied from about $55 to $95 a ton for the period prior to the completion of a rail line into Denver in 1870. Central City *Register,* Nov. 10, 1869; Robert Orchard Old, Bancroft Statement (Georgetown, May 21, 1886), Pacific MS No. 137, Bancroft Library. After the establishment of rail connections with Denver, shipping costs to Liverpool were set at approximately $78 per ton, according to Old. Old to George W. Heaton (Georgetown, Sept. 7, 1870), Teller MSS.

[7] Nov. 10, 1869.

Co-operative Promotion

A second function of the Bureau, when ore values had been established, was to encourage the investment of English capital in smelting and refining works in Colorado. The Denver Board of Trade gave added stimulus with a promise to donate land;[8] the British and Colorado Smelting Works Company, Ltd., was officially incorporated, but capital was never subscribed;[9] and all efforts of the Bureau to foster English-backed smelters in the Rockies collapsed. In the realization of a third avowed purpose—the sale of Colorado mines abroad—the Bureau achieved some success, but was not, as Old stated in 1872, "the means directly and indirectly, of interesting *all* English Capital at this present invested in Colorado."[10] Of the seventeen joint-stock companies registered in England to carry on mining or smelting operations in the Rocky Mountains during the period of the Bureau's life span,[11] only one can be definitely attributed to the agency.[12] There can be no doubt, however, that it served as an important clearinghouse for information and for bringing together mineowners and potential investors.[13]

The story of the British and Colorado Mining Bureau might be repeated many times, with variations of time and locale. Contemporary with it was a sister concern called the London and Colorado Company,[14] which was credited with having sold at least four "valuable

[8] Denver *Tribune*, Dec. 11, 1871; *Rocky Mt. News*, Dec. 27, 1871.

[9] Certificate of Incorporation, Oct. 7, 1872; *Mem. & Art.*, 2; A. W. Wetherell to registrar (London, Aug. 28, 1878), C.R.O. 6654.

[10] *Colorado, U.S.A.*, 3.

[11] Old later stated that the Bureau closed down in 1872 when local smelters were established in Colorado. Bancroft Statement, Pacific MS 137. Advertisements for his revised pamphlet indicate that the London office was still open in February, 1873. *Mining Journal*, Feb. 1, 1873, 121.

[12] This was the sale of the Terrible mine near Georgetown to the Colorado Terrible Lode Mining Co. in 1870, the first major transfer of a Colorado silver mine to a British concern. *Mem. & Art.*, 25, C.R.O. 4804. It is not unlikely that the Bureau was connected with the sale of mines to the Snowdrift Silver Mining and Reduction Co. in 1871. John Collom of Empire concluded the transaction, but Old reported on the property and held shares in the company. Memo. of Agreement (July 5, 1871) between John Collom and James A. Morgan; Summary of Capital and Shares to June 9, 1876, C.R.O. 5537.

[13] See John Innes to George Heaton (Georgetown, Jan. 4, 1871); Charles N. Leland to Heaton (Central City, Sept. 29, 1870), Teller MSS. For a more detailed treatment see Clark C. Spence, "The British and Colorado Mining Bureau," *Colorado Magazine*, XXXIII (April, 1956), 81–92.

[14] First mention of this concern is found in a letter from William Byers, requesting that the *Weekly Central City Register* be sent to the firm's London

properties" in London.[15] Others, like the Wyoming Mining Agency or the American Bureau of Mining Information for Utah, were evanescent and highly unsuccessful; they soon faded away unheralded.[16] Some dealt not only in mines, but in rail, gas, and water ventures as well.[17] A few were primarily defensive, to safeguard the interests of British brokers and their clients.[18] Still others, like the Mining Bureau of the Pacific Coast, managed to achieve considerable publicity and to embroil themselves in entanglements on both sides of the Atlantic. Under the tutelage of Colonel J. Berton, the French vice-consul at Sacramento, and with the foreign consuls resident on the Pacific Coast as ex officio directors,[19] this last organization represented interests in California, Nevada, Arizona, and Utah [20] and maintained branch offices in both Salt Lake City and London.[21] Among other accomplishments it drew down a storm of criticism upon Territorial Governor George L. Woods, who endeavored to support its schemes with his official position.[22] Oblique references indicate that the entire project came to

office. To the editors of the *Register* (Denver, Sept. 13, 1870), Byers Letterbook (1868–1871). First advertisements appeared in British mining periodicals in April, 1871. *Mining Journal,* April 15, 1871, 309. For a description of the company's activities see Georgetown *Miner,* April 25, 1872.

[15] William Larned to George Heaton (Central City, Aug. 28, 1871), Teller MSS.

[16] The Wyoming Mining Agency offered 3,000 shares of the Wyoming Sweetwater Mining Co. in England in 1871. *Mining Journal,* Oct. 29, 1871, 913. The American Bureau of Mining Information for Utah was headed by Warren Hussey, one of the principals in the Emma silver mine fiasco of the early seventies. *Sci. Press,* March 30, June 8, 1872, 193, 360; *E. & M. Jour.,* May 7, 1872, 297.

[17] The European and American Agency, opened in 1871, had such a broad base. *Mining World,* June 24, 1871, 257.

[18] An example was the Stock Exchange Mining Bureau, a London organization of the early seventies. *Mining Journal,* Aug. 12, 1871, 697.

[19] *Mining Bureau of the Pacific Coast* (San Francisco, 1872), 1–2, 8–9.

[20] *Ibid.,* 12.

[21] *Mining Journal,* Jan. 18, March 16, 1872, 81, 254. London offices were with Elkin, Goetz & Co., 5 Great Winchester Street Buildings. London *Times,* Jan. 16, 1872. By 1874 the agency also employed an agent in Paris. *Mining Journal,* Aug. 15, 1874, 881.

[22] Woods promised that engineering reports made for the Bureau would be certified with the seal of his office and that of Territorial Secretary George A. Black. To editor (Salt Lake, May 18, 1872), London *Times,* June 12, 1872. Periodicals at home and abroad assailed him for this announcement. *Investors' Guardian,* June 15, 1872; *Salt Lake Daily Herald,* July 7, 1872. Black made haste to disavow any connection with the Bureau; others threw the entire blame on Woods. See

an abrupt and ignominious end at the hands of an American court, but details are lacking.[23]

The flurry of promotional organizations which characterized the early seventies subsided somewhat in the next two decades yet never completely disappeared.[24] In the eighties Alexander Del Mar of Del Mar's Agency in London advised Americans as to what they might expect when floating mines in England.[25] The Anglo-American and Australasian Mining, Land, and Finance Agency heartily endorsed the Black Hills mines of Dakota and endeavored to operate on a global scale.[26] In the nineties interested Britons called for the establishment of a central bureau in London which would act as "not only a protection and safeguard to investors, but the center of much permanent profitable business." [27] There was at this time one agency fulfilling at least part of this role, although on a limited scale. This was the Anglo-Colorado Mining and Milling Agency, which was founded in 1898 and which directed its energies almost exclusively to the pushing of Colorado mines in England through its monthly publication, the *Anglo-Colorado Mining and Milling Guide*, edited by Edward Toye.[28] But this was a small organization, operating with scanty capital and doubtful effectiveness.

During the nineties emphasis was on another type of agency—the so-called "parent" company, which actively purchased options or titles outright and occasionally undertook development work before transferring the mines to subsidiary or wholly independent companies, if

Black to Hamilton Fish (Salt Lake, July, 9, 1872); Thomas Fitch to Fish (Salt Lake, Aug. 8, Sept. 6, 1872), Territorial Papers: Utah, II, National Archives.

[23] An Englishman in California in 1874 referred to the Bureau and its efforts at blackmail. It was pronounced a swindle by the courts, he insisted. J. Barr Robertson to J. M. Walker (n.p., Nov. 2, 1874), Robertson Letterbook. For a more detailed treatment see Clark C. Spence, "The Mining Bureau of the Pacific Coast," *California Historical Society Quarterly*, XXXV (Dec., 1956), 335–344.

[24] There were complaints in the seventies directed against "bureaus" which collected free samples from miners, set up their displays, then decamped with the ore, leaving only unpaid bills. *E. & M. Jour.*, Sept. 22, 1877, 219.

[25] *Mining Journal*, Oct. 26, 1878, 1185; *Sci. Press*, Oct. 1, 1881, 218.

[26] *Mining Journal*, Aug. 18, 1883, 965.

[27] *Georgetown Courier*, Aug. 27, 1898.

[28] The Western States (U.S.A.) Finance Syndicate was incorporated in 1900 to take over the work of this agency. Toye continued to edit the *Guide*, but operations were still on a limited scale. *Mem. & Art.*, 1, C.R.O. 64868.

such could be formed. For example, Henry Bratnober and T. A. Bennett, both mining engineers, were the key figures in the Mining and Financial Trust Syndicate, Ltd., which was responsible for floating two successful concerns, the Elkhorn Mining Company, Ltd. (Montana), and the De Lamar Mining Company, Ltd. (Idaho), as well as one unsuccessful one, the Harquahala Gold Mining Company, Ltd. (Arizona).[29]

This was probably not a "typical" parent company, in that its degree of success was higher than most. A number of projected parent companies failed even to raise their own capital.[30] Others managed to keep their heads above water only briefly. The North American Exploration Company, Ltd., reported in 1896 that more than 450 mining propositions had been put before it since its incorporation in September of the previous year.[31] Yet for various reasons this concern failed and was forced to abandon a number of its options in Colorado and Arizona.[32] Baron Walter von Richthofen's Anglo-Colorado Exploration Syndicate, Ltd. (1896), succeeded in leasing one property and selling another to a subsidiary,[33] but the death of its promoter and a subsequent lack of capital brought increasing difficulties, although the concern managed to survive for another decade.[34]

At the end of the century the most important British promotional company for western mines was probably the Venture Corporation, Ltd. This powerful syndicate was the key to the sale of Stratton's Independence in London [35] and was active in negotiating for properties

[29] Memo. of Agreement (Jan. 28, 1890) between the Mining and Financial Trust Syndicate and William Turnpenny, Elkhorn Mining Co., C.R.O. B-30756; *ibid.* (March 2, 1891) between the Mining and Financial Trust Syndicate and Thomas Major, De Lamar Mining Co., C.R.O. B-33492; *Report of the Annual Meeting of the Harquahala Gold Mining Company, Limited, Held on December 23rd, 1896,* Stock Exchange Archives, London.

[30] Among company prospectuses in the London Stock Exchange with the words "not floated" penned across them are those of the Cripple Creek and Western Development Corp. (1896) and Cripple Creek Mines (Jan. 31, 1896), both projected as promotional enterprises.

[31] *Directors' Report,* Sept. 26, 1895 to Dec. 31, 1896.

[32] *Annual Report,* year ending Dec. 31, 1897. For another typical example see Alfred Caillat to registrar (London, Sept. 23, 1901), Cripple Creek Agency Syndicate, C.R.O. B-46244.

[33] *Directors' Report,* Feb. 26, 1896 to Dec. 31, 1898.

[34] *Ibid.;* Dissolution Notice, Feb. 25, 1910, C.R.O. B-26995.

[35] Above, 28.

in almost every trans-Mississippi state and territory.[36] It was even rumored that Queen Victoria had money invested in the concern.[37]

It should be noted, too, that British and American brokerage houses were exceedingly active in the late 1890's and frequently reached over into each other's territory. Walters Brothers and Kitchener, for example, maintained broker's offices in both London and Denver in 1900, and Kitchener, the brother of the famed British general and war minister, sought to promote the sale of Colorado mining shares in his native land.[38] On the other hand, American brokerage houses were equally active. At least five Colorado Springs brokerage and investment firms had London branches in the period from 1898 to 1900,[39] and all were primarily concerned with the disposal of shares in American mining companies, rather than with the sale of mining property itself.

The task of evaluating the relative importance of individual and co-operative promotional efforts in any quantitative sense is not an easy one. Too often the official records of Anglo-American joint-stock companies give no indication of the activities which preceded incorporation. Often figureheads appear as vendors or promoters, with no reference to the true intermediaries. But be that as it may, whether individual or co-operative, open or concealed, promotion still depended very largely upon the efforts of one or a few men. It was Robert Old who made the British and Colorado Mining Bureau an

---

[36] The Venture Corporation reorganized two of its subsidiary companies in Australia to take over mines in Boulder County, Colo., in 1898. It also held an interest in and an option on all shares of the Moon-Anchor Consolidated Gold Mines, which was registered to acquire property at Cripple Creek. Venture Corporation, *Annual Report*, year ending Dec. 31, 1899. For other negotiations see Report of the Director of the Mint upon the Production of the Precious Metals in the United States during the Calendar Year 1899, *Ho. Doc.* No. 239, 56 Cong., 2 Sess. (1900–1901), 106; *Anglo-Colorado Mining Guide*, II (June 24, 1899), suppl. iv; III (Jan. 27, 1900), 7; IV (Jan. 30, 1901), 9; V (Jan. 31, 1902), 1.

[37] *Anglo-Colorado Mining Guide*, II (May 27, 1899), 72.

[38] *Ibid.*, III (Nov. 30, 1900), 170.

[39] The Crosby-Ehrich Syndicate plugged the Portland, Gold King, Vindicator, and Cripple Creek Gold Exploration—all well-known Colorado properties. The Approved Investment Co. was agent for Gold Coin, Mount Rosa, Cameron Lands, Columbine Victor Tunnel, and Battle Mountain Consolidated. Bonbright and Co. pushed Lillie, Ingham, Royal, Twenty-Six, Good Will Tunnel and Mining, and the Work Co. The Woods Investment Co. and the Reed and Hamlin Investment Co. were also active in London. *Ibid.*, I (March 26, Nov. 26, 1898), 27, 151; III (May 30, 1900), 80.

active concern; it was Baron von Richthofen who breathed life into the Anglo-Colorado Exploration Syndicate, Ltd. Without the driving force of such men these joint operations would have been stalled at the beginning. Without the impulse of such figures the entire movement to dispose of mines and mining shares abroad would have dragged. They and their prototypes were the individuals who provided the momentum to move the investment wheels from dead center and to keep them turning in times of good fortune and poor.

: CHAPTER IV :

Promotional Methods and Techniques

PUBLICITY is a handmaiden of salesmanship. Once a mine was "brought" to England and placed on the market, there still remained the task of convincing the public that the enterprise was one worthy of investment. Sharp promoters, operating individually or co-operatively, could be depended upon to cater to the wishes of the English investor and to prey upon his weaknesses. If we may believe Rossiter W. Raymond of the *Engineering and Mining Journal,* there were plenty of weaknesses. "Of all the large class of idiotic capitalists," said Raymond in 1881, "the 'Britisher' shows the least symptom of intelligence." [1] William Weston, then in London endeavoring to dispose of Colorado mines, readily endorsed those sentiments with complaints against "the Astute and Conservative Britisher": "The average Britisher is far too astute to go into anything really good because it is American, does not in the least object to being swindled, provided it is done by one of his own countrymen, and if by a body of them with a Duke's name as a director; it is positively delightful." [2]

Here Weston was referring to those characteristics which colored British company promotion throughout the last half of the nineteenth

[1] July 23, 1881, 53.

[2] To editor (London, May 30, 1881), *ibid.,* June 18, 1881, 415.

century. The "lord-loving public," as one critic phrased it,[3] was easy prey for undertakings set up with boards of directors composed of well-known, respectable persons, preferably English but acceptable if of high station even though foreign. The titled "guinea pig," as he became known, was no isolated phenomenon, and his presence was not confined to the mineral industry.

His presence brought criticism both early and late, but he was as much a part of joint-stock organization as limited liability. A publication of 1883 satirically described the main function of the director as being "to confirm all arrangements entered into by the promoter and vendor"; his main qualifications were listed as being "an absence of special knowledge of anything in particular."[4] These conditions could be met by practically any M.P., any gentleman with a title, or any retired military officer who now desired to test his mettle on the field of financial battle.

Discerning observers quickly saw the folly of such an arrangement and insisted that

the name of one thoroughly good man of business, especially if he has gained his own position in cognate undertakings, is worth on a Board, and as a guarantee to investors, more than the titles of fifty young or middle-aged gentlemen, who find it an agreeable relief from the monotony of club life to have a pretence of business once a week in the City.[5]

Or a skeptical English engineer might pose the question:

Why should a prospectus with a sprinkling of peers, or a report with a preface of M.P.'s, such as those of the Californian and Nevada mines, or rather quarries, on the tops of hills, in many cases inaccessible for want of roads and powers of locomotion, command, as if by magic our universal confidence, and absorb the proceeds of our toil from our breeches pocket?[6]

In determining a case concerning the Nevada Freehold Properties Trust, Vice-Chancellor Bacon of the Court of Chancery termed the enterprise "a bubble and a cheat" and turned on the highly respectable

[3] *Mining Magazine and Review,* I (Jan., 1872), 40.

[4] "Jaycee," *Public Companies from the Cradle to the Grave (Or How Promoters Prey on the People)* (London, 1883), 8. For another typical contemporary assault on guinea pig directors see Malcolm Ronald Laing-Meason, *Sir William's Speculations; or, The Seamy Side of Finance* (London, 1886).

[5] *Mining Magazine and Review,* I (Jan., 1872), 46.

[6] R. Tredinnick to editor (London, n.d.), *Mining Journal,* Aug. 12, 1871, 706.

Promotional Methods and Techniques

Englishmen connected with the board. "They ought not to have put their names on that prospectus," he said, "because in point of fact, by so doing, they went beyond the ordinary *role* of a directors' list as guinea pigs and by some new Darwinian process, whether of advance or retrogression, became 'decoy ducks.' " [7]

Probably a bit peeved as a result of his own lack of success in disposing of Colorado mines, William Weston soundly disapproved of the whole system and remarked snidely that

Sir George Deadbroke, Bart., Lord Arthur Pauper, Viscount Damphule, Major-General Haw-Damme, late of H.M. Forty-first Fall-backs, and others of that ilk, are always ready to lend the charm of their great names to these enterprises, and attend the board meetings, for the moderate consideration of one guinea per meeting; the British snob, who, I regret to say forms a large proportion of the population of the "tight little island," snaps at the bait, only too proud to be hooked by such august fishermen. [8]

Such influential journals as the *Statist* and the *Economist* made the same point in less emphatic, if more disinterested, fashion, referring contemptuously to "company mongers" and "Titled Decoy Ducks" and showing the interlinking directorates in literally dozens of British mining companies operating in all parts of the world. [9] Even at the end of the nineteenth century popular books on mining company promotion indicated that if changes had occurred they were so slight as to be unnoticeable. [10]

The prospectuses of almost any proposed mining company in the period from 1860 to 1900 invariably carried at least one or two names of added weight, affixed for their effect upon the investing public. That of the Emma Silver Mining Company, Ltd. (1871), was the most conspicuous example, with an original board made up not only of the United States minister to the Court of St. James and a United States senator, but also three members of Parliament, a commander of the Bath, and the future Lord Stanley. [11]

Some companies, however, such as the Reese River Silver Mining

[7] *In re* Nevada Freehold Properties Trust—Gadsden's Claim, reported in *Mining World*, Jan. 25, 1873, 161.

[8] To editor (London, May 30, 1881), *E. & M. Jour.*, June 18, 1881, 415.

[9] *Statist* (London), July 9, 1891, 32–33; *Economist*, Dec. 6, 1902, 1883–1884.

[10] See Burton S. James, *An Analysis of Modern Mine Promotion* (London, 1900), 5.

[11] *Prospectus* (Nov. 9, 1871). See also below, 146.

Company, Ltd., of 1865, were satisfied with a mere naval captain, a lieutenant colonel and M.P., an Anglican minister, and a former accountant-general of Inland Revenue.[12] Others, like the Atlanta Silver Mining Company, Ltd., organized half a dozen years later to operate in Idaho, had a directorate composed entirely of members of the London Stock Exchange.[13] Or the ill-fated Mineral Hill Silver Mines Company, Ltd. (1871), felt secure in selecting two M.P.'s as trustees for the debenture holders and throwing in another on the board of directors. But it was undoubtedly the presence of the John Taylors, junior and senior, of the highly respected London firm of mining engineers, John Taylor and Sons, on the board [14] that inspired the confidence of many investors. Yet even the presence of such established experts could not prevent speedy failure as the result of the purchase of worthless property.[15]

When the prospectus of Crooke's Mining and Smelting Company, Ltd., was issued in 1882, it could point out that the Hinsdale County, Colorado, property had been inspected by four different individuals, among them Professors J. S. Newberry of the Columbia School of Mines and James E. Thorold Rogers, the eminent Oxonian and M.P., who also joined the board.[16] Time was to prove that Thorold Rogers was much better versed in the history of prices than in mines and mining companies. By 1885 he was describing the company as a "gigantic swindle" and ruing the day he became connected with it.[17] His remarks elicited no sympathy from the *Economist*, however, as that organ cited this as another evidence of a time-honored evil:

But however unpleasant it may be to say it we cannot but think he is somewhat to blame in the matter. Mr. Thorold Rogers is not a mining expert, nor, so far as we know has he had any special experience in mining affairs. What those who approached him wished, therefore, was not the benefit of special experience in the conduct of the business of the company, but the advantage of a name which would favourably impress investors and induce them to engage in a speculation of which they might otherwise have fought shy. Of this Mr. Rogers could hardly have been ignorant, and we do think that men of standing such as he ought not to lend their names to undertakings of which they can know little, but of whose *bona fides* they, by becoming prominently

---

[12] *Prospectus* (1865).
[13] Prospectus published in the London *Times*, Jan. 16, 1871.
[14] *Prospectus* (1871).   [15] *Economist*, June 8, 1872, 709.
[16] *Prospectus* (April, 1882).   [17] *Economist*, June 6, 1885, 693.

associated with them, are supposed by investors to afford some guarantee. This is the moral of Mr. Rogers' story, and it is to be hoped that it will be taken to heart.[18]

One of the most flagrant examples of the misuse of titled "decoy ducks" occurred in the floating of the Sapphire and Ruby Company of Montana, Ltd., which was placed before the British public in October, 1891. Having a normal "guinea pig" directorate with the customary sprinkling of illustrious names, the concern issued 400 founder's shares along with its 450,000 ordinary shares, the former to bear special privileges.[19] The prospectus, inviting subscriptions to half the ordinary shares, stated that the founder's shares had all been subscribed and would be allotted in full to some 128 prominent individuals whose names graced an entire page. Among them were such personalities as the Marquess of Lorne, the Duke of Portland, the Earl of Clarendon, and a veritable host of others. Moreover, the prospectus announced specifically that the subscribers of the founder's shares "have guaranteed subscriptions for Ordinary Shares amounting in the aggregate to the whole of the Ordinary Shares now offered." [20]

A subsequent committee of investigation damned the device of founder's shares and their manipulation as "undoubtedly calculated to induce investors to believe that these gentlemen were substantially interested in the capital and welfare of the Company." [21] Of the entire list of names on the prospectus, only twenty-one had been allotted shares other than the privileged ones, to a total number of 9,755.[22] The committee found the statement that the founders had guaranteed the whole of the issue of 225,000 ordinary shares "open to grave animadversion" and it showed that the bulk of these shares had been underwritten by less influential and less responsible "men of straw," as the *Economist* called them,[23] who forfeited a total of 161,732 shares, which

[18] *Ibid.*

[19] When 20 per cent per year had been paid in dividends on ordinary shares, founder's shares were to receive half the surplus profits over that percentage. *Mem. & Art.*, 33, C.R.O. B-35044.

[20] *Prospectus* (Oct. 28, 1891).

[21] *Report of the Investigation Committee* (Nov. 29, 1894), 5, Stock Exchange Archives, London.

[22] In 1894, 1,000 of these had not been paid for. Two of the defaulters were company directors receiving pay. *Ibid.*, 5–6.

[23] Dec. 8, 1894, 1509.

were then re-allotted to the vendors.[24] Apparently public response to the entire project was not good,[25] but the case stands as a broad illustration of the use of important names to convey the belief that solid backing stood behind a newly introduced enterprise.

The stamina of guinea-pig directors was often amazing. Henry Hess's *Black Book* for 1901–1902 showed Claude Theodore James Vautin, a most versatile individual, as then being on the directorates of no fewer than twenty-three companies, including at least six which operated in the western portion of the United States.[26] In the same source the Earl of Chesterfield could boast of twenty-five, including the huge Colorado venture, Stratton's Independence, Ltd.[27] Sir Henry Seton-Karr was credited with thirty-three,[28] Edward Thomas Reed, fifty-eight,[29] but Percy Tarbutt of the engineering firm Tarbutt and Quintin led the pack with a total of eighty-one.[30] These are but a few examples out of many illustrative of the "professionalism" which came to be attached to the boards of directors of mining companies, as with joint-stock companies in general.

Nor were secretaries always far behind the guinea-pig directors. A biting editorial of the *Stock Exchange Review* late in 1874 sharply criticized one William J. Lavington and listed eighteen mining companies, eight of them in western America, for which Lavington was acting as secretary. No wonder John Longmaid, the harassed manager of one of them—the Utah Silver Mining Company, Ltd.—complained that the London office was indifferent to his correspondence.[31]

The normal publicity techniques included the appropriate newspaper blurbs and the issuance of a prospectus extolling the virtues of the particular property and the contemplated company. One English authority notes that of a total of 9,221 mining companies registered in Great Britain between 1880 and 1904, 1,648 issued prospectuses— roughly one for every five concerns.[32] It would appear that Anglo-

[24] *Report Invest. Com.*, 11–12.

[25] In January, 1896, cash paid in from calls totaled £48,424 16s. and there were 840 shareholders. Summary of Capital and Shares to Jan. 14, 1896, C.R.O. B-35044.

[26] In 1898 Vautin had been arrested for fraud and had spent six months in prison. He went bankrupt in 1890 and again in 1900. I, 1327–1328.

[27] *Ibid.*, 253–254.

[28] At least three of these were in Colorado and Wyoming. *Ibid.*, 1148–1149.

[29] *Ibid.*, 1055–1059.   [30] *Ibid.*, 1241–1248.   [31] IV (Dec., 1874).

[32] Edward Ashmead, *Twenty-Five Years of Mining, 1880–1904* (London, 1909), 149.

American companies maintained an average in this respect higher than the general run of joint-stock concerns. Prior to about 1890 shares were usually allotted publicly; in the later period private underwriting placed a resulting de-emphasis on the original prospectus.[33]

All too many of these early Anglo-American prospectuses were masterpieces of deception and evasion which held out the flimsiest of concrete inducements, yet the most imaginative of promises. Normally they came before the public early on Saturday morning, to coincide with the fanfare appearing in the major mining and financial periodicals of London.[34] A few painted such optimistic pictures as to defy credulity.

When a tempting project called the Pyramid Range Silver Mountain Company, Ltd., was set before the British investor early in 1871 by the firm of Coates and Hankey, its prospectus represented a new high in creative fiction. The *Stock Exchange Review,* the organ of Asbury Harpending, who was to act as vendor in the transaction involving "fabulous" mines in Grant County, New Mexico, stated simply that "one pauses for want of breath at the contemplation, and we will merely add that the enterprise is introduced under such thoroughly respectable auspices that there can be no shadow of suspicion of intentional exaggeration."[35] The "thoroughly respectable auspices" turned out to be Harpending himself, soon to be famous in the great diamond scandal of 1872, and Baron Albert Grant, one of the most questionable of London's financial wizards and a leading figure in the Emma Silver Mining Company debacle of the same period! Years later Harpending did admit that the prospectus "had put the tales of Baron Munchausen in the shade."[36] Another contemporary termed it a "preamble of traditional yarns, collected from Jesuit manuscripts."[37] The financial editor of the *Hour* a few years later waxed even more eloquent in describing it:

Now, through the whole period of the South Sea Bubble, and from the first to the last pages of "Don Quixote," "The Arabian Nights," "Baron Mun-

---

[33] *Ibid.,* 154.   [34] *Statist,* May 7, 1881, 504.   [35] I (Jan., 1871).

[36] Asbury Harpending, *The Great Diamond Hoax and Other Stirring Incidents in the Life of Asbury Harpending,* ed. by James H. Wilkins (San Francisco, 1913), 177. Harpending insists on calling this project the New Mexico Land and Silver Mining Co., but the facts are obviously those of the Pyramid Range enterprise.

[37] "Enfant Terrible" to editor (London, March 7, 1871), *Mining Journal,* March 11, 1871, 211.

chausen," and the writings of Dumas, no exaggeration ever approached the statements in this prospectus. It gave the go-by to the search after the Philosopher's Stone, to Cagliostro, and the whole race of alchemists.[38]

The prospectus had been drawn up by an enthusiastic Briton, one Henry Morgan, who had visited the mines earlier and who, according to Harpending, "looked like the president of the Bank of England and the Prince of Wales rolled into one." [39] In it a net profit was predicted of £560,000 per year or more than 100 per cent on a proposed capital of £500,000.[40] Accompanying was a sketch of the "mountains of silver" controlled by the company-to-be, ranging in height from 18 to 11,000 feet, with the most important mine, the General Lee, looming up, Matterhornlike, in the desert air. No shafts were needed—ore was solid quartz and could be quarried like limestone! Silver values of up to $4,861.09 per ton were cited and, according to the prospectus, the "Pater Argenti" of the whole world had been discovered.[41]

Such flagrant claims brought down the wrath of the *Times*'s all-powerful city editor, Marmaduke Sampson, who was credited by some with having more financial influence than the Queen. "Five lines favorable from Samson's [sic] pen in the financial columns of the *Times* assured the success of an enterprise," wrote Harpending later. "Five lines unfavorable were equivalent to a death warrant." [42] In no uncertain terms Sampson blocked the floating of the Pyramid Range Silver Mountain Company, Ltd., and slew it with a single editorial jawbone.[43]

When the Republican Mountain Silver Mines, Ltd., was promoted in 1880, its prospectus estimated net profits of £116,640 per year— no more, no less—and the description of its Colorado property was as colored as the bright reproduction of Republican Mountain that graced the elaborate announcement. Although company officials in America supposedly stood behind the estimates of future profit, avowing them

---

[38] *Hour* (London), Jan. 21, 1876.
[39] Harpending, *Great Diamond Hoax*, 174.
[40] Pyramid Range Silver Mountain Co., *Prospectus* (Jan., 1871).
[41] *Ibid.*   [42] *Great Diamond Hoax*, 177.
[43] London *Times*, Jan. 28., 1871. The property was then withdrawn from the market, and all subscriptions were returned after promotion fell flat in the city. Harpending, *Great Diamond Hoax*, 178. Harpending had his revenge. He and a confederate exposed secret links between Sampson and financier Albert Grant which brought the editor's disgrace and dismissal. *Mining Journal*, Jan. 23, 1875. 100.

Promotional Methods and Techniques

"true and trustworthy to the best of our knowledge and belief," [44] subsequent investigation uncovered so many misstatements that American officers were forced to disavow the entire prospectus. It had been drawn up in London by one Frederick Von Stech without the knowledge of the responsible "advising committee" in New York, they said, and to prove their good faith they promptly and permanently severed the connection of Von Stech with the company.[45]

While most Anglo-American prospectuses were not as obvious in their misrepresentations, all followed the same general approach, but seldom were scruples allowed to interfere with the presentation of information to the public. Obviously it was necessary that the potential investor be made aware of the lush fruits being offered merely for the taking. Almost all prospectuses gave estimates of future profits, for no device was thought more effective than simple appeal to the individual pocketbook. High dividends were promised, to be paid as soon as possible or, occasionally, to be guaranteed by various devious arrangements. When, in 1865, a trio of Anglo-Nevada mining companies blossomed out in London, the prospectus of one estimated that the development and operation of but two of its four mines would yield an annual profit equal to the whole of the subscribed capital.[46] Another of the three promised "probable dividends of 200 to 300 per cent" on a nominal capital of £100,000.[47] The third concern merely described its lodes as "containing pure silver, varying from 25 to 87 per cent." [48]

Seldom did results reach the high level of expectation set by the prospectus. None of the above-mentioned companies ever paid a penny in dividends. The majority of others followed the same pattern. For example, the Nevada Freehold Properties Trust advertised in 1869 that its mines would bring in £69,165 per year in rentals and royalties, with no need of working capital.[49] Four years later the official liquidator was announcing "a complete loss of the whole of the subscribed capital, and no asset left representing it." [50]

The Flagstaff silver mine in Little Cottonwood, Utah, was taken up by an English company in 1871. The prospectus of the new concern,

[44] *Prospectus* (Sept., 1880).   [45] *Weekly Miner,* Sept. 10, Dec. 17, 1881.
[46] Austin Consolidated Silver Mines Co., *Prospectus* (June, 1865).
[47] Lander City Silver Mining Co., *Prospectus* (June, 1865).
[48] Reese River Silver Mining Co., *Prospectus* (June, 1865).
[49] *Prospectus* (July, 1869).
[50] *Investors' Monthly Manual* (London), III n.s. (Jan. 25, 1873), 31.

the Flagstaff Silver Mining Company of Utah, Ltd., emphasized the proximity of the property to the illustrious Emma mine and estimated annual net profits at 36 per cent. Furthermore, it was announced, dividends would be paid monthly and would commence promptly in exactly two months.[51] The Flagstaff did pay substantial dividends for a time, but when payments were suspended in August, 1873, after £123,-000 had been distributed, it was discovered that only £50,000 of that amount had been earned; the remainder had been borrowed from the vendor and was still owed.[52]

The same tradition was carried into the eighties and nineties. The Montana Company, Ltd., one of the most successful concerns operating from London, was presented to the public with a great flourish in 1883 as about to acquire the Drumlummon at Marysville, Montana, "believed to be one of the Greatest Silver and Gold Mines in the World." The Drumlummon was a great mine—it returned more than £600,000 in dividends during its period of British ownership[53]—but it did not, as the prospectus insisted, contain ore "sufficient to keep the mine at work for the next one hundred years."[54] A sister concern, the Anglo-Montana Mining Company, Ltd., was more modest in its pretensions. Its prospectus estimated annual returns of £40,000 for the next sixty years;[55] its life span barely covered two.[56] In 1890 the appearance of a prospectus issued by the Silver Bell Mining and Smelting Company, Ltd., contemplating yearly dividends of 50 per cent from the firm's Arizona mines,[57] brought jeers of derision from London critics:

We have no evidence as to title, and we have no evidence *whatever* of the proportions, if any, in which the Silver, Lead, Copper, Rags, Bones, and Kitchenstuff exists. . . . The promoters must be under the same impression as the grave digger in "Hamlet" as to the sanity of the English race of *investors.*[58]

Despite this, the Silver Bell was floated, but its career in Arizona was anything but successful.[59]

[51] Abridged prospectus, *Mining Journal*, Dec. 2, 1871, 1069.
[52] Thomas Skinner (ed.), *The Stock Exchange Year-Book and Diary for 1875* (London, n.d.), 162.
[53] Below, 124.   [54] *Prospectus* (Jan., 1883).   [55] *Prospectus* (July, 1886).
[56] Compulsory wind-up order, High Court of Justice, Chancery Division (July 25, 1888), C.R.O. B-22978.
[57] *Prospectus* (July 12, 1890).   [58] *Financial Observer*, July 12, 1890.
[59] Arizona operations were suspended in 1892, and the concern then invested

Promotional Methods and Techniques

Not only were substantial dividends offered, but many concerns also promised immediate profits. The Gold Mining Company of Yuba, Ltd., for example, predicted in 1869 that its Idaho property could be put in working order in from three to four months and that profits could commence at that time.[60] The Emma Silver Mining Company, Ltd., of Utah promised in November, 1871, that 18 per cent monthly dividends would begin on December 1 of the same year.[61] What the prospectus did not explain was that these dividends would be paid largely out of capital and borrowed funds, contrary to law. Other concerns operating in Colorado in the 1880's and the 1890's promised "returns made this year" [62] or advertised their property as an "Immediate Dividend Payer." [63]

Occasionally a company offered a guaranteed dividend of some sort, although few were successful. Sometimes this guarantee took the form of depositing for a specified period part of the purchase money due to be paid the vendor; [64] sometimes this deposit was to be made in shares of the company; [65] sometimes, as in the case of the Dexter, Colorado, Gold Mining Company, Ltd. (1886), the vendor agreed to deposit "suitable government bonds" with the company's bankers in order to ensure dividends of 10 per cent for two years.[66] In looking over this particular arrangement, one London periodical quipped: "If the vendor gets what he asks, we should call him a 'dexterous Colorado vendor.' " [67] Apparently potential vendor George Armstrong did not prove particularly adroit, for the company soon faded into the London mist, with even the registrar of companies ignorant of its whereabouts.[68]

---

in the West Australian Mining Co. Silver Bell Mining and Smelting Co., *Annual Report,* year ending Sept. 30, 1892; *Annual Report,* year ending Sept. 30, 1893.

[60] Abridged prospectus, *Mining Journal,* July 31, 1869, 550.

[61] *Prospectus* (Nov. 9, 1871).

[62] Gilpin Gold Placers, *Prospectus* (July, 1886).

[63] Gilpin Gold, *Prospectus* (Nov. 30, 1895).

[64] One Anglo-Nevada concern stipulated that £6,000 of the cash payable to the vendor was to be held on deposit by the company for two years, to guarantee the payment of dividends at the rate of 10 per cent per annum during that period. Austin Consolidated Silver Mines Co., *Prospectus* (June, 1865).

[65] See Memo. of Agreement (Nov. 7, 1883) between Thomas Carmichael (on behalf of vendor Edward Pray) and Joseph Land, Jr., Richardson Gold and Silver Mining Co., C.R.O. E-1341.

[66] *Prospectus* (June, 1886); Memo. of Agreement (March 1, 1886) between George P. Armstrong and Leonard B. Northcote, C.R.O. B-22298.

[67] *Financial Critic,* June 12, 1886.

[68] George Chead to registrar (London, Oct. 16, 1891), C.R.O. B-22298.

British Investments and American Mines

In addition to promising immediate dividends or, occasionally, pledging guaranteed returns, the normal prospectus also endeavored to prove the doctrine of richness by association. The fact that a company's mines were located in a district or territory of known mineral wealth automatically made them of undeniable value. Thus, when Colonel William Sydney O'Connor brought Nevada property to England in 1864, the prospectus of a British concern incorporated to take over his mines insisted that the location was itself an assurance of success. In Washoe "almost every investment is yielding enormous returns," it stated. "Indeed, it may be fearlessly affirmed that where capital is judiciously employed failure is impossible as the sources of wealth themselves are inexhaustible." [69] Within three years this Washoe United Consolidated Gold and Silver Mining Company, Ltd., had constructed seven and a half miles of canal "capable of carrying the whole Truckee River," [70] had built a £20,000 twenty-stamp mill, had returned no dividends, but had accumulated a £20,000 mortgage debt and was on the verge of extinction.[71]

Prospectuses of three other Anglo-Nevada mining companies formed in 1865 dwelt in glowing terms on the "great success" of the Washoe United Consolidated Gold and Silver Mining Company, Ltd., and on the richness and productivity of Comstock mines taken as a whole.[72] One went so far as to cite the records of a number of well-known mines on the Comstock and even in California.[73] This emphasis was grossly misleading and undoubtedly designed to prey on the geographical ignorance of potential investors, for all the three new companies were organized to acquire property in the Reese River District of Nevada, halfway across the state from the Comstock Lode. "Why," said the Nevada state mineralogist in 1866, "it would be just as absurd to quote mines in Cornwall, England, to increase the value of one in Northumberland, two hundred miles away." [74]

[69] Washoe United Consolidated Gold and Silver Mining Co., *Prospectus* (June, 1864).

[70] *Mining Journal*, Oct. 30, 1897, 1280.   [71] *Ibid.*, March 16, 1867, 177.

[72] Prospectuses of Austin Consolidated Silver Mines Co., Lander City Silver Mining Co., and Reese River Silver Mining Co., all June, 1865.

[73] Reese River Silver Mining Co., *Prospectus* (June, 1865).

[74] The state mineralogist also protested against misleading statements concerning the availability of railroads in the regions and costs of mill construction and operation, which were set much too low. *Annual Report of the State Mineralogist of the State of Nevada for 1866* (Carson City, 1867), 111.

Promotional Methods and Techniques

While numerous other concerns throughout the period emphasized the mineral worth of the areas in which their mines were located, some examples were more flagrant violations of veracity than others. Probably the most distorted use of geography was in the prospectus of Herbert C. Drinkwater's Old Guard Mining Company, Ltd., issued in 1887.[75] This document elaborated on an Arizona mine, emphasizing its "virgin" character and the fact that Arizona's climate allowed year round work. Then it made reference to the tremendously successful Montana Company, Ltd., and casually observed that the Old Guard was about the same size and looked even more promising.[76] Not a word appeared to indicate or even hint that the Old Guard property and the Drumlummon mine of the Anglo-Montana concern were separated by some 1,500 miles of western terrain!

Even in selecting a name for new concerns, it was possible for the promoter to emphasize regions of known wealth.[77] No fewer than seventeen different Anglo-Colorado concerns, promoted in the years 1895–1898, carried the name "Cripple Creek" as a part of their official titles, again endeavoring to sell specific mines on the reputation of a boom region. One of these called itself the Cripple Creek (Bull Hill) Finance and Development Company, Ltd., but the mines it was to purchase were located not on rich Bull Hill, as the name implied, but on Big Bull Hill, a purely speculative and untested area in the Cripple Creek district.[78]

Invariably there were efforts to capitalize on the success of other British companies in America. Even before the sale of the Emma, Utah's "show" mine, in Britain, the prospectus of the Saturn Silver Mining Company of Utah, Ltd., emphasized not merely that "this LODE is represented to be ELEVEN FEET THICK, solid silver and lead-bearing ore," but also that it was located just across the valley from the legendary Emma.[79] Likewise, soon after the Emma was sold, other

---

[75] One hostile editor of the day referred to this undertaking as the "Old Guard Mining diabolical, cold-blooded thieving conspiracy." *Financial Observer*, Aug. 30, 1890.

[76] *Prospectus* (May 14, 1887).

[77] The Comstock Mining Company, Ltd., for example, was organized to operate in Utah, capitalizing on the name of a more renowned area. *Prospectus* (Feb., 1888).

[78] *Prospectus* (1896); Claud Sachs to editor (Colorado Springs, Nov. 30, 1897), *Mining Journal*, Dec. 11, 1897, 1467.

[79] *Prospectus* (July, 1871).

concerns placed favorable stress on the proximity of their mines in Little Cottonwood Canyon.[80]

In promoting mining companies, the vendors sometimes found it necessary to explain why the owners were willing to part with their extremely valuable mines for reasonable prices. Why weren't good mines snapped up by American investors? asked the skeptics in London. Remarked one 1872 observer sarcastically,

It would really appear that investors have of late begun to believe in the return of the golden age, where every man interests himself, not in his own concerns, but in promoting the worldly prosperity of others—or that the possessors of princely properties underground have imbibed Communist principles, and have resolved to set a good example by sacrificing a large portion of their wealth in order to raise those who are poorer to their level of riches.[81]

Those who drew up prospectuses, however, had different explanations. Sometimes property was offered on the British market because of a simple lack of capital in the West; because of illness or even death on the part of the owner; [82] because joint ownership made for such diverse interests that local operation proved impossible; [83] because a mine owner wished to provide a steady future income for his family in case of his demise.[84] In two cases, at least, property in Wyoming was offered "only after considerable negotiation" and because of the vendor's "personal friendship" with the owners.[85] In another instance valuable mines were offered in Britain at bargain prices because the property in Nevada had been lost to the owner through the foreclosure of a mortgage and the forecloser had been willing to sell cheaply.[86] Whatever the justification given to the English public, it invariably tried to convey the impression that the British were being given the opportunity to profit from fortuitous circumstances. No one

[80] Abridged prospectus of the Flagstaff Silver Mining Co. of Utah, *Mining Journal*, Dec. 2, 1871, 1069.

[81] *Mining Magazine and Review*, I (Jan., 1872), 46.

[82] Lander City Silver Mining Co., *Prospectus* (June, 1865).

[83] Toiyabe Silver Mining Co., *Prospectus* (July, 1871).

[84] Cortez Mines, *Prospectus* (Sept. 14, 1888).

[85] Golden Eagle Syndicate, *Prospectus* (Jan. 24, 1898); Charter Oak Copper Mines, *Prospectus* (June 17, 1898).

[86] MS report of William Cope on the Alvarez Mines (May 16, 1871), Alvarez Silver Mining and Smelting Co., C.R.O. 5519.

ever mentioned the less commendable desire of American mineowners and intermediaries to line their own pockets.

It was an advantage, of course, if a mine could be presented as a going concern with facts and figures on past production, rather than on future predictions. Production figures played an important role in the sale of the Emma in 1871; [87] Alturas Gold, Ltd., was formed in 1886 to acquire an unnamed but "celebrated dividend paying Gold Mine" in Idaho; [88] the Elkhorn Mining Company, Ltd., in its 1890 prospectus, pointed out that £258,000 had previously been taken out of the mines acquired in Jefferson County, Montana.[89]

If it was not possible to show that a mine had been in the past or was at present a producer, the promoter sometimes stressed the virgin character of the property. "For several years tradition has pointed to the existence of mountains of silver in the neighbourhood of Arizona, in the United States," said the prospectus of the Pyramid Range enterprise in 1871, "but until a very recent period their exact position could not be ascertained in consequence of the district being in the possession of Indians." [90] The recent "control of the natives" now laid the area open for easy exploitation. When the Yankee Girl Silver Mines, Ltd. (1890), announced its intention of acquiring the Yankee Girl, the Orphan Boy, and the Robinson mines—all wholly unexploited [91] —one skeptical editor commented, "The 'Robinson' may be regarded as a 'Virgin' mine, at least so the prospectus says, and it would, we take it, be ungentlemanly to ask any impertinent questions about the female mine." [92]

Another device frequently used was to associate richness with the size or number of mines to be acquired. The Nevada Freehold Properties Trust, for example, boasted in 1869 of its possession of twenty-two mining properties, totaling 52,200 lineal feet, plus large tracts of what the prospectus termed "fine pine woodlands" [93] but which were deemed "wasteland" by less sympathetic sources.[94] About the same time the Arivaca Mining Company, Ltd., was formed to acquire "about seven-

[87] Emma Silver Mining Co., *Prospectus* (Nov. 9, 1871).

[88] *Prospectus* (Feb., 1886).   [89] *Prospectus* (Feb. 4, 1890).

[90] Pyramid Range Silver Mountain Co., *Prospectus* (Jan., 1871). See also Wyoming Sweetwater Mining Co., *Prospectus* (1870).

[91] Yankee Girl Silver Mines, *Prospectus* (July, 1890).

[92] *Financial Observer*, July 5, 1890.   [93] *Prospectus* (July, 1869).

[94] New York *Herald*, quoted in *Mining World*, Jan. 25, 1873, 161.

teen thousand acres of mineral, arable, and pasture lands" in Arizona, including a minimum of thirty mineral veins and "very probably" a hundred in all.[95]

Any prospectus might be expected to avail itself of favorable comments made in the press or other literature to sustain its own claims. Occasionally companies cited the reports of the United States commissioner on mines, sometimes distorting innocent material grossly out of perspective; [96] others relied similarly on reports of the director of the Mint.[97] When the "California" Gold Mine Company, Ltd., appealed for capital in 1881, it could quote from Frank Fossett's *Colorado* to prove that its mine near Central City "cleared more money in 1879 than any other mine north of Leadville." [98] Likewise, the prospectus of the Quartz Hill Consolidated Gold Mining Company, Ltd., contained excerpts from the first edition of the same work glorifying the Quartz Hill.[99] The prospectus failed, however, to note that Fossett's second edition, published nine months before, reported that "the most valuable ore [in the Quartz Hill mine] has been nearly all worked out." [100] Nor did it mention that the property had originally belonged to another British concern long since bankrupt.[101]

Purchase agreements customarily made completion of the transaction contingent upon the conveyance of valid title. The promoter, therefore, did his best to leave the impression that the title of a particular property was clear. Sometimes the vendor could be persuaded to make a deposit which would be forfeited if perfect title were not produced.[102]

[95] Arivaca Mining Co., *Prospectus* (1870); *Mem. & Art.*, 1, C.R.O. B-4643. See also the detailed box score showing total number of feet to be acquired by the Silver Star Mining Co. in Nevada a year later. Silver Star Mining Co., *Prospectus* (July, 1871).

[96] The Atlanta Silver Mining Co. used this report in 1871 to show that its mines must be rich because the commissioner praised the Atlanta (Idaho) district in general. London *Times,* Jan. 16, 1871.

[97] See Charles Dickens Mining Co., *Prospectus* (1886).

[98] *Prospectus* (1881).

[99] *In re* Quartz Hill Consolidated Gold Mining Co.—Young's case. London *Times,* Feb. 14, 1883.

[100] *Ibid.;* Fossett, *Colorado* (2d ed., 1880), 325.

[101] Quartz Hill Consolidated Gold Mining Co. *v.* Beall, 20 *Chancery Appeals* (1882), 504.

[102] Memo. of Agreement (Nov. 1, 1871) between Henry Altman and Edwin Miller, South Utah Mining Co., C.R.O. 5807.

Sometimes prominent Americans in England would be called upon to assure the public that title or patent was good.[103]

But technically an English citizen or an English company could not hold title prior to the issuance of a government patent, and this drawback worked to deter some investors from sinking their savings in American mines. There were those, however, with more ambition than scruples who sought to mislead the British public as to the right of an alien to hold title to mining land. Shortly before Christmas of 1872 Benjamin Moran noted the appearance of a "big, coarse fellow, calling himself Col. J. H. Taylor of Utah," at the United States Legation in London. Taylor was seeking a lawyer who would say that an English company could hold mining property in Utah Territory. He was reminded by Moran that no alien or alien concern could do so until after a government patent had been issued. Taylor fully acknowledged this but expressed his belief that the law would soon be altered, and until it was, "as he has mines to sell, he don't [*sic*] want it known here." "And," commented Moran, "he has an idea that an English lawyer's opinion that a foreigner can hold property in the U.S. will put him all right & enable him to swindle people here out of their money." [104]

After 1887 and the passage of the Alien Land Law preventing foreign corporations from acquiring real estate in the territories, the problem became still more serious for promoters. The Buster Mines Syndicate, Ltd., was chartered in 1892 to acquire property in Arizona, and its prospectus casually assured the public that as soon as Arizona was admitted to statehood absolute title would be vested in the concern.[105] The syndicate was to go out of business years before Arizona became the forty-eighth member of the Union.[106]

If prospectuses of Anglo-American mining companies were often notorious for what they did say, they might frequently be criticized for what they did not say. The prospectus of Crooke's Mining and

---

[103] Judah P. Benjamin, formerly a high Confederate official who spent the rest of his life in self-imposed exile, performed such a service for the Flagstaff Silver Mining Co. of Utah in 1872. London *Times,* June 15, 1872.

[104] Moran Journal, XXXIII (Dec. 18, 1872), 344.

[105] *Prospectus* (1892), in C.R.O. 36215.

[106] E. Wilding to registrar (London, March 7, 1911), *ibid.*

Smelting Company, Ltd. (1892), dwelt lovingly on potential dividends of 15 per cent per annum but failed to mention a mortgage of £40,000 on the Colorado property.[107] When the English promoter, Thomas Gilbert, agreed to sell six hundred acres of placers to the "Gold Queen," Ltd., he was silent about the fact that the title was never his to convey. "It was a mistake," he confessed in 1891, shortly before his arrest for manipulations in this and other shady transactions in American mines.[108] In his policy of silence he was not unique.[109]

That the average prospectus left much to be desired is obvious. It had been composed with but one objective in mind—to promote the subscription of shares and thus infuse life into the company so that the purchase transaction could be completed, with a profit for the owner and the various intermediaries. Too often facts were inconsequential; sales were of first importance.

The bulk of the western mining properties transferred to British hands during the period 1860–1900 simply did not come up to the levels predicted in company prospectuses. Only about 11 per cent of the companies registered returned any dividends at all; an even smaller group returned dividends of importance. If anything, this only serves to emphasize the nature of risk in the extractive industries. But there were some examples—exceptions, perhaps, to the general rule —of honest promoters, using restrained, well-balanced appeals, who sold paying property to the British investing public. The De Lamar Mining Company, Ltd., paid more than 267 per cent in dividends from its Idaho mines between 1891 and 1905. Camp Bird, Ltd., paid 177 per cent in the eleven years following 1900. Cortez Mines, Ltd., a concern promoted honestly, without extravagant appeals, paid regular dividends totaling 49 per cent for five years after 1888 until the low price of silver forced its liquidation and the sale of its property to an American company.[110] But these and such illustrious concerns as the Arizona

---

[107] *Prospectus* (1882); *In re* Crooke's Mining and Smelting Co., reported in London *Times,* Aug. 3, 1885. For another example see W. J. Lavington to registrar (London, May 2, 1893), Ouray Gold Mining Co., C.R.O. B-24513.

[108] London *Times,* Oct. 23, 1891.

[109] For a case where prospectuses issued in England misled investors into believing that title was clear when actually it would not be transferred until $450,000 had been paid out of profits to the original owners, see Wiser *v.* Lawler, 189 *U.S. Reports* (1902), 263.

[110] See Appendix IV.

Copper Company, Ltd., or the Richmond Consolidated Mining Company, Ltd., were few and far between.

Final transfer of property usually hinged on favorable reports by "competent" engineers. Normally engineers or interested parties would make preliminary reports to be included in the prospectus, but full consummation generally depended upon the report of English experts either already in the West or sent out especially for the purpose. Mining "experts" were in superabundance in trans-Mississippi America. As one Cornishman in Colorado warned his fellow countrymen late in 1871, "Every person who can wheel a barrow or drive a span of mules over the road is an 'M.E.,' and persons who can put a stick of wood into the fire-door of an engine is an 'Engineer,' and think they know as much of mining and engineering as the most practical men of the day." [111]

The New York *Daily Bulletin* in the following year commented on "the faith of these London investors in the testimony of some obscure person dubbed 'professor,' or member of some mining bureau or college or institute." [112] In a general critique of Cornish, Indian, and American mining enterprises, "The Most Risky of All Investments," the *Economist* put its finger on the same spot in 1881:

A company is formed, two or three mining captains' reports are readily obtained, some picked lumps of ore are assayed, (by means of which assays possibly the name of the Bank of England actually makes its appearance on the face of the prospectus,) and an allotment is made to a small sprinkling of gulled investors.[113]

William Weston, himself trained at the Royal School of Mines in London [114] and a reputable promoter of Anglo-American mining ventures, voiced his opinion of the experts' reports in 1898. They were documents produced "by some former high official in the local Government, who knows as much about a mine as a pig does of waistcoat pockets, the same thing endorsed by local butchers, bakers, and candlestick makers, who put M.E. to their names." [115]

[111] H. B. Grose to editor (Central City, Nov. 27, 1871), *Mining Journal,* Dec. 30, 1871, 1173.

[112] Quoted in London *Times,* Dec. 9, 1872.   [113] June 18, 1881, 756.

[114] Biographical sketches of Weston are found in *Portrait and Biographical Record of Denver,* 698, and in Frank Hall, *History of the State of Colorado* (Chicago, 1891), IV, 607.

[115] To editor (Cripple Creek, n.d.), *Anglo-Colorado Mining Guide,* I (Oct. 29, 1898), 141.

Whether the situation was generally as bad as represented by such critics is debatable. To be sure, much room for improvement was apparent. Unqualified "experts" were available on all sides and were sometimes relied upon much too heavily. One can cite many obvious misfits: a Royal Artillery officer, a London lawyer, a clerk in a mining company office—these men had not gone to "the proper school to perfect the education of a first-class mining expert." [116]

But probably the average inspection was made by personnel with either formal training or practical experience in the field. Particularly in the early period the majority were men dispatched from the British Isles, despite the insistence of Her Majesty's consul in San Francisco that resident engineers were far more dependable than itinerants who were not necessarily familiar with the West.[117] Many of those sent out from England, especially the Cornish mining captains, remained to provide a hard core of mine managers and superintendents.[118]

Established British engineering firms sometimes handled the prepurchase inspection for prospective buyers. According to the few of their records which survived the 1940 blitz, John Taylor and Sons of London inspected and reported upon at least a dozen mining properties in the American West between 1883 and 1900.[119] Bewick, Moreing and Company, another exceedingly stable and able concern, performed the same tasks,[120] and occasionally a reputable metal broker did likewise.[121]

Engineers employed by such firms were usually experienced and well trained, yet often unacquainted with local western problems. Ex-

[116] See *Rocky Mt. News*, Nov. 19, 1866; Charles Douglas, *Report on Certain Mines, Owned by the Pacific National Gold-Mining Company of Colorado, and Edward J. Jaques of New York, Situated near Central City, Colorado* (New York, 1877); *Sci. Press.*, Dec. 11, 1886, 374; MS report of William Cope on the Alvarez Mines (May 16, 1871), C.R.O. 5519; Cope to George Heaton (London, Dec. 17, 1869), Teller MSS.

[117] Annual Report of Consul Booker on the Trade of California (MS), 1871 (San Francisco, March 8, 1872), Diplomatic and Consular Papers, 1872, F.O. 115/540.

[118] See below, 101–102.

[119] Included were four in Colorado, three in Idaho, two in Arizona, and one each in Dakota, Wyoming, and New Mexico. MS Index Book of Inspections (1883–1900), Offices of John Taylor and Sons, 2 White Lion Court, London.

[120] Pittsburgh Consolidated Gold Mines, *Prospectus* (May 17, 1887).

[121] The Utah representatives of Lewis and Son, Liverpool metal brokers, in 1873 inspected property to be purchased by the Chicago Silver Mining Co. Chicago Silver Mining Co., *Prospectus* (1873).

ceptional in this respect were such men as Thomas A. Rickard, trained in the Royal School of Mines, London, or John Hays Hammond, with a Freiberg background, both destined to become top-level engineers with world reputations.[122]

Generally the expert undertook the task of inspection for a flat fee. Frequently, however, he had a stake beyond mere impartial inspection. Often the expert who examined property took over as manager for the new British owners. John Longmaid, for example, investigated mines acquired by the Carlisle Gold Mining Company, Ltd., in 1886 and when the purchase was completed took over as general manager in New Mexico.[123] Nicholas Maxwell, an English engineer who inspected mines in Utah ultimately purchased by three British concerns, became manager of the property owned by all three.[124] Nor did he confine his activities to Utah: he was active in Colorado as well. It was Maxwell who reported on the Champion and California mines in Gilpin County for the vendors, Thatcher and Standley, in 1871.[125] Subsequently he threatened to make public the fact that he had overvalued the property on the vendors' fraudulent misrepresentation of past proceeds and that they had agreed to pay him £1,800 if he produced a report which would ensure a sale.[126] Most of this soiled linen was laundered in private, however, and when Maxwell showed signs of disclosing the arrangement Thatcher promised to "hoist him in a balloon, to be seen not only in England & here but all the way to Utah—if he begins exposing." [127]

This incident does not prove that all inspections of mining property were fraudulent. It was by no means uncommon for a mine to be turned down after negotiations had been completed because of an

---

[122] Below, 103.

[123] Carlisle Gold Mining Co., *Prospectus* (1886) and *Annual Report,* year ending Dec. 31, 1888. For other examples see Big Creek Mining Co., *Prospectus* (Jan. 31, 1891); Sapphire and Ruby Co. of Montana, *Prospectus* (1891) and *Report Invest. Com.,* 9–10.

[124] Last Chance Silver Mining Co. of Utah, *Prospectus* (April, 1872); Tecoma Silver Mining Co., *Prospectus* (Jan., 1873); Memo. of Agreement (Nov. 23, 1871) between the Salt Lake Mining Co. of Utah and Horace Nelson Wilkinson, Flagstaff Silver Mining Co. of Utah, C.R.O. 5861.

[125] Georgetown *Miner,* March 28, 1872; Maxwell to Thomas Green (Georgetown, Aug. 31, 1871), William Miles Read MSS, Bancroft Library.

[126] Thomson Business Diary, Sept. 26, 1872, 70.

[127] *Ibid.,* Sept. 24, 1872, 69.

adverse report by an engineer. Hiram Johnson was in England in 1871 endeavoring to sell the Illinois lode in Colorado. The property was purchased conditionally, and an engineer was dispatched to give the final seal of approval before the purchase became binding.[128] Johnson waited impatiently for the telegraphic report, confiding to an associate that "if the report is favorable I shall make some money here *double quick* by the organization of an additional Company on property owned mostly by Teller and myself and then propose to begin to close out for return home."[129] A week later Johnson's dreams were rudely interrupted. "I have just heard that the report of Engineer is unfavorable," he groaned. "DAM THE LUCK." [130]

Though an unfavorable engineering report normally might be expected to bring a flat rejection of the property under consideration, there were exceptions to every rule. When the Utah Silver Mining Company, Ltd., was incorporated in London in 1871, it proceeded to purchase nine locations in Bingham County, some twenty-five miles southwest of Salt Lake, despite the adverse report of an American engineer, who had been overruled by the enthusiastic endorsement of two British experts, James Nancarrow and Henry Sewell.[131] Both time and the federal commissioner of mineral statistics pointed out the folly of this action, for the "mines" turned out to be nothing more than "irregular pockets" in locations "staked out on imaginary veins running in all conceivable directions." [132]

In the same year Henry Sewell had an opportunity to redeem himself. William Cope, the ambitious director of the British and Colorado Mining Bureau, made a very sanguine report on the Alvarez mines in Nye County, Nevada, in which he urged prospective investors to support a proposed company in acquiring this property, the profits of which would be "simply enormous." [133] The Alvarez Silver Mining and Smelting Company, Ltd., was thereupon registered, and Sewell inspected the mines before contracts became final. His report disagreed with Cope's and was generally regarded by most of the shareholders as unsatisfactory. As a result the subscribers refused to sanction the com-

---

[128] Johnson to Carpenter (London, June 17, 1871), Johnson MSS.
[129] The same (July 11, 1871), *ibid.*   [130] The same (July 22, 1871), *ibid.*
[131] *Mining Journal,* July 1, 1871, 559; Jan. 6, 1872, 20.
[132] Statistics of Mines and Mining in the States and Territories West of the Rocky Mountains, *Ho. Exec. Doc.* No. 211, 42 Cong., 2 Sess. (1871–1872), 315.
[133] MS report of Cope on Alvarez Mines, C.R.O. 5519.

pletion of the purchase. The trustees, however, accepted a revised offer of the vendor and set out to complete the transaction despite shareholders' protests.[134] In the end it was the shareholders who had the final word: early in 1872 they voted to wind up the company voluntarily and company officials found themselves without jobs, capital, or mines.[135]

In a few cases the British followed the advice of their own engineers in rejecting a property and later regretted their hasty action. When several producing Nevada mines, known collectively as Bateman's Eureka, were offered for sale early in 1869,[136] George Batters, an English broker associated with a number of Anglo-American ventures, organized a "scientific and practical commission" to investigate.[137] As a result a provisional company, the Champion Mining Company, Ltd., was formed to purchase the property,[138] and Captain Frank Evans was sent out from Cornwall to report on it. Evans' examination indicated that the mines were not worth the £50,000 asked for them, and the transaction was "allowed to fall through by sundry wiseacres, who preferred the testimony of a Cornish mining captain before that of men resident on the spot and thoroughly conversant with the different characteristics of Nevada Silver Mines." [139] A San Francisco concern, the Eureka Consolidated, then acquired the property, which proved its worth many times over—to the consternation of the frustrated Englishmen.[140] The unfortunate Captain Evans was made to bear the brunt of the error,[141] and thereafter when American properties were introduced on the London market the ghost of the Champion was invariably invoked to convince the potential investor that here lay another El Dorado waiting to be exploited.

Usually, however, the situation was the other way round. Instead of failing to grasp opportunity as it came by, British companies more often grabbed at something which might fall under the classic definition of "bonanza"——"a hole in the ground owned by a d——d liar." [142]

[134] *Mining World,* Dec. 23, 1871, 1085.

[135] *Special Resolution,* passed March 6 and confirmed March 26, 1872, C.R.O. 5519.

[136] *Mining Journal,* Jan. 7, 1871, 19.   [137] *Ibid.,* Feb. 19, 1869, 144.

[138] *Mem. & Art.,* 1–2, C.R.O. 4775.

[139] "P" to editor (London, Jan. 25, 1871), *Mining Journal,* Jan. 28, 1871, 78.

[140] *Ibid.,* Jan. 21, 1871, 58.   [141] *Ibid.,* Jan. 7, 1871, 19–20.

[142] *Anglo-Colorado Mining Guide,* VII (July 30, 1904), 104.

Sometimes the difference between bonanza and *borrasca* was discovered before investors' losses were appreciable; [143] more often shareholders learned the lesson later and at their own heavy expense.

In a few instances, particularly in the 1880's, agreements included clauses designed to reduce the hazards involved in acquiring western mines. The purchase contract of one Anglo-Colorado concern, for example, endeavored to "almost entirely eliminate the risk usually attached to the purchase of mines by giving a whole season's trial before the purchase money is paid." [144] Operations during the probationary period were frequently not encouraging, and purchase was never completed in this instance.[145] When the Kaiser Gold Mines, Ltd., took a ninety-nine-year lease on twelve claims of the Vulture Lode in Arizona late in 1888,[146] it was agreed that in order "to provide against the possibilities of error" the company was to work the mines for six months on a trial basis. If at the end of that period results did not confirm the estimates of production made by the vendor, H. A. W. Tabor, all capital expended in proving the property would be refunded and the transaction would be canceled. Moreover, if the vendor failed to comply with these stipulations, the directors were empowered to sell the mines and machinery at public auction, the company was to be remunerated from proceeds of the sale, and Tabor would receive the surplus, if any.[147] On paper this arrangement seemed like an adequate guarantee; in practice it meant little. When the mines did not prove satisfactory and the directors rendered an account to the vendor for return of the capital expended, the latter refused to pay and the company was forced to turn to the courts.[148]

[143] The Spanish term *borrasca* was commonly used in the western mining camp to indicate that pay dirt had not materialized. For examples of *borrasca* disclosed before British companies had progressed very far, see Charles Goodyear to registrar (London, Feb. 15, 1892), Santa Catalina Gold and Silver Mining Co., C.R.O. B-26365; Skinner, *Mining Manuel* (1889), 325; seven original subscribers to registrar (London, April 15, 1889), San José Gold Mining Co., C.R.O. B-27960.

[144] *Mem. & Art.*, 1, Colorado Mines Development Co., C.R.O. B-16415; *Mining Journal*, April 8, 1882, 416.

[145] *Special Resolution*, passed March 30 and confirmed April 14, 1883, Colorado Mines Development Co., C.R.O. B-16415.

[146] *Prospectus* (Sept. 17, 1888); Certificate of Incorporation, April 15, 1888, C.R.O. B-26370.

[147] Memo. of Agreement (Sept. 7, 1888) between H. A. W. Tabor and the Kaiser Gold Mines, quoted in *Prospectus* (Sept. 17, 1888).

[148] J. D. Pattullo to registrar (London, Dec. 21, 1891), C.R.O. B-26370.

Occasionally such guarantees were kept by the vendor. For example, David H. Moffat of Denver sold the Henriett lode, near Leadville, to an English concern in 1882.[149] The prospectus of the purchasing company set the mine's reserves at £200,000, its annual profits at £94,000, according to the estimates of George Henty.[150] Moffat supported these statements and made himself responsible to the firm, the Henriett Mining and Smelting Company, Ltd. After small initial returns, the ore dropped off in value, and the company discovered that the vaunted ore reserves existed only in the imagination of certain interested parties. Under pressure Moffat agreed to buy back all shares of the English concern at par.[151] Thus the Englishmen who had subscribed to a total of 144,550 shares at £1 each [152] received not only their subscriptions back, but also the initial profits amounting to 4 per cent interest in dividends. Moffat and his American associates bore all expenses of organization and liquidation.[153]

The Henriett episode was, however, not common. "It is a pleasure, and a rare one," commented the editor of the *Financial & Mining News*, "to record one case connected with foreign mining enterprises where failure to make good the representations of vendors has been met in a most honourable manner by a prompt refund of shareholders' subscriptions at par." [154]

Few would contend that the various techniques of promotion described in the preceding pages were entirely commendable. But these were no isolated phenomena peculiar to the American mining frontier. Rather they were devices geared to the mind of the British investing public—or, in fact, to any investing public. Promotional literature, even in modern advertising, goes to extremes on occasion. The approach was much the same, whether the object was capital for the gold mines of Nevada, Aruba, Mysore, or Coolgardie. And it did not differ notice-

---

[149] Memo. of Agreement (Sept. 25, 1882) between David H. Moffat and the Henriett Mining and Smelting Co., C.R.O. B-17332.

[150] *Prospectus* (1882).

[151] Report of meeting of Henriett Mining and Smelting Co. (June 27, 1883), *Mining Journal,* June 30, 1883, 749.

[152] A total of 270,000 shares had been taken up—112,450 by Americans, 8,000 by Frenchmen, 5,000 by Belgians, and the remainder by Englishmen. Summary of Capital and Shares to Jan. 26, 1883, C.R.O. B-17332.

[153] *Mining Journal,* June 30, 1883, 749; *Financial & Mining News,* June 18, 1884.

[154] June 18, 1884.

ably from that used in earlier attempts to induce investment in American canal projects in the 1830's, Latin American rail enterprises in the 1860's, or penny uranium stocks some ninety years later.

Certainly these promotional methods differed only in degree rather than in kind from those used to effect investment in the thousands of limited companies of all types registered in London during the same period.[155] Many of these—even domestic ventures—were like the foreign mining schemes, pigs in pokes sold by skillful hucksters to simple or greedy buyers. But at least the western hogs were much farther away. It was therefore more difficult for the potential investor to hear the grunt or the squeal, much less open the sack to see what was inside.

[155] Some idea of the broad picture of British company promotion for all types of ventures is found in H. A. Shannon, "The First Five Thousand Limited Companies and Their Duration," *Economic History,* II (Jan., 1932), 396–424, and in his "The Limited Companies of 1866–1883," *Economic History Review,* IV (Oct., 1933), 290–307.

: CHAPTER V :

Capitalization Problems

THERE were several channels through which British capital normally flowed into western mines during the era 1860–1901. An indeterminable amount was invested through companies incorporated in the United States and controlled by American directors. Hundreds of such concerns made efforts to dispose of shares or debenture bonds in England, and many achieved some degree of success in their attempts to do so. It is extremely difficult, however, to discuss this movement of capital comprehensively, for existing records are usually inadequate to do more than indicate in general terms that Englishmen did pour substantial amounts into western mines through firms organized on this side of the Atlantic.

An example or two will illustrate the problems involved. When the Sierra Madre Tunnel Company was organized in Colorado in 1873 to drive a twelve-mile tunnel under Seaton Mountain between Black Hawk and Middle Park,[1] some British capital was interested. Alexander Brogden, M.P. and a "man of enlarged experience" in mining,[2] was committed to provide up to £10,000 and actually did furnish at

[1] *Boulder County News*, June 20, 1873; Corbett, *Colorado Directory of Mines*, 235.
[2] *Mining Journal*, Aug. 29, 1868, 622. Brogden sat as M.P. for Wednesbury for a total of eighteen years. A graduate of King's College, London, he was owner of mining property at Ulverstone, Staffordshire, and a partner in the Tondu Iron Works at Bridgend, South Wales. *Mining Journal*, Dec. 5, 1868, 869; London *Times*, Nov. 29, 1892.

least £2,000 before caution triumphed over his optimism.[3] How much was contributed by other Englishmen is not known.

Another instance, though scantily documented, of investment in American mining companies concerned the Anaconda Copper Mining Company in the mid-1890's. A mining periodical announced in 1895 that 30,000 shares of $25 each—one-fourth of the total capital of that great concern—had been acquired by the Exploration Company, Ltd., a creature of the Rothschilds, and would be introduced on the English market.[4] Two years later it was stated in Britain that "the securities of this huge copper producing mine are now largely held in this country and on the Continent."[5] This was about as definite a statement as was normally found on the amount of American mining shares held in Britain at any one time.

To the average stock-buying Englishman there were disadvantages evident in this form of investment. Under normal conditions British control was either completely lacking or slight, since a small number of English shareholders among a mass of Americans could not exert much influence. Frequently, in cases where considerable shares were held in Britain, companies registered in the United States virtuously added an English director or two and even established a separate "advisory board" for the British shareholders, but these were mere sops thrown out to appease and could not be regarded as effective machinery for determining company policy. At the same time investors in England were frequently frustrated by delay and complications in receiving information and payment of dividends from concerns organized in America. British investors consequently looked with favor upon companies organized in their homeland as vehicles for plunging capital into western ventures. Shareholders might exert direct control over boards of directors sitting in London, Manchester, or Edinburgh, and division of dividends was simplified. Even so, problems of distance and of management were not eliminated or even minimized by establishing the seat of direction at the source of capital.

The concerns organized in England fell into two fairly clear-cut categories—unincorporated associations or partnerships and joint-stock companies. The first must be dismissed with only brief comment, pri-

[3] Alexander Brogden to George W. Heaton (London, June 18, 1873), Teller MSS.
[4] Skinner, *Mining Manual* (1896), 830; *Statist,* Oct. 10, 1895, 477.
[5] *Statist,* Jan. 2, 1897, 6.

marily because they, like the American firms with shares held abroad, have left behind little substantial information. Partnerships, trusts, and other loose associations were not required to register with the Board of Trade, and probably the number operating in western mines was never very great. Scanty evidence, however, points to a few. Robert Old mentioned in 1868 "an association of friends and others in England, called the 'Mineral Mines Co.'" which had acquired property near Jamestown, Colorado.[6] Since the records of both the registrar of joint-stock companies and the registrar of friendly societies fail to disclose an organization of this name,[7] it is fair to assume that it was an unregistered association of partners without the benefits of incorporation.

A more detailed example of the unincorporated organization in the sixties is seen in the Nevada Freehold Properties Trust, which was formed in 1869. This particular concern endeavored to appeal widely and to raise its capital by the issue of two-pound trust certificates bearing 12.5 per cent interest payable at the end of a prescribed seventeen-year period. At the expiration of this time proceeds were to be divided and the concern was to be dissolved.[8] Unfortunately for all concerned, this association fell upon evil days and expired long before the allotted seventeen years.

The second category—joint-stock organization—undoubtedly provided by far the more important medium for British investment. Since 1856 British Companies Registration Acts provided increasing, although sometimes imperfect, protection to the investor and laid down requirements and regulations that must be met before incorporation could be completed and the advantages of a corporate existence attained. The process was a slow, cumulative one, but by 1900 rules governing prospectuses, organization, direction, capitalization, and insolvency were clarified and improved to provide substantial safeguards to the individual. But during the period under consideration loopholes and leniencies often made for easy joint-stock organization and for abuses and manipulation on the part of unscrupulous promotional ex-

[6] Old to editor (Ward District, May 15, 1868), *Rocky Mt. News,* May 19, 1868.
[7] Others later referred to this group as the "Mineral Mines Discovery Company." Charles S. Richardson to editor (Central City, n.d.), *Mining Journal,* Jan. 24, 1874, 103; *Weekly Central City Register,* Nov. 9, 1870. No registration is indexed.
[8] *Prospectus* (1869). There is no indication that liability was limited for shareholders.

perts. Imperfect though the laws were, some measure of control did exist. Furthermore, the comparative ease of registration and the legal advantages of incorporation, including the benefits of limited liability, made the joint-stock company the natural form of organization for all types of investment in every part of the world after 1856.

Company law in Britain demanded the filing of a *Memorandum of Association* stating the purpose and general outline of the proposed company, to be followed by the filing of an *Articles of Association* giving a more concise and detailed statement of capital, organizational structure, and the rules and regulations under which the company was to operate. By law, these familiarly called *"Mem. and Arts."* were to be signed by seven persons subscribing to shares, thus making public the names of those interested in promoting the concern. In practice, however, the actual promoters chose to remain in the background. The seven original signatories proved to be mere puppets fronting for those who pulled the strings behind the scenes. Usually signers turned out to be junior clerks or others having no interest in the undertaking beyond the single share subscribed to in order to comply with legal requirements. A typical list of original subscribers to the *Memorandum and Articles* of an Anglo-American joint-stock mining company would include one solicitor, one real-estate agent, one shorthand writer, two solicitors' clerks, and two law students.[9]

Technically speaking, these seven constituted the company until shares had been allotted. To be sure, numerous instances may be cited in which the original subscribers were bona fide investors who sometimes accounted for a quarter, a half, or even the total of the nominal capital of a company.[10] But these were the exceptions rather than the general rule, and the signatories all too frequently had no interest beyond that of lending their names at the outset.

Almost all Anglo-American mining concerns formed on the joint-stock basis followed a fairly standardized pattern.[11] Liability was

[9] *Mem. & Art.,* 9, Golden Horn Consolidated Mining Co., C.R.O. 49518.

[10] Original subscribers of the Crown Prince Mine Syndicate, a Colorado venture of 1888, took almost half the contemplated capital of £7,500. *Mem. & Art.,* 7, C.R.O. 26607. Original subscribers of the Utah Mining and Smelting Co. of 1871 accounted for the total capital (£5,000). *Mem. & Art.,* 3–4, C.R.O. B-5289.

[11] The four deviations uncovered were either "dummy" concerns to hold property temporarily or arrangements involving loans or voluntary participation in specific projects. See *Mem. & Art.,* 7–8, Exploration Co., C.R.O. 23378; *Mem. & Art.,* 5, 8,

limited, corporate life was continuous, denominations of shares were set, and the total nominal capital was stated. One pound sterling was the common par value assigned to shares throughout the period, although great variation was to be found between the one shilling preferred shares of the Mineral Assets Company, Ltd., of 1898 [12] and the £500 shares offered by the Clifton Arizona Copper Company, Ltd., two years later.[13] Denominations of two, five, ten, and twenty pounds were also common, along with a few larger ones,[14] but the small one-pound unit appealed to a broader segment of the population.[15]

If the amount of nominal capital was set at registration, it might vary greatly from company to company, ranging from the £100 of the Doris Syndicate, Ltd., of 1888 [16] to the £2,000,000 of the Harney Peak (Dakota) Tin Company, Ltd., in 1887.[17] Between these two extremes, which were decidedly atypical, lay the more normal capitalizations of from £50,000 to £500,000.

It must be pointed out, however, that frequently a vast difference existed been the nominal and the actual capital. In the first place, there was no guarantee that all the nominal capital would be subscribed. Many companies registered in London or Edinburgh fell by the wayside because the public was skeptical and refused to take sufficient shares to justify the firm in starting operations. Many others succeeded in "going to allotment," according to the common expression, but were not able to dispose of all their shares. The nominal capital of the Ophir Mining and Smelting Company of Utah, Ltd., was listed

---

Doris Syndicate, C.R.O. 27338; *Mem. & Art.*, 6, Star Syndicate, C.R.O. 30303; *Mem. & Art.*, 3, 6, Victorian Mines Syndicate, C.R.O. 32232.

[12] Along with 200,000 preferential shares of this denomination, the company authorized 180,000 ordinary shares of 2s. 6d. each. Statement of Nominal Capital, Nov. 18, 1898, C.R.O. 59582.

[13] Statement of Nominal Capital, Dec. 24, 1900, C.R.O. B-68711.

[14] Nominal capital of the White River, Colorado, Coal Syndicate was to be £12,480 in 120 shares of £104 each. Statement of Nominal Capital, March 10, 1890, C.R.O. B-31004. This was one of the few instances in which both nominal capital and share denominations were not rounded off. Another exception was the Wyoming Coal and Coke Co. with a nominal capital of £50,001 in shares of £2 12s. 6d. each. *Mem. & Art.*, 4, C.R.O. B-21693.

[15] For an excellent study emphasizing the increasing popularity of the pound share see J. B. Jefferys, "The Denomination and Character of Shares, 1855–1885," *Economic History Review*, XVI (1946), 45–55.

[16] *Mem. & Art.*, 5, C.R.O. 27338.

[17] Statement of Nominal Capital, May 10, 1887, C.R.O. B-24391.

in 1873 as £120,000, yet only £59,000 was subscribed.[18] A Colorado venture, the Denaro Gold Mining Company, Ltd., was nominally capitalized at £60,000 in 1886, but by 1889 when the concern was voluntarily liquidated only £32,877 in shares had been taken.[19]

If the total amount of capital was rarely subscribed, it was equally true that the number of shares allotted was generally far in excess of the number sold for cash. This disparity is readily explained by the fact that a majority of British joint-stock companies paid for at least part of their property with shares issued as fully paid-up. Edward Ashmead estimates in a survey of all English mining companies between 1880 and 1904 that at least 75 per cent of the full nominal capital went to vendors in this fashion.[20]

A few concerns issued the whole or very nearly all of their shares to the vendors fully paid, then fell back on other sources for operating capital. Two large concerns incorporated in 1871 to operate in Utah, the Emma Silver Mining Company, Ltd., and the Flagstaff Silver Mining Company of Utah, Ltd., both paid over their entire capital to the vendors, intending to keep work in motion by the proceeds of ores in transit or being removed from the mines.[21] Other concerns issued the bulk of their shares as part of the purchase price, then depended upon the issue of mortgage debentures for working capital.[22]

Some Anglo-American corporations paid cash outright for their mines in the West; a few agreed to installment payments, to be made from profits from the property, although this sometimes led to complications.[23] Most, however, preferred to pay as much in shares as possible,

---

[18] Summary of Capital and Shares to Aug. 8, 1873, C.R.O. B-5289.

[19] *Mem. & Art.*, 3; Summary of Capital and Shares to March 21, 1889, C.R.O. B-23418.

[20] *Twenty-Five Years of Mining*, 152.

[21] *Mem. & Art.*, 2; Memo. of Agreement (Nov. 23, 1871) between the Salt Lake Mining Co. of Utah (by Groesbeck) and Horace N. Wilkinson, C.R.O. 5861; Memo. of Agreement (Nov. 4, 1871) between Trenor W. Park and George Henry Dean, C.R.O. 5809.

[22] Mineral Hill Silver Mines Co., *Prospectus* (June, 1871); Memo. of Agreement (June 21, 1871) between the Mineral Hill Silver Mines Co. and the California Mining Co., Mineral Hill Silver Mines Co., C.R.O. B-5496; *Mem. & Art.*, 3, Boulder Valley Collieries Co. of Colorado, C.R.O. 8312; Bear Creek Alluvial Gold Co., *Prospectus* (Feb. 1, 1894).

[23] The Silver Plume Mining Co. acquired Colorado mines from an American concern in 1872, agreeing to pay a total of £30,000—£5,000 in cash and the remainder from "time to time" out of half the profits set aside for that purpose.

thus eliminating the necessity of finding subscribers. Not infrequently purchase agreements were modified to allow payment in shares rather than cash,[24] and when contracts gave companies the option of paying a portion in cash or in shares settlement invariably was made in the latter.

It was customary to point to the acceptances of fully paid shares as an indication of real faith on the part of the vendor.[25] But often no restrictions were placed on the transfer of the vendor's shares, and he was free to dispose of them at whatever rates he saw fit. When Winfield Scott Stratton sold his famous Independence mine to a British concern at the end of the century, he shrewdly took his due in one million shares of one pound each.[26] Then by another agreement negotiated with the Venture Corporation, Ltd., he disposed of all his vendor's shares at premium prices. Stratton netted $10,000,000 for his pains [27] and did it in such a fashion that some of the finest legal minds in both England and the United States were unsuccessful in having the sale nullified and the purchase price returned.[28]

Many times restrictions were imposed to prevent the vendor from parting with his shares within a specified period or until prescribed dividends had been returned. Sometimes special dispensations would be given, allowing the vendor to part with the bulk of his holdings in

---

Memo. of Agreement (July 3, 1872) between George E. H. Gray and the Silver Plume Mining Company, C.R.O. 5552. The American vendors insisted this meant one-half the proceeds of ore sales; the English contended it meant one-half the net profits. As a result, the two factions were in constant strife until 1880, when an amalgamation was effected. *Mining World,* March 28, 1874, 598; *Mining Journal,* June 17, 1876, 660; *E. & M. Jour.,* Aug. 7, 1880, 93.

[24] The contract of one British firm acquiring Nevada mines was modified so that the vendor accepted £285,000 in paid-up shares instead of £285,000 in cash as originally provided. Memo. of Agreement (Aug. 27, 1872) between Hermann Heynemann and the Ruby Consolidated Mining Co., C.R.O. B-6247.

[25] *Mining Journal,* Aug. 31, 1872, 816.

[26] Memo. of Agreement (April 27, 1899) between Stratton and George Butcher, Stratton's Independence, C.R.O. B-61817.

[27] Stratton was to receive £1 19s. each on the first 666,666 shares and £2 10s. each on the remaining 333,334. Par value was £1. On April 18, 1900, when 592,000 shares had been sold by the Venture Corporation, Stratton sold the balance of his holdings to that concern "at such a price as with the cash already received on account of sale of stocks and dividends . . . to make up the total inclusive sum of $10,000,000. Waters, *Midas of the Rockies,* 219, 227.

[28] Below, 132–133.

order that the company might receive a quotation on the London Stock Exchange, since the rules of the Exchange required that at least two-thirds of the capital must have been taken up by the public.[29] Nor was it unknown for a vendor to disregard the limitations placed on his shares and to dispose of all or part for whatever he could obtain at the moment. Matthew Graham of New York accepted 4,000 shares of five pounds each from the Lucy Phillips Gold and Silver Mining Company, Ltd., in 1866 with the understanding that there should be no transfer until a stipulated percentage of dividends had been paid.[30] No profits were forthcoming from the Idaho mines, but despite this Graham began to sell his shares at the modest price of two shillings apiece, to the great consternation of bona fide shareholders who had paid fifty times as much for theirs.[31] The vendor of certain processing patents and rights in western America managed to unload some £100,-000 in shares received from the Cassel Gold Extracting Company, Ltd., in the 1880's, despite his earlier agreement to hold them for three years.[32] "This," noted a London financial organ in disgust, "is gold extracting with a vengeance." [33]

Responsible observers regarded the vendor's share as "often a delusion and a snare." [34] As the editor of the *Economist* insisted in 1888, if the owner or vendor retained any measure of faith in his property, he would most likely endeavor to raise capital on a mortgage rather than sell. But if he did sell, taking the large part of his pay in vendor's shares, he retained considerable control while the investing company provided the funds. If the enterprise proved successful, he reaped the lion's share of the profits: if it failed, he lost nothing.[35]

Another device occasionally utilized was the issuance of what were termed "founder's shares," carrying a disproportionately greater percentage of participation in profits than ordinary shares. In almost every instance such shares went fully paid up to the vendor or the promoter and must be distinguished from preferred shares, which also gave holders priority on profits. The preferred share was normally sold to the public; the founder's share was not, except in rare instances where

[29] Below, 155.

[30] *Mining Journal,* May 22, 1869, 370; Summary of Capital and Shares to Nov. 1, 1867, C.R.O. B-3298.

[31] *Mining Journal,* Feb. 12, 1870, 120.   [32] *Economist,* June 12, 1886, 741.

[33] *Financial Critic,* June 30, 1886, 424.   [34] *Economist,* Dec. 8, 1888, 1541.

[35] *Ibid.*

such were issued to important guinea-pig subscribers for the value of their influential names on the prospectus.[36]

A typical example of using the founder's-share device was Crooke's Mining and Smelting Company, Ltd., incorporated to operate in Colorado in 1882 with a nominal capital of £301,000 in 60,000 ordinary and 200 founder's shares of five pounds each. Founder's shares were to receive no dividends in any year until a 15 per cent cumulative dividend had been paid on all the ordinary shares, but after that the remaining profits were to be divided equally between holders of shares of both types.[37] Thus, theoretically, if in a single year the company were to pay dividends totaling £75,000 on its entire capital, ordinary shareholders would receive a return of 20 per cent on their investments, while those holding founder's shares would receive a return of 1,500 per cent.[38] Details might vary, but this was the standard arrangement for founder's shares.[39] Criticism of such schemes stemmed largely from the belief that in any successful venture, founder's shares would absorb too large a share of the profits. Moreover, since there was frequently no provision for paying them off, the company found itself with a millstone around its neck for an indefinite time.

If both the vendor's and founder's shares might be regarded as disadvantageous to the average joint-stock enterprise, another common detriment was the fact that British firms expended too great a proportion of their total capital on the purchase of property, leaving insufficient funds for defraying operating expenses. Frequently as much as 90, 95, or occasionally even 100 per cent of the total nominal capital was thus invested. Consequently, one of the commonest cries heard during the period was the plea for additional working capital. Companies

---

[36] The one such instance coming to light involved the Sapphire and Ruby Co. of Montana in 1891. Above, 55–56.

[37] *Mem. & Art.*, 4, 7–8. This provision was repealed late in 1883 and the founder's shares reverted to the status of ordinary shares. *Special Resolutions,* passed Dec. 3, 1883 and confirmed Dec. 21, 1883, C.R.O. B-16664.

[38] Fifteen per cent, or £45,000, would be set aside for ordinary shareholders. The remaining £30,000 would be divided equally between holders of ordinary and founder's shares, giving £15,000 for each category. Holders of ordinary shares would thus have received £60,000 or 20 per cent on the £300,000 in ordinary shares, while holders of the £1,000 worth of founder's shares would have received £15,000 or 1,500 per cent.

[39] See, for example, *Mem. & Art.*, 11–12, Mine Owners' Trust, C.R.O., B-33175; *Mem. & Art.* 7–8, Rocky Mountain Milling Co., C.R.O. B-43811.

resorted to all possible stratagems—borrowing, issuing debentures, mortgaging, reconstruction, and the leasing of part or all of their property—in usually futile efforts to raise supplemental funds for exploration and development.

On the other hand, the old bogy of overcapitalization arose to plague Anglo-American mining companies, just as the same problem tended to disturb the activities of practically all other types of joint-stock enterprise. The huge capitalizations of the Emma Silver Mining Company, Ltd., of 1871 (£1,000,000), of the Harney Peak (Dakota) Tin Company, Ltd., of 1887 (£2,000,000 but later raised to £3,000,000), or of Stratton's Independence, Ltd., in 1899 (£1,100,000) made it almost impossible to return substantial dividends on such large investments unless ore deposits proved fabulously rich. Unluckily this proved not to be the case.

If companies were overcapitalized and tended to pay too high a percentage of their capital for property, this was often simply the result of exorbitant prices asked for mines worth only modest sums. It was agreed by many observers on both sides of the Atlantic that Brother Jonathan was a shrewd operator and would very neatly separate the Englishman from his hard-earned shillings at the slightest opportunity. Any Briton in the mining regions of the West provided a sitting target for the local "sharps," who closed in from all sides with property for sale, like hungry wolves moving in on their isolated prey. That one of Her Majesty's subjects deserved special consideration was illustrated by a letter written by a self-styled Coloradan to a prospective British promoter early in 1871: "When you come here I should advise you to say nothing about buying mines as these Yankee fellows are all anxious to sell and the price they ask is all in proportion to the ability of the purchaser. I could buy a mine for 5000 dollars that they would ask you 50000 for." [40]

Even the transplanted Englishman occasionally seemed to catch the spirit of "these Yankee fellows" after having been exposed to the western atmosphere. After living in California a few years, J. Barr Robertson could write to an associate in Gold Hill, Nevada, late in 1875, paving the way for an English friend who was soon to visit the Comstock. "I wish him to examine the *Atlantic*," said Robertson, "and I think he will take shares in it, *but be careful not to say too much to*

[40] W. West to George Heaton (Black Hawk, Colo., March 8, 1871), Teller MSS.

him. He has been at Virginia City before, so he understands mining matters somewhat." [41] Robertson also cautioned against high-pressuring his friend and against raising his hopes too high. He warned against endeavoring to interest the visitor in certain specified Comstock mines because "I do not wish parties in Virginia to think that this is a rich Englishman likely to invest in any of these, because that would only raise the price higher against myself." [42]

Although a few Yankees, even some interested in promoting mine sales, honestly advised British capitalists to proceed with wariness,[43] all too frequently Englishmen in the West failed to heed such warnings and burst into the mining towns with such fanfare that mineral property naturally and suddenly shot upward in value. A competent mining man from Manchester, Thomas Tonge, complained in 1899 that the operations of London exploration and development syndicates in Colorado "were conducted on a similar plan to that of 'hunting bumble bees with a brass band.'" In at least two instances, he said, "titled persons from London stayed in the best rooms of the best hotels in the Colorado mining districts, and their purposes were practically proclaimed from the housetops." [44] Engineer-promoter William Weston also noted in 1900 that the agents of interested companies sent out from London usually arrived in riding breeches and leggings, carrying with them paraphernalia of all sorts marking them as capitalists from the moment they appeared, with the result that prices were promptly multiplied by five.[45]

Perhaps difficulties would have been greatly minimized had all Englishmen showed an awareness as acute as that of the itinerant Allayne Beaumont Legard, who visited the Rocky Mountain region in 1872. Viewing matters philosophically, Legard sought to establish a mathematical formula to cover transactions involving western mining prop-

---

[41] To Jesse W. Brown (San Francisco, Dec. 30, 1875), Robertson Letterbrook.
[42] *Ibid*.
[43] The first editor of the Denver *Rocky Mt. News* informed J. Valentine Smedley of London in 1870 that a young friend of the latter had arrived in the Rockies. "I advise him not to be in too great haste about putting money into the business," he wrote. "Experience is sometimes worth more than money & if observant—as I believe him to be—he can acquire a great deal of that in a few months and cheaply." Byers to Smedley (Denver, July 22, 1870), Byers Letterbook (1868–1871).
[44] Quoted in the *Anglo-Colorado Mining Guide*, II (Dec. 30, 1899), 182.
[45] In *Mountain Sunshine*, quoted in *ibid.*, III (Feb, 24, 1900), 21.

erty and made known to the British public the proper course in bargaining with a Yankee over a mine. "To reduce the thing to a rule," he said, "*halve the sum he asks, and divide the result by three.*" Then, he added, "you will get pretty near what he will take." [46]

If there was a tendency to boost prices to meet what the traffic would bear when an Englishman wandered innocently into the mining camps, there was likewise an inclination for prices to rise severalfold when mines were placed on the London market. This mystical process of inflation during the Atlantic journey was well recognized and brought adverse comment from both unofficial and official sources. A perceptive Cornishman from Nevada in 1872 wrote: "That confusion is itself confounding has been sufficiently evidenced by the way in which mines, so-called—skeletons of their former selves alone remaining—have been selected and purchased at sums which actually stagger reason, and almost defy credence." [47]

Official recognition of the dualism between prices in London and in the West came in the annual reports of the British consul at San Francisco throughout the period. Consul Booker gave express warning in 1872:

A good many California and Nevada Mines have been sold during the past year on the London Market, and the price paid for these has generally been far in advance of their recognized value here. The almost insatiable demands of the California and Nevada "Operators" and the London Stock Exchange have in some instances caused the par value of the shares of a Company to be five times or more what the Mine has or should have cost. Good mines are to be purchased at a reasonable valuation if the same sagacity and caution are displayed in securing them as would be in any ordinary commercial transaction.[48]

Two decades later Her Majesty's vice-consul at Los Angeles reiterated the caution, advising English agents in the Southwest to purchase undeveloped mines at comparatively low costs rather than to purchase property which might conceivably be worked out.[49]

[46] *Colorado* (London, 1872), 67.

[47] Robert Knapp to editor (Ellsworth, Nevada, n.d.), *Mining Journal*, April 27, 1872, 394.

[48] Annual Report of Consul Booker on the Trade of California (MS), 1871 (San Francisco, March 8, 1872), Consular Papers, 1872, F.O. 115/540.

[49] Report of the San Francisco Consulate, 1892, Foreign Office, *Annual Series*,

Capitalization Problems

Such warnings may have had some effect, for numerous western mines offered in London at fabulously high prices were rejected by the investing public, simply because of "the owners opening their mouths too wide," as one commentator put it.[50] The Comet, of Yellow Pine District, Nevada, which was offered for $12,000 at home, was put on the English market at the asking price of $1,500,000 but found no takers.[51] When the Copper Queen mine of Arizona was offered in London for £350,000 in 1884 and 1885,[52] the investing public steered clear of the proposal when American mining periodicals disclosed that the price was thrice that which had been asked in the United States.[53]

In many other instances, however, sales were not rejected. Only too often English concerns snapped up the bait almost as soon as it was dangled before their noses. As a matter of fact, the great majority of western mines sold in Britain went at prices they could never have commanded at home.

There seems little evidence to suggest, though, that the more hazardous western ventures were pushed off on the more remote British markets. Prices may have been jacked up, but in terms of property and risk, the British investing public was fed much the same general diet that was being given to American investors during the same period.

Thoughtful Englishmen and Americans were in essential accord in placing much of the blame for inflated prices on "the excessive greed of the promoters, who often place the mine on the market at ten to twelve times the amount the mine was bought for from the original vendor."[54]

No. 1251 (1893), 83. See also Report of the San Francisco Consulate, 1893, Foreign Office, *Annual Series,* No. 1452 (1894), 78.

[50] *Anglo-Colorado Mining Guide,* II (June 29, 1899), 105.

[51] J. White to editor (San Francisco, Aug. 13, 1871, *Mining Journal,* Sept. 9, 1871, 800.

[52] *Mem. & Art.,* 1–2, Copper Queen, C.R.O. B-20210; *Mem. & Art.* 1 and Memo. of Agreement (Feb. 2, 1885) between Richard L. Ogden, James T. Browne, and Francis Hutley, Copper Queen United, C.R.O. B-20767.

[53] *E. & M. Jour.,* Aug. 29, 1885, 141. In 1885 the Copper Queen United was organized to acquire the property, but almost immediately the purchase contract was repudiated and the company wound up, with the capital returned to the subscribers. Special *Resolutions,* passed July 15 and confirmed July 30, 1885, C.R.O. B-20767.

[54] "An Englishman" to editor (Salt Lake, Aug. 26, 1873), *Mining World,* Sept. 27, 1873, 651.

There was fairly general agreement also that such greed was not limited by national boundaries but that John Bull and Brother Jonathan both transgressed in this respect.[55] Americans did not hesitate to condemn the practices of their fellow countrymen. While appraising the sale of mines to the Cripple Creek (Bull Hill) Finance and Development Company, Ltd., a western editor in 1897 strongly deprecated the scandalous boosting of the purchase price to £130,000 by a fellow Coloradan and felt confident that he "could duplicate the properties for £1000 and most probably a good deal less." [56] On the other hand, British editors found themselves in complete sympathy with the Cripple Creek owner, who after a visit to England in the nineties to dispose of mineral property reached the conclusion that "to call a London promoter a hog was an insult to the swine family." [57]

Regardless of who was responsible, the fact remains that prices were inordinately high and that profits were shared by middlemen along the way. One former mineowner confided to William Weston that he had received but $30,000 from his property which sold in England for $300,000: the remaining $270,000 had been absorbed by three groups of intermediaries in Denver, New York, and London.[58] This was not at all unusual, for the margin of profit received by a successful vendor or promoter was fantastic. On December 14, 1885, one James Williams of Surrey acquired five lodes from a Denver "operator" for $180,000 or approximately £36,000. Less than twenty-four hours later he transferred this property to the agent of a British firm then in the process of being formed for a total of £136,000.[59] Thomas Gilbert of London later acquired four claims in Montrose County, Colorado, for £4,500, then

[55] Indeed, "in this particular," wrote one English editor, "it must be as freely conceded that English promoters have sinned far more deeply than American mine owners." *Ibid.*, Jan. 18, 1873, 113.

[56] Claud Sachs to editor (Colorado Springs, Nov. 30, 1897), *Mining Journal*, Dec. 11, 1897, 1467. Only £6,000 was to be in cash. The remainder was to be in fully paid-up shares. Cripple Creek (Bull Hill) Finance and Development Co., *Prospectus* (1896).

[57] Quoted in Waters, *Midas of the Rockies*, 206.

[58] Weston in *Mountain Sunshine*, quoted in *Anglo-Colorado Mining Guide*, III (Feb. 24, 1900), 21.

[59] *Statist*, Sept. 17, 1887, 321; Memo. of Agreement (Dec. 15, 1885) between James F. Williams and Percy Merfield, United States Gold Placers, C.R.O. B-22323.

promptly disposed of them to the "Gold Queen," Ltd., for £165,000 in cash and shares.[60]

It would appear that the average Anglo-American mining company labored under disadvantages from the onset. Frequently the capitalization process was accomplished in such a way that a firm was grossly overcapitalized, possessed insufficient actual capital for sustained operations, or had paid such an excessive sum for its property that it could not hope to return profits. Sometimes a combination of these factors plagued the company; in such a case the concern usually met an early demise, sadly lamented by a host of discontented mourners.

[60] Memo. of Agreement (Feb. 3, 1888) between Thomas Gilbert and the "Gold Queen," Ltd, C.R.O. B-25811.

: CHAPTER VI :

Management Problems

IF overcapitalization, high prices, and inferior or worked-out property were disadvantages under which many Anglo-American mining companies labored, another perplexing major problem was management. Actual operation of western mines was an intriguing and complex business in itself, but where British corporations were concerned it was further complicated by questions springing from absentee ownership and factors of time and distance.

Basic issues were raised immediately. How might honest, competent, and experienced men be obtained to handle affairs that were difficult under any conditions but especially so when encountered under new and strange circumstances? How might control be exercised over supervisory personnel from a London or Edinburgh office five or six thousand miles away so that shareholders could be certain a mine manager in Utah or Idaho would act according to instructions and transmit satisfactory information in return? These questions were frequently asked; not so frequently were they answered to the gratification of the British investor.

Although the pattern of management might vary in detail from company to company, ordinarily it followed a set outline. The board of directors determined broad policy in England, but in almost all instances a single man was in charge of operations in the West.[1] By

[1] There were a few examples of joint responsibility at the mine, but these generally proved unsatisfactory. See report of meeting of the Kansas Mining Co. (Sept. 18, 1873), *Mining World*, Sept. 20, 1873, 584.

whatever name he was known—agent, general manager, manager, or superintendent—his task was to supervise all operations, frequently with freedom to accumulate debts, to hire and to discharge subordinates, and to give full expression to his own ideas or lack of ideas at the mine.

In addition, many British concerns maintained managing directors, usually men originally interested in the property before transfer or shareholders with a reputation for knowing something about the unpredictable science of mining. Although some managing directors were full-time employees and were actually in charge of operations, the majority received the same monetary benefits as ordinary directors and their duties were limited to periodic inspections and co-ordination of affairs between London and the United States.[2]

There was a noticeable tendency among British directors to place small faith in American engineers or mine managers, and the bulk of English companies depended on men sent from the home isles. After all, were not all Yankees interested only in "mining" the English investor? Had they not, in the words of one Englishman of experience, "discovered a vein in British pockets which is nearly as remunerative, and promises to be quite as lasting, as any yet worked in the entire State of Nevada"?[3] There was a commonly accepted feeling, moreover, that Americans lacked the training and the technical skill necessary for effective, economical management.

Certainly the Britisher could cite plenty of examples to illustrate the inferiority of American supervision so far as Anglo-American mining companies were concerned. The poet James Thomson ("B. V."), in Colorado in 1872 as agent for a British mining firm, expressed profound contempt for the company's former manager, Theodore Hikes Lowe of Idaho Springs but commended two English representatives subse-

[2] J. Warren Brown, the vendor and one of the leading shareholders, became managing director for the Republican Mountain Silver Mines early in the 1880's. He later brought suit against the company to collect £3,000 allegedly due him for services, contending that he had been in charge of actual operations. The company proved, however, that a regular superintendent had been in charge and that Brown's contribution had consisted of biannual trips to Colorado and several jaunts to London—with all expenses paid in each case. The court consequently decided against the New Yorker, maintaining that he had been paid as a regular director and was entitled to no more. Brown *v.* Republican Mountain Silver Mines, 17 *Colorado Reports* (1892), 422, 426.

[3] Rae, *Westward by Rail* (2d ed. 1871), xxiii.

quently sent out by his own and another British concern. These latter two, noted Thomson, "I verily believe can be trusted, & I scarcely know any Americans here of whom I can say as much." [4]

It soon developed that the poet had every reason to be distrustful of Lowe. The American, he discovered, had used company funds for private speculations and consistently refused to account for the money for nearly five months.[5] Thomson expressed the fear that "the doubt of T. H. L.'s honesty in this matter might break off all negotiations with capitalists & prevent any settlement" of differences between his own company and the vendors in Colorado.[6] That Lowe's attitude served to block other transactions in Britain in 1872 is almost certain. Hugh H. Roche of the European and American Agency in London wrote to one Dr. Adduddell of Colorado with regard to the Nimrod lode: "Have destroyed bond. Lowe's infamous conduct as regards California Mine spoils anything with which his name is connected." [7]

News of this and other defalcations or chicanery spread rapidly among mining and investment circles abroad. Englishmen were quick to pass on word of the shortcomings of the Americans in charge of Colorado property for the Red Mountain Mines, Ltd., and the Henriett Mining and Smelting Company, Ltd., in the early 1880's.[8] A later generation was warned against the likes of Nicholas Treweek, the Yankee manager of the Dickens Custer Company, Ltd., in Idaho, who took advantage of federal restrictions on aliens in the territories to exploit the company at every opportunity.[9] Such episodes, plus innumerable instances of poor mines pushed off on British investors at exorbitant prices, helped persuade English companies to rely heavily on British personnel to supervise mine operations.

But there were other factors making for the same tendency. English directors were often subject to pressure when such appointments were made. Occasionally large shareholders became managers, not by virtue of knowledge or ability, but simply because of influence within

---

[4] Business Diary, Nov. 7, 1872, 87.

[5] Lowe admitted that he had invested $8,500 belonging to the company but refused to give details. On the day that Thomson left Colorado in December, 1872, after months of haggling, the Englishman was finally informed that the money had been handed over to the vendors. *Ibid.*, July 27, Aug. 16, Dec. 26, 1872, 40–41, 49, 108.

[6] *Ibid.*, Aug. 16, 1872, 49.   [7] *Ibid.*, Dec. 3, 1872, 94.

[8] *Mining Journal,* Dec. 30, 1882, 1574; June 30, 1883, 749.   [9] Below, 209.

the company. One "expert" was sent out to carry on work for the La Plata Mining and Smelting Company, Ltd., in Colorado primarily because he owed money to the chairman.[10] Nepotism was common in all periods, with mixed results. Sometimes the second or third sons of respectable English families—the remittance men of the West—were sent out by fathers in influential positions on boards of directors.[11] The manager of the Eberhardt and Aurora Mining Company, Ltd., in Nevada during the early seventies was Thomas Phillpotts, brother of one of the largest shareholders.[12] When Phillpotts was ousted in 1873 after a prolonged and heated internal struggle,[13] he did not join the ranks of the unemployed but was made general manager of the Davenport Mining Company, Ltd., a British concern operating in Utah. This time the appointment came through the influence of another brother, who was chairman of the Davenport board of directors.[14] The manager of the Montana Company, Ltd., in the early 1880's was an appointee of the chairman—the nephew of "a very dear old friend of mine," confessed the latter.[15] Young Tom Rickard, fresh from the Royal School of Mines at London, received his first job with an Anglo-Colorado concern in 1885 through the influence of his "Uncle Alf," who managed several properties for English companies near Idaho Springs.[16]

The inevitable result of selection on such irrational bases was that many inexperienced or inept men were placed in charge when qualified personnel were needed. No wonder the average westerner could view with disdain the so-called British mining "expert." "We had quite a variety of them here in the course of the last four years," said a Utah resident in 1874, "and the best that can be said for them is that they were quite harmless."[17]

James Thomson of the Champion Gold and Silver Mines Company

[10] Thomas A. Rickard, *Retrospect* (New York and London, 1937), 35.

[11] "Equitas" to editor (Salt Lake City, n.d.), *Mining Journal*, Aug. 29, 1874, 931.

[12] George Attwood to Thomas Phillpotts (Hamilton, Nev., Sept. 2, 1870, Read MSS; *Mining World*, Oct. 12, 1872, 1545–1546.

[13] *Mining World*, Oct. 19, 1872, 1590–1591; Aug. 16, 1873, 364.

[14] *Ibid.*, Aug. 16, 1873, 364.

[15] Montana Co., *Report of the Proceedings at a Special General Meeting of the Shareholders held at the City Terminus Hotel, Cannon Street, London, E.C., Wednesday, 19th November, 1884*, 5–6, Stock Exchange Archives, London.

[16] Rickard, *Retrospect*, 29.

[17] "Equitas" to editor (Salt Lake City, n.d.), *Mining Journal*, Aug. 29, 1874, 931.

of Colorado, Ltd., might be classified in the "quite harmless" category, but it is clear that he was prepared neither for financial nor mining transactions. Like other English literary figures of his day, he probably had little interest in and less knowledge of Colorado prior to his becoming secretary and agent to this particular concern in 1872.[18] If his diaries are any indication, "B. V." enjoyed himself immensely in the Rockies and diligently represented his company at practically every social event held in Gilpin County for a period of six months. Yet what the company needed was not someone who could write "The City of Dreadful Night" or declaim at length over the wonders of Colorado's mountain scenery but a practical, hard-headed businessman who knew something about mines and mining.

A Nevada venture, the South Aurora Silver Mining Company, Ltd., had by 1872 handed over management to a shareholder, one Dr. Goodfellow, a British dentist whose previous experience with precious metals seems to have been confined to the gold fillings of cringing patients.[19] Goodfellow's salary of £2,000 a year brought protests from fellow shareholders, who commented freely on his independence of action when so far from the board of directors. "Dr. Goodfellow," said one, "gets a large salary, and there is a sort of carelessness comes over a man when he finds he has neither a soul to be saved nor a stern to be kicked." [20] Despite these protests and the directors' admission that he was overpaid,[21] it was a full two years before he was dismissed.[22]

The Thomsons and the Goodfellows were frequent enough, but few Anglo-American concerns were as consistent in obtaining inadequate and inexperienced personnel as was the Clifton Silver Mining Com-

[18] Before leaving England, Thomson wrote his friend, William M. Rossetti: "I may be very probably called to start at two or three days notice in search of the Heathen Chinee among the Rocky Mountains, on business of the Company of which I am the unworthy Secretary *pro tem.*" (London, April 21, 1872.) Rossetti, to whom the Rockies were as alien as the Tsingling Range, believed that Thomson was about to depart for China. Rossetti to Thomson (London, April 28, 1872), MS Don c. 73a. (fol. 1), Bodleian Library.

[19] *Mining Journal*, Feb. 3, 1872, 95.

[20] Report of meeting of the South Aurora Silver Mining Co. (Nov. 6, 1872), *Mining World*, Nov. 9, 1872, 1681.

[21] See *ibid.;* also reports of meetings of South Aurora Silver Mining Co. (March 4, May 6, 1874), *ibid.*, March 7, May 9, 1874, 476, 842–843.

[22] His services terminated at the end of 1874, when the concern was contemplating leaving the Nevada scene for more lucrative pursuits in Corsica. *Mining Journal*, Jan. 16, 1875, 59.

pany, Ltd. Operating in Colorado, this firm in 1871 sent out Edward Dowlen and Thomas Rodham, the former as manager and the latter as mining captain.[23] Rodham died within a year [24] but not before criticism of Dowlen had begun.[25] One shareholder characterized him as an office boy with only a month's experience in assaying before he assumed supervision of the Clifton property. It was charged that when the mine crew struck a new type of rock Dowlen immediately telegraphed the board of directors, but when it turned out to be of no value he explained his hasty action in cabling by saying, "It looked so beautiful." [26]

Dowlen was released in the spring of 1872,[27] but no replacement was named until early the following year. At that time the company sent out William McCree, a British druggist "whose only recommendation was that he understood medicines." [28] McCree proceeded to leave the directors without news for nearly eight months [29] and was ultimately removed [30] in favor of Hiram F. Sawyer, a Coloradan described by a competent judge as "a green country farmer." [31] By June, 1874, Sawyer, too, had been released, with one of the promoters (who was now also a creditor) supervising unofficially while the property was being leased on a share-the-profit basis.[32]

It need not be inferred that semi- or, indeed, totally inexperienced men in charge at the mines invariably spelled disaster to the British

[23] *Ibid.,* Nov. 11, 1871, 988; July 10, 1875, 744.

[24] James Thomson mentions the funeral of Captain Rodham in late September, 1872. Diary of a Visit to Colorado, Sept. 30, 1872, 61, MS Don e. 46, Bodleian Library.

[25] Report of meeting of the Clifton Silver Mining Co. (Dec. 13, 1872), *Mining World,* Dec. 14, 1872, 1909.

[26] *Ibid.*

[27] F. Andrews to editor (London, July 9, 1875), *Mining Journal,* July 10, 1875, 744.

[28] "A Shareholder" to editor, *ibid.,* July 3, 1875, 732.

[29] Report of meeting of the Clifton Silver Mining Co. (Nov. 24, 1873), *Mining World,* Nov. 29, 1873, 1096.

[30] McCree charged that company officials in London had consistently refused to co-operate and that someone had "schemed" to have him discharged in mid-winter five thousand miles from home. To editor (Central City, March 25, 1874), *Mining Journal,* April 18, 1874, 424.

[31] Charles S. Richardson to editor (Central City, July 21, 1874), *ibid.,* Aug. 15, 1874, 889.

[32] Report of meeting of the Clifton Silver Mining Co. (June 15, 1874), *Mining World,* June 20, 1874, 1138.

97

concern, although certainly success under such circumstances was more the exception than the typical case. For nearly a quarter of a century the eminently successful Richmond Consolidated Mining Company, Ltd., was managed in Nevada by an "amateur," Edward Probert, an ordained minister and formerly chaplain to the Duke of Northumberland.[33] A shareholder and a nonprofessional geologist, Probert visited the company's mines in the early seventies and was asked to remain as manager.[34] Under his supervision the concern prospered despite ups and downs and charges of ineptitude which coincided with the lean years.[35] Criticism was particularly strong in 1878, when the two-hundred-page report of a specially appointed committee of investigation reflected seriously on Probert's management, charging him with maladministration in general and more specifically with the purchase of property rights on his own account rather than for the company and with poor and uneconomical construction of "hydrocycle" furnaces.[36] This report evoked a lengthy reply by Probert and precipitated a serious internal squabble that raged within the company for several months.[37] In the end, however, the shareholders accorded Probert a vote of confidence and the storm subsided.[38] For nearly two decades thereafter he continued in charge of the Richmond Consolidated, performing his duties capably without serious criticism.[39]

Inexperienced men of Probert's ability were few and far between. More typical was the neophyte manager who proved only too surely and at company expense that mine administration was not his particular forte. To the end of the century British companies never completely discarded the idea "that a man having been a Sunday school teacher,

---

[33] *Mining Journal*, Jan. 18, 1873, 60; *Statist*, Dec. 3, 1887, 625.

[34] Report of meeting of the Richmond Consolidated Mining Co. (Feb. 20, 1873), *Mining World*, Feb. 22, 1873, 386.

[35] *Mining Journal*, May 22, 1875, 570.   [36] *Ibid.*, Nov. 9, 1878, 1232.

[37] Begun in Aug., 1877, the investigation cost a total of £4,098 18s. *Ibid.*, June 15, 1878, 667. Probert's reply filled 132 pages. *Ibid.*, Nov. 9, 1878, 1232.

[38] Report of meeting of the Richmond Consolidated Mining Co. (Nov. 12, 1878), *ibid.*, Nov. 16, 1878, 1278–1279.

[39] The company in 1895 joined the exodus to Australia but retained its Nevada property until 1905. Probert remained with the concern until it ceased active work in the West and died in San Francisco in 1900. Richmond Consolidated Mining Co., *Annual Report*, year ending Feb. 28, 1895; *ibid.*, year ending Feb. 29, 1900; Herbert Akins to J. A. Torrens Johnson (London, Sept. 21, 1905), Stock Exchange Archives, London.

or a most exemplary tradesman, or a needy relative of the president, or one of the directors is sufficient qualification to enable him to manage a mine successfully." [40]

Inexperience was normally a handicap and frequently disastrous to a company manager or agent, although not always. Conversely, experience as an engineer or superintendent was no ironclad guarantee that a man might do well in the American West. It was imperative that the experience be of the proper sort. When complaints were made in 1871 that the Nevada mines of the Pacific Mining Company, Ltd., were "grossly mismanaged," [41] investigation disclosed that the superintendent sent out from England was well-trained in copper and tin mining but knew nothing about silver—the only metal with which the company was concerned on Lander Hill.[42] Francis Fowler, who served Anglo-American companies in Utah and Colorado, was a civil engineer, not a mining engineer, and was regarded by competent mining men as "a pretender." [43]

Not infrequently purchase contracts provided that the vendor be employed for a specified period of time as mine manager. Some, like William S. Godbe, the vendor and subsequent general manager of the Chicago Silver Mining Company, Ltd. (Utah), agreed to give their services in exchange for a percentage of dividends paid.[44] Others, like Samuel Newhouse of Denver, who sold Utah property to the Boston Consolidated Copper and Gold Mining Company, Ltd., in 1898, were to receive an annual minimum with additional remuneration based on the amount of profit available for distribution.[45] Still others acted as

[40] William Weston to editor, *Mining Journal*, May 7, 1881, 561. See also *ibid.*, July 25, 1896, 954.

[41] This was the charge of Director Francis Cope, a London stockbroker just back from the mines, who probably knew as much about mine management on Saturn as in Nevada. *Ibid.*, Feb. 4, 1871, 84.

[42] *Stock Exchange Review*, I (Oct., 1871).   [43] Rickard, *Retrospect*, 35.

[44] Godbe agreed to serve as general manager for two years at a salary equal to 2 per cent of any dividends paid. Memo. of Agreement (March 14, 1873) between William S. Godbe and J. Henry Richardson, Chicago Silver Mining Co., C.R.O. 7003.

[45] While annual profits were under £20,000, Newhouse was to receive a salary of £2,000 a year; when net profits jumped to between £20,000 and £60,000 per annum, he was to receive his base salary, plus one-tenth of the profits; when net profits went over £60,000 a year, he was to receive an additional one-twentieth of this surplus. Memo. of Agreement (May 14, 1898) between Samuel Newhouse and Charles Luff, Boston Consolidated Copper and Gold Mining Co.,

vendors, then took over as managers or managing directors on a flat salary basis. Even canny old Winfield Scott Stratton, who exchanged his Independence mine for ten million dollars in the English market, could not resist the offer of a managing directorship at a salary of £4,000 a year for two years.[46]

Some vendors turned manager for the salary involved; many probably did so in hopes of instilling confidence into actual or potential shareholders. Some proved to be capable administrators, but a significant number of Anglo-American mining concerns ultimately found their vendor-manager a source of grief. Some such officials were simply not qualified for their posts; [47] others displayed little interest in their work.[48] In a few cases companies discovered to their dismay that American vendors or former owners retained in a managerial capacity sought to use their official positions to line their own pockets.

The not inappropriately named Crooke brothers, vendors of Colorado properties to Crooke's Mining and Smelting Company, Ltd. (1882), not only threw in an unbargained-for mortgage in the transaction but continued to supervise operations and endeavored to bull the London market from across the Atlantic. About eight months after the company was launched, "profits" were forwarded from Colorado sufficient to pay a 15 per cent dividend but were accompanied by no accounts. Consequently the directors refused to declare a dividend; instead they dispatched one of their members, James E. Thorold Rogers, to the mines to investigate. Thorold Rogers—"a fine, big, loud-mouthed, rough, profane old Parliamentarian war-horse" [49]—discovered that the "proceeds" were unearned and apparently had been sent to induce British investors to take up the remaining unsubscribed shares. When the directors appointed certain officials in Colorado, friction ensued between them and

---

C.R.O. B-57354. In 1904 the company purchased this contract from Newhouse for $60,000. It still had four years to run. Boston Consolidated Copper and Gold Mining Co., *Annual Report,* year ending Sept. 30, 1904.

[46] Memo. of Agreement (April 27, 1899) between Winfield Scott Stratton and George Butcher, C.R.O. B-61817.

[47] See *Mining Journal,* July 20, 1872, 687; *Mining World,* March 1, 1873, 430.

[48] For an example pertaining to the Colorado Terrible Lode Mining Co., see *Mining Journal,* June 28, 1873, 691. For a more detailed survey of the difficulties experienced by this concern and its attempts to rid itself of a vendor-manager, see Clark C. Spence, "Colorado's Terrible Mine: A Study in British Investment," *Colorado Magazine,* XXXIV (Jan., 1957), 56–58.

[49] Furniss, *Some Victorian Men,* 90.

the Crooke brothers and the former were ousted. When the company raised an additional £10,000 by the issue of mortgage bonds, the Colorado management incurred debts on behalf of the concern which absorbed the bulk of the new capital almost as soon as it was obtained.[50]

It is apparent that in many instances the selection of mine superintendents was not carried out in accordance with sound business principles. Nepotism sometimes brought inexperienced men or incompetents; the hiring of vendors, ex-owners, or tools of promoters frequently brought men of the same caliber and in addition provoked efforts to manipulate shares. But it does not necessarily follow that all mine managers were selected on these bases or that they were inefficient or corrupt. On the contrary, there were many capable men in the employ of British concerns in the West who forged to the top or who never found an opportunity to display their abilities because their employers lacked operating capital or because the property was worthless.

Throughout the period British mining companies relied heavily upon English—and especially Cornish—experts. A comparatively small percentage of these were engineers trained in respectable schools on the home islands or on the Continent. In this category were such men as John Arthur Phillips, educated at the École des Mines in Paris and noted for his original field research for English concerns in the West during the late 1860's.[51] The name of Minos Claiborne Vincent, "Fellow of the Geological and Royal Geographical Societies; Professor of Economic Geology & Metallurgy," crops up again and again among those active in management during the seventies and eighties.[52]

Phillips and Vincent were examples of experts who came to the United States only temporarily on behalf of British concerns. Numerous other trained engineers came in the service of English firms, then remained to make reputations in western mines. Ernest Le Neve Foster, for example, one of a prominent British mining family, studied both at the Royal School of Mines in London and at Freiberg, the Mecca of top-caliber mining engineers the world over.[53] Coming to

---

[50] *Economist*, June 6, 1885, 693.   [51] London *Times*, Jan. 7, 1887.

[52] *Memorandum of Association*, 1–2, San Juan Reduction Co., C.R.O. 11494; report of meeting of the Flagstaff Silver Mining Co. of Utah (July 9, 1880), *Journal of the Shareholders' Corporation, Limited*, July 14, 1880, 68–69.

[53] Frost, "History of Clear Creek County," in *History of Clear Creek and Boulder Valleys, Colorado*, 511. A brother, Sir Clement Le Neve Foster, was

Colorado in 1871 in the employ of two English mining companies, Foster pursued a subsequent career as a mining expert that affiliated him with half a dozen Anglo-American concerns [54] and made him one of the most highly respected men in his field.[55]

That Foster's success was not unique is indicated by a glance at the life of Richard Pearce, a Cornishman whose progress went even farther. With a wealth of practical experience in Cornish tin mines and study at both London and Freiberg behind him, Pearce came to Colorado in 1871 as metallurgist for the Swansea Smelting and Silver Mining Company, Ltd.[56] Within two years he had joined an American, Nathaniel P. Hill, in building reduction works which used successfully processes as yet untried in the United States.[57] Considered by competent authorities as "the pioneer of copper-smelting practice in the Rocky Mountain region," [58] Pearce was deemed one of the most eminent metallurgists in the world at the time of his death in 1927.[59]

Another British name well known in the West was Rickard. Beginning with James Rickard, who in 1850 brought one of the first stamp mills to California for John Taylor and Sons,[60] members of this family were to play important roles in mineral development down to the present date. At one time there were eight members of the family who

---

from 1890 until his death in 1904 a professor at the Royal School of Mines in London. *Who Was Who* (1887–1916) (London, 1920), 225.

[54] Foster was associated in one capacity or another with the Snowdrift Silver Mining and Reduction Co., the Silver Plume Mining Co., the Astor Alliance Mines, the Cinnamon Mountain Gold and Silver Mining Co., the Planet Silver Mining Co., the Quartz Hill Consolidated Gold Mining Co., the Nouveau Monde Gold Mining Co., and the Slide and Spur Gold Mines—all Anglo-Colorado undertakings.

[55] Foster was appointed state geologist of Colorado in 1883. See *Report of E. Le Neve Foster, State Geologist, Colorado* (1883–1884).

[56] William N. Byers, *Encyclopedia of Biography of Colorado* (Chicago, 1901), 233–234; *DAB*, XIV, 353.

[57] *DAB*, XIV, 353.

[58] Rickard, *History of American Mining*, 120.

[59] Pearce was British vice-consul at Denver for many years, a fellow of the Geological Society in London, and president of the American Institute of Mining Engineers; he was awarded an honorary Doctor of Philosophy degree by Columbia University. In 1902 he returned to England, where he spent the rest of his days. *DAB*, XIV, 353; *Who's Who in Mining and Metallurgy* (1908), 72.

[60] Rickard, *Retrospect,* 9.

belonged to the American Institute of Mining Engineers.[61] Thomas Arthur Rickard was undoubtedly the most famous of the group, although his father and at least two of his uncles were also active in managing Anglo-American ventures in the 1880's and 1890's.[62] A graduate of the Royal School of Mines, London, Rickard acted as consulting engineer for some of the largest Colorado concerns at the end of the century [63] and subsequently became editor of the leading mining periodicals of the United States and England.[64] He was a prolific writer, lectured on mining geology at Harvard University, and was indisputably one of the world's foremost mining specialists in the half-century following 1890.[65]

British firms also employed some highly skilled American engineers, but most of these tended to specialize in inspection of properties rather than in managerial or consultive work. Probably the best known was John Hays Hammond, the most famous of all American mining engineers save only Herbert Hoover. With a background combining both Yale and Freiberg, Hammond filled engagements in almost every part of the world, stopping briefly in Colorado at the turn of the century as consulting engineer for Stratton's Independence, Ltd., and Camp Bird, Ltd., before moving on to wider pastures.[66]

[61] "My father, grandfather, and great-grandfather were mining engineers," wrote Thomas Rickard, who also had four brothers in that profession. *Ibid.*, vii, 8–9.

[62] For the affiliation of his father, Thomas Rickard, and his two uncles, Reuben and Alfred, with British mining firms in the West, see Skinner, *Mining Manual* (1887), 210, 217; Corregan and Lingane, *Colorado Mining Directory*, 147–148, 267, 287; Memo. of Agreement (March 1, 1881) between Reuben Rickard and the Eureka (Nevada) Silver Mining Co., C.R.O. B-14527.

[63] Included were Camp Bird, Stratton's Independence, and the Moon Anchor Consolidated Gold Mines—all in Cripple Creek district.

[64] After a career of mine inspection and management in France, the United States, and Australia-New Zealand, Rickard became state geologist of Colorado (1895–1901). Subsequently he was editor of the *Engineering and Mining Journal* (1903–1905), the *Mining and Scientific Press* (1906–1909, 1915–1922), and the London *Mining Magazine* (1909–1915). *Who's Who in America*, XXIV (1946–1947), 1977.

[65] Among at least thirty articles and books that he wrote, his *History of American Mining* (1932) is today a classic in its field. Rickard died in 1953 in Victoria, B.C.

[66] Completing his work at Freiberg in 1879, Hammond gained experience with the United States Geological Survey and in mines in the West, in Mexico, and in Central America before casting his lot with Cecil Rhodes in Africa in the 1890's. It was there that he built his reputation as a mining engineer. According to his own statements, he was later boomed briefly as Taft's running mate in 1908, was

Such well-educated and technically trained engineers were undoubtedly definitely in the minority. The backbone of Anglo-American mine management was the self-educated, self-made mining "expert," who tended to dominate the scene throughout the period. It is safe to say that a substantial majority of British concerns placed their western property under the supervision of these practical "engineers by experience," who usually had Cornish backgrounds. When Herbert Hoover left college in the mid-nineties, he found Pacific mines predominantly under the management of Cornishmen who had risen through the ranks. They were, relates Hoover, competent mining men but skeptics about "them college educated fellers." [67]

Examples of the Cornish mining captain advanced to a supervisory capacity appear on all sides, in all periods, and in all western regions. Experienced in all parts of the world, these pragmatic specialists spread the Old World heritage throughout the New and contributed a great deal to the mineral frontier. George Teal, of the Colorado Terrible Lode Mining Company, Ltd., was the first in the Rocky Mountain region to show the practicality of treating low-grade ores. [68] A stocky Scotch-Irishman, Philip Argall, with a mining background in Ireland, Cornwall, New Zealand, Mexico, and France, in 1887 became manager of the La Plata smelter in Colorado, then owned by an English concern, and went on to design, erect, and manage the first large custom mill to treat Cripple Creek ores by the cyanidation process. [69]

---

offered numerous diplomatic posts under Taft, Harding, and Coolidge, and was one of the leading exponents of international peace and the World Court in the post-World War I period. A fascinating account is his *Autobiography* (2 vols., New York, 1935). With the exception of this work, biographical data on Hammond is disappointingly scarce.

[67] *The Memoirs of Herbert Hoover* (New York, 1951), I, 25.

[68] Teal first came to Colorado in 1869 on mining business for a Manchester engineering firm. Two years afterward he took charge of the Terrible and later became one of Colorado's substantial citizens. Georgetown *Miner*, Dec. 23, 1869; *Portrait and Biographical Record of Denver*, 753.

[69] Argall was first affiliated with the La Plata Mining and Smelting Co. at Leadville, then with the Red Mountain Silver Mines; by 1906 he had stepped into the shoes vacated by the fabulous Hammond as consulting engineer to Stratton's Independence, a position he retained until 1915 when the firm disposed of its Colorado property. *DAB*, I, 344; New La Plata Mining and Smelting Co., *Directors' Report*, Aug. 28, 1886 to June 30, 1887; Stratton's Independence, *Annual Report*, year ending June 30, 1906; *ibid.*, year ending June 30, 1915; Skinner, *Mining*

Management Problems

It was the Rickards, the Argalls, the Teals, and scores like them who bore the responsibility for British companies in America. Some were good men, some were poor; some displayed versatility and ingenuity in adapting old processes to new situations or in devising improvements to fit the new western environment. In many instances their technological contributions were of lasting benefit. In others their experiments were unsuccessful or at best premature. Witness the manager of the Pittsburgh Consolidated Gold Mines, Ltd., in Lander County, Nevada, who in 1882 endeavored without avail to circumvent the high cost of fuel by using sage brush for smelting.[70] Another visionary, equally unsuccessful but at greater expense, late in the nineties added another £2,050 to his company's already staggering debit balance by experimentation in hauling ore by steam traction engine and wagons over ordinary dirt roads in Nevada.[71] Similarly the efforts of Alexander Hill, "A.M.I.C.E., M.E., F.C.S.,"[72] of the Ray Copper Mines, Ltd., to utilize gasoline power for milling in Arizona failed miserably in 1899,[73] indicating only that Hill was in advance of his contemporaries and that the internal combustion engine had not yet reached perfection.

That even trained and experienced mining men had their shortcomings was all too obvious. British complaints against their managers in America ran the gamut from dishonesty to incompetence and independence and were directed at men with all types of background. Nicholas Maxwell, in charge of operations for the Last Chance Silver Mining Company, Ltd., in the first years of the seventies, was charged

---

Manual (1891–1892), 325. For a listing of at least twenty technical articles written by Argall see Olive M. Jones, "Bibliography of Colorado Geology & Mining," *Colorado State Geological Survey Bulletin* No. 7 (Denver, 1914), 17–19.

[70] "The expense was perhaps a trifle less, but there is a great doubt of there being a continuous supply of suitable brush, and the risk of fire is materially increased when large stacks of this inflammable fuel are stored in close proximity to the Mill." Pittsburgh Consolidated Gold Mines, *Annual Report,* year ending Sept. 30, 1892.

[71] This was Otto Stallmann of Salt Lake City. The equipment proved totally worthless in the soft terrain between the company's mill and mines. Adelaide Star Mines, *Annual Report,* year ending Oct. 31, 1899; Glasgow and Western Exploration Co., *Annual Report,* year ending Oct. 31, 1901.

[72] Ray Copper Mines, *Annual Report,* year ending June 30, 1900; Skinner, *Mining Manual* (1900), 1074.

[73] Ray Copper Mines, *Annual Report,* 1900.

with sinking three shafts which missed the lode completely and "might as well have been sunk in Hyde Park." [74] It was Maxwell who purchased furnace sites for the Tecoma Silver Mining Company, Ltd., which were located at Truckee, Nevada, some five hundred miles from the company's Utah mines. Maxwell paid $26,000, although the same sites had been offered shortly before to an American concern for only $15,000. He then proceeded to erect furnaces costing £20,000 while the mines were still undeveloped.[75]

Critics of John R. Murphy of the Utah Silver Mining Company, Ltd., openly called for his dismissal in 1872, charging that his blundering and wastefulness had plunged the company £10,000 into debt and had given nothing but misleading reports in exchange.[76] Murphy, in his "midsummer madnesss," was accused of having purchased flux from afar at a cost of twenty-five dollars a ton when it was readily available on the company's own property. "Had he been digging for the favourite vegetable sometimes called by his name," muttered one unkind commentator in 1874, "he could hardly have made greater mistakes than he did in searching for Utah ore." [77] If, as represented, Murphy "was the most able smelter on the Pacific Coast, then heaven help that Coast, for the sooner it ceases to smelt the better." [78]

Directors of the Kohinoor and Donaldson Mining Company, Ltd., forced the resignation of Alfred Rickard in June, 1886,[79] replacing him with Samuel J. Vivian, a Cornish import with a broad mineral background. Vivian arrived at the Colorado mines to find little or no ore in sight and "the mill, tramways, and machinery in a very neglected and dilapidated state, and not at all in the condition the Directors ex-

[74] John P. Sewell to editor (London, Dec. 17, 1873), *Mining Journal,* Dec. 20, 1873, 1403–1404. A brother of the engineer who replaced Maxwell, Sewell was not exactly an impartial critic.

[75] *Mining World,* March 7, 1874, 470.

[76] *Mining Journal,* Sept. 21, 1872, 904; report of meeting of the Utah Silver Lead Mining Co. (Feb. 17, 1874), *Mining World,* Feb. 21, 1874, 374. By the latter date the company had been reorganized under this name.

[77] "Englishman" to editor (London, Feb. 17, 1874), *Mining World,* Feb. 21, 1874, 371.

[78] *Ibid.*

[79] Kohinoor and Donaldson Consolidated Mining Co., *Annual Report,* year ending Dec. 31, 1885 (with supplemental statement of accounts in London to Dec. 31, 1885).

pected he would have found them." [80] Vivian set to work and employed a large number of men to break down poor-grade ore which should never have been taken from the mine. The results were so disappointing that the directors sent a special agent to the mine in 1889 and Vivian was replaced.[81]

Frequently the plight of the Vivians or the Murphys resulted from a combination of unfamiliarity with conditions in the West, miscalculations, and circumstances beyond the superintendent's control. Sometimes, however, there were other causes. In at least one instance a well-trained, experienced engineer found himself under fire because he had failed to check the validity of information from subordinates that he passed on to the directors as his own. In this case the British firm, Stratton's Independence, Ltd., had purchased Cripple Creek property on original inspection reports by State Geologist Thomas A. Rickard in 1899. "The Mine shows no signs of exhaustion—possibilities unlimited," said Rickard at that time.[82] In later official estimates he calculated 250,000 tons of ore in sight, worth at least £2,800,000.[83] But, in October—five months after the original inspection—Rickard cabled the London office that the valuation of ore reserves previously furnished was "seriously over-estimated." [84]

In the following spring John Hays Hammond, "that American superman of the Nineties," [85] arrived to inspect the Independence, wearing the "highest and shiniest boots, and carrying the longest candlestick ever seen in the gold camps." [86] The thorough, efficient Hammond refused to be misled by minor officials, insisted on making a detailed personal survey, and reported there were not more than 120,000 tons in sight, worth a total of £460,000.[87]

Hammond's findings brought down abuse upon the head of the hapless Rickard. The mine had been gutted before being sold to the

[80] Kohinoor and Donaldson Consolidated Mining Co., *Directors' Report*, two years ending Dec. 31, 1887.

[81] Kohinoor and Donaldson Consolidated Mining Co., *Annual Report*, year ending Dec. 31, 1889.

[82] Stratton's Independence, *Prospectus* (May 11, 1899).

[83] *Statist*, Dec. 8, 1900, 936.

[84] Stratton's Independence, *Directors' Report*, May 1, 1899 to June 30, 1900.

[85] Sprague, *Money Mountain*, 212.   [86] *Ibid.*, 314.

[87] *Statist*, Dec. 8, 1900, 936; Hammond, *Autobiography*, II, 492.

British, charged critics.[88] "Rickard the Reckless" was a brother-in-law of the chairman of the Venture Corporation, which had promoted the undertaking. Rickard was English, hence unfamiliar with Colorado mines. Furthermore, insisted his opponents, he spent the bulk of his time in local barrooms rather than attending to business. "It would be better if he leaves mining to those who understand it, and devotes his time to geology and the writing of papers," suggested the incensed editor of the *Anglo-Colorado Mining and Milling Guide*.[89]

Rickard hastened to explain his own miscalculation. His report, he acknowledged, had been written on the basis of information supplied by the foreman at the mine, not from personal inspection.[90] The final outcome saw Rickard being replaced as consulting engineer by Hammond, who "consented" to accept a year's engagement at a salary of £10,000.[91] The faith of the British shareholder was given a severe jolt and, although charges of fraud remained unproven, the Independence failed to live up to expectations.[92] Rickard's error, while it did not affect the mine's output, unfortunately placed him under the scrutiny of the public eye. His reputation was tarnished temporarily, but he survived the episode to become one of the most respected of the world's mining experts.[93]

If some difficulties stemmed from too heavy a reliance on the word of subordinates, others came from attempts of the manager to do too much. It was not uncommon practice for one man to serve two or even three companies simultaneously, dividing his time among them. The Snowdrift Silver Mining and Reduction Company, Ltd., and the Silver Plume Mining Company, Ltd., both operating near George-

[88] *Anglo-Colorado Mining Guide*, III (Dec. 29, 1900), 178.

[89] IV (Jan. 30, 1901), 9–10.

[90] Report of meeting of Stratton's Independence (Dec. 7, 1900), *Financial Times* (London), Dec. 8, 1900.

[91] For the second year this salary was cut in half. Stratton's Independence, *Annual Report*, year ending June 30, 1901.

[92] Still, down to 1915, when the Colorado property was sold, the British concern took a total of $19,635,288 from the mine for a net profit of $5,714,624. Stratton's Independence, *Annual Report*, year ending June 30, 1915.

[93] In 1937 Rickard commented: "The Stratton's Independence affair caused me much worry, and chagrin. I might go into the details of the fiasco, but to do that would involve censure of the performances of three prominent men. That I do not care to do, and it would not be as interesting today as it might have been 36 years ago, when I was prevented, by feelings of loyalty and decency, from hitting out." *Retrospect*, 76.

town, Colorado, during the early 1870's, shared the services of the British engineer Ernest Le Neve Foster and one Captain Bennett with no complaints from either concern.[94] In the next decade Alfred Rickard was at once in charge of the California, the Kansas, and the Kent County lodes—all owned by separate British concerns—plus "other mines" near Leadville.[95]

There were many examples, but one of the most notorious was to be found in Utah where three companies were closely tied together in various ways during the seventies. The Flagstaff Silver Mining Company of Utah, Ltd., the Last Chance Silver Mining Company of Utah, Ltd., and the Tecoma Silver Mining Company, Ltd., all boasted a number of common directors, including Chairman Alexander Malet, an outstanding British statesman and diplomat; they also shared the same manager in America, Nicholas M. Maxwell.[96]

It was soon obvious that the directors and the shareholders of these concerns were not pleased with Maxwell's work. Charges of inefficiency, laxity in forwarding accounts, extravagance, and "deficiencies in organic regulations" flew like shrapnel at meetings of all three companies.[97] The three combined in 1873 to send to Utah one Captain Forbes, an officer in Her Majesty's Navy, "therefore thoroughly competent to undertake the management of the mine," according to a skeptical but sarcastic shareholder.[98] Once having dropped anchor in Utah, the nautical Mr. Forbes distinguished himself by purchasing equipment at prices double those normal in the region and by sending back sensational reports of the properties in language obviously calculated to enhance share values in London.[99] Soon "private sources" informed the directors that "the eyes of the mines were picked out"—that almost no development and exploration had been carried out prior to the end of 1873.[100] Within a short time shareholders were cursing both Forbes

[94] *Mining World,* June 21, 1873, 1171.   [95] Rickard, *Retrospect,* 34.

[96] *Mining Journal,* Jan. 20, Aug. 10, 1872, 52, 743; *Mining World,* May 17, 1873, 980.

[97] *Mining Journal,* Dec. 20, 1873, 1403–1404; *Mining World,* April 30, 1873, 436; Feb. 7, 21, March 7, 1874, 278, 363, 470.

[98] Report of meeting of the Tecoma Silver Mining Co. (Feb. 2, 1874), *Mining World,* Feb. 7, 1874, 278.

[99] Forbes had earlier received a number of fully paid shares free from the American vendor. *Ibid.,* 276, 278.

[100] *Mining Journal,* Feb. 28, 1874, 422.

and Maxwell in the same breath as "that hole somewhere up in the Utah mountains." [101]

Faced with mounting debts, all three of these Utah concerns fell on evil days. In need of operating funds, the directors of the Flagstaff and the Tecoma companies clandestinely borrowed from vendor Erwin Davis, circumventing legal limitations on borrowing by the simple expedient of contracting to deliver ores to Davis in the future.[102] But as part of the agreement Davis was permitted to appoint his own Utah agent and manager, who was to remain in control until ore taken out of the mines paid off all debts.[103] When the Davis appointee, J. N. H. Patrick, assumed charge, self-righteous shareholders rent the air with howls of protest and demanded that the property be returned to English supervision immediately. Overnight Davis was transformed from friend and savior to "Mephistopheles," [104] "a sleek sly Jew . . . who can pick your pocket with such thorough grace that you scarcely know it." [105]

The Tecoma did not yield up management of its property without a fight, however. The Britisher, Captain St. Stephens, who stepped into the breach left by the release of both Forbes and Maxwell, was without instructions when Patrick arrived to take charge in 1874. According to the English account of the affair, Patrick met stiff opposition from St. Stephens and was obliged to enforce his words with a loaded pistol. Whereupon the Englishman promptly knocked him to the floor, placed one foot on his chest in a manner that would have done justice to Theodore Roosevelt, and voiced his feelings in a clipped British accent: "Now, Sir, who shall have the mine, me or you? I stand here as the representative of the Tecoma Company. I have received no

[101] Report of meeting of the Tecoma Silver Mining Co. (Feb. 2, 1874), *Mining World*, Feb. 7, 1874), 278.

[102] The company's *Articles* prohibited the board from borrowing more than £10,000 without consulting the shareholders. Directors evaded this restriction in December, 1873, by contracting to deliver a total of some £58,000 worth of ore at a future date. Part of the money obtained on this "ore contract" was used by the Flagstaff company to pay unearned dividends. *Mining World*, Feb. 28, 1874, 422–423; Davis *v.* Flagstaff Silver Mining Co. of Utah, 2 *Utah Reports* (1877), 86–87.

[103] Flagstaff Silver Mining Co. of Utah *v.* Patrick, 2 *Utah Reports* (1877), 305.

[104] Report of meeting of the Tecoma Silver Mining Co. (April 17, 1874), *Mining World*, April 18, 1874, 720.

[105] *Ibid.* (March 17, 1874), *Mining World*, March 21, 1874, 567.

advice from the directors to deliver up the mine to you, and until that is done I will not part with the trust that has been given to me." [106] The American version of the same episode unfortunately seems never to have been recorded for posterity. St. Stephens, despite his heroic defense of justice against the swaggering Yankee, was ordered by the company to hand over the property to Patrick and was himself forced to cajole and plead for his salary after his return to England in the spring of 1874.[107]

The Flagstaff submitted more gracefully than the Tecoma, and Patrick was in charge for at least three years before the company managed to secure his ouster. Even then it took legal action and a decision of the Utah Supreme Court finally to resolve the controversy in favor of the British owners. This tribunal discarded the contract that had allowed Davis to select a manager on the ground that shareholders had not been consulted and that the directors had no legal right to sign away their own power to appoint and remove supervisors in Utah. The court further decided that Patrick had not lived up to the agreement because he failed to submit required monthly reports to the London office.[108] The Flagstaff Company was not relieved of all its miseries by this decision, but the control of Davis was broken.

The distance from the seat of ultimate authority tended to give mining experts a laxity and an independence never enjoyed nearer the British Isles and to lend credence to the common English belief that the honesty of a manager varied inversely with the distance between London and the mine. If the mines of the Flagstaff Company were located in England, commented the chairman in 1874, there would be plenty of men available who would remain honest. "But," he added, "somehow or other there is something in the atmosphere of Utah so extraordinary that they no sooner get there than they become utterly corrupted." [109]

Western critics complained of the weaknesses of the Britishers sent out who spent their time "loafing around the streets and the whisky shops, making themselves a laughingstock to the Yankees, and a dis-

[106] *Ibid.*

[107] *Ibid.*, 568; report of meeting of the Tecoma Silver Mining Co. (April 17, 1874), *Mining World*, April 18, 1874, 720.

[108] 2 *Utah Reports* (1877), 317–318.

[109] Report of meeting of the Flagstaff Silver Mining Co. of Utah (April 16, 1874), *Mining World*, April 18, 1874, 715.

grace to their own countrymen." [110] Nicholas Maxwell was pictured by officials of the Tecoma Silver Mining Company, Ltd., as a ne'er-do-well who sipped claret and enjoyed life in general while he neglected his duties in Utah.[111] A Salt Lake City editor, pondering the difficulties of the Flagstaff Company, commented sarcastically that "the 50,000 dollars superintendent sent out by the directors, who spends his time playing billiards, is not yet an extinct biped." [112]

Sometimes liquor was not the only temptation. English agents or managers might be inclined to devote much time to driving, sporting, or engaging in what one writer termed "gallant pursuits." [113] Henry Sewell, as superintendent of the mining and milling operations of the Camp Floyd Silver Mining Company, Ltd., was accused of mixing an overcostly combination of business and pleasure. Sewell had placed four bars of bullion in a jeweler's window under a large-sized photograph of May Howard, the current darling of the Salt Lake theater, with the caption, "Miss May Howard astonished at the purity of this bullion from Sunnyside mine. $307 per ton, 995 fine. Her sweet smile indicates the impression of the purity of this silver." [114] Few would have complained at this demonstration of public relations had it stopped at this point. What brought condemnation was the postscript Sewell appended in a note to the Camp Floyd mill foreman: "Please send me a $100 brick to present to Miss H., 997 if possible, as soon as you can." [115] In the eyes of the British shareholder, this was carrying Anglo-American friendship entirely too far.

If distance often meant lax ties with Britain and caused some managers to stray from the narrow path, the frequency of turnover in Anglo-

[110] John Johns to editor (Central City, Nov. 27, 1872), *Mining Journal,* Jan. 4, 1873, 23.

[111] Report of meeting of the Tecoma Silver Mining Co. (March 17, 1874), *Mining World,* March 21, 1874, 568. The Saturn people also castigated their manager, Francis Fowler, for his extravagance in insisting on carpeted floors in the Utah office and for including whisky on his accounts under "incidental expenses." Report of meeting of the Saturn Silver Mining Co. of Utah (Jan. 12, 1874), *Mining World,* Jan. 17, 1874, 139.

[112] Quoted in *ibid.,* Dec. 6, 1873, 1151.

[113] "Equitas" to editor (Salt Lake City, n.d.), *Mining Journal,* Aug. 29, 1874, 931.

[114] Henry Sewell to [?] Baxter (n.p., Nov. 17, 1873), *ibid.,* Nov. 14, 1874, 1253. Notarized copies of this and other incriminating letters were sent by George Attwood to the *Mining Journal.*

[115] *Ibid.*

American concerns was also a definite weakness. True, some companies managed to retain good men for substantial periods of time. But others saw personnel of all types come and go with alarming regularity. An ex-underground foreman of the Flagstaff Company complained in mid-1874 that the concern had employed five different smelter foremen in twenty months—each with his own ideas and operational plans.[116] The Colorado Terrible Lode Mining Company, Ltd., came under the supervision of five different men during the period from 1870 to 1879.[117] During the eighties Alturas Gold, Ltd., experienced upheavals that placed four different superintendents in charge, each for a period of approximately a year.[118] Under such circumstances production could hardly be expected to remain at peak level.

In most cases the London office was heavily dependent upon its engineer or agent for information from the West. Yet it was often extremely difficult to determine whether the information that came— often very infrequently—was accurate or deliberately misleading. Mining experts sometimes had a distressing way of leading directors onward, urging that more capital be raised, more property purchased, or more development undertaken.[119] Speaking of Anglo-American mining enterprises in general, the editor of the *Mining World* in 1871 offered pointed advice on this subject:

Take care that your working capital is sufficient and have your mining captains sharply looked after and pushed to bring ore to the banks and whenever his "Report" speaks of "developing" and the "lower adit," button up your pockets and call out "mad dog!" until you have put another man in his place.[120]

This was indeed sage counsel. All too often experts and engineers in charge of property for British concerns were prone to follow their directors' lead in building false hopes in the minds of naïve shareholders.[121] Almost as often the gap between prediction and performance

---

[116] *Ibid.*, Aug. 15, 1874, 879.

[117] See Spence, "Colorado's Terrible Mine," *Colorado Magazine*, XXXIV (Jan. 1957), 50–57.

[118] Alturas Gold, *Directors' Report*, Feb. 25, 1886 to Oct. 31, 1887; Alturas Gold, *Circular to Shareholders*, March 5, 1888; Memo. of Agreement (March 9, 1888) between Alturas Gold and John B. Kyshe, C.R.O. B-22252.

[119] See Alfred H. Oxenford to William Read (London, July 10, 1891), Read MSS.

[120] Aug. 5, 1871, 413–414.

[121] An excellent example is discussed in Tarryall Creek Gold Co., *Annual Report*, year ending June 30, 1891.

was entirely too broad. Yet to the end of the period mine managers continued to tender optimistic reports and recommendations for additional capital to protect already existing investments.[122]

But whether engineers, agents, or managers were British or American, experienced or inexperienced, efficient or inefficient, honest or dishonest, the fundamental problem of dealing with them was the same. How to bridge the distance gap was the major difficulty. "A too careful supervision of the local management cannot be exercised," said the London *Mining World* in 1871.[123] "If you do not direct, manage, and control your enterprises here personally," advised another British observer after a visit to Colorado in 1876, "you will regret that your money was not subscribed to the Indian Famine Relief Fund or some other patriotic object." [124]

But the question to be answered was "How?" Slow and often unsatisfactory communications frequently kept London officials ignorant of affairs in the West for weeks. Such a situation necessitated cloaking the man in charge at the mine with broad powers of attorney so that he might act quickly in any emergency without reference to the English directors. Yet the power of attorney could be a two-edged sword: without it the mine manager would have been seriously limited in power; with it, he might abuse his power and go far beyond the bounds contemplated by the company. One vendor-manager even went so far as to mortgage his company's Cripple Creek mines in order to obtain funds owed him by the concern.[125] What the Anglo-American mining company sought to attain was a balance allowing control of the manager, yet also allowing him freedom to operate in vital affairs.

Many directorates believed that requiring frequent and regular reports and accounts from the mines served to keep agents and managers in line. Thus supervising officials in America were repeatedly hedged in on every side by a mass of regulations demanding strict accountability for every action and every shilling. Sometime in the early 1870's a committee of the Eberhardt and Aurora Mining Company, Ltd., drew up an elaborate plan designed to make all personnel at the mine more

[122] See the typical plea made by the manager of an Anglo-Idaho company in 1901. Poorman Gold Mines, *Circular to Shareholders,* June 28, 1901.

[123] Aug. 19, 1871, 473.   [124] Townshend, *Colorado,* 88.

[125] Caledonia (Cripple Creek) Gold Mine, *Directors' Report,* April 9, 1897 to June 30, 1899; *ibid.,* June 30, 1899 to Dec. 31, 1901.

responsible to the London office. The arrangement proposed such an intricate maze of weekly, fortnightly, and monthly reports from manager, accountant, storekeeper, and the mine and mill superintendents that, if ever placed into effect, it must certainly have made mining and milling operations secondary to written work and accounting procedure.[126] Such regular reports were "required" by dozens of companies. Yet an almost invariable complaint was that accounts and news from the mines were long overdue.

Most Anglo-American companies endeavored to exert a closer supervision over their managers in the West through the periodic sending of directors to view the local situation. At the same time others attempted to reach the same objective by retaining roving managing directors, often Americans, who were to inspect operations occasionally. Normally visits by directors were sporadic and often came only when an emergency presented itself, although throughout the entire period the number of British subjects trekking across the Great Plains on mining business was very large.

A few concerns cultivated a policy of dispatching someone to their mines at definite intervals. The board of the Last Chance, for example, resolved in 1872 that each year one director should travel to Utah and visit the company's property.[127] A scant six months later the chairman of the Flagstaff board urged the addition of a seventh director—a man who journeyed to the United States occasionally.[128] When the Silverton Mines, Ltd., was incorporated in 1887 to consolidate several holdings in the San Juan area of Colorado, its prospectus emphasized a managerial arrangement under which a financial agent and a superintendent were to be sent out as permanent employees but were to be subject to an engineer's inspection at definite, stated intervals.[129]

It may well be assumed that excursions by London directors did not always prove satisfactory. Inspections might be years apart in some instances, and directors were not always sufficiently informed on min-

---

[126] Eberhardt and Aurora Mining Co., Committee's report on system of returns on working at mines (n.d.), Read MSS. Internal evidence indicates that this was drawn up prior to March 15, 1873, but there is no documentation revealing whether or not the arrangement was adopted.

[127] *Mining Journal*, Aug. 10, 1872, 743.

[128] Report of meeting of the Flagstaff Silver Mining Co. of Utah (Feb. 3, 1873), *Mining World*, Feb. 8, 1873, 284–285.

[129] Silverton Mines, *Prospectus* (April, 1887).

ing affairs in general. Critics charged that English direction was "too effete, too supine, and too ready to take for granted facts of paramount importance." [130] While Thomas A. Rickard was a neophyte engineer in Colorado, a British director arrived to visit the mines. Since the visitor was "a kindly Scot," Rickard "took care to provide good oatmeal for breakfast" but soon discovered that his guest "was a simpleton on mining matters." "Then," said Rickard, "I had a bully time. I talked to him as if I had been consulting engineer to the Almighty when he made rocks, veins, and ores." [131] There is another delightful, though probably apocryphal story of a director of an Anglo-Colorado mining company who, when informed that a new shaft must be sunk, wanted to know if a second-hand one could not be bought! [132] Perhaps in this era of titled guinea pigs and decoy ducks such an error was excusable, but men of this caliber were not likely to improve conditions when sent out to check on a mining superintendent in Colorado or Idaho.

Yet good men, sent out on inspection tours, were capable of bringing about real improvements. In 1884 Chairman Mervyn Herbert Nevil Story-Maskelyne of the Montana Company, Ltd.,[133] traveled to Montana with another director to examine the company's property near Marysville and to investigate the reasons for high operating costs and a falling off in the richness of ore. The two found manager George Attwood "wanting in the business faculty indispensable for economical management" [134] and pointed out numerous examples of laxity and inefficiency at the mines, all costing the company much money. The firm's two stamp mills and compressor machinery had been erected at fabulous expense; supplies were normally purchased at prices beyond their market values; stores were kept with no system of care; large amounts of mercury, amalgam, and retorted metal had been stolen, but records were so scant that it was impossible to determine how much was missing. The two Englishmen ordered the immediate erection of a storehouse and instituted a system of double checks on stores. Attwood was given stringent orders to record every bit of mercury used

[130] *Mining World*, Aug. 24, 1872, 851.   [131] *Retrospect*, 29–30.

[132] *Anglo-Colorado Mining Guide*, III (Oct. 31, 1900), 154.

[133] Story-Maskelyne was an outstanding mineralogist who lectured at Oxford for a number of years and also did much work for the British Museum. He sat as M.P. for Cricklade, North Wiltshire. *DNB*, Suppl. 2, III, 434.

[134] Montana Company, *Report of Messrs. N. Story-Maskelyne and J. R. Armitage to the Board of Directors* (Nov. 12, 1884), 9, Stock Exchange Archives, London.

and amalgam obtained at every stage of retorting and melting and to submit detailed monthly reports on all aspects of operation.[135] But the fumbling manager was retained, amid caustic objections from shareholders. Within a short time, however, he resigned,[136] and better days were ahead for the Montana Company, in part because the concern now maintained a closely regulated system of periodic inspections by a competent managing director and in part because much of the development work was now out of the way and the mine ready for sustained production.

Another means of encouraging more efficient management practiced by a handful of English companies was to rely upon an established engineering firm for advice and even actual supervision. The old respected firm of John Taylor and Sons did not limit its activity to prepurchase inspection of property in the seventies and eighties but also endeavored to promote companies and manage mines in all parts of the world. This partnership was responsible for the unfortunate Mineral Hill Silver Mines Company, Ltd., of 1871,[137] and later was charged with the management of mines belonging to British concerns in Montana,[138] Colorado,[139] and Dakota.[140]

In the same fashion the London partnership of Bewick, Moreing and Company, another British firm of international reputation,[141] was active in western America, supervising mines in Colorado and Nevada.[142]

[135] *Ibid.*, 8–10.

[136] Montana Company, *Annual Report,* year ending Dec. 31, 1884; *Circular to Shareholders,* Jan. 29, 1885.

[137] Mineral Hill Silver Mines Co., *Prospectus* (June, 1871); *Mem. & Art.,* 16, C.R.O. B-5496.

[138] One such concern was the Broadway Gold Mining Co. in Montana. *Mining Journal,* Dec. 3, 1881, 1508.

[139] Silver Peak Mining Co., *Prospectus* (1880).

[140] John Taylor and Sons were listed in 1887 as consulting engineers and brokers for the monumental Harney Peak (Dakota) Tin Co. Skinner, *Mining Manual* (1887), 494.

[141] This concern commenced first in Cornwall and Derbyshire and has now been in operation for nearly a century and a half. At the end of the nineteenth century it maintained offices in London, New York, Kalgoorlie, Melbourne, and Johannesburg. It was this partnership that first gave Herbert Hoover an opportunity to prove himself as a mining engineer. Hoover, *Memoirs,* I, 28, 73, 74.

[142] Among other properties managed were those of Farrington Mines in Nevada and the Pay Rock Silver Mines in Colorado. Pay Rock Silver Mines, *Prospectus* (Nov. 1890); Farrington Mines, *Prospectus* (Feb., 1886). See also Garfield, Ltd., *Circular to Shareholders,* Oct. 23, 1886.

Bainbridge, Seymour & Company of Sheffield were in 1889 listed as consulting engineers to the "Minah Consolidated" Mining Company, Ltd., which operated in Montana.[143] By the end of the century the firm of Edmund Spargo and Sons of Liverpool had also established a reputation for its work beyond the Mississippi on behalf of British mining companies.[144]

If English concerns sought to assure honest management by requiring frequent reports, by periodically sending roving inspectors to keep a wary eye on superintendents, and by turning to well-known engineering firms at home, a good many also operated on the assumption that higher salaries necessarily meant superior personnel. Salaries varied, of course, with the period and with the company, but frequently they were in excess of those paid by corresponding American concerns. The £760 a year received by the able Ernest Le Neve Foster from the Snowdrift Silver Mining and Reduction Company, Ltd., and the Silver Plume Mining Company, Ltd., in 1872 [145] was probably normal for a general manager in Colorado at that time but was undoubtedly below the average paid by Anglo-American concerns in general. Nicholas Maxwell received an annual salary of £2,000 from the three British firms he represented in Utah during the same year.[146] At the end of the eighties Simeon Wenban was being paid £2,400 per annum by Cortez Mines, Ltd., in Nevada,[147] but in the same state in 1891 William Read received $416.67 per month or roughly £1,000 a year as manager of the property of the New Eberhardt Company, Ltd.[148]

These were normal sums. The highest salary paid by any Anglo-American mining company during the entire period was probably the £10,000 which went to John Hays Hammond in 1900 for his year's work as consulting engineer for Stratton's Independence, Ltd.[149] This

[143] Skinner, *Mining Manual* (1891–1892), 222.

[144] *Who's Who in Mining and Metallurgy* (1908), 86–87.

[145] This figure is projected from monthly salary payments and was met by a like amount from the Silver Plume people. See Ledger of the Snowdrift Mining and Reduction Co. (Dec. 27, 1871–March 31, 1873), University of Colorado Libraries.

[146] Report of meeting of the Flagstaff Silver Mining Co. (Feb. 3, 1873), *Mining World*, Feb. 8, 1873, 283.

[147] Memo. of Agreement (Sept. 14, 1888) between Simeon Wenban and Cortez Mines, C.R.O. B-27410.

[148] Alfred H. Oxenford to William Read (London, May 29, 1891), Read MSS.

[149] Stratton's Independence, *Annual Report*, year ending June 30, 1901.

figure bore out the common conviction in the West that British outfits paid entirely too much. Americans had complained for years,[150] and in this instance Hammond further bolstered the opinion by agreeing to accept a salary of only half that amount for 1901.[151]

To keep in touch with the situation, then, to exert a maximum of influence over personnel who were not always the most talented available, and to outline general, long-range policies were the functions of directors in London. Naturally such boards were first and foremost interested in dividends as the final objective. Naturally, also, such boards frequently sought to absolve themselves of responsibility by shifting blame onto the shoulders of their representatives in the West. But there were at least a few who evidenced concern over the welfare of their staffs in America. When J. H. Collins suggested to his company, Alturas Gold, Ltd., in February, 1888, that additional property be purchased near its Idaho holdings, he appended a brief note:

Although not strictly a technical matter, I should like to add a few words as to the provision of some means of recreation for the men. It is a very isolated locality—especially in the winter—and the men have no place of resort after working hours, except the drinking saloons, or worse, at Rocky Bar. It would cost very little to provide a warm and well-lighted reading room, and to assist a committee of the men to provide papers, games, coffee, etc. Such a provision would be an attraction for steady and well-behaved men, and would enable your superintendent to gradually gather round him a staff of men who could be relied upon during the winter months. It would be well also to encourage the advent of married men with the same object.[152]

Secretary Oxenford of the New Eberhardt Company, Ltd., could express his solicitude a few years later when an epidemic of influenza struck the camp in Nevada. "We are glad of your assurance that the men are well cared for," he informed the manager, "as we think just as much of their welfare as of the weekly output & a good deal more." [153] Along similar lines Francis Muir, chairman of the Harquahala Gold Mining Company, Ltd., visited the firm's newly acquired property in Arizona in 1893 and showed particular concern about the unhealthful

[150] For a typical complaint see *Utah Mining Gazette*, May 23, 1874.
[151] Stratton's Independence, *Annual Report*, 1901.
[152] Alturas Gold, *Directors' Report*, Feb. 18, 1888.
[153] To William Read (London, April 2, 1891), Read MSS.

condition of the camp, even to advocating a new vegetable garden and boarding house to ward off the dysentery and digestive troubles which had sorely plagued personnel at the mines.[154]

If responsible officials took cognizance of such small points, they were undoubtedly not wholly unaware of the larger picture. But that many were ill-informed seems a certainty. It took a long time for London directors to appraise the situation across the Atlantic, to reach a decision, and to transmit that decision back to the company's western agent. When mine superintendents were inefficient or negligently independent, the difficulties were magnified manyfold. And if an English corporation did, by chance, emerge with a satisfactory combination, as few did, of an adequate working capital, a capable superintendent, and a producing mine, it found that there were still problems to be solved. If British directors were too far from their American managers, they were at the same time too close to their own shareholders for competent, impartial control. Directors knew the shareholders, took a personal interest in them, and were in turn swayed by their biased, uninformed opinions at general or special meetings. This was the analysis of the American economist, Edward Taussig, who in 1891 attributed the failure of Anglo-American mining companies in part to such a situation in the British Isles.[155]

[154] Harquahala Gold Mining Co., *Report of the Chairman, Francis Muir, on His Visit to the Mines* (Dec. 14, 1893), Stock Exchange Archives, London.
[155] To editor (St. Louis, n.d.), *Economist,* Nov. 7, 1891, 1434.

: CHAPTER VII :

Litigation Problems

ON the American frontier in general the lawyer occupied a place in the eyes of the pioneer only one notch above the wily redskin, the sidewinder, or other lowly "varmints." From the Regulators to the Populists probably no other class of men was so traditionally regarded with distrust and suspicion by the average westerner. On the mining frontier, however, the lawyer was often financially successful far beyond his fondest expectations and frequently rose in stature to be rated at least as a coequal of the local saloonkeeper! Indeed, such top-flight legal intellects as William M. Stewart and Henry Teller amassed substantial fortunes from mining litigation and advanced to national prominence.

Litigation was admittedly the "curse of this country," according to a Nevadan in 1865. "Until recently, at least one in every ten of the male population of Virginia City was either a lawyer or a hanger-on of law courts." [1] The mineral industry in America has always been encumbered with more than its share of legal entanglements. Mining law proved inextricably complex and its interpretation difficult and confusing at best. As J. Ross Browne once expressed it, "Everybody's spurs were running into everybody else's angles." [2] New strikes invariably drew from all sides hordes of new claimants with conflicting pretensions. Although federal legislation in 1866 and 1872 made substantial

[1] "P" to editor (Virginia City, Nev., Nov. 16, 1865), *Mining Journal*, Jan. 6, 1866, 2.
[2] Quoted in Shinn, *Story of the Mine*, 127.

121

improvements in the statutes, much remained to be clarified by future generations.

Fortunate indeed was the mining company, domestic or foreign, that managed to survive for any length of time without being dragged through some form of legal proceedings. And woe unto the corporation unlucky enough to have acquired mines that proved valuable! [3] From all corners flocked the vultures of the mining world, eager to pick its corporate bones clean. "The disgraceful state of American mining law, rendered still more confused and misleading by clever legal knaves, has given rise to thousands of suits involving the expenditure of hundreds of thousands sterling in legal expense," complained the editor of the *Mining World* in the autumn of 1871.[4] Samuel Nugent Townshend, an English visitor to Colorado in 1876, expressed opinions of a similar nature:

Nothing can possibly be more disgraceful to a country than the systematic manner in which all titles, and especially English mining titles, are questioned in this district. Lawyers in high offical positions actually buy claims adjacent to English ones to raise a disputed boundary question; and the only court in America in or for which Englishmen have the slightest confidence or respect —the Supreme Court of the United States—, has until this year, been practically closed to them owing to Colorado being a Territory only.[5]

To the average British investor, the legal system in operation in the West left much to be desired. It was generally contended by most "informed" Britons that in the United States there existed a dual standard of justice—one for native Americans, another for foreign mining companies. When lawsuits developed it was always the Yankee who was the intruder on British property. When former Governor Henry Blasdel of Nevada clashed with the Eberhardt and Aurora Mining Company, Ltd., in 1871 over title to the Ward Beecher, the British saw the matter clearly: "With that disregard of others' rights, peculiarly the property of Brother Jonathan, he [Blasdel] has encroached on the Ward Beecher." [6]

[3] Two perils were involved in American mines, observed the London *Times* philosophically in 1872: the mines might prove worthless, or they might prove exceptionally valuable, in which case expensive litigation was almost certain to follow. June 12, 1872.

[4] Sept. 30, 1871, 665.   [5] *Colorado*, 63.

[6] *Mining World*, Nov. 4, 1871 850.

The *Mining World* complained in the late seventies that it could not recall a single instance in which an English mining company had been successful against an American individual or corporation in an Ameri can court action. The editor of the *Engineering and Mining Journal*, however, pointed out from New York the inaccuracy of this sweeping generalization and insisted that ignorance of the nature of mining titles, adverse claims, and local regulations were the reasons for many of the widespread legal difficulties of British companies in America. Besides, litigation and mining went hand in hand, and miners' juries tended to strike hard at corporations of any kind, American or English.[7]

To the British the contention that prosperity brought "all the swindling sharks for fifty miles round" to give legal battle [8] was nowhere more graphically illustrated than in the history of the Montana Company, Ltd. For nearly twenty-five years following 1889 this important corporation was engaged in an expensive legal war with Charles Magyar and the St. Louis Mining and Milling Company of Montana.

The conflict began with minor challenges to the concern's title to certain properties, but these were mere preliminary skirmishes. In 1889 the St. Louis Mining and Milling Company began its major attack by calling for an official survey of the neighboring portion of the Montana Company's workings. The Britishers, on the advice of "the most eminent authorities in the United States," decided to "fight it out" in the courts to the bitter end.[9]

With the sanction of the state judiciary, the official survey was completed, and litigation commenced over possession of the Nine Hour lode, ostensibly in the hands of the Montana Company, Ltd.[10] The British concern reorganized as the Montana Mining Company, Ltd., in 1892 in order to raise additional capital to pay off an outstanding loan and to fight the case.[11] From a long, complex series of lawsuits and appeals between 1893 and 1906 the English firm emerged in possession

[7] Aug. 9, 1879, 87–88.

[8] For lengthy comments on this characteristic of American mining see Townshend, *Our Indian Summer*, 40; *Mining World*, March 6, 1873, 476.

[9] Montana Co., *Semi-Annual Report*, half year ending Dec. 31, 1889.

[10] St. Louis Mining and Milling Co. *v.* Montana Co., 9 *Montana Reports* (1890), 308.

[11] *Mem. & Art.*, 1–3, Montana Mining Co., C.R.O. B-37766; Montana Company, *Circular to Shareholders*, Nov. 18, 1892, Stock Exchange Archives, London.

of the contested ground.[12] But the St. Louis company renewed its attack on another part of the property, claiming damages of $1,000,000 for ore illegally taken out by the Montana Company.[13] This time the case went badly for the British firm and ultimately, when a judgment of $203,129 was handed down against it,[14] it was forced to let the Drumlummon go under the sheriff's hammer for £30,000.[15]

Even this did not satisfy all of the judgment, and the St. Louis company endeavored unsuccessfully to attach property in Nevada for the remainder.[16] Finally in February, 1913, the English company obtained a full discharge from liabilities connected with the litigation and the long legal tussle formally terminated.[17] But the Montana Mining Company, Ltd., was finished, and in early June, 1914, liquidation proceedings were started.[18] During its existence it had paid out about £630,000 in dividends, mostly from the Drumlummon. For all that, the mine was so nearly worked out when lost by the company that it probably would not have sustained operations for any length of time, even had the property been retained.[19]

The Montana Mining Company, Ltd., provides an example of a British corporation which refused to compromise with the "swindling sharks" and "blackmailers" so common in America. Time and time again, however, English mining companies were willing to throw a sop to these wolves rather than run the expense of carrying a case

[12] For this intricately involved contest see the cases between the St. Louis Mining and Milling Co. and the Montana Mining Co. reported in 58 *Federal Reporter* (1893), 129–132; 20 *Montana Reports* (1897), 406; 23 *ibid.* (1899), 312–318; 104 *Federal Reporter* (1900), 665–669; 113 *ibid.* (1902), 903; 148 *ibid.* (1906), 450; also, Montana Mining Co., *Annual Report,* year ending Dec. 31, 1906.

[13] Montana Mining Co., *Annual Report,* year ending Dec. 31, 1907; Montana Mining Co. *v.* St. Louis Mining and Milling Co., 204 *U.S. Reports* (1907), 204–220.

[14] Montana Mining Co. *v.* St. Louis Mining and Milling Co., 183 *Federal Reporter* (1910), 51–71; Montana Mining Co. *v.* St. Louis Mining and Milling Co., 220 *U.S. Reports* (1910), 611.

[15] *Report of the Thirtieth Ordinary General Meeting of the Montana Mining Company, Ltd. held October 4th, 1911, at Exchange Chamber, St. Mary's Axe,* Stock Exchange Archives, London.

[16] *Report of the Extraordinary General Meeting of the Montana Mining Company, Ltd., held March 18th, 1913,* Stock Exchange Archives.

[17] Montana Mining Co., *Directors' Report,* Aug. 1, 1912 to Sept. 30, 1913.

[18] *Special Resolution,* passed June 5 and confirmed June 24, 1914, C.R.O. B-17787.

[19] *Report of the Extraordinary General Meeting of the Montana Mining Company, Ltd., held March 18th, 1913.*

through the courts in a land where the legal machinery was felt to be costly and hostile to English interests.

The Richmond Consolidated Mining Company, Ltd., an unusually successful foreign firm in the West, provides several typical examples of this willingness to make concessions rather than rely on legal procedure. Late in 1871 Nevadans owning the adjoining Tip Top mine brought claims against Richmond Consolidated, contesting the boundary on the basis of an older, prior claim.[20] The British company dispatched to the scene one of its London managers, J. J. Corrigan, an ex-Californian well acquainted with litigation. On the advice of Corrigan, who estimated that it would cost at least £10,000 to defend the suit, Richmond Consolidated decided to purchase Tip Top, thus removing the claim. To do this it was necessary to pay £15,000 for the property.[21] "We would suggest, for the future guidance of our 'English Cousins,' " said the editor of the *San Francisco News Letter* amiably, "that they be a little more careful in examining into titles to mining properties." [22]

Hardly had the Tip Top dispute been settled when the Eureka Consolidated Mining Company, an American concern, brought proceedings against Richmond Consolidated in a dispute over title to the Look Out lode bordering between the two. Immediately the sheriff seized the mines of the Richmond, including bullion, furnaces, and ore in the dumps, and the company was compelled to post a £20,000 bond.[23]

This new development brought shrill screams of anguish from British mining editors, who cited it as a typical example of American "justice," which protected "jumpers" against foreign concerns. "Do we not also hear continually of managers walking about the mines protecting themselves with revolvers, when the laws of the country should enable them to prosecute their work in peace of mind and perfect security?" asked Chisholm of the *Mining World,* demanding that American statutes be reformed.[24]

[20] Report of meeting of the Richmond Consolidated Mining Co. (Dec. 3, 1872), *Mining World,* Dec. 7, 1872, 1878.

[21] Settlement had first been set at £10,000 but due to delay caused by a snowstorm an additional £5,000 was added. *Ibid.*

[22] June 8, 1872.

[23] Report of meeting of the Richmond Consolidated Mining Co. (Dec. 3, 1872), *Mining World,* Dec. 7, 1872, 1879–1880; *Mining Journal,* Nov. 30, 1872, 1140.

[24] Dec. 7, 1872, 1858.

Although the Richmond Company soon managed to win the release of its mine, the ore in the dumps and the bullion were still held by a replevin suit. "Knowing" Americans estimated for British benefit that the company's chances of winning were 999 in 1,000, although it was further estimated that the suit would cost approximately £30,000.[25] In order to cover the cost capital was increased by £50,000,[26] and while awaiting the hearing the English concern had ten men "armed to the teeth," hired at £20 a day, to hold the mine behind barricades.[27]

The case was heard in the Nevada courts in February, 1873, but the jury deadlocked and a retrial was ordered. When an offer was made to compromise the suit by selling the Look Out location to the British company for £17,000, the latter accepted with alacrity, feeling that litigation might otherwise drag on for years.[28] Manager Edward Probert reflected the Englishman's common sentiment when he explained that this acceptance was based on necessity. He had seen the jury, he said—"a jury picked up in the streets—holding out their hands to both sides. . . . Our counsel might as well have spoken to the winds as to that jury." [29]

Under the settlement of 1873 the Look Out went to Richmond Consolidated, and the two companies drew a line between their properties which they agreed not to cross. Such a compromise held for a few years until the Richmond Company followed a lode across the boundary underground. Eureka Consolidated promptly obtained an injunction to halt progress and was upheld by a United States Circuit Court in 1877.[30] "A Looker-on" saw this decision as merely "one more instance of the folly of the British public in entrusting their capital to the tender mercies of Brother Jonathan. The paramount design of the American

[25] Report of meeting of the Richmond Consolidated Mining Co. (Feb. 5, 1873), *ibid.*, Feb. 8, 1873, 288.

[26] *Ibid.; Special Resolution,* passed Feb. 4 and confirmed Feb. 20, 1873, C.R.O. B-5606.

[27] Report of meeting of the Richmond Consolidated Mining Co. (Feb. 5, 1873), *Mining World,* Feb. 8, 1873, 289.

[28] *Ibid.* (Nov. 18, 1873), *Mining World,* Nov. 22, 1873, 1043.

[29] *Ibid.* (Jan. 27, 1874), *Mining World,* Jan. 31, 1874, 214.

[30] Eureka Consolidated Mining Co. *v.* Richmond Mining Co. of Nevada, 4 *Sawyer* (1877), 302–326; *Mining Journal,* Jan. 27, Aug. 25, 1877, 87, 937. The suit was in the name of the American subsidiary company of the Richmond Consolidated.

judges seems to be to favour their own countrymen, and to refuse justice to all aliens." [31]

The injunction was lifted temporarily,[32] and though with only slight hopes of a favorable decision the Richmond people appealed to the United States Supreme Court, which ultimately handed down its findings in 1881, upholding the opinion of the lower court against the English company.[33] Richmond Consolidated agreed out of court to pay over $100,000 and a "small piece of ground" in dispute to the Eureka Company. "When it is remembered that the Eureka Company laid their damages at $2,500,000 or £500,000 sterling," said the directors of the Richmond consolingly, "this settlement will be looked upon by the shareholders as satisfactory." [34]

In the meantime litigation had commenced with another American concern, the Albion Company, over possession of the Albion mine. The Richmond Company won the first round in the district court in a decision handed down in July, 1881, but this was reversed by the Nevada Supreme Court in March of the following year.[35] Carried to the Supreme Court of the United States, the decision was sustained in 1884, with $13,250 in damages assessed against the British concern. But the Albion Company demanded more, and the threat of a new suit was in the air.[36] The Richmond Company averted this threat by paying £17,000, whereupon the Albion people dropped all claims and transferred the disputed mines to their former adversary.[37]

Another instance of compromise, not so prolonged and so complex, may be seen in the history of the Colorado Terrible Lode Mining Company, Ltd., organized in 1870 to work one of the show mines of the Rockies. Early in 1875 the east level of William A. Hamill's Silver

[31] *Mining Journal*, Sept. 1, 1877, 964.

[32] Eureka Consolidated Mining Co. *v.* Richmond Mining Co. of Nevada, 5 *Sawyer* (1878), 121–128.

[33] Richmond Mining Co. of Nevada *v.* Eureka Consolidated Mining Co., 103 *U.S. Reports* (1881), 839–847.

[34] Richmond Consolidated Mining Co., *Annual Report*, year ending Feb. 28, 1882.

[35] *Ibid.*

[36] Richmond Mining Co. of Nevada *v.* Rose, *et al.*, 114 *U.S. Reports* (1885), 576–587; Richmond Consolidated Mining Co., *Annual Report*, year ending Feb. 28, 1885.

[37] Richmond Consolidated Mining Co., *Annual Report*, year ending Feb. 28, 1886.

Ore broke into the fourth level of the Terrible, and litigation commenced, soon curtailing all activity at the mine.[38] More than one observer believed that Hamill had deliberately pushed exploration and development in the Silver Ore in the hopes of creating a legal dispute and inducing the British concern to purchase his interest.[39] Whether this charge was true or not, the outcome was that the Terrible Company was maneuvered into acquiring the Silver Ore and half a dozen other lodes from Hamill and Jerome Chaffee for £200,000 in shares.[40]

Undoubtedly the purchase of adjoining claims to halt the threat of real or potential litigation was commonplace in the mining world, but British companies, because of their general lack of familiarity with mining laws, and particularly local regulations, seem to have been caught up to a greater degree than normal in this well-known but expensive pastime. The examples of the Richmond and the Terrible companies illustrate well that the old adage of "if you can't lick 'em, join 'em" had its application in the mineral field. But the joining process was not one to be undertaken without supporting cash, and there is no doubt that litigation or the threat of litigation was sometimes used as a lever with which to pry additional pounds and shillings from British investors.

While a great deal of legal activity centered on the defense of titles, lawsuits were by no means limited to that narrow field. Another common type usually originated in England and endeavored to force restitution of all or part of the price originally invested in western property. If the comments of disappointed British shareholders and directors were taken at their face value, it would be immediately concluded that nine out of ten western mining ventures floated on the English market were unmitigated frauds. In innumerable company meetings cries of "knaves," "swindle," and "gulled investors" filled the air. Some of the blame for failure was cast on the shoulders of management, but vendors

[38] Statistics of Mines and Mining in the States and Territories West of the Rocky Mountains, *Ho. Exec. Doc.* No. 159, 44 Cong., 1 Sess. (1875–1876), 298. Shortly before a court order was issued closing the area in dispute, the Terrible manager reported the situation tense and that he was maintaining armed guards at the mine. George Henty to H. M. & W. Teller (Georgetown, April 1, 1875), Teller MSS.

[39] *Ho. Exec. Doc.* No. 159, 44 Cong., 1 Sess. (1875–1876), 298.

[40] Memo. of Agreement (May 17, 1877) between Jerome Chaffee, William A. Hamill, and the Colorado United Mining Company, Ltd., Colorado Terrible Lode Mining Co., C.R.O. 4804; Corbett, *Colorado Mining Directory*, 140.

and promoters were equally popular targets. Had there not been mis-representation by the vendor or promoter in the original prospectus, contended unhappy shareholders, no investment would have been made in the first place. Englishmen even spoke with tiresome frequency of American mines that had been "plastered," or "salted" as Americans called it.

That there were frauds is undeniable. But the number of lawsuits actually commenced fell far short of what one might expect from reading company discussions. The number of lawsuits which terminated successfully for Englishmen was even smaller. For the sake of sim-plicity these suits charging fraud or misrepresentation may be divided roughly into two categories: cases brought by individuals or companies in Britain against the vendor or promoter and asking rescission of the purchase contract and the return of all or part of the purchase price; suits brought by the individual within the British company, charging deception or negligence, usually by company directors, and demanding that his name be struck off the register as a shareholder and his money refunded.

While there were numerous cases of the first type—most unsuccess-ful, some not even completed [41]—there is one outstanding well-documented example of an unquestionable case of mine "salting" per-petrated on unsuspecting British investors during the period. In this instance federal courts did not hesitate to rap the American vendors' knuckles sharply and order them to refund the purchase money. The occasion was a decision handed down in 1894 by a United States Court of Appeals in a case involving the sale of property to the Mudsill Min-ing Company, Ltd. Chartered in London, the Mudsill Company had been incorporated in 1888 to acquire the Mudsill mine and ten other lodes located, ironically enough, near Fairplay, Colorado.[42] At the time of the transaction title was vested in one Orville Watrous, with Stewart A. Van Deusen, another American, acting as agent for the sale. After preliminary negotiations, arrangements were completed for transferring the mines, subject to favorable inspection and reports.[43]

[41] See *Special Resolution*, passed July 9 and confirmed July 29, 1897, Jersey Lily Gold Mines, C.R.O. B-45507; Jersey Lily Gold Mines, *Annual Report*, year ending June 30, 1897; Anglo-Continental Gold Syndicate, *Directors' Report*, 15 months ending March 31, 1899; London *Times*, April 8, 1899.

[42] *Mem. & Art.*, 5, C.R.O. B-25721.

[43] Mudsill Mining Co. *v.* Watrous, *et al.*, 61 *Federal Reporter* (1894), 164.

Van Deusen declared the property was worth half a million dollars. According to his calculations, the average assay of ore would run thirty-five ounces of silver to the ton, and there were an estimated 30,-000 tons in sight. Inspection by Walter McDermott, a competent engineer, corroborated these figures on ore value, for McDermott's samples assayed thirty-four ounces of silver per ton. The transaction was completed on the basis of this evidence.[44]

When the Mudsill Mining Company, Ltd., was formed early in 1888, it took over the property at an agreed price of £58,000, of which £25,-000 was to be in shares.[45] Additional ore samples taken after the company was in possession showed only seven ounces of silver to the ton, and company officials quickly realized that something was radically amiss. No formal demand for rescission of sale was made until more than a year later, in April, 1889, but in the meantime the concern constructed a small mill, reduced token quantities of ore, carried out moderate exploration and development, and, according to the directors, sought evidence of fraud.[46]

The average value of ores reduced during this interim period proved to be a mere four ounces of silver per ton rather than the thirty-four shown in presale tests. When the vendors refused to make restitution of the purchase price outside court, the British company took legal action in America, asking that the purchase contract be set aside and all money and shares returned.[47]

In the lower courts the company lost its case.[48] But on appeal the vendors began to emerge with tarnished reputations. Two thousand pages of evidence were collected, and the United States Court of Appeals, Eastern District of Michigan, found much to say about the evils of mine promotion. It was the court's contention that although Van Deusen's representations of the richness of the Mudsill property had been verbal, he could not hide behind the argument that they were merely "opinions." His statements had been made with a purpose —to facilitate the sale of mines—and as such must be considered

[44] McDermott was a mining engineer with the firm McDermott and Duffield of New York and London and had agreed to help organize the company in England, *Ibid.*, 164–165.

[45] *Ibid.*, 164; Mudsill Mining Co., *Prospectus* (Jan. 21, 1888).

[46] 61 *Federal Reporter* (1894), 167.   [47] *Ibid.*

[48] *Ibid.;* Mudsill Mining Co., *Circular to Shareholders*, Dec. 23, 1892, Stock Exchange Archives, London.

"puffing" or "trade talk" designed to influence capitalists and investors.[49]

Moreover, in the eyes of the court there was no doubt that the ore samples taken by McDermott had been "salted."[50] They had contained a high percentage of almost pure silver in the form of a fine powder. Ores taken from the Mudsill vein in their natural state contained no silver in this form and only a little in chlorides and sulphides. This, contended the bench, could not have been mere chance.[51] Although the exact method of "salting" could not be fixed,[52] there was no doubt that the vendors had had both the opportunity and the incentive and that a multitude of English investors had been hoodwinked. It was clear that the fraud had been instrumental in bringing about the sale abroad, and the court did not hesitate to point its finger directly at the culprits. Upsetting the decision of the lower tribunal, it ordered Watrous and Van Deusen to hand back with interest the payments already received in cash and shares, and the case was closed.[53]

Such clear proof of outright swindling was a rare occurrence in courts on both sides of the Atlantic, so far as Anglo-American mining companies were concerned. "Salting" cases were extremely difficult to prove—particularly after the transaction had been completed. Besides, there were more subtle means to misrepresent mining property than to "graft" minerals where nature had not intended them to be. The whole array of high-pressure sales techniques cultivated and perfected throughout the period proved safer and more effective.

These techniques—and especially statements contained in prospectuses—fostered litigation, but again with striking lack of success. One case resulted from the issue by a New Jersey concern, the Seven Stars Gold Mining Company, of 80,000 copies of a prospectus for the British public in 1892. The prospectus implied, but did not specifically state,

---

[49] 61 *Federal Reporter* (1894), 168.

[50] McDermott was one of the plaintiffs in the suit and as such presumably was absolved of suspicion.

[51] 61 *Federal Reporter* (1894), 168–169, 172.

[52] Sealed with wire and with lead seals, the sacks of ore samples had been left in the mine for four days, then locked overnight in an old crushing mill belonging to Van Deusen. It was the belief of the court that silver powder could have been forced through the mesh of the sacking with a syringe at any time during this period or that Van Deusen might well have accomplished the deed while McDermott was occupied feeding the crusher as the ore was being prepared for shipment to New York for testing. *Ibid.*, 175, 177.

[53] *Ibid.*, 190.

that property in Arizona was held under federal patent by the company. Actually the title stood in the name of John Lawler and Edward Wells, the original owners. Nor did the prospectus mention an earlier agreement which stipulated that the only interest of the company was an equitable right to the mines after $450,000 had been realized from the profits and paid to Lawler and Wells; rather it implied that the net proceeds would be distributed as dividends. No mention was made of provisions in this contract which stipulated that if a payment was missed, previous payments, improvements, and credit for ore taken out were to be forfeited.[54]

When perturbed shareholders demanded redress and brought suit against the original owners, the United States Supreme Court upheld two lower decisions. Lawler and Wells were not chargeable, because of their silence, with the fraud perpetrated on subscribers of Seven Stars Gold Mining stock by misstatement or omission in the prospectus, since the document had been written and circulated abroad without their knowledge, although later they became aware of its contents.[55]

Equally fruitless were the efforts made by Stratton's Independence, Ltd., to reclaim a major part of the purchase price paid for W. S. Stratton's Cripple Creek property in 1899. The company contended that at the time of the transaction Stratton had represented the ore exposed and in sight as being worth $7,000,000 and the total property as being reasonably valued at $10,000,000. The latter figure had been set as the purchase price, insisted the concern, although Stratton well knew that only $2,000,000 was in sight and that the entire mine was worth only $4,000,000. Consequently the company brought suit against Stratton's estate to collect $6,000,000, the difference between the represented and the actual value.[56]

Even though the Independence employed a formidable battery of legal talent, headed by Samuel Untermeyer of New York, its case proved to be untenable. The defense calmly pointed out that the Cripple Creek millionaire had not sold directly to Stratton's Independence, Ltd., for his $10,000,000. Instead he had taken his price in shares, which

[54] Wiser *v.* Lawler, 189 *U.S. Reports* (1902), 263.   [55] *Ibid.*, 274.
[56] Stratton's Independence *v.* Dines, *et al.*, 126 *Federal Reporter* (1904), 969–970.

"constituted but a change in the manner whereby Stratton held the ownership and possession of the property." [57] The fact that he had made immediate arrangements to dispose of his shares for $10,000,000 through the Venture Corporation, Ltd., had no bearing on the case at hand. The defense, moreover, denied misrepresentation, showing that the company's own agents had inspected the mine prior to purchase and that the concern had taken out and sold more than $10,100,000 worth of ore up to August 1, 1907. [58] The case was settled when federal courts in Colorado handed down decisions against the British company. [59]

If litigation brought by English firms to set aside purchase on charges of fraud or deception were in most instances unsuccessful, what of those proceedings brought by individual shareholders to obtain a restitution of personal investments on similar complaints directed primarily against company officials? Contemporary records show many such cases, some decided favorably and some unfavorably by English courts.

One of the earliest examples stemmed from activities of the promoters and directors of the Reese River Mining Company, Ltd., in the middle sixties. The purpose of this company, as stated in its prospectus issued in early 1865, was the acquiring of some fifty acres of mineral land in the Reese River District of Nevada. [60] But when two directors inspected the contemplated purchase and pronounced it worthless, [61] the board bought another mine, the Confederate Extension, instead. [62] At least one individual shareholder subsequently demanded through the British law courts that he be relieved of his shares and his obligation to pay the remaining calls on the ground that the prospectus had

[57] *Ibid.*, 973.   [58] *Ibid.*

[59] *Ibid.*, 980–981; Stratton's Independence *v.* Dines, *et al.*, 135 *Federal Reporter* (1905), 449–465. The first decision is that of the U.S. Circuit Court for the District of Colorado; the second is that of the U.S. Circuit Court of Appeals, Eighth District.

[60] *Prospectus* (June, 1865).

[61] Investigators found the mine situated "on the slope of a hill, where its own and all other workings had been abandoned months ago." *In re* Reese River Silver Mining Co.—Smith's case, 2 *Chancery Appeals* (1867), 606.

[62] According to engineers, the Confederate Extension was "one of the best (if not the finest) mines in the *Reese River* district." Smith *v.* Reese River Silver Mining Co., 2 *Equity Cases* (1866), 266.

misrepresented the original property and that the directors lacked authority to purchase alternate mines at their own discretion. English justice favored the protesting investor in this instance.[63]

The Quartz Hill Consolidated Gold Mining Company, Ltd., was another concern which experienced upheavals from within—probably more than the normal number. Formed in 1881 to acquire Colorado mines once owned by another British firm,[64] the Quartz Hill organization almost immediately encountered opposition in the form of a circular issued by solicitor Edward Beall casting aspersions on promoters and directors and on the manner in which the company had been floated. Quartz Hill officials attempted unsuccessfully to prove that the spreading of such a broadside constituted libel and was the work of "bears" attempting to depress shares further than they already were.[65]

About the same time, while the company was in the process of voluntary liquidation with a view to reconstruction as the Denver Gold Company, Ltd., a shareholder named Robert Young lost his case against the firm for restitution of his investment on the ground that he had been induced to take shares by false and misleading statements in the original Quartz Hill prospectus.[66]

This action was still under consideration when the company brought legal proceedings against another shareholder whose major crime had been to advertise and present a petition for liquidation of the concern under supervision of the courts. This in itself was not contrary to statute, except that the petition contained statements to which the company strenuously objected.[67] In a thorough airing before the bench, evidence quickly revealed that irregularities had indeed accompanied

---

[63] *Ibid.*, 269; 2 *Chancery Appeals* (1867), 616–617.

[64] From the Kansas Mining Co., the property had passed into the hands of James C. Fagan, who sold through an agent to the new concern. Memo. of Agreement (Feb. 5, 1881) between William W. Temple and Edward Jenkins, Quartz Hill Consolidated Gold Mining Co., C.R.O. B-15023.

[65] Quartz Hill Consolidated Gold Mining Co. *v.* Beall, 20 *Chancery Cases* (1882), 502–503, 505–509.

[66] London *Times*, Feb. 14, Dec. 3, 1883; Quartz Hill Consolidated Gold Mining Co.—*ex parte* Young, 21 *Chancery Cases* (1882), 642–646.

[67] London *Times*, Feb. 2, 1883; Quartz Hill Consolidated Gold Mining Co. *v.* Eyre, 11 *Queen's Bench Division* (1883), 674–676.

the floating of the company; also that the prospectus had been misleading; and that the promoters had overnight added £70,000 to the selling price as the Colorado property changed hands. Hence the jury's decision vindicated the shareholder; [68] but in this, as in other cases, the courts did not order any refund of investments to the individuals who had loosed the charges of misrepresentation.[69]

The legal defense of titles and efforts to bring about readjustments of original purchase price or share allotments were but two of the many problems encountered by British companies operating in the West. It would be almost impossible, as well as wearisome, to classify neatly all the various types of lawsuits which filled the period under consideration. Many of them were actions common to mining and milling operations in all parts of the world. There were suits over damages done to neighboring property by improper handling of water [70] or by debris from waste dumps; [71] over water rights; [72] over right of way claimed by railroad companies; [73] and over the interpretation of contracts.[74] Legal proceedings often resulted when vendors or managers sought to obtain remuneration [75] or to enforce agreements presumably already in effect.[76] Companies that had fallen upon evil financial days faced a host of lawsuits brought by mine foremen or laborers deter-

---

[68] *Ibid.*, 694–695.

[69] See Foakes *v.* Quartz Hill Consolidated Gold Mining Co., Queen's Bench Division (1885), reported in London *Times*, March 28, 1885. For other cases stemming from internal discontent of one kind or another see *In re* Flagstaff Silver Mining Co. of Utah, 20 *Equity Cases* (1875), 268–269; *In re* Crooke's Mining and Smelting Co., 31 *Chancery Cases* (1886), 420–424; London *Times*, Aug. 3, 1886.

[70] See Clark *v.* Nevada Land and Mining Co., 6 *Nevada Reports* (1870), 527–530.

[71] See Colorado Silver Mining Co., *Annual Report*, year ending Dec. 31, 1890.

[72] See annual reports of San Bernardo Mining Co. for years ending Aug. 31, 1901 and 1902.

[73] See annual reports of Twin Lakes Hydraulic Gold Mining Syndicate for years ending Dec. 31, 1886, 1887, and 1888; Twin Lakes Placers, *Annual Report*, year ending Dec. 31, 1894.

[74] See Kohinoor and Donaldson Consolidated Mining Co., *Directors' Report*, Nov. 29, 1883.

[75] See Kimber and Ellis [Solicitors] to the directors, Eberhardt and Aurora Mining Co. (London, March 31, 1873), Read MSS.

[76] See annual reports of Slide and Spur Gold Mines for years ending Sept. 30, 1890 and 1894.

mined to collect back wages when defunct corporations would not or could not meet their obligations.[77]

Taken one by one these examples of litigation were perhaps not too disturbing. But all too frequently legal troubles came in large, multiflavored doses. One illustration—possibly an extreme—will suffice. In the year 1877 the Flagstaff Silver Mining Company of Utah, Ltd., had to parry thrusts from all sides. It was appealing a decision relating to a managerial squabble with one of the vendors, Erwin Davis.[78] At the same time Davis was claiming repayment of funds from certain "ore contracts," by which he had loaned money to the concern.[79] A suit had just been commenced by Helen Tarbet, asking that a receiver be appointed to take over the company's property to satisfy a $45,000 judgment awarded in an earlier decision.[80] Papers had been served in a suit brought by an English shareholder to have all leases canceled and a receiver appointed. Two sets of creditors were attempting to sell the property to settle prior judgments, and one had attached and sold the office furniture. An American named McCormick was commencing another suit to test his right to follow the Flagstaff ledge.[81] Not to be outdone or kept entirely on the defensive, the company was pressing an old claim against a fellow British concern, the Last Chance Silver Mining Company, Ltd., for the return of $25,000 loaned in more prosperous days.[82]

It must again be emphasized that most of these examples of litigation were in no way restricted to British mining companies, for American concerns encountered the same troubles. But the tangible combined result was to help discourage English investment in western mines. There is no escaping the fact that litigation of any kind was expensive. When the Nevada attorney of the Eberhardt and Aurora Mining Company, Ltd., was asked in 1871 to estimate the cost of a suit defending

---

[77] It was necessary for George Cullins, foreman of the Flagstaff Silver Mining Co., to fight his case against the company through the Supreme Court of the land before receiving satisfaction—and ultimately the $1,530 owed him in back salary. Flagstaff Silver Mining Co. of Utah v. Cullins, 104 *U.S. Reports* (1881), 176–177.

[78] Flagstaff Silver Mining Co. of Utah v. Patrick, 2 *Utah Reports* (1877), 305–318.

[79] Davis v. Flagstaff Silver Mining Co. of Utah, *ibid.*, 74–87.

[80] *Mining Journal*, Jan. 5, 1878, 5; Flagstaff Silver Mining Co. of Utah v. Tarbet, 98 *U.S. Reports* (1879), 463–470.

[81] *Mining Journal*, Jan. 5, 1878, 5.   [82] *Ibid.*, March 10, 1877, 256.

the title to a portion of the corporation's property, he calculated that lawyers' fees and other expenses would range between $10,000 and $50,000.[83] Actual figures from a number of Anglo-American concerns indicate that this was no wild or idle guess. Cash statements for the Eberhardt and Aurora show legal expenses of $28,121.72 for the period between September 30, 1870, and September 1, 1872.[84] The official balance sheet of the Arizona Copper Company, Ltd., as of September 30, 1886, showed legal costs aggregating $23,544.42 for the twenty-seven months prior to that date.[85] In its quarter of a century of running litigation with the St. Louis Mining and Milling Company, the Montana Mining Company, Ltd., expended, it is estimated, about $400,000 in defense of its property.[86]

This drain on the corporate purse, along with the loss of property to adverse claimants, quickly brought home to the British investor one of the disadvantages of western mines. Brokers played sharply on that particular weakness, cautioning Londoners against the "uncertainty of title, and the chances of having to fight for possession at enormous costs in the law courts, or to buy out for a large sum every filibuster who chooses to make a claim." [87]

Undoubtedly a fear of American litigation directly hindered the investment of English capital in trans-Mississippi mining. When court action prevented the Colorado Terrible Lode Mining Company, Ltd., from removing ore from the ground in dispute with William A. Hamill in 1875, the London *Standard* regarded the injunction as unjust. "The episode may be expected to increase the disposition to avoid investments in American securities, especially mining shares," promised the editor.[88] James Teal, returning to the Rockies from England in May of the same year, reported that the litigation had discouraged British shareholders and had already prevented the sale of several Colorado mines on the London market.[89] When the North American Exploration

[83] Thomas Wren to Thomas Phillpotts (Hamilton, Nev., June 13, 1871), Read MSS.

[84] Eberhardt and Aurora Mining Co., Cash Statement from Sept. 30, 1870, to Oct. 1, 1871, and from Oct. 1, 1871, to Sept. 1, 1872, Read MSS.

[85] *Annual Report,* year ending Sept. 30, 1886.

[86] *Report of the Extraordinary General Meeting of the Montana Mining Company, Ltd., held March 18th, 1913,* Stock Exchange Archives, London.

[87] T. Thompson's circular in *Mining World,* Jan. 4, 1873, 15.

[88] April 29, 1875.   [89] *Weekly Miner,* May 15, 1875.

Company, Ltd., encountered unexpected lawsuits in 1898 over possession of its Colorado property, its directors decided to acquire no more mines in America. Said they, "The intricacies of the American Mining Law are chiefly to blame for this." [90]

[90] *Annual Report,* year ending Dec. 31, 1898.

⁑ CHAPTER VIII ⁑

The Emma Silver Mining Company, Limited: A Case Study

INASMUCH as more than five hundred British mining companies were formed between 1860 and 1901, it is impossible to select a single one and label it as "typical" of concerns operating in the American West. General problems and broad patterns may be discerned, yet the course of each individual company proved somehow unique. But if any may be chosen for a case study to illustrate the details of organization and operation of the English joint-stock corporation in western mining, the Emma Silver Mining Company, Ltd., serves best.

The Emma was more than an "average" Anglo-American company. It was by far the most famous—or infamous—of all such projects brought before the British public in the seventies, and its reputation long exceeded its productive life. It was an exceptional concern in that its scandalous background kept it in the public eye for several decades and precipitated international complaints. Yet beneath the extraordinary publicity most of its problems were the common ones faced by a great number of companies during the same period. Promotion and organization were different in this instance only in their magnitude and complexity. Operation brought the same obstacles, the same complaints, the same disappointments as those experienced by other unsuccessful concerns. In London the bulls and the bears gored and clawed one another and the shareholders of the Emma with a ferocity more intense than, but certainly not basically different from, that stemming from other companies. And the lawyers on both sides of the Atlantic reaped their rewards in a score of expensive lawsuits which spanned a quarter of a century.[1]

Situated in Little Cottonwood Canyon, near the Utah town of Alta, the Emma was located in 1868 by two prospectors[2] who, for lack of working capital, were compelled to enlist the aid of several others, including James E. Lyon of Racine, Wisconsin. As the mine developed, the new partners organized the Emma Company of Utah and by spring, 1871, had given Erwin Davis of San Francisco an option to purchase the property for $1,500,000, subject to the settlement of Lyon's claim of one-third interest.[3]

After several futile endeavors[4] Davis managed to interest Trenor W. Park of Vermont[5] and General H. Henry Baxter of New York,[6]

[1] There is no detailed account of the Emma episode. For a brief treatment see W. Turrentine Jackson, "The Infamous Emma Mine: A British Investment in the Little Cottonwood District, Utah Territory," *Utah Historical Quarterly*, XXIII (Oct., 1955), 339–362.

[2] The mine was named for the daughter of one of the discoverers. James E. Lyon, *Dedicated to William M. Stewart, My Attorney in the "Emma Mine" Controversy in 1871* (n.p., n.d.), 1–2; *E. & M. Jour.*, May 13, 1876, 467.

[3] James E. Lyon testimony (Feb. 28, 1876), Emma Mine Investigation, Ho. Rpt. No. 579, 44 Cong., 1 Sess. (1875–1876), 46. Cited hereafter as *Ho. Rpt. No. 579.*

[4] For accounts of these abortive attempts see Lyon, *Dedicated to W. M. Stewart,* 7; Harpending, *Great Diamond Hoax,* 172; *Mining Journal,* Oct. 28, 1871, 956.

[5] Park (1823–1882) was born in Vermont and was trained as a lawyer. Moving to California in 1852, he became interested in the firm of Halleck, Pechy, Billings, and Park, specializing in land titles. In 1863 he helped form a company to take over Frémont's Mariposa Estate at an immense valuation, but when it was discovered that the mines were being ruthlessly exploited without pretense of development the enterprise collapsed. Park returned to Vermont where he established the First National Bank of Bennington and interested himself in several steamship and railroad ventures. *DAB,* XIV, 208–209.

[6] A native of Vermont, Baxter was educated for the law but went into the railroad business, becoming ultimately a director, and for a time president, of the New York Central. He was considered "one of the heaviest operators" on Wall Street and as one possessed of "a princely fortune and unbounded liberality." Matthew Hale Smith, *Bulls and Bears of New York, with the Crisis of 1873, and the Cause* (Hartford and Chicago, 1874), 432–438.

who combined to purchase a half-interest for $375,000.[7] Because of
unsettled territorial laws in Utah, a new company was organized in
New York, to be known as the Emma Silver Mining Company of New
York, with Park and Baxter holding between them one-half the shares.[8]
Park saw an opportunity to make a tidy profit by taking the mine to
England for sale, but the unliquidated claim of Lyon blocked any
early hope of disposal there until, after prolonged bickering, it was com-
promised [9] and the way opened to offer the mine on the London market. By this time—late in the summer of 1871—the Emma was as well
known in England as in the United States. The federal commissioner
on mining statistics called it "one of the most remarkable deposits of
argentiferous ore ever opened." [10] The London *Mining Journal* described it as "par excellence, the mine of Utah," [11] and the "Potosi
mine" of the Wasatch.[12] Normally a large amount of its ore was shipped
to bullion brokers in England, especially the firms of Lewis and Son
and Bath and Sons, both of Liverpool.[13] Whenever particularly rich
shipments arrived, the press was duly informed and the information
was relayed to the public.[14] Whether this display of wealth was or
was not intentional is debatable. But Senator William M. Stewart of
Nevada, Lyon's attorney, wrote his client in August of 1871, "They have
worked the mine up in England by the ore they have sent, and the

[7] L. E. Chittenden, *The Emma Mine* (New York, 1876), 7.

[8] Nominal capital of the company was $5,000,000 in $100 shares. Park and
Baxter originally held 12,500 shares each, while ten others divided the rest. Park
then bought an additional 3,125 shares from James M. Day just before the mine
was sold abroad. *Ibid.*

[9] *Ibid.*, 9. Lyon had originally demanded $1,000,000, but he settled for an ar-
rangement which was based on the sale of the mine but which in no case would
give him more than $500,000. Memo. of Agreement (Aug. 18, 1871) between
H. H. Baxter (for the Emma Silver Mining Co. of New York) and James E. Lyon,
in *Ho. Rpt.* No. 579, 52.

[10] Statistics of Mines and Mining, *Ho. Exec. Doc.* No. 211, 42 Cong., 2 Sess.
(1871–1872), 321.

[11] Aug. 12, 1871, 710.   [12] *Ibid.*, Oct. 7, 1871, 872–873.

[13] Between Sept., 1870, and May, 1871, Lewis and Son had received and sold
2,217 tons of Emma ore, of £72,868 net value. From July 20, 1871 to Aug. 19,
1871, the firm handled 1,894 tons, worth £58,931 net, and received a commission
of 2.5 per cent on all. London *Times*, June 27, 1878.

[14] See *Mining Journal*, Sept. 30, Oct. 21, 1871, 867, 933; *Mining World*, Oct.
14, 1871, 756.

manner of sending it, that I have no doubt of a sale from five to eight millions." The brokers, said Stewart, "are crazy about the mine." [15]

It was mid-September of this year when Park and Stewart arrived in London. Park had come to sell the Emma; Stewart was there ostensibly to look after Lyon's interests, but he was to be instrumental also in disposing of the property. The two immediately joined the colony with headquarters in the Langham Hotel.

Soon they were introduced to the brokerage firm of Coates and Hankey in London, primarily through Cyrus M. Fisher, a young New York attorney who had done legal business for the United States Legation [16] and who was at the same time busy promoting the sale of American rail and mining securities.[17] Coates and Hankey immediately informed the Americans that British clients were waiting for negotiations to proceed as soon as authorized. Although Stewart "thought that was a little fast," [18] an understanding was quickly reached whereby Coates and Hankey were to form a joint-stock company to purchase the Emma for £400,000 in cash and £500,000 in shares.[19]

Coates insisted that, though the British knew the mine well, an official inspection and report be made by a competent American expert. The name of Benjamin Silliman, a Yale professor of chemistry, was suggested, and instructions were flashed to Baxter in New York to

---

[15] Stewart to Lyon (New York, Aug. 5, 1871), *Ho. Rpt.* No. 579, ii. William Morris Stewart early taught school in New York and studied law briefly at Yale University. Drawn to California in the early 1850's, he soon became one of the finest mining lawyers on the Pacific Coast. As Republican senator from Nevada from 1864 to 1875, he was instrumental in the passage of the mining laws of 1866 and 1872 and responsible for the final wording of the Fifteenth Amendment. From 1887 to 1905 he served again in the Senate, where he was an ardent champion of the Free Silver cause. *DAB*, XVIII, 13–14. It is interesting to note that none of the standard accounts of the life of Stewart make any mention of the Emma mine episode. See *Reminiscences of Senator William M. Stewart of Nevada*, ed. George Rothwell Brown (New York and Washington, 1908); Effie Mack, "Life and Letters of William Morris Stewart, 1827–1909," unpublished Ph.D. dissertation, University of California.

[16] *Ho. Rpt.* No. 579, ii. Fisher was a close friend of Benjamin Moran, the veteran secretary of the Legation in London, and went down on the liner *Atlantic* off Nova Scotia in 1873. Moran Journal, XXXIV (April 2, 1873), 254.

[17] See Brayer, *William Blackmore*, I, 31–32, 35.

[18] Stewart testimony (March 21, 1876), *Ho. Rpt.* No. 579, 152.

[19] *Ibid.*; Chittenden, *Emma Mine*, 13–14.

engage his services. Silliman agreed to undertake the project, having been invited to "name his own terms." [20]

The inspection, made immediately, established "beyond all reasonable doubt" that the Emma was a true fissure vein and "in the category of the great mines of the world." [21] Silliman's report, dated October 16, 1871, was telegraphed from Corinne to Coates and Hankey in London at a cost of $3,012,[22] so that it might be in time to accompany the prospectus when the proposed company was announced. For this and additional services Silliman received a total fee of $25,000, but, contrary to subsequent charges, his pay was not contingent upon a favorable report and sale of the mine abroad.[23]

Meanwhile the negotiations by Coates and Hankey faltered. On the basis of information supplied by Park, a prospectus had been printed and held in readiness,[24] but it soon became evident that the brokerage firm had attempted a transaction beyond its capacity. Unable to meet a deadline set by Park and Stewart,[25] Coates and Hankey were forced to call in one of the most influential and certainly one of the most controversial of London's contemporary promoters, Albert Grant.

Born Albert Gottheimer, Grant floated company after company in the period from 1865 to his death in 1899 [26] and appeared almost as frequently in the bankruptcy courts. Described as the "pioneer of modern mammoth company promoting," [27] he was for nearly three decades

[20] Silliman testimony (March 9, 1876), *Ho. Rpt.* No. 579, 125.

[21] *Report of Professor B. Silliman on the Emma Silver Mine* (Salt Lake City, Oct. 16, 1871), 3, Western Americana Collection, Yale University.

[22] Baxter testimony (April 20, 1876), *Ho. Rpt.* No. 579, 777–778.

[23] Silliman's terms were $5,000 in advance, plus not less than $10,000 nor more than $20,000 in addition, "depending on the estimate I might form of the value of the service." He was paid a total of $25,000, but for the same fee made a second inspection of the Emma as well as of other mines in Utah and California. Silliman testimony (March 9, 1876), *ibid.*, 126.

[24] For a copy of this see *ibid.*, 467–470.

[25] Park and Stewart to Coates and Hankey (London, Oct. 21, 1871; Oct. 24, 1871), *ibid.*, 471, 473.

[26] London *Times*, Aug. 31, 1899. As early as April, 1874, Grant had promoted at least thirty-seven companies, among them the Emma Silver Mining Co., the Mineral Hill Silver Mining Co., and the South Aurora Silver Mining Co. *A Selected List of Companies, Foreign Loans, and Miscellaneous Projects, Many of Which Were Issued under the Auspices of Albert Grant* (London, 1874), frontispiece chart.

[27] Albert Gottheimer (1830–1899) was born in Dublin, educated in London and

one of the leading figures of the "City" as well as one of the most detested. The bestowal of an Italian barony upon him rankled the British; his endless and unsuccessful financial schemes made him the natural target for abuse. When he donated land in central London to establish Leicester Square in 1874, his opponents charged that this was done in order that his name might for once be connected with something "square."[28]

Grant proved very definitely interested in the Emma mine, despite his protests later that he approached it with caution, thrice refusing to introduce the mine on the market until convinced by Coates and Hankey that this was no ordinary property.[29] But it was Grant—probably the only man in London capable of so doing—who ultimately floated the Emma.

Acting together as vendors, Park and Stewart on November 2 concluded a secret agreement with Grant whereby the latter pledged himself to organize a company to take over the Emma for the purchase price of £1,000,000, half to be paid in cash and half in fully paid-up shares. Grant further agreed to offer the remaining £500,000 in shares for public subscription in exchange for a 20 per cent commission on the total allotted and taken up. Those shares reserved for the vendors as part of the purchase price were not to be transferable for a period of nine months without the consent of Grant. Moreover, the agreement stipulated that Grant must keep an accurate accounting of expenses of organizing the company and of "sustaining the market"—this sum to be deducted from his commission profits.[30]

On the basis of this contract Grant organized the Emma Silver Mining Company, Ltd., but kept always in the background, ever manipulating and lubricating the financial machinery until the task was completed. A subsequent agreement between Park and a representative

---

Paris, and assumed the name of Grant in 1863. King Victor Emmanuel conferred the title of Baron upon him for his contributions to the Galleria Vittorio Emanuele at Milan. He was M.P. for Kidderminster in 1865 and was re-elected in 1874. London *Times*, Aug. 31, 1899; *DNB*, Suppl. II, 338–339.

[28] Furniss, *Some Victorian Men*, 84.

[29] Albert Grant, Circular to the Shareholders of the Emma Silver Mining Co. (Jan. 5, 1876), *Ho. Rpt.* No. 579, 32.

[30] Memo. of Agreement (Nov. 2, 1871) between Trenor W. Park and William M. Stewart (vendors) and Messrs. Grant and Co., *ibid.*, 252–253. Albert Grant and his brother Maurice operated under the name Grant and Co. for a brief period. Emma Silver Mining Co. *v.* Grant, 11 *Chancery Appeals* (1879), 919.

of the proposed company (November 4) made no mention of Grant's role in floating the concern. It did provide that 2,400 feet of the Emma and 600 feet of the Emma Extension should be transferred, along with all plant and equipment, all ore in and about the mine or in transit, and all bullion on the premises as of October 12. This included 2,800 tons of first-grade ore en route or ready for shipment, 8,000 tons of second-grade ore, and £46,300 of the proceeds on hand from ore sold since the agreed date.[31]

Incorporated on November 8, the Emma Silver Mining Company, Ltd., boasted a nominal capital of £1,000,000, divided into 50,000 shares of twenty pounds each. Of these, 25,000 shares went fully paid to the vendors under the agreement of November 4.[32] Since the total purchase price equaled the total capitalization, the concern would have no operating capital save what was realized on ore then in transit or that taken out of the mine immediately. But since the Emma was undoubtedly rich beyond description, operational problems could surely not be great!

As a practiced promoter of the widest experience, Grant issued a prospectus which represented the acme of sensationalism. "The most dazzling and seductive literature was scattered broadcast through the length and breadth of the United Kingdom," maintained Asbury Harpending, himself no neophyte in the gentle art so adroitly practiced by the London financier. The Emma's fabulous wealth was described "in the vivid language that fires the speculative spirit latent in every man and in most women."[33]

The prospectus carried substantial excerpts from Silliman's report; indeed, copies of the report were attached to the first edition. It pointed out that the mine had produced £298,438 in ore during the four months prior to September 1, 1871, with a net profit of £231,059. Thus a net yield of nearly £700,000 per year might be expected on the basis of past performance—almost twice the estimate in the prospectus drawn up by Coates and Hankey. Ore already taken out and being handed

[31] The purchase price of £1,000,000 was payable half in paid-up shares and half in cash, the latter to be paid in equal monthly payments commencing Dec. 1, 1871. This was subject to the making over of a clear title and proper conveyance before the money was transferred. Memo. of Agreement (Nov. 4, 1871) between Trenor W. Park and George Henry Dean, C.R.O. 5809.

[32] Certificate of Incorporation (Nov. 8, 1871); *Mem. & Art.,* 2, *ibid.*

[33] Harpending, *Great Diamond Hoax,* 188.

over to the new company was valued at £144,000, and first-class ore already developed in the mine, according to Silliman's estimate, was worth £357,750. Dividends were to be limited to 18 per cent per annum until the concern had built up a reserve fund of £180,000 to assure their payment a year in advance. But, it was pointed out, the distribution of dividends was to commence immediately on a monthly basis as of December 1, 1871.[34]

Quoting from a letter written in July, 1871, by William Blake, an American mining engineer, the prospectus lauded the Emma in glowing terms:

The wonderful extent of this mass of ore, the rapidity and ease with which it is extracted, and its high value, make this mine unique in the history of mining in the United States, while it compares with the most brilliant and magnificent developments in the silver regions of Mexico and South America.[35]

Blake later contended that this excerpt was used without his consent and that a second letter predicting that the mine would soon be stripped at the current rate of extraction was ignored completely.[36]

What caught the public eye besides the promise of immediate dividends and the description of dazzling wealth was the distinctive array of imposing names presented as trustees and directors. Included on the board of directors were such dignitaries as George Anderson, M.P. from Glasgow, listed by Stewart as a coppersmith of "large wealth"; Edward Brydges-Willyams, M.P. for Cornwall, banker and smelter; Edward Leigh Pemberton, M.P. for West Kent, a "large landed proprietor"; John C. Stanley, "heir to Lord Stanley of Alderney," also "very wealthy." In addition to these titled guinea pigs, Park, Stewart, and Baxter were on the board, adding whatever prestige a banker, a United States senator, and an ex-railroad president might convey to the British public.[37] But the crowning touch, the *pièce de résistance*, of this enticing display was the name of General Robert Cumming Schenck, United

---

[34] *Prospectus* (Nov. 9, 1871). For a comparison with the Coates and Hankey prospectus, see Alexander Macdougall, *Emma Mine* (London, 1876), 1–28, Western Americana Collection, Yale University.

[35] *Prospectus* (Nov. 9, 1871).

[36] Blake testimony (April 18, 1876), *Ho. Rpt.* No. 579, 708–709.

[37] *Prospectus* (Nov. 9, 1871); Stewart to Schenck (London, Nov. 3, 1871), *Ho. Rpt.* No. 579, 29.

States minister at the Court of St. James.[38] Here was supreme proof of the value of the Emma mine. Here was ground for confidence in super-abundance. What British investor could refrain from plunging his savings into such an enterprise when it carried the solemn endorsement of the American minister?

Behind the selection of these names, particularly Schenck's, lay a story not known to the prospectus-reading public. Originally Park had sought the services of Colonel John J. Puleston, who was in charge of the London office of Jay Cooke, McCulloch & Company. Puleston was willing to join the board of directors, but McCulloch protested and he limited his connection to acting as trustee along with Schenck.[39] For the use of Puleston's name as a member of Jay Cooke, McCulloch & Company £25,000 was paid to the latter concern,[40] much to the disturbance of Cooke himself. "Had I been consulted," he wrote, "I should have preferred paying $75,000 out of pocket rather than to have linked our name with it." [41]

This payment was one of many made with similar benefits in mind. "Every man we met on the street wanted a commission for everything," complained Stewart later. "Everybody in England wanted a 'pull.' . . .

[38] Schenck (1809–1890) graduated from Miami University of Ohio and practiced law in Dayton. A member of the national House of Representatives from 1843 to 1851, he then became the American minister to Brazil until 1853. Active in Lincoln's 1860 campaign, he fought at both battles of Bull Run and emerged as a major general only to resign his commission in order to serve again in the House, where he became chairman of the Committee on Military Affairs and later of the Committee on Ways and Means. He failed of re-election in 1870 and in the following year was appointed to the post in England. After 1876 he practiced law in Washington. Among other accomplishments Schenck was the author of a book on draw poker. *DAB*, XVI, 427–428. There is no full-length biography of Schenck, although Professor Fred Joyner of Miami University is at work on one. For sketches of his life see Joyner, "Robert Cumming Schenck, First Citizen and Statesman of the Ohio Valley," *Ohio State Archaeological and Historical Quarterly*, LVIII (July, 1949), 286–297; Epiphanie Clara Kokkinou, "The Political Career of Robert Cumming Schenck," unpublished M.A. thesis, Miami University, Ohio.

[39] Chittenden, *Emma Mine*, 64.

[40] Stewart explained that Cooke, McCulloch & Co. wished to float the company themselves and that when they did not get the task they asked for a percentage of the sale price for the use of their own and Puleston's name. The £25,000 was paid mainly to avert a clash, said Stewart. Stewart testimony (March 22, 1876), *Ho. Rpt.* No. 579, 179.

[41] To Hugh McCulloch (Nov. 22, 1871), quoted in Ellis Paxson Oberholtzer, *Jay Cooke* (Philadelphia, 1907), II, 290.

I never had seen such a place in my life." [42] Hiram Johnson informed
Henry M. Teller early in 1872 that

what is here termed a syndicate was formed[,] headed and organized by an
apostate Jew now bearing the name of Albert Grant, formerly Moses Deish-
pecker, or some other jawbreaking name, who was to receive and did receive,
the lump sum of $500,000 Cash. Schenck, our immaculate honest representa-
tive at the Court of St. James, a Member of Parliament, Messrs Cook Mc-
Coulack [*sic*] & Co. and other stinkers divided another $500,000.[43]

Subsequent investigation revealed that though Johnson's figures were
not quite accurate,[44] neither were they entirely fictitious, for Baron
Grant had indeed dispensed funds with a liberal hand in promoting and
organizing the concern. He paid a total of £29,000 to various brokers,
solicitors, or accounting firms, while Park contributed at least another
£20,000. Considering the fact that Grant was to receive £100,000 for
the original promotion, it would appear that the initial total for forming
the company and getting it on its feet was at least £120,000, probably
an unusually high fee for such a service. This does not include commissions later paid to Grant for disposing of the vendor's shares to the
public.[45]

In the meantime the choice of directors was being made, and Robert
Schenck found himself involved in the new company. Introduced to
Stewart and Park by William Evarts, Schenck listened with interest
when the topic of the Emma mine was brought casually into dinner
conversation.[46] Like other diplomatic officials the minister found his
salary inadequate to meet the desired standards. With three daughters
to keep in the height of London's fashions, he was easy prey to suggestions that he invest in the profitable new venture soon to be set before the English people.[47]

When Schenck pointed out that he lacked the necessary funds, Park
agreeably offered assistance. By a secret agreement he advanced
Schenck £10,000 on the latter's note, the loan to be secured on shares

[42] Stewart testimony (March 21, 1876), *Ho. Rpt.* No. 579, 155.

[43] To Teller (London, Jan. 9, 1872), Teller MSS.

[44] Report of Sole, Turner & Knight, Solicitors (London, Nov. 5, 1875), *Hour*,
Jan. 18, 1876.

[45] Park testimony (April 19, 1876), *Ho. Rpt.* No. 579, 758.

[46] Schenck testimony (June 27, 1875), *ibid.*, 12.

[47] Schenck to Hamilton Fish (Finale-Marina, Italy, Nov. 30, 1872), *ibid.*, 303.

taken by Schenck or, if Park desired, on the further security of Schenck's house in Washington. At the same time Schenck was guaranteed a monthly dividend.[48] Park agreed that, on Schenck's request, he would take over the shares, paying him their par value. It was stipulated, however, that if at any time Park offered to take the shares at par and Schenck refused, the former was released from the agreement.[49]

What all this meant was that Park furnished the funds, guaranteed dividends, and insured Schenck against loss if the shares dropped in price. Schenck paid no interest on his loan for the first year and was protected on all sides. The relationship of this agreement with Schenck's presence on the board of directors was much disputed in the 1870's but seems obvious to observers in the twentieth century.

Park, Stewart, and Schenck all maintained later on that the diplomat was approached to become a director after he had already arranged to take shares on his own through Park's aid.[50] Lyon insisted that this was untrue, and Grant declared that he undertook to float the company only after Park had informed him the American minister was willing to join the directorate.[51] On the basis of evidence before it in 1876, the House Committee on Foreign Affairs was inclined to side with Grant, although questions still remained unanswered.[52]

Park explained his beneficence toward Schenck as the result of an instinctive liking for the man and of the desire to have a capable person in London to protect American interests in the company.[52] The weight of Schenck's official position was not unimportant, however, and Park was not acting for philanthropic reasons. This was all the more evident

[48] This was originally 2 per cent per month but by an amendment of Dec. 2, 1871, Schenck agreed that it should be scaled down to 1.5 per cent per month or 18 per cent per annum. Park to Schenck (London, Nov. 1, 1871) [Agreement, with endorsement], ibid., 280.

[49] Ibid.

[50] Park testimony (April 12, 1876); Stewart testimony (March 22, 1876); Schenck testimony (March 28, 1876), ibid., 161, 281, 642.

[51] Grant, Circular to shareholders of the Emma Silver Mining Co. (Jan. 5, 1876), ibid., 34.

[52] Park's secret agreement with Schenck was dated Nov. 1, 1871, more than a week before the announcement of the officers of the company, but lacking was the customary stamp giving legality to such documents in England. Under pressure, Park admitted that arrangements with Albert Grant were verbally completed before Schenck was asked to sit on the board, but the actual contract with Grant was not signed until afterward. Ibid., iii, v, 310, 650.

[53] Park testimony (April 12, 1876), ibid., 646.

when he promised, out of the goodness of his heart, to hand over to Schenck half of what he made on independent purchase and sale of Emma shares on the London market. Schenck did receive £1,894 in this fashion, which was credited on his promissory note late in 1872.[54] It was done, contended Park, because Schenck had incurred losses on Emma shares and needed help.[55]

The prospectus released to the public on November 9 gave no indication of the engineering that had gone on behind the scenes. Initial public reaction was mixed, if the press may be taken as an accurate reflection. In London the *Iron Times* saw the Emma as "one of the Great Mines of the World—brought out under auspices of no ordinary character."[56] A full-page editorial in the *Mining World* applauded the "strongest board of direction ever perhaps associated with any joint-stock company, and certainly with any mining venture."[57] The more conservative *Economist* expressed surprise and regret at Schenck's participation and recommended that he withdraw his name from the enterprise immediately. A diplomat, said the *Economist*, "ought not to have time for such occupations, and even if his material interests might not sometimes clash with his official duties, the dignity of his office . . . is infringed with his contact with the rough world of commerce."[58] Similar sentiments were echoed by the *Daily Telegraph*, which rationalized Schenck's action on the ground of inexperience but could find no precedent for it and concluded with the warning: "Let the Minister beware lest his high name and position be a topic for scandal and a butt for the poisoned shafts of calumny."[59]

In the London Legation Benjamin Moran noted that feeling in the "City" toward Schenck's being a director was "intense and hostile." "A storm on the subject will come from Washington," he predicted, "or I am in error."[60] Feelings in the United States, however, were at first divided. The *Wall Street Journal* printed the story under the caption "How an Honest Silver Mine Was Sold in London" and predicted that "its success will go far to counterbalance the outrageous swindles which have, during the present year, been thrust upon unsuspecting pur-

---

[54] Promissory note (London, Nov. 1, 1871), *ibid.*, 279–280.
[55] Park testimony (April 21, 1876), *ibid.*, 805.
[56] Nov. 11, 1871.   [57] Nov. 11, 1871, 881–882.
[58] Nov. 11, 1871, 1365.   [59] Nov. 24, 1871.
[60] Moran Journal, XXX (Nov. 13, 1871), 275–276.

chasers." [61] The *Engineering and Mining Journal* believed that too great a price had been asked for the mine and, predicting possible trouble in the future, asserted that Schenck's position was indefensible.[62] In essential harmony was E. L. Godkin, the editor of the New York *Nation*, when he painted the following picture of what might happen:

Supposing, too, as is not impossible, the scheme should prove, like hundreds of the same kind that have gone before it, one of those failures closely bordering on a swindle, or prove wholly a swindle and the strong arm of the English law should lay hold of his brother-directors, what a nice position the American eagle would be in flapping its wings over Mr. Schenck's head to save him from the legal consequences of conduct on the moral guilt of which the world would be unanimous.[63]

The New York *Evening Post* early asked for the recall of Schenck, and Moran in London thought it not unlikely that this demand might be met.[64] Although the London *Observer* carried the news that there would be no recall,[65] the *Times* contended that Schenck would be brought home by his government unless satisfactory explanations were forthcoming.[66] This news caused Schenck "great distress of mind" [67] and prompted him to cable Secretary of State Hamilton Fish on November 27, explaining his position in self-righteous, if not completely punctilious, terms.

Have no pecuniary interest except some shares for which, after investigation fully, I paid dollar for dollar. Having thus decided and raised means to invest was solicited by respectable Americans to act with gentlemen of known high character as director, to protect their interest and my own in what I believe very valuable property. Perhaps made mistake in consenting. Want only honorably and usefully to serve my government and countrymen, but have not deemed it wrong to try to make something honestly for myself and family. Will withdraw from board or do whatever you advise. Will not embarrass administration.[68]

The attention of Fish had already been called to the *Economist's* criticism of Schenck, and the Secretary of State brought these comments

---

[61] Quoted in *Mining Journal*, Dec. 9, 1871, 1102.
[62] Dec. 12 & 19, 1871, 377, 393.   [63] Nov. 30, 1871, 345.
[64] Moran Journal, XXX (Nov. 23, 1871), 299–300.
[65] *Ibid.*, (Nov. 27, 1871), 307.   [66] Nov. 27, 1871.
[67] Moran Journal, XXX (Nov. 27, 1871), 309–310.
[68] Schenck to Fish (London, Nov. 27, 1871), Dispatches, Great Britain, CXII.

before the Cabinet, explaining that although no law or departmental regulation prohibited a diplomat from being connected with a business undertaking of this nature, it was "unfortunate" that his name had been used in London advertising "an inchoate and possibly speculative concern." [69]

After consultation with President Grant [70] Fish notified Schenck that, though all citizens had full right to invest in honest enterprises as they saw fit, his action in helping advertise the Emma was "ill-advised and unfortunate" and would bring criticism. Fish "earnestly advised" that Schenck withdraw his name from the management of the concern.[71] While the language used was not bluntly final, it really gave Schenck two choices: either resign from the directorate or resign from his post as minister.

Schenck made his decision immediately and confided in Benjamin Moran as early as November 29,[72] but not until a week later did he write a note resigning from the board,[73] and not until January 12 of the new year was this made public.[74] There is ample ground to believe that this time lag was to provide an opportunity for all shares to be taken up before Schenck's name was withdrawn. Even then the resignation was couched in terms expressing great confidence in the Emma mine,[75] and strong evidence suggests that it was at least revised, if not written in its entirety, by Park.[76] Schenck's parting statement that his resignation was "upon grounds purely personal to myself" was anything but accurate. In view of the recommendations of his government he actually had little choice.[77]

Various newspaper reports predicting his recall or rumoring his

---

[69] Fish Diary, III, Nov. 24, 1871, 143, Fish correspondence, Library of Congress. Nevins erroneously cites this as an entry of Nov. 4. Allan Nevins, *Hamilton Fish* (New York, 1936), 650.

[70] Fish Diary, III, Nov. 24, 1871, 145.

[71] Fish to Schenck (Washington, Nov. 28, 1871), Fish Letter Copy Book, V, 38–39, Fish Corr. On the very same day the British chargé in Washington confidentially informed his government of this advice. Pakenham to Granville (Washington, Nov. 28, 1871), F.O. 5/1218.

[72] Moran Journal, XXX (Nov. 29, 1871), 315–316.

[73] Schenck to Fish (London, Dec. 9, 1871), Fish Corr., LXXXIV, 13251.

[74] London *Times,* Jan. 12, 1872.

[75] Schenck to George Anderson (London, Dec. 6, 1871), *ibid.,* Jan. 12, 1872.

[76] *Ho. Rpt.* No. 579, xiii.

[77] Schenck to Fish (London, Dec. 10, 1871), Fish Corr., LXXXIV, 13254.

resignation as minister distressed the general a great deal.[78] Particularly disconcerting was the news appearing in the *Times* on December 20 that the Senate had adopted a resolution calling for an inquiry into the role of diplomatic personnel in foreign business ventures.[79] Schenck immediately telegraphed Fish, asking about such a resolution,[80] and received a reassuring answer flashed back on the same day: "No such resolution, to my knowledge." [81]

Evidently the Secretary was not fully abreast of current affairs in Washington, for the Senate had passed such a resolution, introduced by Francis Blair of Missouri, on December 19,[82] but the inquiry—if one was actually undertaken—appears to have applied the whitewash with a liberal hand, exonerating Schenck without searching investigation at this time.[83]

In the meantime, while Schenck remained the center of controversy, Park and Stewart moved ahead with the company, consolidating their position rapidly. Organization was completed, the shares were quickly taken up by the public, and, on the surface, quiet reigned. James E. Lyon, who arrived in London badly in need of funds, was persuaded to settle his claim to a third interest in the Emma for a cash sum. "The Emma is not so *rose colored* as it looks," commented Hiram Johnson to a friend a few days before Christmas, 1871. "I think Lyon has been done in by his American Associates." [84] In any event Lyon withdrew his claim in return for a lump payment of $250,000,[85] but later received an additional $50,000, paid as "blackmail money," according to Stewart, to prevent litigation and adverse notoriety.[86]

It was also necessary to deal with the ten remaining shareholders in the old Emma Silver Mining Company of New York who still retained

---

[78] London *Times*, Dec. 13, 1871; Jan. 5, 1872; Moran Journal, XXX (Dec. 14, 1871), 365.

[79] Dec. 20, 1871.

[80] Schenck to Fish (London, Dec. 20, 1871), Dispatches, Great Britain, CXII.

[81] Fish to Schenck (Washington, Dec. 20, 1871), *Ho. Rpt.* 579, 7.

[82] For this resolution see *Congressional Globe*, Dec. 19, 1871, 211.

[83] See Luke P. Poland testimony (April 21, 1876); Park testimony (April 19, 1876), *Ho. Rpt.* No. 579, 758–759, 795; Moran Journal, XXXIV (Feb. 17, 1873), 143.

[84] To Carpenter (London, Dec 21, 1871), Johnson MSS.

[85] Stewart and Curtis J. Hillyer each received $50,000 of this for legal fees. Stewart testimony (March 21, 1876), *Ho. Rpt.* No. 579, 158.

[86] Stewart testimony (March 23, 1876), *ibid.*, 229–230.

21,875 shares in that concern and hence were entitled to a proportionate interest in the new British company.[87] Shortly before the end of 1871 Stewart succeeded in purchasing these American holdings for Park for $50 per share,[88] at a time when shares in the British Emma were quoted at the equivalent of $115 on the London market. Park was the chief gainer from this coup: what his profits were was never revealed, but an estimate of $1,000,000 would probably not be too high.[89] Stewart admitted that his rewards from Park for all services pertaining to the Emma mine totaled between $270,000 and $290,000, although his memory on his personal finances proved to be as hazy as his book-keeping.[90]

With minor American interests taken care of, the next step was for Park to dispose of his £500,000 worth of vendor's shares. Part of the technique employed was for Grant to buy on the market and sustain Emma prices until Park could unload.[91] Hiram Johnson, an avowed speculator in the shares, contended that $500,000 of the purchase money had to be kept in London to meet dividend payments and to bull the market.[92]

Park yielded to no one in bulling activity. "I am satisfied the ore will hold out," he told shareholders in March, 1872, "and if I had a guarantee I would hold out as long as the ore will, I would not want a better life-insurance." At the same time he denied categorically that Grant had received a commission of £100,000 and personally offered to reimburse any investor who wanted his money back.[93] While he admitted that his own purse had not suffered, he expressed regret that he had not asked more than £1,000,000 for such a rich prize as the Emma.[94]

[87] Old shareholders were entitled to one £20 share of the British company for every $100 share of the original. Memo. of Agreement (Dec. 9, 1871) between H. H. Baxter, *et al.* and T. W. Park, *ibid.*, 271.

[88] *Ibid.*

[89] The difference between Park's price of $50 each and the par value of $100 each would total $1,093,750. At the market price of the exchanged British shares, they would be worth $328,125 more.

[90] Payment was made in cash advances to Stewart or his wife or in the form of Canadian or Utah Southern railroad bonds. Lyon contended that Stewart, in league with Park, had cheated him out of "nearly a million dollars." Lyon, *Dedicated to W. M. Stewart*, 80.

[91] Stewart testimony (March 23, 1876), *Ho. Rpt.* No. 579, 191.

[92] To Teller (London, Jan. 9, 1872), Teller MSS.

[93] Report of meeting of the Emma Silver Mining Co. (March 7, 1872), *Mining World*, March 9, 1872, 451–452.

[94] *Ibid.* (May 8, 1872), *Mining World*, May 11, 1872, 749.

Park had offered to pay the expenses of the entire board to visit Utah, but only Edward Brydges-Willyams took advantage of the opportunity and toured the mine in February, in company with "a literary gentleman," George Alfred Lawrence, who proposed to write a résumé of his travels west.[95] Both were present early in 1872 when Silliman made his second inspection and reported that explorations had added at least two years to the life of the mine and that fully three years' ore was in sight at the workings.[96] Brydges-Willyams, deeply impressed, cabled Park to purchase a thousand more shares on his account.[97] Upon his return to London he reiterated his faith in the property and its possibilities. "I can only repeat," he said, "that I believe the mine will be paying larger dividends than it is at the present time, after every person hearing me now is dead and gone."[98]

Late in March excerpts appeared in English mining and financial periodicals taken from a pamphlet titled *The History of a Great Investment, Illustrated from Mining Enterprise in America,* which described with enthusiasm the Emma and its developments. While the pamphlet, its author unknown, was printed in an edition of only eighteen copies, Emma shareholders or potential shareholders reading extracts in the journals believed they were perusing portions of a substantial work published by reputable experts. Behind it, however, some saw "the master-hand of Mr. Park," with London underlings filling out the details.[99]

On April 1, two days after the pamphlet received publicity, the directors of the company announced that the London Stock Exchange regulations prohibited giving an official quotation unless at least two-thirds of a concern's shares had been offered to the public. The benevolent Park at this juncture magnanimously offered 8,500 of his shares

[95] Samuel T. Paffard, *The True History of the Emma Mine* (London, 1873), 17–18; *Mining Journal,* Jan. 27, 1872, 76.

[96] *Supplemental Report of Professor B. Silliman on the Emma Mine in Little Cottonwood Canyon, Utah Territory* (Salt Lake City, Feb. 29, 1872), 1–3. See also the printed letter, Silliman to George Anderson (Salt Lake City, April 2, 1872). Both of these items are in the Western Americana Collection, Yale University.

[97] To Park (Salt Lake City, Feb. 8, 1872), in *Suppl. Report of Silliman on the Emma Mine,* 3–4.

[98] Report of meeting of the Emma Silver Mining Co. (May 30, 1872), *Mining World,* June 1, 1872, 844.

[99] Paffard, *True History,* 20, 56. For the excerpts see *Mining World* and *Mining Journal,* March 30, 1872, and the *Stock Exchange Review* for April of the same year.

in order to reduce the vendor holdings to the required one-third but protested that he did so only at the insistence of the board of directors and only after Silliman had again pronounced the property sound.[100] In offering this block of shares, with the blessing of Grant, who was to handle the transaction, Park found it necessary to sell at the current market price of twenty-three pounds a share—three pounds above par.[101] But though he disposed of his shares and returned to the States in mid-May,[102] the company failed to receive a quotation on the *Exchange Official List* because of discrepancies in the original prospectus.[103]

Americans in London played the markets, dealing in Emma shares for speculative purposes. Park later admitted that he made a profit of £16,700 from market transactions outside his original holdings.[104] In June, 1872, Moran noted in his Legation journal that Schenck had lost £6,000 in speculation in Emma shares "entered into by that blockhead Woodhull." [105] "That blockhead," Maxwell Woodhull, was soon replaced as second secretary of the Legation by his uncle, Colonel William H. Chesebrough, who likewise quickly succumbed to the seductive wiles of the Emma, as frequent references by the frugal Moran attest.[106]

Schenck had retained the bulk of his original investment and had joined Woodhull to purchase additional shares, using money advanced by Park.[107] In Paris during December, 1872, he received word from Park that dividends would be discontinued and immediately attempted to sell two thousand shares short. This failed, but only because sub-

[100] Chittenden, *Emma Mine,* 29; Park testimony (April 7, 1876), *Ho. Rpt.* No. 579, 502.

[101] Paffard, *True History,* 19; Park Testimony (April 13, 1876), *Ho. Rpt.* No. 579, 683.

[102] Park later stated that he held 5,450 shares when he left England on May 11 but that practically all had been purchased on the open market and were not part of the vendor's issue. Park testimony (April 13, 1876), *Ho. Rpt.* No. 579, 502, 683.

[103] For an acrimonious dispute over this between Chairman Anderson and the secretary of the Exchange see London *Times,* June 6, 1872; *Economist,* June 8, 1872, 709.

[104] Park testimony (April 21, 1876), *Ho. Rpt.* No. 579, 805.

[105] XXXII (June 18, 1872), 165.

[106] See *ibid.,* XXXIII (Dec. 21, 1872), 357.

[107] Schenck testimony (March 28, 30, 1876), Park testimony (April 19, 1876), *Ho. Rpt.* No. 579, 293, 351, 749.

ordinates failed to carry out his orders. Schenck later estimated his deficits in the Emma affair at $41,700.[108]

From the lobby of the Langham Hotel other Americans followed Emma shares closely. Hiram Johnson after an unsuccessful stint of trying to dispose of Colorado mining properties in England, decided it might be worth his while to remain a bit longer and keep a wary eye on Emma shares. In early February, 1872, he wrote a friend in New York:

The Emma stock has made no move since I wrote you last. Nor do I expect any until the report of Brydges Williams [*sic*] and others who have been dispatched by Park, is received, which will come about the 12th or 13 Inst. When I expect or at least they promise to advance the stock to £ 25. When it has reached that figure or sooner if I shall think proper, I shall sell the stock short. I hope to get out a good line of stock. There never was a stock so utterly worthless as this selling for so high a figure. I will keep you posted and you must keep all dark.[109]

Johnson also wrote Henry Teller at the same time that "if the mine is as worthless as I am sure that it will prove, there will be a panic in the stock now, certainly as soon as its condition can be understood. . . . I feel confident that from Lyon and from the Emma shares, I shall make a few thousand dollars." [110]

What Johnson needed to cause a decline was adverse information regarding the mine. Already there had been charges, small rumblings of discontent, which were ominous portents for the future. As early as December, 1871, Godkin's *Nation* had cautioned its American readers that the " 'monthly dividend' of the Emma Mine which sounds so attractive is not to be relied upon for the support of a family." [111] A week later the London *Times* quoted the *White Pine News* as authority for

---

[108] Schenck testimony (March 28, 1876), Statement of Losses, *ibid.*, 293, 375, 377, 806. Nevins mentions Schenck's financial transactions, stating that "when he received inside information that dividends would cease, he had not only disposed of his holdings at high prices but had tried to sell the stock short." *Hamilton Fish*, 814. This is misleading, because Schenck appears to have lost some £ 13 a share on the sale of 500 shares after the market fell. Moreover, he retained 475 of his original 500 shares throughout subsequent reorganizations until his death in 1890. See Summary of Capital and Shares to Sept. 26, 1890, Emma Company, C.R.O. 31459.

[109] To Carpenter (London, Feb. 6, 1872), Johnson MSS.

[110] To Teller (London, Feb. 19, 1872), Teller MSS.

[111] Dec. 28, 1871, 410.

the statement that the Emma Silver Mining Company, Ltd., "will have some of the tallest lawing ever known in the country," for it was rumored that "those working the mine gutted it, and can afford to let the other party stock it." [112] Naturally, such an allegation evoked an immediate refutation from Chairman Anderson. "If the mine has been 'gutted,'" he said, "the operation has been somewhat incomplete, for besides the large masses of ore known to remain at the date of purchase, more has been discovered since, and of a still richer character." [113]

Such assertions did not quiet rumors that "a large portion of the best of the cream had been skimmed." [114] Flushed by a few initial successes in selling short,[115] Hiram Johnson added his voice to the small chorus of dissidents and commenced a private bearing campaign through the distribution of circulars to shareholders. It was he who first made public the New York contract of December 9, whereby the interests of the American shareholders had been purchased at half price. If Americans who knew the situation regarding the Emma had been willing to sell at such a loss, why, then, asked Johnson, should the British public be gullible enough to buy at prices above par? [116] "Every shilling" of dividend paid had been out of capital, contrary to the *Articles* of the concern, he charged.[117] Silliman's reports were inaccurate and misleading and had been influenced by the promise of a salary largely contingent on the sale of the property. Was it mere coincidence, Johnson asked, that large discoveries of first-class ore should be announced in London the very evening before the public was invited to subscribe to Park's 8,500 shares at twenty-three pounds each? This discovery, pointed out Johnson, turned out to be on ground claimed by other parties, so that "for all practical purposes, a development in the interior of China would have been quite as interesting to the shareholders of this company." [118]

[112] Jan. 5, 1872.

[113] Anderson to editor (London, Jan. 10, 1872), *Mining World*, Jan. 13, 1872, 54.

[114] *Stock Exchange Review*, II (Jan. 1872).

[115] Johnson to Carpenter (London, March 12, 1872), Johnson MSS.

[116] Hiram A. Johnson, *The Emma Silver Mining Company, Limited* (London, April 20, 1872), *ibid.*

[117] *Ibid.* (London, May 6, 1872).

[118] Johnson insisted that Silliman had been paid $5,000 outright and $45,000 conditional to the sale. See Hiram A. Johnson circular (May 23, 1872), *Ho. Rpt.* No. 579, 857–858.

James E. Lyon, who was likewise selling short, co-operated with Johnson in bearing the market and took particular delight in attacking Park and Stewart. Park he described as "a sweet-scented pup"; the pair of them, "a damn set of villains." "I mean to raise hell with these fellows and get even with them," he is supposed to have written an associate in Utah.[119]

Officials of the Emma company were not unaware of these efforts to depress stock; they urged shareholders to disregard all circulars being issued by the "bear conspiracy."[120] Let investors beware of sharp operators and libelous charges of "gutting" the mine, cautioned editor Chisholm of the *Mining World*. In time Emma shares would climb to £50 or more.[121]

But the bears were aided by events in Utah, and reports began to filter into London that all was not well at the mine. Lyon passed on to the public information received from associates in Salt Lake City. "Emma badly caved—200 feet water—six months before ore can be raised," read one cable published in June.[122] Moreover, insisted Lyon, the Emma company was working land not within its patents but owned by the Illinois and Cincinnati Tunnel Company.[123] On June 14 a telegram stated: "Cave bad as possible—all ore now held by Illinois Tunnel, who are holding it by armed force—Emma ground 300 feet off Emma patent."[124] Two days later Lyon received the words, "Foreman of Emma shot by Illinois."[125]

The directors deprecated such "sensational" telegrams and at first refused to believe them, expressing mystification as to why the company was receiving no information.[126] The price of shares fell from £28 on June 1 to £15 3s. 4d. on June 22,[127] and the company was hard pressed to counteract the rumors flying on all sides. Finally, eleven

---

[119] To Sylvester Almy (London, May 31, 1872), *ibid.*, 199, 200.

[120] Report of meeting of the Emma Silver Mining Co. (May 8, 1872), *Mining World*, May 11, 1872, 745.

[121] *Ibid.*, April 6, 27, 1872, 512, 586–587.

[122] William Dalton to Lyon (n.p., June 10, 1872), *ibid.*, June 22, 1872, 998.

[123] To editor (London, June 6, 1872), *Mining Journal*, June 8, 1872, 538.

[124] Dalton to Lyon (n.p., June 14, 1872), *Mining World*, June 22, 1872, 998.

[125] Sylvester Almy to Lyon (n.p., June 16, 1872), *ibid.*

[126] As soon as Lyon and Johnson publicized word of a cave-in, Park immediately cabled from New York: "Mine all right. Johnson's circular a tissue of lies." *Ibid.*; London *Times*, June 18, 1872.

[127] *Ho. Rpt.* No. 579, 385.

days after the cave-in occurred, officials admitted that there had been "some leakage" in the mine, although nothing serious.[128] Directors then shrugged off share fluctuations as the "result of ignorance far from creditable to investors in mines" and tried to bolster hopes by announcing that quotations had been given on the Manchester and Glasgow Stock Exchanges.[129]

Although shares had dropped in the first half of June, they moved upward again at the end of the month and after mid-July were below their par value only once throughout the remainder of 1872.[130] Hiram Johnson was finding it more difficult than he expected to reap a profit. Early in July he confided that he was "still in a muddle with Emmas and Erie, especially the former." [131] A few days later he issued another circular, reiterating the unpalatable facts which had now been corroborated by the directors. It was now definitely established—and admitted—that mining operations had ceased at the Emma, that there had been a cave-in on June 3, that the Illinois Tunnel Company had taken possession ten days later and still retained possession, and that on July 2 the Emma Company had commenced suit to recover its property.[132] Johnson sharply criticized engineer William Blake, who had insisted that the cave-in clearly demonstrated the absence of non-ore-bearing limestone formations and only served to indicate more than ever the mine's richness. Why, asked Johnson, had all this passed unobserved before? Why had it not been mentioned in "the greatest financial *Man-Catcher of the age*—the Emma Prospectus," or by Silliman, "whose eye penetrates deep into the bowels of the earth"? [133]

Probably it was Johnson who about this same time issued a fictitious playbill advertising the Anglo-American comedy "Bubble and Squeak, or The Emma-sculated Mine of Utah," featuring the "American National Anthem" specially arranged to be sung under the leadership of Trenor Park:

> Yankee Doodle sold a mine
> Which wasn't worth a cent, boys

[128] Directors explained that the regular weekly telegram from Utah had been sent to the offices of the Ebbw Vale Company by mistake; thus they were not informed. *Mining World*, June 22, 1872, 998.

[129] *Ibid.*, July 6, 1872, 1050, 1062.   [130] *Ho. Rpt.* No. 579, 385.

[131] To Carpenter (London, July 6, 1872), Johnson MSS.

[132] *The Emma Silver Mining Company, Limited* (London, July 8, 1872), *ibid.*

[133] *Ibid.*

The Emma Silver Mining Company

To Johnny Bull for a million pounds,
And back to Vermont went, boys.

Yankee Doodle he's the lad,
He's smart and slick and handy;
Poor Johnny Bull was had so bad,
Oh Yankee Doodle dandy.[134]

On July 20 the company acknowledged that the Illinois Tunnel Company had been in possession but was now dispossessed by an injunction which would probably be made permanent during the fall session of court.[135] Park, Stewart, and a battery of other legal minds represented the Emma case before Judge McKean of the Utah bench, where, according to the *Scientific Press*, the arguments on both sides were "able and exhaustive, yet in one way the least said about them the better, as they abound in personalities not expressed in the choicest or most elegant language. 'Scoundrel,' 'thief,' and 'swindler' are not the most dignified terms for counsel to address to each other." [136]

On a subsequent visit to Utah, Chairman Anderson called litigation the "principal difficulty" of the company:

Every mine of any value here has to encounter it and as the Emma ranks in public estimation as the mine of the district, it has excited the rapacity of the black-mailers to an unusual degree. Some mines buy them off; others fight them. We have taken the latter course, and I have little doubt will succeed; but there is a very strong organization of them, and they may try other suits against us and keep us in hot water for some time. . . . Public feeling is decidedly with us: they want an accession of English capital to develop the remarkable resources of this territory, and they see that if our company was heavily robbed by "black-mailers," English capital would shun Utah for the future.[137]

By mid-November the company could report that it had won the verdict, with $5,000 awarded as damages. At the same time it announced

---

[134] This interesting broadside, undoubtedly designed for bearing purposes, is found among the Johnson MSS with no indication of its authorship.
[135] London *Times*, July 20, 1872.   [136] Aug. 3, 1872, 72.
[137] To W. Tooke (Salt Lake City, Sept. 25, 1872), Emma Silver Mining Co., *Circular to Shareholders* (n.d.), 1–2, Western Americana Collection, Yale University.

161

the purchase of the disputed Illinois tunnel.[138] Three months before that
tunnel had been described by officials as "of no value to us, being entirely barren." [139] Now in November, once purchased for £19,000, it
became "valuable for immediate extraction of ore." [140] Chairman Anderson explained the transaction by contending that, although the
claims of the Illinois Tunnel Company were "perfectly baseless," that
concern "had the power to appeal to the territorial court, and if they
failed there, they had it in their power to appeal to the United States'
Senate"—a process which might take considerable time.[141] Gone was
the talk of "fighting the blackmailers"; compromise was the order of
the day.

The armistice on the legal front was anything but welcome to the
bears, American and British alike. Several of the "Bears, Lions, Wolves,
and other Circular-writing individuals, and curbstone brokers from
America" who were after the Emma failed in July.[142] British brokers
became more deeply embroiled, sending out circulars filled with
"bloomy imaginations," through which "the paw of the 'bear' now and
then inadvertently protrudes itself." [143] But at the end of 1872 Emma
shares were holding up well.

In December the *Nation*, which could never be regarded as a friendly
critic, admitted that favorable reports from the mine and continuing
dividends were gratifying and might do much to offset foreign opinion
of American financial manipulations in other fields.[144] Hard on the
heels of this salutary, if grudging, acknowledgment came the announcement in England ("as a nice Christmas greeting") [145] that "in
prudent anticipation of winter obstruction," monthly dividends would
be deferred and a proposal submitted at the next meeting for the pay-

---

[138] London *Times,* Nov. 12, 1872.   [139] *Ibid.,* July 20, 1872.

[140] *Ibid.,* Nov. 12, 1872; *Mining Journal,* Dec. 14, 1872, 1212.

[141] Report of meeting of the Emma Silver Mining Co. (March 6, 1873), *Mining
World,* March 8, 1873, 451. Anderson was obviously more familiar with appeals
to the House of Lords in England than he was with procedure in the United
States.

[142] *Mining Journal,* Aug. 3, 1872, 734.

[143] *Ibid.,* Aug. 3, 1872, 734; Jan. 22, 1873, 365. An interesting, if ridiculous,
libel suit ensued when Messrs. Grobecker, Son & Company, who were bearing
the market, were described as "Grubeater, Son & Co." by a rival concern attempting to bull Emma shares. See *Mining World,* June 15, Nov. 9, 16, 1872, 952,
1705, 1754.

[144] Dec. 19, 1872, 399.   [145] Paffard, *True History,* 32.

ment of quarterly dividends.[146] It was to be a long, cold winter for Emma's shareholders.

This was the break for which Hiram Johnson had been waiting—except that it came too late. As early as July, Johnson had been certain that the directors would have to pass the August dividends, that the market would then break, and that he could then pick up the shares needed to meet his obligations.[147] Again in late August he wrote hopefully to a friend that the directors "cannot pay more than one or two more dividends at the most." [148] In September he was "watching the Stock with an eagle eye waiting for the stoppage of dividends." [149] But when the shares did finally drop, he was already wrecked on English rocks. By mid-December he was back in New York, "stirring around," as he put it, "endeavoring to get my grappling irons onto something or somebody where I can squeeze out some money." [150]

By the end of 1872 the company had paid thirteen monthly dividends of £15,000 each, a total of £195,000. Many shareholders "whistled in the dark," hoping against hope that suspension of monthly payments would be only temporary. Under the simple title "Emma," one shareholder from the west of Scotland expressed a blind faith in doggerel far more optimistic than enduring:

> Emma's faith and Emma's trust
> Write their characters in "dust"·
> Stamp them on the Mormon stream,
> Weigh them on the Miners' beam.
> Of her fluctuating scrip
> I will hold a firmer grip;
> She's less changeable I ween,
> Than faint-hearted suitors deem.
>
> Her I wooed in her début,
> Followed when in fame she grew;
> When the Bears her downward bore,
> Then I sought her more and more.

[146] *Mining World*, Dec. 28, 1872, 2001.
[147] To Andrew Gross (London, July 13, 1872), Johnson MSS.
[148] To Carpenter (London, Aug. 27, 1872), *ibid.*
[149] The same (Sept. 10, 1872), *ibid.*
[150] To Teller (New York, Dec. 12, 1872), Teller MSS.

Th' average of my scrip, I ween
Cost me less than seventeen,
And my dividends, I'm sure,
Are enough, and will endure.

Comrades! toast our Emma dear
Midst our New-Year's festive cheer.
Henceforth in no monthly driblets,
But in handsome quarter triplets,
Shall our Emma's gains be quoted—
So her guardians sage have voted.
Emma! best of tochered lasses!
Emma! drain in peace your glasses.[151]

On January 16, 1873, came the announcement that no dividend would be paid for February. Production had fallen off, explained the board, additional expenses had been incurred in litigation, and the mine required a great amount of retimbering. But even the directors were not wholly satisfied by their own explanations and acknowledged that further investigation was required.[152]

The displeasure of the shareholders was quickly manifest. "Let us take the bull by the horns," demanded one, "and insist on having more than sleeping directors, who are content to let the shareholders feed on the few crumbs which now and then get blown across the Atlantic from their wide-awake American cousins." [153] Others urged that the directors be made responsible for Park's misdeeds, including the "tremendous system of puffing and bulling" which enabled him to dispose of his own shares.[154] "What a history is that of 1872, with its numberless American mines, utter failures, resulting in a loss to England greater than the *Alabama* compromise," lamented an investor. "Alas! are we come to such a pass that English honour is no better than American?" [155]

Possibly half the Emma shares were held in Scotland. "Even our canny friends north of the Tweed could not resist the bait," said one

[151] By "L.G.H." of Lochgilphead (Dec. 27, 1872), *Mining World*, Jan. 4, 1873, 41.

[152] London *Times*, Jan. 16, 1873.

[153] *Mining Journal*, Feb. 1, 1873, 127. See also *Mining World*, Jan. 25, 1873, 190.

[154] *Mining Journal*, March 1, 1873, 240; Paffard, *True History*, 19.

[155] *Mining Journal*, March 1, 1873, 240.

broker's circular early in 1873. "Well! The mountain bellowed in right royal style, when lo! behold, scarcely after a twelve-month had elapsed, out creeps a very poor little mouse indeed."[156] Embittered Scots demanded action: the appointment of a commission to hire an engineer and inspect the mine independently; the transfer of the company's offices from London to Glasgow, where a more rigid supervision could be exercised; Scottish representation on the board of directors —and meanwhile the holding of a "protest" meeting in Glasgow and the sending of two delegates to the company's meetings in London.[157]

At the second annual meeting in early March the air crackled with charges and countercharges. Shareholders angrily asked why the balance sheet showed that 2,790 tons of ore sold in England and Germany bore expenses of £19 per ton when the prospectus had estimated such costs would be only £8 15s. a ton.[158] Chairman Anderson found himself embarrassed to explain why London expenses were £12,420 and why the company owed £50,000 to the Illinois Tunnel Company and to Trenor Park. He did finally admit that the final dividend had been paid from funds remitted by Park from Utah, that the ore had fallen off in value, and that nothing but discouraging words now came from the mine.[159] Archibald Orr-Ewing, one of the Glasgow emissaries, made what his colleagues termed a "slashing speech" in which he "out-Heroded Herod" and demanded that Park be ousted from the board of directors, an action which was promptly taken.[160]

As early as December, 1872, there had been complaints about the handling of affairs in Utah. A new foreman reported that on his arrival in November he found the mine "in a most dilapidated and miserable state," with no levels being driven, no shafts being sunk, and every bit

---

[156] *Mining World*, Feb. 8, 1873, 280.

[157] "A Bona Fide Shareholder" to editor (Glasgow, Jan. 17, 1873), *ibid.*, Jan. 25, 1873, 190; "A Shareholder" to editor (Glasgow, Jan. 6, 1873), *ibid.*, Jan. 11, 1873, 87; report of independent Glasgow meeting (Feb. 24, 1873), *ibid.*, March 1, 1873, 404–405.

[158] Report of meeting of the Emma Silver Mining Co., (March 6, 1873), *ibid.*, March 8, 1873, 451.

[159] Apologizing for the lack of information, Anderson explained that a nephew of Sir Selwyn Ibbetson had been sent out in the summer of 1872 to investigate but had unfortunately succumbed from sunstroke shortly after arriving in Little Cottonwood. *Ibid.*, 449, 453.

[160] Report of independent Glasgow meeting (March 13, 1873), *ibid.*, March 22, 1873, 579; *Mining Journal*, March 8, 1873, 270.

of ore in sight removed.[161] Hardly three months later the board announced that an English engineer, George Attwood, was replacing resident manager Warren Hussey, whose administration "partook too freely of an amateur character." [162]

Investigations by Attwood yielded most discouraging reports about the mine,[163] and subsequent comments by Edward Blackwell and Clarence King were equally glum. King reported in June, 1873, that "a maximum of 300 to 350 tons is all that is left of the famous Emma reserves." Asking why the "eyes of the mine had been picked out" without any countervailing development or exploration, King stated bluntly that the Emma "is with insignificant exceptions worked out, and the future of your company is hung on a mere geological chance which may be eternally against you, and if in your favor may only be secured by the wise expenditure of much time and money." [164]

It became increasingly clear to English shareholders that there would be no more dividends. The evidence piled up to prove that the Emma had really been gutted and that a gigantic fraud had been perpetrated on the investors. The Park-Schenck secret agreement was brought to light. The figures, properly analyzed, indicated that since the mine had passed into British hands it had produced less than £30,-000 in profits in fourteen months; yet thirteen dividends totaling £195,-000 had been paid during that period. The source of these dividends was laid bare. Part had been paid out of £46,300 in cash taken over from the vendor as proceeds on hand.[165] Part had been provided from the more than £76,000 taken over in ores.[166] Finally, the directors had simply borrowed £33,848 from Park to cover payment of the last two dividends.[167]

As abuse rained upon his head, Park tried to defend his actions in a

[161] J. W. Kemp to editor (Austin, Nev., Dec. 26, 1872), *Mining Journal*, Jan. 25, 1873, 102.

[162] *Mining World*, March 1, 8, 1873, 408, 449.

[163] Report of George Attwood (March 25, 1873) in Emma Silver Mining Co., *Circular to Shareholders* (April 21, 1873), 1–6. Western Americana Collection, Yale University.

[164] To W. Tooke (Salt Lake City, June 11, 1873), *Ho. Rpt.* No. 579, 634.

[165] Park had borrowed £45,000 to cover this payment and had repaid it three days later out of the purchase money for the mine. Park testimony (May 4, 1876), *ibid.*, 874–875.

[166] Park testimony (April 5, 1876), *ibid.*, 483–484.

[167] Paffard, *True History*, 33.

published letter. Insisting that all the information originally given about the Emma had been true and that the unpredictability of silver mines and ores was well known, he explained that he had sold his own shares—except a bare twenty-five—only because of suspicious and malicious comments about him on the part of British shareholders.[168] It should be noted, however, that Park was careful to divest himself of his shares before the suspension of dividends and the resulting fall in price.[169]

To irate shareholders this defense was a "most sublime piece of impudence" offered by a "modern, ill-treated Jeremiah." [170] The mine was a hoax—worthless and fraudulently introduced to the British public. "It is humiliating to one's feelings," wrote the editor of the *Railway News*, "to be told that the capitalists of the country have been cheated out of their money by one of the boldest and most impudent swindles attempted in modern times." [171] If acting with intent, the perpetrators of the scheme were "not one whit less guilty of swindling than the punished Bank of England forgers lately," cried the *Mining World*.[172]

The original prospectus was dragged out and scrutinized so that promises could be compared with performance. Schenck—although no longer a director—was asked to explain why the ore cost five times as much to extract as initially estimated; also to account for the difference between the gross of £86,400 taken out in fourteen months and the total net yield of nearly £700,000 per year set down in the prospectus. Since the company owed over £30,000 to Park, but had no unpaid calls or accrued earnings to fall back upon, there was strong fear that Park might seize the mine, and Schenck was urged to use his influence to prevent such action. If the mine were confiscated, it was contended, the directors might be held legally as well as morally responsible in the courts.[173]

The attack on Schenck was well sustained. In the summer of 1873, hardly a month before the general financial panic was to break, Samuel

---

[168] Park to directors and shareholders of the Emma Silver Mining Co. (New York, April 12, 1873), *Mining World,* May 2, 1873, 886–887.

[169] Park acknowledged that he was rid of his shares by Nov. 9, 1872. Park testimony (April 8, 1876), *Ho. Rpt.* No. 579, 553.

[170] "A Shareholder" to editor (London, May 6, 1873), *Mining Journal,* May 10, 1873, 514.

[171] Aug. 23, 1873.   [172] Nov. 22, 1873, 1020.

[173] *Ibid.,* May 17, 1873, 950–951.

T. Paffard, a small shareholder apparently operating as a "front" for some more interested person,[174] published a biting sixty-page pamphlet, *The True History of the Emma Mine*, laying bare the "facts" of this most brazen scandal. Paffard badgered Schenck persistently, demanding that the minister disavow the acts of his fellow Americans in floating the mine and threatening to send incriminating letters to influential newspapers and to President Grant and Lord Granville.[175]

Schenck did explain his position to Paffard in "a courteous and candid manner," [176] but before long he was again being condemned for his "semi-official explanation" of his connection with the company. "It is all very well as far as it goes," wrote Paffard, "but will you allow me to suggest that it does not go far enough?" [177] When Schenck studiously ignored his letters, Paffard protested to Lord Tenterden, permanent under-secretary for foreign affairs, stating that he had already laid the Emma episode before John Bright and was prepared to do likewise with President Grant.[178]

The booklet leaned heavily on the arguments of Lyon and Johnson; in fact, Park's legal adviser later called it "the Lyon story in the long clothes of babyhood." [179] But Paffard went a step farther than the two Americans, contending that the Emma had been "plastered" with rich ore before being sold on the English market.[180]

On both sides of the Atlantic *The True History of the Emma Mine* received wide attention. The *Railway News* was sympathetic,[181] but

[174] Paffard, a railway employee, described himself as "a man of moderate means." *True History*, 3. Company files show that in March, 1872, he held but two shares. Summary of Capital and Shares to March 28, 1872, C.R.O. 5809. Since these files have been weeded of all Summaries save those of every fifth year, it is impossible to judge his 1873 holdings, but they were probably small. Possibly Paffard was fronting for Alexander Macdougall.

[175] Paffard, *True History*, 42–43. See also *Mining Journal*, May 31, 1873, 604; *Mining World*, June 21, 1873, 1188.

[176] Paffard, *True History*, 45–46.

[177] Paffard wanted Schenck to persuade William Evarts, the United States counsel at the Geneva Arbitration, to hand down a legal opinion as to whether measures might be taken to obtain restitution of lost investments. *Emma Silver Mine* (printed circular, Oct. 21, 1873), F.O. 5/1452.

[178] To Lord Tenterden (Wandsworth, Nov. 7, 1873), F.O. 5/1452. On the back of this letter is a notation, signed "G," "I suppose I need take no notice of this." A brief survey of the eleven volumes of Bright papers in the British Museum shows no correspondence concerning the Emma mine.

[179] Chittenden, *Emma Mine*, 72, 74.   [180] Paffard, *True History*, 7, 8.

[181] Aug. 23, 1873.

the *Mining World* labeled it "truth highly seasoned with fiction." [182] In the United States both Godkin's *Nation* and the *Mining and Scientific Press* supported the British position,[183] while the *Utah Mining Gazette*—as might be expected—expressed a typically western viewpoint in reiterating its faith in the mine and asking if making a large profit was illegal. Although its editor could not definitely prove that Paffard was working with others who sought to control Emma shares, he saw at least "a palpable squint in that direction." [184]

Surviving an exchange of inky blows with several Americans, including Park, Stewart, and Baxter,[185] Paffard, "the Quixotic historian of the Emma Mine," [186] undauntedly issued a second Emma pamphlet early in 1874, this one adorned with a cartoon showing an eagle carrying off a dying lion, branded " £1,000,000." [187]

In the meantime attention was being focused on Schenck at home. The *Nation* thought that the gentleman had outlived his usefulness in England since "the commercial morality of the United States [was] sufficiently represented abroad without him." [188] When Louis Jennings of the New York *Times* returned from London in the summer of 1873, he imparted disturbing reports to President Grant, and as a result Schenck's case was warmly discussed in several Cabinet meetings.[189] But realizing the possible embarrassment which might stem from pressing the minister for an explanation, Grant refused to investigate,[190] and the ultimate day of reckoning was postponed.

[182] Aug. 23, 1873, 408.

[183] *Nation*, Dec. 18, 1873, 402–403; *Sci. Press,* Jan. 10, 1874, 19.

[184] Oct. 18, 1873. See also the issue for Jan. 10, 1874.

[185] *Mining Journal,* March 21, 1874, 320–321. Both Park and Paffard subsequently became embroiled in questions of libel over statements made by the editor of the *Nation* and repeated by other publications. See *Monetary and Mining Gazette,* Feb. 20, 1875; London *Times,* Oct. 21, 1874; New York *Tribune,* Dec. 4, 1875.

[186] Henry Sewell to editor (Salt Lake City, Dec. 30, 1873), *Stock Exchange Review,* IV (Jan., 1874).

[187] The title was *The Emma Silver Mining Company Scheme. How It Was Foisted on the British Public. Were the English Public Defrauded—and How? Parliamentary, Senatorial, and Professional Aid.* In the Western Americana Collection at Yale University is what appears to be a second edition of the Emma prospectus, offering 25,000 shares. On it is a curious picture showing an eagle flying off with a lion labeled £1,000,000.

[188] June 12, 1873, 393. [189] Fish Diary, IV (Aug. 5, 6, 1873), 78, 83–84.

[190] *Ibid.,* (Aug. 6, 1873), 82.

Public opinion would not, however, let the Emma die. Utahans refused to believe that the mine would not pay if its management was competent. One of the difficulties, according to a Cornish miner in Utah, was not simply that the "Yankee company took in the English tight enough" in the sale, but that "they have got the mine full of Yankees and men that scarcely ever saw a mine, or know any more about mining than an infant." The superintendent, charged the Cornishman in 1873, "didn't know the ore from any other kind of rock: he asked me and I told him, and showed him all about it." [191]

George Attwood, who replaced Warren Hussey, quickly came under fire from those in the territory. The local smelters complained that his work was wasteful,[192] and "the celebrated English, Freiberg, Chilian, Peruvian and Mexican expert in the limestone formation, Mr. Henry Sewell," [193] criticized management on both sides of the Atlantic. In several letters reprinted in the mining press and in a pamphlet published in 1875, Sewell held that British management was generally inferior to American and that the Emma had not paid substantial dividends simply because it had been led astray by wastrels in charge.[194]

Utahans seemed generally agreed that the mine was good [195] but that the sale price had been too high and that skullduggery abroad was responsible for evil days. The vein may have been pinched out, but Manager Attwood could find it again "when convenient," it was insisted. "We believe that Mr. Park, Mr. Attwood, Mr. Anderson, Brydges Williams [*sic*] and others, are alike interested in 'pinching' the stock as well as the ore," said the *Utah Mining Gazette*.[196] If swindling had been accomplished, it had been done by directors and officials of the shareholders' own choosing, insisted the *Salt Lake Herald*.[197] At the mine Attwood was "exceedingly generous, not to say lavish," in disbursing the company's funds. The *Herald* could point to more than £11,000 paid for hauling some five thousand tons of ore from the mine

[191] John Kitto to editor (Alta, Utah, March 24, 1873), *Mining Journal,* April 19, 1873, 430.

[192] *Utah Mining Gazette,* June 13, 1874.   [193] *Ibid.,* April 15, 1873.

[194] *Sci. Press,* Jan. 3, 1874, 2; *Mining Journal,* Jan. 17, 1874, 77. The pamphlet was titled *The Emma Mine. Its Past and Present Mismanagement, and Its Future Prospects.* Complete with illustrations of the mine and the young lady after whom it was named, its main purpose was to show the superiority of American management. *Monetary & Mining Gazette,* April 24, 1875.

[195] *Utah Mining Gazette,* Nov. 1, 1873.   [196] March 14, 1874.

[197] March 6, May 27, 1874.

to the railroad—a rate of about eleven dollars a ton. "We should think the teamsters ought to feel particularly grateful," snorted the editor.[198]

Nor were other Americans unaware of the damage done by the Emma episode. The *St. Louis Democrat* was of the opinion that the sale of the property and the manner in which it was accomplished had "done more injury to the mines and mining in the Territory of Utah than years of large discoveries and successful development can efface." [199] Certainly it did work as a detriment to British investment in Utah and in other western regions. B. A. M. Froiseth, late in 1873, mentioned that English capitalists were now so skeptical of Utah enterprises that they were refusing to invest until confidence had been restored—all because of "the rascality of a few dishonest speculators, who, like Esau, have sold their birthright for a mess of pottage." [200]

In California J. Barr Robertson was considering entering into an arrangement with Senator Jones of Nevada whereby the latter might try to float a California mining scheme in London. The only drawback, confided Robertson to a friend in England, was that "one objectionable man"—Senator Stewart—was connected with the proposed undertaking.[201] A week later Robertson had made a decision. "I find on enquiry," he said, "that Mr. Trenor W. Park is associated with Senator Stewart & Senator Jones in the Panamint business, so I think I have gone far enough into that project." [202] A British observer saw the influence of the Emma as far afield as Colorado in 1876. "Since the 'Emma' swindle," wrote Samuel Nugent Townshend, "English capital has been steadily withheld from these mines; and there is very little machinery in this San Juan district." [203]

Meanwhile, as if mismanagement and nonpayment of dividends were not enough, Park demanded the £33,848 owed him by the company, and when it failed to materialize he attached the mine in September, 1874.[204] A new directorate promptly instructed the firm of Shipman, Barlow, Larocque & MacFarland in New York to bring action against the American promoters for £1,000,000 and other damages,[205] thus commencing a suit that was to drag on for more than five years.

[198] May 27, 1874.   [199] Jan. 12, 1874.
[200] *Utah Mining Gazette,* Aug. 30, 1873.
[201] To J. W. Walker (n.p., Nov. 30, 1874), Robertson Letterbook.
[202] The same (n.p., Dec. 7, 1874), *ibid.*   [203] *Colorado,* 11.
[204] *Mining Journal,* Jan. 30, 1875, 109; *Economist,* Jan. 15, 1876, 65.
[205] *Mining Journal,* Jan. 30, 1875, 109; London *Times,* April 1, 1875. For cor-

This litigation helped keep alive the controversy and to keep Schenck in the public eye, for the general gave voluntary testimony which could be used in defending his fellow Americans. On one hand, friends like Reverdy Johnson, himself a former minister to Britain, went out of their way to support the belabored diplomat,[206] while, on the other side, both the *Nation* and the *New York Tribune* loudly demanded governmental investigation and, if necessary, action on behalf of British shareholders.[207]

In response to this agitation Representative Pierce of Massachusetts in February, 1876, introduced a resolution in the House, which was adopted, calling for the Committee on Foreign Affairs to ascertain what executive action had been taken in regard to Schenck's connection with the Emma mine.[208] The report submitted by the committee was brief and colorless,[209] yet sufficiently revealing to warrant further investigation. Consequently, on February 28 Thomas Swann, Maryland Democrat, procured the passage of a resolution in the House authorizing the Committee on Foreign Affairs to inquire further into Schenck's part in the Emma scheme.[210]

As soon as the Pierce resolution came to Schenck's ears, he cabled the Secretary of State offering to resign if the adverse publicity of the affair had embarrassed the administration.[211] Fish at first rejected this offer [212] but two days later reversed his position, informing Schenck that while the administration had not lost faith in him his connection with the Emma was an "unfortunate indiscretion" and that a resignation would relieve any embarrassment.[213]

---

respondence handing over information and evidence to the American law firm see *Emma Silver Mining Company, (Limited)* (n.p., 1876), 1–14, Western Americana Collection, Yale University.

[206] Reverdy Johnson to editor (London, Dec. 13, 1875), *Baltimore American and Commercial Advertiser,* Dec. 31, 1875.

[207] *Nation,* Jan. 6, 1876, 5–6; New York *Tribune,* Nov. 24, 1875; Jan. 15, Feb. 1, 1876.

[208] *Congressional Record,* Feb. 7, 1876, 921.

[209] Connection of Hon. Robert C. Schenck with the Emma Mine and Machado Claim, *Ho. Rpt.* No. 123, 44 Cong., 1 Sess. (1875–1876).

[210] *Congressional Record,* Feb. 28, 1876, 1345.

[211] To Fish (London, Feb. 8, 1876), Copy, Dispatches, Great Britain, CXXVIII.

[212] To Schenck (Washington, Feb. 9, 1876), *ibid.*

[213] To Schenck (Washington, Feb. 11, 1876), *ibid.,* CXXIX.

Within a week Schenck mailed his resignation to the State Department,[214] then cabled asking for a leave of absence to appear in Washington before the Foreign Affairs Committee.[215] His resignation was
promptly accepted, despite his last-minute request that it be set aside
while the investigation was under way.[216] Probably Republican stalwarts who deemed such action politically necessary forced acceptance
upon Grant.[217]

As testimony piled up in Washington, Schenck left England with
indecent haste.[218] Although Fish defended him, rumors were prevalent
in London that Schenck had been recalled at the request of the British
government, and Under-Secretary of State for Foreign Affairs Bourke
was called upon to deny such a rumor in the House of Commons.[219]
The *Times,* on the other hand, reported that it was believed in Washington that Fish strongly expected an English claim against the United
States on behalf of Englishmen who had suffered in the Emma fiasco.[220]
No such claim was ever made, however, although Parliament threatened to investigate the entire affair.[221]

Testimony before the House Committee on Foreign Affairs began
on February 28 and continued throughout March and intermittently
into early May. All major participants in the promotion of the company
were present save Albert Grant, who tendered written testimony. The
verdict of the committee, predominantly Democratic in make-up, after
weighing a mass of conflicting evidence, was not favorable to Schenck.
He had acted indiscreetly and by identifying himself with the company without consulting the State Department he had placed himself
"in a false position with his own government." By accepting special

[214] To Grant (London, Feb. 17, 1876), *ibid.*
[215] To Fish (London, Feb. 21, 1876), *ibid.*
[216] Fish to Schenck (Washington, Feb. 23, 1876); Schenck to Fish (London,
March 2, 1876), *ibid.;* Fish to Schenck (Washington, April 5, 1876), Fish Letter
Copy Book, XV, 294.
[217] See Thornton to Derby (Washington, March 13, 1876), F.O. 5/1538; Fish to
James A. Garfield (Washington, Feb. 10, 1876), Fish Letter Copy Book, XV, 214.
[218] *Hour,* March 30, 1876; Wickham Hoffman to Fish (London, April 15, 1876),
Fish Corr., CXIII, 19564.
[219] Fish to Thomas Swann (Washington, Nov. 19, 1876), *Ho. Rpt.* No. 579, 4;
Hansard's Parliamentary Debates, 3d ser., CCXXVII, 1798.
[220] March 10, 1876.
[221] *Hansard's Parliamentary Debates,* 3d ser., CCXXIX, 1352–1353.

favors from the vendors and by lending his name to the prospectus, he had "placed himself in a further false position with the public." [222] While Schenck was absolved of fraud or fraudulent intent, the committee saw his relations with the vendors as casting suspicion on his motives and subjecting him to unfavorable criticism.[223] Finally, the committee deemed his subsequent speculative dealings in Emma shares "not compatible with his diplomatic usefulness at the court near which he was accredited." [224]

These unanimous findings led to the submission of a resolution condemning Schenck's relation with the company "as ill-advised, unfortunate, and incompatible with the duties of his official position." [225] This censure resolution was adopted by the House in July,[226] but not before petitions from the "honest miners of Utah" had been sent to Congress, complaining that the published reports of the investigation "misled the public in respect to the mines of Utah and are most unjust to the Emma mine." [227] The mines of the territory were extremely valuable, continued the memorials: "The only cause of failure has been the very wasteful, negligent, and unskillful management in the hands of a foreign corporation." [228]

By adopting the resolution the legislative arm of the federal government saw fit to reprimand Schenck, whereas the executive branch had been unwilling to do so for a period of more than four years. The United States had a new minister to Great Britain; at the same time another scandal had been officially added to the growing list of the Grant administration. A reprimand was given, true, but no restitution of money was demanded. As he dispatched copies of the committee's 883-page report and comments from the *Congressional Record* to the British Foreign Office, Sir Edward Thornton could categorize these documents sardonically under the heading of "Preservation of American Honour." [229]

While "American Honour" was being preserved, the company was having its difficulties and upheavals at home as well as in America. A

---

[222] *Ho. Rpt.* No. 579, viii.　　　[223] *Ibid.*, xvi.　　　[224] *Ibid.*　　　[225] *Ibid.*

[226] *Congressional Record,* July 12, 1876, 4520.

[227] Two memorials carried a total of 252 signatures. *Congressional Record,* March 24, 1876, 1964.

[228] *Mining Journal,* April 15, 1876, 428.

[229] To Derby (May 29, 1876), F.O. 5/1539; the same (June 5, 1876), F.O. 5/1540.

rebellion led by Alexander Macdougall, "an obstinate and pugnacious Scotchman, with a long purse and an unpleasant temper," [230] assumed control on a program of suing all parties connected with floating the company.[231] After surviving a petition to wind up the company, the board under General R. M. Gardiner was thrown out late in 1875 as the Macdougallites rode into power.[232]

The new Macdougall directorate, as part of its avowed policy, pressed the case pending in the New York courts against the American vendors, issuing debentures to provide funds.[233] In April, 1877, however, the case was decided against the company, the court holding that no fraud was perpetrated in the Emma sale.[234] The circuit court denied petitions for a new trial but did admit that "the evidence discloses many circumstances connected with the sale of the Emma Mine, which strongly impeach the honor and morality of the transaction, but which are to be entirely eliminated from the case, except as far as they bear upon the question of fraud in law." [235]

"The vindication goes beyond the parties in the suit," commented the New York *Evening Post.* "It relieves Ex-Minister Schenck and Professor Silliman from the taint of fraud." [236] Macdougall, however, felt far less satisfied and insisted that the verdict had been unfairly reached.[237]

In the meantime he had not been idle on the English scene. Early in

[230] New York *Tribune,* Jan. 17, 1876.

[231] See *Mining World,* May 16, June 13, 1874, 882–883, 1108–1109; Alexander W. Macdougall, *The Emma Mine* (n.p., 1874), 6.

[232] Report of meeting of the Emma Silver Mining Co. (Nov. 10, 1875), *Mining Journal,* Nov. 13, 1875, 1265. For the winding-up petition see *ibid.,* May 8, 1875, 496; Emma Silver Mining Co., *Circular to Shareholders* (April 29, 1875), 1–12, Western Americana Collection, Yale University.

[233] London *Times,* March 19, 1877.

[234] *Ibid.,* April 30, 1877. For the great mass of evidence and testimony submitted by both sides see *The Emma Silver Mining Company, (Limited) of London, vs. Trenor W. Park and H. Henry Baxter, Impleaded, Complainants' Testimony* (1088 pp.) and *Defendants' Testimony* (823 pp.). Printed in 1877, these duplicate much of the material in *Ho. Rpt.* No. 579. They are in the Western Americana Collection, Yale University.

[235] The question was not whether individual shareholders were fraudulently induced to buy shares but whether the English directors were induced to purchase the mine by misrepresentation or concealment of material facts. Emma Silver Mining Co. *v.* Trenor W. Park and H. H. Baxter, 14 *Blatchford* (1878), 420–422.

[236] April 30, 1877.

[237] London *Times,* March 6, 1878; *E. & M. Jour.,* Oct. 2, 1880, 225.

1876 he brought legal action against Albert Grant, "the terror of the City," for return of the promotion money on the grounds of fraud. Baron Grant promptly offered to bargain with Park for return of the mine to the company and to provide £10,000 as working capital, providing all suits were dropped.[238] Ignoring this proposal, Macdougall pressed his suit and a few weeks later reported that all the Utah holdings had been sold to an agent of Park by a United States deputy marshal and that the company had no legal property whatsoever.[239] Here was another opportunity for the Stock Exchange wags to bombard their favorite target:

> Titles a King can give, but honour can't.
> Title, without honor, is a barren grant:
> Sad, 'tis true, but a worse dilemma
> To be without a title, like the Emma.[240]

As the concern "descended from a mining company into a lawing company," to use the words of Macdougall,[241] it brought and won a suit against Lewis and Son, Liverpool metal brokers, charging that this firm conspired with Park to sell them the Emma while knowing that the mine was worth but a fraction of the price asked on the English market.[242] At the same time the Macdougall machine moved against the promoters, the original directors, and certain of the firms that had

[238] *Hour,* Jan. 18, 20, 1876; report of meeting of the Emma Silver Mining Co. (Jan. 21, 1876), *Mining Journal,* Jan. 22, 1876, 85. Grant's offer is printed in *Ho. Rpt.* No. 579, 40–43.

[239] Report of meeting of the Emma Silver Mining Co. (Feb. 5, 1876), *Mining Journal,* Feb. 12, 1876, 183.

[240] Quoted in Furniss, *Some Victorian Men,* 85.

[241] Report of meeting of the Emma Silver Mining Co. (Nov. 24, 1876), *Mining Journal,* Nov. 25, 1876, 1306.

[242] Lewis and Son were ordered to pay damages of £8,188 in restitution of profits gained by their activities in the Emma undertaking. London *Times,* June 29, 1878; May 15, 1879; Jan. 13, 1880; Emma Silver Mining Co. *v.* Lewis and Son, 4 *Common Pleas Division* (1879), 396–410. Arthur Lewis had written his father from the mine in the summer of 1871: "At present nearly all the kidney has been taken out of the suet in the desire to extract ore." He denied, however, that this was meant as an unfavorable comment and insisted that although the firm had received 250 fully paid Emma shares as compensation for reduced commissions on ore and that his father had been asked to introduce Park to prospective buyers, they had actually played no part in forming the company. London *Times,* June 26, 27, 1878.

received exorbitant fees in floating the company.[243] Most of these settled out of court, leaving Albert Grant to fight the case alone.[244] Despite Grant's protests the court's decision went against him. In summing up the judgment, the Master of the Rolls pointed out that it was fraud to tell the public that the mine was being sold for £1,000,000, when actually there was a secret agreement that £200,000 of this sum was to be retained by the promoter for his and others' expenses.[245] The defendant was thereupon ordered to pay over to the company £105,938 6s. 11d., but there is some doubt that he was able to do so.[246]

By mid-December, 1879, Chairman Macdougall could inform the shareholders that all suits in English courts were completed and that under his leadership the company had realized a total of £32,850 13s. 10d. In addition, another £148,657 had been legally recovered but not yet realized.[247] Not every battle had been won, for the company failed in its £1,000,000 recovery suits on both sides of the Atlantic. Still, something had been salvaged from the wreck, and except for pending appeals the "lawing" was over.[248]

But what of the property—the "fabulous" Emma mine—during this time? As Macdougall explained in 1877, the only "property" the company had owned for two years was litigation.[249] Park had taken over

---

[243] In one suit action was brought against Albert and Maurice Grant, George Anderson, J. H. Puleston, Park, Baxter, Schenck, Stewart, a Mr. Lincoln (who had purchased the mine for Park), and the Emma Silver Mining Co. of New York. Emma Silver Mining Co. v. Grant, et al., 11 Chancery Appeals (1879), 918. Since all but Anderson and the Grant brothers were in the United States, they could not be touched.

[244] The old directors agreed to pay £14,775, plus guarantees for part of the costs of American litigation. Bishoff, Bompas, & Bishoff, the original solicitors, returned their entire fee of £2,000, while the auditing firm paid over £1,500. Ibid., 931; report of meeting of the Emma Silver Mining Company, Ltd. (Oct. 16, 1877), Mining Journal, Oct. 20, 1877, 1162; report of meeting of the Emma Silver Mining Company, Ltd. (Dec. 10, 1878), ibid., Dec. 14, 1878, 1392.

[245] Emma Silver Mining Co. v. Grant, et al., 11 Chancery Appeals (1879), 935.

[246] Ibid., 940–941. Grant filed bankruptcy proceedings and was apparently able to wiggle out of paying. See Emma Silver Mining Co. v. Grant, 17 Chancery Division (1880), 122; Financial Critic, Feb. 6, 1886.

[247] Report of meeting of the Emma Silver Mining Co. (Dec. 17, 1879), Mining Journal, Dec. 20, 1879, 1302.

[248] For several lawsuits among Americans connected with the Emma see New York Evening Post, April 30, 1877; E. & M. Jour., Aug. 1, 1885, 83.

[249] Mining Journal, Feb. 24, 1877, 212.

the mine and in October, 1877, had organized the American Emma Company, a New York concern, with Schenck as one of the leading lights.[250] An English expert who visited the property about this time found nineteen men at work "and the premises marked, alas, only by a few tumble-down wooden sheds on a very small scale, presenting no external appearance of much outlay." [251] Since 1874 the mine had been worked little, and it had deteriorated. Directors' fees had been cut back during these idle years, as the company grimly hung on, hoping against hope for better days.

After 1872 Emma shares became worth little on the English market. Their price on New Year's Day, 1876, ranged from £1 to £1 5s., and by the end of the year from 7/6 to 12/6.[252] Their low esteem is indicated by an advertisement appearing in the *Mining Journal* in January, 1875:

SHARES WANTED;—CEDAR CREEK, EMMA, WEST ESGAIR LLE, or others, marketable. A Gentleman has a large collection of OIL and WATER-COLOURED DRAWINGS which he WISHES TO EXCHANGE. An easy way of acquiring a collection.[253]

For a mining company with no mine and very little capital the future seemed far from bright.

In 1880, however, it seemed faintly possible that the property might pass into English hands again. In November of that year Park and the American Emma Company consented to hand back the mine and £49,663 in exchange for shares in a reorganized British company, a guarantee that all proceedings against the American defendants and Albert Grant would be discontinued, and mutual releases on both sides.[254] In mid-October, 1881, Macdougall was able to announce that the British company now had clear title to the mine and that the formation of a new concern might be undertaken.[255]

Consequently, in January of the following year the New Emma Silver

---

[250] *The New York Mining Directory* (New York, 1880), 1.

[251] Henry Hussey Vivian, *Notes of a Tour in America* (London, 1878), 112.

[252] *Mining Journal*, Sept. 16, 1876, 1029; Feb. 24, 1877, 197.

[253] *Ibid.*, Jan. 23, 1875, 77.

[254] Memo. of Agreement (Nov. 9, 1880) between O. A. Gager (attorney for T. W. Park and the American Emma Co.) and Alexander W. Macdougall. This was incorporated into a subsequent Memo. of Agreement (March 15, 1882) between Macdougall and the New Emma Silver Mining Co., C.R.O. 16300.

[255] London *Times*, Oct. 17, 1881.

Mining Company, Ltd., was incorporated in London, acquiring from the old company, now in liquidation, the mine, the plant, and the lease of a tunnel granted by a Utah concern.[256] The British shareholders were now back in business, but as work progressed the risks and uncertainties of mining became more and more apparent. Although rays of hope shone dimly through gloomy *Annual Reports,* the Emma never prospered. Here was the old story of will-o'-the-wisp riches always in the immediate future, but never nearer.

Ore bodies did not develop. In 1884 and again in the following year snowslides swept across the property, killing in all seven employees, causing expensive damage, and bringing a loss of more than a year's working time to the company.[257] These avalanches also brought the need for further capital, raised at first through the issue of additional mortgage debentures,[258] then later by means of reorganizing as the New Emma Silver Mining Company, 1886, Ltd.[259]

But difficulties continued. Miners refused to remain at the mine during the early winter months;[260] the manager had to be dismissed for making exaggerated statements about resources and results.[261] Another reorganization in 1890 [262] also proved to no avail, nor did a complete turnover of personnel at the mines bring improvement. Ruinous pumping costs forced work at the Emma to be abandoned; the new Grizzly and Lavinia group of claims, purchased "at a reasonable

[256] *Mem. & Art.,* 1. Nominal capital was £700,000 in 70,000 shares of £10 each, of which 67,493 were to be issued fully paid. Memo. of Agreement (March 15, 1882) between Alexander Macdougall and the New Emma Silver Mining Co., C.R.O. 16300.

[257] Annual reports of the New Emma Silver Mining Co. for years ending Dec. 31, 1884 and 1885.

[258] A total of £22,470 in debentures were issued at 50 per cent discount. New Emma Silver Mining Co., *Annual Report,* year ending Dec. 31, 1885.

[259] Nominal capital was £350,000 in £1 shares. By exchanging new shares, partially paid up, for old ones, some £15,000 was raised. *Mem. & Art.,* 6; Memo. of Agreement (May 29, 1886) between the New Emma Silver Mining Co. and Richard L. Hobbes, C.R.O. 22546.

[260] New Emma Silver Mining Co., 1886, *Annual Report,* year ending June 30, 1889.

[261] The new manager was Charles Bennett, a shareholder and "a gentleman of high position" in Salt Lake City, *ibid.*

[262] This was the Emma Company, with nominal capital of £125,000 in shares of 5/– each. Memo. of Agreement (May 23, 1890) between the New Emma Silver Mining Co., 1886, and the Emma Company, Emma Company, Ltd., C.R.O. 31459.

price," [263] failed to live up to expectations. Efforts to lease them also proved unproductive.[264]

In the face of the low price of silver and the depression of 1893 officials hesitated to sink further capital into the mines. In 1894 the directors could see but two choices: either sell the property and go out of business or raise more funds and transfer operations to Africa or Australia, retaining the Utah holdings until the price of silver rose and mining could be resumed with profit.[265]

The latter course was taken. The shareholders voted to wind up voluntarily and reconstruct—for the fourth time since the original incorporation of 1871. Little wonder that the editor of the *Economist* protested vigorously against another attempt to keep this "shocking example" of limited-liability enterprise alive. The Emma mine, said the *Economist*, was "an historic institution," which in its time had "gone through as many vicissitudes as most mundane things." [266]

Thus in the summer of 1895 the newly reorganized Emma Company, Ltd., acquired sixty acres in Coolgardie, Western Australia, and thirty-two acres in New South Wales, retaining the Utah property but making no attempts to work it.[267] This and the final reorganization, the Emma Company (1900), Ltd., were interested only in disposing of the Emma and concentrated on the New South Wales operations until the company voted voluntary liquidation in 1902.[268]

From 1882 till activity ceased in Utah in 1895, the English company consistently operated at a loss, as the following figures show:

[263] The "reasonable price" was £6,449 19s. Annual reports of the Emma Company for years ending June 30, 1892 and 1893.

[264] Annual reports of the Emma Company for years ending June 30, 1893 and 1894.

[265] Emma Company, *Annual Report,* year ending June 30, 1894. Directors implied that low prices were the basis of the company's ills. Actually, very little ore was available, and even had silver been as high as in 1871 the concern would have continued to suffer.

[266] Jan. 13, 1894, 45; April 6, 1895, 455.

[267] Memo. of Agreement (July 8, 1895) between the Emma Company and the Emma Company [1895], C.R.O. 44457; Skinner, *Mining Manual* (1896), 937; annual reports of the Emma Company for years ending June 30, 1896 and 1899.

[268] Certificate of Incorporation (May 30, 1900). Shareholders voted to wind up in 1902, but the final meeting was not held until 1908. At that time it was voted that all company records and papers be retained for three months, then destroyed by the liquidator. *Special Resolution,* passed Dec. 3, 1908, Emma Co. (1900), C.R.O. 66097.

The Emma Silver Mining Company

Year	Total loss incurred [269]
1882	£ 4,972
1883	11,744
1884	9,486
1885	20,813
1887	15,020
1888	16,537
1889	12,878
1891	9,480
1892	8,682
1893	10,245
1894	5,657
Total	£ 125,514

The grand total for this period was about £125,500. The greatest deficit, in 1885, was caused largely by snowslide damages and loss of working time. London expenses also contributed to the sad results of some years. Of the total deficit for 1892, for example, £3,368 of the total of £8,682 was put down as loss on the British side of the Atlantic.[270] In 1894 the London figure was actually greater than the losses incurred at the mine.[271]

It took nearly a quarter of a century for English shareholders to become convinced that the Emma mine was not a paying proposition; it took another decade before the hapless wench was abandoned to American concerns.[272] But before that happened the Emma had had her day and left an imprint on the British mind that was not soon

[269] Compiled from annual reports, 1882–1894. The figures for 1887 include the period from April 28, 1886, to Dec. 31, 1887, leaving a gap from Dec. 31, 1885, to April 28, 1886. The entry for 1888 is for the year ending June 30, 1888, and thus overlaps six months on the previous figure. The figure for 1891 covers the period from April 30, 1890, to June 30, 1891, leaving a gap of ten months which is not covered.

[270] Emma Co., *Annual Report*, year ending June 30, 1892.

[271] The mine lost £2,396 11*d.* for the twelve months; the total deficit was £5,656 15*s.* 8*d.* Emma Co., *Annual Report*, year ending June 30, 1894.

[272] In the autumn of 1916 the Emma Consolidated Mines Co. was formed in Delaware to acquire the stock of companies then owning title to the property. J. J. Beeson, *Report on the Property of the Emma Silver Mines Company in Little Cottonwood Mining District, Alta, Utah* (n.p., 1919), 16, 31. By 1940 "Mayor" George H. Watson of Alta was the owner of the Emma, consolidated with thirty-three other locations. Federal Writers' Project, *Utah* (New York, 1941), 287.

erased. It was a Mormon historian who wrote that after the initial transfer of the mine to English ownership, "Its subsequent history was not enviable." [273] So far as the Emma was concerned, such modesty and understatement could only have stemmed from the American side of the Atlantic.

[273] Orson F. Whitney, *History of Utah* (Salt Lake City, 1893), II, 273.

A NEW

NURSERY BALLAD,

EMBELLISHED WITH FINELY-ENGRAVED

PORTRAITS

OF SOME OF THE MOST *EMMANENT*

MEN OF THE DAY.

SEVENTY-EIGHTH EDITION.

———

The earth hath bubbles, as the water has,
And these are of them.—Macbeth.

———

SALT LAKE CITY, UTAH.

PUBLISHED BY AND FOR EMMA A. SELL.

1872.

PRICE TO ENGLISH SUBSCRIBERS, £1,000,000.

Cover of a pamphlet "bearing" Emma shares which was published in 1872, probably by the Lyon-Johnson combination. The rest of the pamphlet follows on pp. 184–190. (Johnson Corr.; courtesy of the Bancroft Library.)

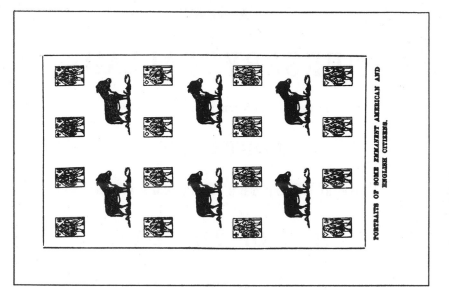

PORTRAITS OF SOME EMINENT AMERICAN AND ENGLISH CITIZENS.

To prevent unnecessary application, it may be mentioned that translations of this work in the following languages are already in the press:—FRENCH, GERMAN, SANSCRIT, IRISH, HEBREW, TURKISH, PENNSYLVANIA DUTCH, CHINESE, SPANISH, CHENOOK, RUSSIAN, TAMUL, and BOHEMIAN.

6

This is the Ore that lay in the Mine that Lyon struck.

5

This is the Mine that Lyon struck.

8

These are the Yanks from the Eastern shore, that joined the Men who had cleaned out the Ore, that lay in the Mine that Lyon struck.

7

These are the Men that cleaned out the Ore, that lay in the Mine that Lyon struck.

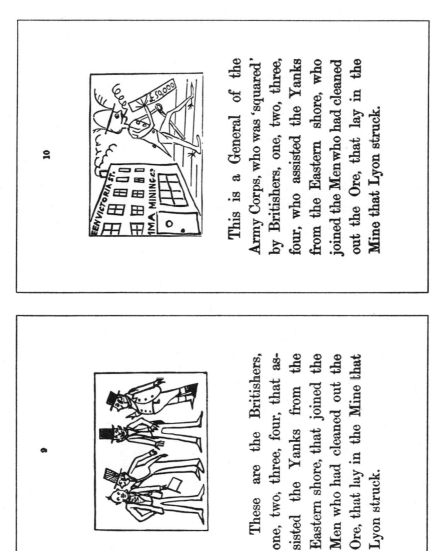

This is a General of the Army Corps, who was 'squared' by Britishers, one, two, three, four, who assisted the Yanks from the Eastern shore, who joined the Men who had cleaned out the Ore, that lay in the Mine that Lyon struck.

These are the Britishers, one, two, three, four, that assisted the Yanks from the Eastern shore, that joined the Men who had cleaned out the Ore, that lay in the Mine that Lyon struck.

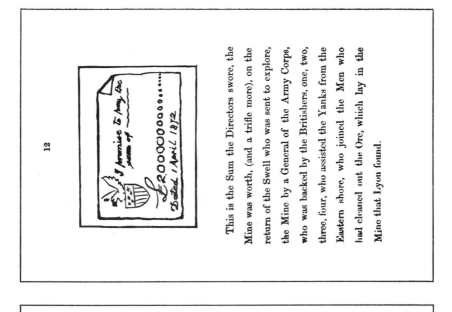

This is the Sum the Directors swore, the Mine was worth, (and a trifle more), on the return of the Swell who was sent to explore, the Mine by a General of the Army Corps, who was backed by the Britishers, one, two, three, four, who assisted the Yanks from the Eastern shore, who joined the Men who had cleaned out the Ore, which lay in the Mine that Lyon found.

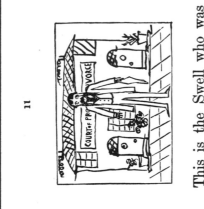

This is the Swell who was sent to explore the Mine by a General of the Army Corps, and was backed by the Britishers, one, two, three, four, that assisted the Yanks from the Eastern shore, that joined the Men who had cleaned out the Ore, that lay in the Mine that Lyon struck.

14

This is the way the Water did pour, into the Mine which *somebody* swore, was worth a Million Pounds or more, on the return of the Swell who was sent to explore, the Mine by a General of the Army Corps, who was backed by the Britishers, one, two, three, four, who went in with the Yanks from the Eastern shore, who joined the Men who had cleaned out the Ore, that lay in the Mine that Lyon found.

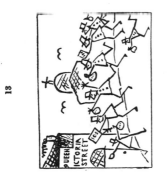

18

These are the Dupes who insanely tore, to subscribe the Sum the Directors swore, was worth a Million of Pounds and more, on the return of the Swell who was sent to explore, the Mine by a General of the Army Corps, who was backed by the Britishers, one, two, three, four, who shared with the Yanks from the Eastern shore, who joined with the Men who had cleaned out the Ore that lay in the Mine that Lyon struck.

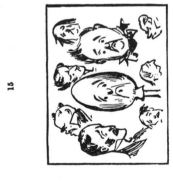

15

These are the Faces the Subscribers wore, after the Water began to pour, into the Mine that *somebody* swore, was worth a Million Pounds or more, on the report of the Swell who was sent to explore, the Mine by a General of the Army Corps, who was backed by the Britishers, one, two, three, four, who winked at the Yanks from the Eastern shore, who joined with the Men who had cleaned out the Ore, that lay in the Mine that Lyon struck.

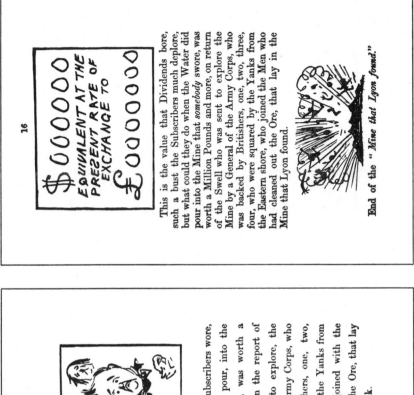

16

$ 000000
EQUIVALENT AT THE PRESENT RATE OF EXCHANGE TO
£ 0000000

This is the value that Dividends bore, such a bust the Subscribers much deplore, but what could they do when the Water did pour into the Mine that *somebody* swore, was worth a Million Pounds and more, on return of the Swell who was sent to explore the Mine by a General of the Army Corps, who was backed by Britishers, one, two, three, four, who were squared by the Yanks from the Eastern shore, who joined the Men who had cleaned out the Ore, that lay in the Mine that Lyon found.

End of the "*Mine that Lyon found.*"

: CHAPTER IX :

Relations with the
Federal Government

IF the Emma Silver Mining Company, Ltd., provides a good insight into most of the problems of organization, finance, and operation faced by Anglo-American western mining concerns, neither it nor any other single company can adequately illustrate the perplexities which often stemmed from the relationship of the alien or the alien corporation to the federal government's policy of disposing of public mineral lands. This relationship was probably even more confusing than some of the other aspects of American mining law and brought wide disagreement in interpretation by the judiciary. Legal experts have noted that decisions in several western localities prior to 1900 showed "differences of opinion, diversity of view, and unharmonious conclusions" where alien ownership was concerned.[1]

Part of the difficulty stemmed from the fact that the federal government consistently pursued a liberal policy toward exploitation of the mineral wealth and enacted only a few laws, relatively simple ones at that, to govern this process. At the same time local regulations and

---

[1] Curtis H. Lindley, *A Treatise on the American Law Relating to Mines and Mineral Lands within the Public Land States and Territories and Governing the Acquisition and Enjoyment of Mining Rights in Lands of the Public Domain* (San Francisco, 1897), I, 278–279. Cited hereafter as Lindley, *Mining Law.*

precedents were given important recognition. Thus the courts found themselves compelled to fall back on a heterogeneous mass of earlier decisions handed down under widely varying circumstances and with interpretations that were equally diverse.

Local regulation was dominant until the early seventies. Indeed, no major federal mining legislation was enacted until 1866, when a congressional act recognized to a great degree the customs that prevailed in various localities.[2] In 1872 the national government reappraised the situation and wrote into the statutes a basic mining law. All valuable mineral deposits and the public lands in which they were found were to be free and open to exploration and purchase from the government "by citizens of the United States and those who have declared their intention to become such."[3] The original bill had provided that "any person" might take up mineral claims under the prescribed rules and conditions, but the Senate struck out that phrase in favor of the more restrictive one,[4] thus excluding aliens from participation.

As a matter of fact debates prior to the passage of the measure indicated that one of the reasons behind it was the fear that large tracts of mining land in the West might fall into the hands of capitalists living abroad who would do nothing to develop it.[5] This along with similar fears of American capitalists and speculators led Congress to require some sort of evidence of development before final title might be obtained from the government.

Consequently, in addition to limiting the size of mining claims and laying down rules governing location and recording, the act of May 10, 1872, prescribed certain conditions to be met before a patent could be issued completing title.[6] On each claim located after the passage of the law not less than $100 in labor or improvements was to be invested each year,[7] and proof that at least $500 had been so expended was made a prerequisite for receipt of patent from the federal

[2] Act of July 26, 1866, 14 *U.S. Statutes,* 251, 253.
[3] Act of May 10, 1872, 17 *ibid.,* 91.
[4] *Congressional Globe,* April 29, 1872, 2898.   [5] *Ibid.,* April 16, 1872, 2459.
[6] Claims were not to be more than 1,500 feet long along the vein or lode and no more than 300 feet in width along both sides of the middle of the vein at the surface. Act of May 10, 1872, 17 *U.S. Statutes,* 91.
[7] On claims located before passage of the act $10 for each 100 feet in length was to be expended per year until patent was issued. *Ibid.,* 93.

Land Office.[8] Citizenship or declaration of intent must be affirmed when application was made.[9]

What practical effect, if any, did this law of 1872 have upon the British subject or corporation interested in acquiring mineral holdings in the West? Englishmen were quick to note the passage of the act and to seek clarification of their own status under it. Hardly a month after its enactment the editor of the *Mining Journal* explained to his readers what a United States patent was, described how it was obtained, and attempted to quiet "disconcerting rumours" percolating in London concerning the validity of titles to American mines.[10] Officials of the Eberhardt and Aurora Mining Company, Ltd., almost as quickly asked the firm's legal representatives in Nevada to clarify the statute's effect on alien holdings in that state. The attorney, the future United States Congressman Thomas Wren, acknowledged that the law seemed intended to exclude all foreigners from holding mines under patent. But if they purchased the possessory right to mineral land from citizens of the United States, what then? Could they maintain action for injuries done to the mine or recover possession from encroachers who were citizens? Wren merely posed the questions: at the time neither he nor the courts had definite answers.[11]

Although the policy which ultimately emerged—if it may be termed a policy—was not always clear-cut, certain fundamental ideas stand out in a distressingly complex picture. By law the alien could not locate

[8] It was first necessary that the locator comply with the regulations on locating and recording, then under oath file application for a patent with the Land Office. Accompanying this application must be plat and field notes of the claim. Plat and notice of application were to be displayed "conspicuously" on the claim and notice published for sixty days in a newspaper chosen by Land Office officials. Affirmation of citizenship and expenditure of $500 on improvements were also necessary. At the end of sixty days, if there were no adverse claimants, the applicant was entitled to final possessory title in the form of a government patent. *Ibid.*, 92–93.

[9] *Ibid.*, 94.   [10] June 1, 1872, 505.

[11] Wren pointed out that Nevada courts had not yet passed upon such a question but that the Supreme Court of California, with Justice Field writing the opinion, had decided that the right of an alien to hold real property was a question between him and the federal government and until officially decided by the government the alien had the same rights as resident owners. To Thomas Phillpotts (Hamilton, Nev., June 10, 1872), Read MSS. For the case mentioned by Wren, see Norris *v.* Foyt, 18 *California Reports*, 217.

and could not obtain a patent directly from the government. But the act of 1872 expressly stipulated that "nothing herein contained shall be construed to prevent the alienation of the title conveyed by a patent for a mining-claim to any person whatever." [12] Thus a foreigner or a foreign corporation was free to purchase a patent issued to a United States citizen and to receive with it all the rights and privileges which would have accrued to the original patentees had they retained their interest in the mine.[13]

There were deviations, but in general practice an alien might even locate or purchase unpatented claims and hold or dispose of them with full rights against all comers except the federal government.[14] And consistently the federal government seldom moved of its own initiative; only when application for patent was made did it challenge and ask proof of citizenship.[15]

Once a patent had been issued, the government was no longer concerned. At that point individual states or territories presumed to sketch out provisions governing aliens and real estate; but in most western regions these proved to be comparatively liberal arrangements. An exception was the law of Territorial Montana, enacted in 1872, which stipulated that no alien could acquire "any title, interest, or possessory or other right to any placer mine or claim, or to the profits or proceeds

[12] 17 *U.S. Statutes,* 94.

[13] 1 *Copp's Land Owner* (1875), 178–179; 3 *ibid.,* (1876), 18. The Montana Supreme Court held that an alien could not take title by purchase from a citizen locator. Wulff *v.* Manuel, 9 *Montana Reports* (1890), 286. The Federal Supreme Court soon reversed this extreme position, however. Manuel *v.* Wulff, 152 *U.S. Reports* (1894), 505.

[14] Territory of Montana *v.* Lee, 2 *Montana Reports* (1874), 137–138; Gorman Mining Co. *v.* Alexander, 2 *South Dakota Reports* (1892), 557. A deviation may be seen when the Nevada Supreme Court ruled that an alien could not locate nor hold claims and that an American citizen might relocate a claim presumed to have been located by a noncitizen. Golden Fleece Gold and Silver Mining Co. *v.* Cable Consolidated Gold and Silver Mining Co., 12 *Nevada Reports* (1877), 327–328.

[15] In all classes of actions between individuals with which the government had no concern, citizenship was not a fact in issue and did not need to be either alleged or proved. Billings *v.* Aspen Mining and Smelting Co., 51 *Federal Reporter* (1892), 338. According to a Land Office decision, a mineral entry by an alien was not automatically void, but only voidable when action was taken by the government. *Decisions of the Department of the Interior and General Land Office in Cases Relating to the Public Lands,* XII (1891), 345. Cited hereafter as *Land Decisions.*

thereof," in the territory.[16] Undoubtedly designed to operate against the detested "Celestials," rather than against English capitalists, this law was nullified by the Territorial Supreme Court two years later [17] and was repealed post haste by the legislature.[18]

Western mining regions might wish to restrict the Chinese, but, being interested in European investment, they were forced to accord generous privileges to aliens in general. The Constitution of the state of Colorado provided in 1876 that "aliens, who are or who may hereafter become *bona-fide* residents of this State, may acquire, inherit, possess, enjoy, and dispose of property, real and personal, as native-born citizens." [19] There is evidence that this provision was honored in the years immediately following statehood [20] but it appears to have been inoperative during the eighties and nineties.

Nevada declared by law that any nonresident alien—individual or corporate—except subjects of the Chinese Empire was eligible to hold property on the same basis as any resident citizen or domestic corporation.[21] By an act of 1885 the territory of Arizona allowed any alien to acquire or purchase mineral lands but placed a limitation of 320 acres, exclusive of mining lands or land used to support mining or milling operations, on what a noncitizen might hold at one time.[22]

Thus, although the alien could not legally patent mineral claims, both local and federal governments tended to encourage aliens and alien corporations to some degree. A foreign concern could always purchase property already patented, and many English companies were careful to follow such a practice. But patented properties were invariably more expensive than unpatented claims, and without the completed title full security was lacking. British concerns cannot be blamed too much

[16] Act of Jan. 12, 1872, *Laws of the Territory of Montana,* 7 Sess., 1871–1872, 594–595.

[17] Territory of Montana *v.* Lee, 2 *Montana Reports* (1874), 137–138.

[18] Act of Jan. 15, 1874, *Laws of the Territory of Montana,* 8 Sess., 1874, 97.

[19] Art., II, Sect. 27.

[20] David H. Moffat, Jr., and Francis Andrews, the former a native-born citizen and the latter an Englishman who had declared his intent to become an American citizen, acted as trustees to hold property for the Colorado United Mining Co. in 1877. Report of meeting of the Colorado United Mining Co. (July 13, 1877), *Mining Journal,* July 14, 1877, 752.

[21] *General Statutes of the State of Nevada,* 1885, Sect. 2655, 689.

[22] Act of Feb. 28, 1885, *Laws of the Territory of Arizona,* 13 Sess., 1885, 40.

for desiring and attempting to circumvent the law by one means or another.

One subterfuge used to obtain patented lands was to purchase western mining claims upon which no patent had yet been issued, then register a company in America to hold the title, with the subsidiary concern being controlled wholly by the British. For example, one such corporation, the Richmond Consolidated Mining Company, Ltd., in 1873 created and maintained the Richmond Mining Company, which operated in Nevada for at least twenty years as the American arm of the English concern.[23]

That the lot of the Richmond Consolidated Mining Company, Ltd., was completely bound up with that of its Nevada subsidiary was indicated in the late eighties when the federal government brought suit against the Richmond Mining Company for the value of timber taken from the public domain since 1873—a sum estimated at $6,246,720 by a special timber agent who investigated the situation.[24] The suit centered on interpretation of the Timber Act of 1878, which permitted bona fide residents to fell trees on mineral lands for purposes of mining, agriculture, or other industries,[25] and was initiated by an impetuous district attorney who wished to earn the fees of his new office by prosecuting these "bold robbers of the public domain." [26] "The case is one," contended the commissioner of the General Land Office, "in which a foreign corporation have appropriated to themselves the liberal provisions of the Government made for the benefit of its citizens only." [27]

Federal action forced a closing down of all operations by the Rich-

---

[23] Report of meeting of the Richmond Consolidated Mining Co., Ltd., (Nov. 18, 1873), *Mining World*, Nov. 22, 1873, 1044; United States *v.* Richmond Mining Co., 40 *Federal Reporter* (1889), 415–416.

[24] It was estimated that since Jan. 1, 1873 the concern had cut and removed pine, cedar, and what was known locally as "mountain mahogany" totaling no less than 21,600,000 bushels of charcoal and 112,320 of fuel wood. Report of George D. Temple, Special Timber Agent (Eureka, July 11, 1888), Report of the Committee on Mines and Mining Concerning United States Suits Brought for Cutting Timber in Nevada, *Senate Report* No. 2, 50 Cong., 2 Sess. (1888–1889), 37.

[25] 20 *U.S. Statutes*, 88.

[26] Thomas Haydon to L. Q. C. Lamar; Haydon to William A. J. Sparks (Reno, April 28, 1887), Report of Suits Brought for Cutting Timber, *Senate Report* No. 2, 50 Cong., 2 Sess. (1888–1889), 33–34.

[27] S. M. Stockslager to William P. Vilas (Washington, July 31, 1888), *ibid.,* 39.

mond Consolidated Mining Company, Ltd., on behalf of its subsidiary and prompted outraged protests from London. "In the face of these suits," warned the directors, "it behoves the Company to be very careful how they invest any further capital in the United States." [28] The Nevada legislature petitioned Congress in protest, asserting that business was paralyzed "and the people are menaced with absolute financial ruin." [29] The Senate Committee on Mines and Mining investigated and found the timber suits "needless and vexatious." In authorizing them, the Attorney General "must have done so under a misapprehension of the facts." [30] As a result, after a test case was decided in November, 1889,[31] the charges were dismissed amid loud sighs of relief from British shareholders.[32] But operations had been suspended for at least two years; Richmond Consolidated shares had dropped from £3 in 1887 to £1 10s. by early 1889; [33] and one of the most successful Anglo-American mining companies had been given a bad fright.

There were also general disadvantages in the creation of an American subsidiary; hence only a few English companies utilized this approach.[34] The London solicitors of the Eberhardt and Aurora Mining Company, Ltd., presented many of the standard arguments against forming a local concern to hold property when the company's Nevada agent suggested such a move in 1878. They pointed out that there were legal problems to be overcome and that additional expenses would

[28] *Directors' Report,* Feb. 18, 1889.

[29] *Congressional Record,* Feb. 20, 1889, 2080–2081.

[30] Report of Suits Brought for Cutting Timber, *Senate Report* No. 2, 50 Cong., 2 Sess. (1888–1889), xi.

[31] United States *v.* Richmond Mining Co., 40 *Federal Reporter* (1889), 415–419.

[32] Richmond Consolidated Mining Co., Ltd., *Directors' Report,* Feb. 18, 1889. Because of the timber suits this report was actually not submitted to the shareholders until Dec., 1890.

[33] *Mining News,* Feb. 23, 1889.

[34] The Utah Consolidated Gold Mines for a number of years after 1897 proceeded to operate through its American subsidiary, the Highland Boy Gold Mining Co. of New Jersey, just as another Anglo-Utah concern, the Boston Consolidated Copper and Gold Mining Co., Ltd., functioned in America through the Boston Consolidated Mining Co. Skinner, *Mining Manual* (1900), 1145; Utah Consolidated Gold Mines, *Directors' Report,* fifteen months ending June 30, 1900; Boston Consolidated Copper and Gold Mining Co., Ltd., *Annual Report,* year ending Sept. 30, 1902. From 1884 the Arizona Copper Co., Ltd., operated in America through two subsidiaries, the Arizona and New Mexico Railroad Co. and the Arizona Copper Co. Arizona Copper Co., Ltd., *Annual Report,* year ending Sept. 30, 1886.

be involved in maintaining a dual corporate structure. Furthermore, the directors or trustees of the American subsidiary might well have to be given broad and important powers at the expense of British shareholders. Control might be considerably more difficult than under a conventional arrangement: "For instance, all questions as to the powers & rights of the shareholders over their property would be determined in America & by American law, in a State in which the legal tribunals can hardly be considered as satisfactorily settled." [35]

Another means of circumventing the mining laws was to leave the legal title in the hands of an American citizen until patent was issued and title completed. Thus Charles S. Richardson held the title to the property of the Clifton Silver Mining Company, Ltd., in Colorado during the early 1870's and could therefore feel secure that the company would pay his back salary alleged to be due for inspection services.[36] The engineer, Clarence King, held the title to the original property purchased by the Richmond Consolidated Mining Company, Ltd., in 1871 until he acquired the patents; then two years later he assigned them to the subsidiary company formed in Nevada.[37]

These practices, though common, did not wholly solve the problem. Sometimes official decisions in the United States endeavored to curb such arrangements and presented additional difficulties for the often already-harassed British mining company. When an Anglo-Nevada corporation, the Ruby Consolidated Mining Company, Ltd., was formed in 1872,[38] it was agreed that the vendor, Hermann Heynemann, "a respectable merchant in California," would hold title to the company's property, obtain the patent, then transfer it to the company.[39] Ultimately, however, Nevada courts decided that the contract to this effect was an evasion of the law and therefore unenforceable.[40]

Other decisions tendered by the courts or by the General Land Office

[35] Henry Kimber & Co., "Solicitors' Report as to Constitution of American Company" (London, March 30, 1878), Read MSS.

[36] Richardson to editor (Central City, July 21, 1874), *Mining Journal*, Aug. 15, 1874, 889.

[37] Report of meeting of the Richmond Consolidated Mining Co. (Nov. 18, 1873), *Mining World*, Nov. 22, 1873, 1044.

[38] *Mem. & Art.*, 1–2, Ruby Consolidated Mining Co., C.R.O. B-6247.

[39] Report of meeting of the Ruby Consolidated Mining Co. (Aug. 28, 1872), *Mining World*, Aug. 31, 1872, 1325.

[40] *Mining Journal*, Oct. 21, 1876, 1148; *Sci. Press*, June 6, 1877, 366, 370.

followed the same line. When an Englishman endeavored to obtain a patent on a Colorado claim in 1885 by transferring the claim to an American for that sole purpose, the Court of Appeals, Colorado District, invalidated not only the transaction but the location as well.[41] A similar incident involving a British company rather than an individual was recorded in the same state. In February, 1884, the Twin Lakes Hydraulic Gold Mining Syndicate, Ltd., of London conveyed the Capricorn Placer near Leadville to Theodore F. Van Wagenen, an American citizen. Van Wagenen and the syndicate entered into an agreement which provided that the former was to hold the claim in trust to the sole end of acquiring a government patent upon it and that when his mission was accomplished he would convey the claim to the Twin Lakes Syndicate. Van Wagenen in December, 1886, applied for a patent, but the Land Office blocked the move. Insisting that by law no alien could patent, the opinion handed down recognized that the trustee in this instance was an agent for that special purpose. If the corporation was incompetent to secure title by proceedings under law, it could not do so through an indirect approach by an agent. Hence entry for patent was canceled.[42]

Yet despite such decisions British firms still continued to leave mines in American hands until the titles were completed. It is difficult to say how widespread the practice was, but undoubtedly it was reasonably common. The federal government, it would appear, made but half-hearted efforts to prevent such arrangements. But from the English standpoint neither this approach nor the use of American subsidiary companies was wholly satisfactory. In the middle seventies Englishmen and Americans urged an amendment to allow foreign capitalists to apply for patents on mines located in the Far West only. The editor of the New York *Engineering and Mining Journal* probably recounted the arguments as neatly as anyone else:

The public lands belong to the people; and they should not be given away, whether for agricultural or for mining purposes, to those who are not citizens. But when a citizen has sold his possessory title to a *bona fide* foreign purchaser, why should not the latter be allowed to enjoy the rights which the former meant to convey? Moreover, even if it were desirable to prohibit the acquisition of mines by alien corporations, the end is not secured by present

[41] Lee *v.* Justice Mining Co., 29 *Pacific Reporter* (1892), 1020–1021, 1024.
[42] 10 *Land Decisions* (1890), 641–642.

law. It is necessary for a citizen only to take out the patent; and then nobody can prevent the legal transfer of title. But many a poor miner cannot incur the expense of procuring a patent before attempting to get aid by loan or sale; and many a foreigner, perplexed or disgusted by the round-about formalities required, will refuse to obtain a title by what seems to be a subterfuge, and to invoke additional perils of irregularity. . . . The net result of our law in this respect is, therefore, that some foreign capitalists are deterred by its unmeaning provisions from investing at all in American mines, while others continue to work the mines they hold, and the United States is deprived of the money they would gladly pay for their patents, if they were allowed to make direct application.[43]

This outcry re-echoed by editor Raymond was not particularly loud nor widespread, yet there is evidence to indicate that interested promoters in the West sought to exert top-level pressure to effect the desired changes. A number of references in British Foreign Office correspondence throw light on one such effort by Lewis Chalmers, an Englishman in charge of the Exchequer Gold and Silver Mining Company, Ltd., in California. Although this study does not embrace the California locale, Chalmers' sentiments and his attempt to bring pressure to bear in Washington reflect clearly the views of the average English investor and, more importantly, those of the British Foreign Office.

Early in 1874 Chalmers complained to the Foreign Office about the difficulties experienced by foreign concerns in obtaining mineral patents in the West and insisted that the United States government not only lost money, but inflicted undue hardship on aliens with investments to protect.[44] Lord Derby transmitted these complaints to the British minister in Washington, Sir Edward Thornton, who informed Chalmers that in his opinion Congress could not at that time be induced to amend the law of 1872 and grant full mineral rights to noncitizens. "Such a step would be entirely opposed to the spirit of recent Federal Legislation," he said.[45]

Undaunted, Chalmers continued to press his arguments, insisting that the foreign owner remained at the mercy of the federal gov-

[43] January 10, 1874, 24.

[44] Lord Derby to Sir Edward Thornton (Foreign Office, Feb. 28, 1874), F.O. 115/566; Chalmers to Thornton (Silver Mountain, Calif., April 30, 1874), F.O. 115/582.

[45] To Chalmers (Washington, March 14, 1874), draft in F.O. 115/583.

ernment. "A mine on which he has expended millions of dollars might be taken from him any day without a word of warning," he protested.[46] At the same time a British colleague, Henry Syme of London, also approached the Foreign Office, bemoaning that the act of 1872 exposed English companies "to a risk of forfeiture, which in its practical bearing is without parallel in this or any other country, wherein the rights of property are respected." [47] Syme suggested that the British minister in Washington might be able to exert influence; if not, the Companies Registration Acts in England should be amended to prohibit the registration of all joint-stock companies proposed to work American mines.[48]

Despite assurances that the law of 1872 adequately protected foreign concerns,[49] Syme subsequently called the attention of the Foreign Office to several bills introduced in Congress to modify the existing statute and suggested that "a word from Sir E. Thornton" to certain western senators might not be out of place in this instance.[50] In the meantime Lord Derby advised the British chargé d'affaires in Washington that Her Majesty's Government could do little more for the protection of British subjects whose mining operations in the United States might be affected by the law of 1872 than "to bring officiously to the notice" of the Secretary of State the possible injurious effect on British interests.[51]

In reply Chargé Watson announced that he had broached the subject with Secretary Fish and that the latter felt such a question was not one for diplomatic treatment. It was the opinion of Fish that if the interests of British subjects were not sufficiently protected by the law itself, as he thought they were, then "it was for them to move in the proper quarter for such legislative measure as might be required in order to avert any unfair action of this law upon their interests." [52]

Such a wordy answer was hardly satisfactory to the Englishman

[46] To Thornton (Silver Mountain, May 26, 1874), F.O. 115/582.
[47] To Derby (London, April 9, 1874), F.O. 115/569.
[48] To Derby (London, June 3, 1874), *ibid.*
[49] Thornton to Derby (London, July 15, 1874), F.O. 115/570.
[50] He suggested either Senator Stewart of Nevada or Sargent or Pratt. Syme to Derby (London, Aug. 19, 1874), F.O. 115/571. Aaron A. Sargent was Senator from California, 1873–1879; the Pratt mentioned may have been either Senator Daniel D. Pratt of Indiana or Representative Henry O. Pratt of Iowa. Wold, *Biographical Directory of the American Congresses,* 1428, 1429, 1494.
[51] To R. G. Watson (Foreign Office, Aug. 8, 1874), F.O. 115/750.
[52] Watson to Derby (Washington, Sept. 3, 1874), F.O. 5/1487.

with a stake in unpatented mineral claims in the West. "Mr. Fish simply talks nonsense," wrote Syme to the Foreign Office.

Mr. Fish then says we ought to apply "in the proper quarter" on this subject, but his meaning is somewhat obscure, unless it is that we are to hire some "hole in the wall" politician to engineer an amendment of the act thru' Congress. If so it is superfluous to remark that the Wash[n] Lobby is too expensive an institution for an English Limited Liability Co. even if that were the proper course for us to adopt wh: I very much doubt.[53]

Back in Washington, Thornton conferred with Fish and reached the conclusion that the best opportunity to bring about modification of the mining law as suggested by Syme and Chalmers would be to solicit personally the aid of one or two senators. Accordingly he called upon the two senators from California, Aaron Sargent and John Hager, and left with them proposals which had originated with Chalmers and had been forwarded to the British minister via Syme.[54] Sargent reworked these proposals into bill form and introduced a measure into the Senate early in 1875 which, if passed, would have enabled foreigners to be granted patents for bona fide mining claims purchased by them from citizens prior to the passage of the 1872 law.[55]

Thornton endeavored to keep his role confidential, explaining that Fish was jealous of direct negotiation of foreign ministers with members of the government other than himself.[56] Lord Derby expressed his approval of the course pursued.[57] Lewis Chalmers showered profuse praise from California.[58] Yet Sargent's bill was lost somewhere along the way and was never enacted.[59]

More than a year later another approach was explored when Syme suggested the negotiation of a convention between Great Britain and the United States by which British subjects, after purchasing mines from American citizens, would be able to apply directly for federal patents on their property. Such a step could obviously be made pos-

[53] To Derby (London, Oct. 5, 1874), F.O. 115/571.
[54] Thornton to Derby (Washington, Jan. 20, 1875), F.O. 5/1516.
[55] Thornton to Chalmers (Washington, Jan. 31, 1875), draft in F.O. 115/596; *Congressional Record*, Jan. 11, 1875, 361.
[56] To Derby (Washington, Jan. 20, 1875), F.O. 5/1516.
[57] To Thornton (Foreign Office, Feb. 4, 1875), F.O. 115/584.
[58] To Thornton (Silver Mountain, Feb. 11, 1875), F.O. 115/595.
[59] It was reported out by the Senate Committee on Mines and Mining late in January, 1875, with amendments. *Congressional Record*, Jan. 25, 1875, 679. After that, there is no mention of the bill.

sible only by modification of the existing law of 1872. Derby requested Thornton to report his opinion as to whether such an agreement would be desirable or possible,[60] and the latter replied that at the moment (March, 1876) it would almost certainly be impossible to induce the American government to negotiate or the Senate to ratify any such convention as was proposed by Syme. Nativism was too strong, observed Thornton, Americans were not anxious to have foreigners reap profits from western resources, and there was an "inordinate and unnecessary fear" that the Chinese might overrun the country.[61] This appears to have ended the matter.

Undoubtedly the whole question of British subjects and American mineral patents was not a major one at this time so far as Her Majesty's Government was concerned. Yet the fact that Thornton was willing to use his influence with members of Congress, at the risk of arousing hostilities, indicates that either the problem was of some importance or that Thornton was not acting as a wise foreign representative should act.

Meanwhile the situation was unchanged: aliens were still not able to obtain patents, but once a patent had been issued to an American citizen there were no restrictions on his disposing of the property to a foreign concern or individual. The middle eighties, however, focused new attention on the alien in the West and brought a tightening of federal laws controlling the disposition of the public domain. From all parts of the country came expressions of fear lest large corporations and foreign exploiters dominate western lands unless checked by action from Washington.

The Land Office, under Commissioner William A. J. Sparks of Illinois, reflected this sentiment between 1885 and 1888 by increasing the emphasis on freeing the public domain from the grip of large operators and companies. As early as 1883 congressmen were viewing with growing concern reports of foreign penetration in the West. In December of that year Irish-American William Eugene Robinson, representative from New York, submitted a resolution of inquiry "concerning the purchase of public lands by foreign noblemen, so called." [62] This was

[60] To Thornton (Foreign Office, March 11, 1876), F.O. 5/1543.

[61] To Derby (Washington, March 27, 1876), *ibid.*

[62] *Congressional Record*, Dec. 11, 1883, 97. Born in County Tyrone, the egotistical, bombastic Robinson had been a supporter of the Young Ireland movement and must be regarded as a professional hater of England. *DAB*, XVI, 57–58.

followed in the next three years by the introduction of eighteen bills in both House and Senate which, if passed, would have prevented aliens from acquiring any title to land either in the territories or in any portion of the United States.[63] Such congressmen as Oates of Alabama, Payson of Illinois, and Plumb of Kansas reported that Europeans —"principally Englishmen—have acquired, and now own, in the aggregate, about 21,000,000 acres of land within the United States." [64]

While such reports were being widely spread and antialien bills discussed in Washington, the London press took cognizance.[65] The British government proved interested enough to call for information on the situation and its minister, Sir Lionel Sackville-West, in 1886 instructed the consuls to report on the mineral industries in the United States, with particular emphasis on the rights of private ownership in mineral lands of each state.[66] Reports were soon forthcoming from Chicago and San Francisco, covering both general and specific laws on mining and giving some account of conditions in each region.[67]

If these laws generally allowed considerable freedom to foreign concerns, Congress soon threw a new impediment into the way of such corporations. On March 3, 1887, when President Cleveland affixed his signature, the act thereafter to be known as the Alien Land Law became effective. Henceforth it was unlawful for noncitizens or those who had not declared their intent to become citizens, or for any corporation not chartered under the laws of the United States or some state or territory thereof, to "hereafter acquire, hold, or own real estate so

[63] One was introduced in 1883; five in 1884; three in 1885; nine in 1886.

[64] Report of the Committee on the Public Lands on Land Titles to Aliens in the United States, *Ho. Rpt.* No. 2308, 48 Cong., 2 Sess. (1884–1885), 1. A similar report made the following year showed 20,747,000 acres held by twenty-nine persons or corporations, all alien and mostly English. This was "not complete by any means," it was stated, for small cases could be cited totaling over 30,000,000 acres. None of those listed involved mining property and only one was shown conclusively to be in the territories. Many were land or cattle companies, some were holders of southern timber lands. Report of the Committee on the Public Lands on Ownership of Real Estate in the Territories, *Ho. Rpt.* No. 3455, 49 Cong., 1 Sess. (1885–1886), 2.

[65] London *Times,* Feb. 26, 28, 1885.

[66] To the British consuls in America (Washington, Oct. 13, 1886), draft in F.O. 115/786.

[67] Report of Consul Hayes Sadler on Mining in the Consular District of Chicago (Dec. 13, 1886); Report of Acting Consul Mason on Mining in the Consular District of San Francisco (Nov. 17, 1886), F.O. 115/787.

hereafter acquired, or any interest therein in any of the Territories of the United States or in the District of Columbia." [68] The new law further stipulated that no corporation or association, more than 20 per cent of the stock of which was owned by noncitizens or alien corporations or associations, could acquire and hold real estate in the same areas after this date. Violation was to mean forfeiture to the United States. [69]

The law of 1887 did not mention mining lands as such; it was designed to prevent foreign grazing concerns from taking up the public domain intended for American homesteaders and settlers. While the bill was being debated in the summer of 1886, those representing the mineral interests of western territories pointed out what they considered to be the inequalities and discrepancies in the proposed law, but to no avail. Delegate Joseph K. Toole of Montana, for example, reflected the typical western viewpoint in his contention that the measure was too extreme, that mineral lands desperately needed foreign capital for their full development, and that amendments should exclude mining land from the law's operation. [70] But in the clamor to protect the public domain nobody heard Toole's feeble, voteless voice.

If mines were not mentioned in the Alien Land Law, Attorney General Garland's early opinion quickly confirmed the worst fears of western miners. Garland held that mines were real estate or inheritable interests in real estate and as such were covered by the act. Aliens could not hold more than 20 per cent of the stock of American corporations owning mineral land in the territories. Under the law the advancement of capital by aliens to develop mineral property was legal, ruled the Attorney General, but no interest in real estate could be acquired by such action and no alien might purchase real estate on any loan made since the passage of the act, even if done on his own security or lien. On the other hand, aliens might lawfully contract with American owners to work mines by personal agreements or bona fide leases for "a reasonable time." [71]

Repercussions of the Alien Land Law were quickly apparent in mining circles on both sides of the Atlantic. Communities in Dakota,

[68] 24 *U.S. Statutes*, 476.   [69] *Ibid.*, 477.
[70] *Congressional Record*, July 31, 1886, Appendix 321–322.
[71] 14 *Copp's Land Owner* (1887), 126–127.

Montana, Idaho, New Mexico, Arizona, and Utah—those territories affected by its provisions—lost no time in making known their sentiments. Newspapers throughout the mineral West called for the law's repeal and the enactment of a new one exempting mines from such restrictions on foreign capital.[72] Important national periodicals took up the cry with equal vigor. The *Engineering and Mining Journal* published information inferring that $10,000,000 worth of sales had fallen through in Idaho alone because English and Scottish capitalists had been discouraged by the Alien Law.[73] In San Francisco the *Scientific Press* cited five specific cases in which the act had been responsible for suspending transactions in Idaho, Montana, and New Mexico totaling some $4,285,000.[74] One important British concern was reported as having turned south of the border from New Mexico when the law was enacted, while the Mines Company, Ltd., a large English promotional agency, insisted that it would refuse to touch mines in the territories even if some means of circumventing the law were discovered.[75] "This measure has awakened among the English a distrust of a people capable of such insane legislation, and not another pound will the British public be likely to invest in the proscribed mining regions so long as this law remains in force."[76] So predicted the editor of *Scientific Press* in the summer of 1887.

The people in the territories affected endeavored to make their impotent voices heard in Washington. Memorial after memorial was sent to Congress by territorial legislatures or by other interested groups. A petition from the Montana Assembly, for example, early protested that the risks of mining entailed heavy expenses and that outside capital was necessary. Prior to the Alien Law capitalists were prepared to make large-scale investments, but now "several million dollars of foreign capital" had been turned aside. It was further pointed out that mineral lands were of necessity limited in area by expenditure of money and labor and that no such thing as a monopoly of this type of property could exist. Since the holding of mines by aliens was indeed a great boon to the territory, contended the petitioners, such land should be exempted from the law's operation.[77]

[72] See, for example, *Great Falls Tribune,* May 3, 1887.
[73] April 2, 1887, 236–237.   [74] June 4, 1887, 364.
[75] *Ibid.,* May 7, 1887, 300.   [76] Aug. 6, 1887, 80.
[77] *Laws of Montana Territory,* 15 Extra. Sess., 1887, 111–112.

A similar memorial from the Idaho legislature said much the same thing.[78] So also did official protests from Utah and New Mexico as well as from unofficial organizations or conventions throughout the mining territories.[79]

In Congress friends of the territories did what they could, but for a decade their efforts went unheeded. Bill after bill was introduced to amend the act and exclude mineral lands, but western votes were too unimportant to prevail.[80] In fact, while interested western spokesmen were endeavoring to liberalize the Alien Land Law, a hard core of conservationists were attempting to push through revisions which would apply its provisions to the states as well as to the territories.[81]

Despite the efforts of congressmen sympathetic to the mineral regions and despite at least one favorable report in the Senate and three in the House between 1888 and 1891,[82] it was not until 1897 that the law was finally amended to exempt "any mine or mining claim, in any of the Territories of the United States." [83] By this time there was but slight discussion on the subject in Congress: only Arizona, New Mexico, and Oklahoma remained outside the pale of statehood and their influence was nil.

That the mining areas were wholeheartedly against the Alien Land Law and that the statute provided another territorial grievance against congressional control is indicated not only from criticisms leveled dur-

[78] *General Laws of the Territory of Idaho,* 15 Sess., 1888–1889, 70–71.

[79] See Memorial to Congress, *Laws of the Territory of Utah,* 28 Sess., 1888, 220–221; Memorial to Congress, *Laws of New Mexico,* 28 Sess., 1889, 364; *Sci. Press.,* Nov. 7, 1891, 300; Resolution of Salt Lake City Chamber of Commerce (Nov. 21, 1888), quoted in Report of the Committee on Mines and Mining Interests of Aliens in the Territories, *Senate Report* No. 2690, 50 Cong., 2 Sess. (1888–1889), 22; *Congressional Record,* Dec. 12, 19, 1887, 43, 111–112; Jan. 11, 1892, 268.

[80] See *Congressional Record,* Jan. 4, 5, 10, Feb. 6, 7, March 8, 1888, 234, 257, 363, 988, 1025, 1878; Dec. 4, 1889, 99; April 16, 1890, 3438; Dec. 10, 1891, 23; Dec. 10, 11, 1896, 77, 78–79, 127.

[81] See *ibid.,* Jan. 9, 16, March 12, 1888, 322, 483, 1974; Dec. 18, 1889, 226; Jan. 21, 1890, 753; Jan. 5, Feb. 1, 1892, 125, 731.

[82] See *Ho. Rpt.* No. 703, 50 Cong., 1 Sess. (1887–1888); *Ho. Rpt.* No. 3014, 50 Cong., 1 Sess. (1887–1888); *Ho. Rpt.* No. 1140, 51 Cong., 1 Sess. (1889–1890); *Senate Report* No. 2690, 50 Cong., 2 Sess. (1888–1889).

[83] Act of March 2, 1897, 29 *U.S. Statutes,* 618. For an excellent treatment of the Alien Land Law in general see Roger V. Clements, "British Investment and American Legislative Restrictions in the Trans-Mississippi West, 1880–1900," *Mississippi Valley Historical Review,* XLII (Sept. 1955), 207–227.

ing its period of operation, but also by the actions of newly admitted states as they left behind territorial status. The constitutions of Montana, Wyoming, and South Dakota all provided that no distinction should be drawn between aliens and citizens in the right to hold property.[84] One of the first laws of the new state of Idaho in 1891 stipulated that all persons except Chinese or Mongolians born outside the United States could hold mining lands. "An emergency exists," said one section of this measure, "and this act shall take effect from and after its passage." [85]

So much for American reaction to the Alien Land Law. What about the British? Just how much did it mean to English investment in the West? When the statute was passed, British periodicals took notice but were far less outspoken than their American counterparts.[86] Representatives of the government also expressed a mild interest, although few pertinent references are to be found in the Foreign Office papers. Consul Sadler of the Chicago district, which embraced much of the area covered by the Alien Act, commented in June, 1887, that both state and federal restrictions on foreign ownership of real estate "may prove to be hard in many cases, be the cause of much litigation, and check the employment of British capital in mining, ranching, and other occupations, more especially in those parts which are the least developed." [87] The Foreign Office was sufficiently interested in the matter to have an official report drawn up and tendered to Parliament early in the 1890's, but there affairs seem to have rested.[88]

If the British government showed only moderate concern, neither were other English sources overexcited, although those closest to west-

[84] Montana's provision was limited to mineral lands. Constit., Art. III, Sect. 25. The sections in the organic acts of Wyoming and South Dakota were almost identical and applied to all types of property. Constit. South Dakota, Art. VI, Sect. 14; Constit. Wyoming, Art. I, Sect. 29.

[85] Act of March 2, 1891, *General Laws of the State of Idaho*, 1 Sess., 1890–1891, 119. In North Dakota, by law any person, citizen, or alien was entitled to hold property. *Revised Code of North Dakota* (1895), Sect. 3277, 722. Utah's constitution made no mention of aliens and property, hence did not discriminate.

[86] London *Times,* July 25, 1887; *Mining Journal,* Dec. 31, 1887, 1583.

[87] To Marquess of Salisbury (Chicago, June 13, 1887), F.O. 5/1989.

[88] Preliminary reports were sent to Parliament in 1887 and 1888 and were later drawn together into an official summary which covered the federal law and those restricting nonresident aliens in the various states. Reports on Status of Aliens and Foreign Companies in the United States, 1886–1888, F.O. 5/2043.

ern investments were naturally most aware of the law's existence. Directors of the Montana Company, Ltd., immediately expressed their "great satisfaction" that the passage of the act was not, "in any way, detrimental to the interests of this company; inasmuch as the Act is *not retrospective* or *retroactive,* and the Company had acquired all the adjoining properties of any known value, which they desired to possess, *before* the act was passed." [89] Sir Charles W. F. Craufurd, who was associated with several other Anglo-Montana mining concerns, expressed his opinion about the importance of the law to British companies and its adverse effect in general.[90] The London *Economist* saw fit to comment on the attention being given English investors and their holdings in the American West but did "not recall any objection that has been publicly raised to investments by foreigners in American silver and gold mines, particularly if such mines happened to be awaiting development." [91]

It is difficult to determine how much the Alien Land Law actually did affect the course of British mining investments in the territories. Undoubtedly it placed an additional barrier in the way of a smooth capital flow, and some Englishmen may have suffered. Directors of the Dickens Custer Company, Ltd., for example, became dissatisfied with their Idaho manager, one Nicholas Treweek, in 1889, but because the title to their property had been placed in Treweek's name in order to circumvent the Alien Law they were forced to tread warily. Treweek not only threatened to invoke the statutes if the company made any effort to remove him, but also kept hauling out additional mining claims for the concern to purchase.[92] Fortunately for the Dickens Custer people Idaho became a state in the following year.

The law undoubtedly caused additional litigation problems for at least a few English subjects. A Reuter's news report from New York announced in 1894 that the Pichaco mines in Arizona, "which belong to non-resident Englishmen, have been occupied by American citizens, on the ground that the mines were owned by aliens in contravention of the law. The case will be taken to the Law Courts." [93] Regardless of the outcome of the contemplated litigation, such reports could hardly be

[89] Montana Co., *Semi-Annual Report,* half year ending June 30, 1887.
[90] To editor (n.p., Feb. 10, 1888), *Mining Journal,* Feb. 11, 1888, 157.
[91] July 27, 1889, 965.   [92] *Mining News,* March 2, 1889.
[93] London *Times,* Oct. 13, 1894.

expected to foster an atmosphere of trust and confidence on the part of the British investing public.

In reality, it was possible to circumvent the Alien Land Law. It was still feasible to do so in practice by forming subsidiary companies in the United States to hold title, and some concerns announced openly their plans to use this device.[94] Although the statute applied to American corporations in which more than 20 per cent of the stock was held in foreign hands, lax interpretation tended to make its practical operation in this respect a dead letter. According to Land Office regulations, when a corporation made entry for a patent after 1887, it had to present not only its certificate of incorporation, but also evidence showing that aliens did not own more than the maximum percentage of shares set by law.[95] From an official point of view the stockholders of a company were those originally registered on the books of the concern. If they were all or predominantly American citizens at the outset, the corporation was outside the operation of the Alien Land Law, even though a majority or all of the shares might subsequently pass into foreign hands. This was the broadest possible interpretation of the law and it illustrates the government's reluctance to enforce the statute with even comparative mildness where mining was concerned. "We are not aware of a single instance where the government has intervened and sought to enforce the forfeitures provided for by the act," wrote one legal expert in 1897.[96]

But there was another method of evasion which was technically legal and effective and which was utilized by British companies in the territories after 1887. This was the simple expedient of taking long-term leases on mining property, leaving the titles in the hands of original owners. The Attorney General had expressed his opinion as to the validity of alien leases for "a reasonable time," and the government viewed with liberality leases of thirty, forty, and even ninety-nine years.

Thus the Harquahala Gold Mining Company, Ltd., had no difficulty in 1893 in taking the Harquahala group of mines in Yuma County, Arizona, under a working agreement with an American concern for forty-

[94] The Gold-Basin Mining Co. openly announced intentions to register a company in America to hold title to property in Arizona and contravene the act of 1887. *Prospectus* (May, 1896). This Scottish concern was quickly liquidated, however, "in view of the unfavourable reports from the mine." *Special Resolution,* passed Sept. 2 and confirmed Sept. 30, 1896, C.R.O. E-3200.

[95] 16 *Copp's Land Owner* (1889), 110.

[96] Lindley, *Mining Law,* I, 304–305.

two years, paying £270,000 in exchange for 97.5 per cent of the profits for the prescribed period.[97] Five years before, the Kaiser Gold Mines, Ltd., had acquired twelve claims in the same territory, paying a nominal rent of ten pounds a year on each, but also paying a total of £180,000 for equipment which went with the property.[98] The Buster Mines Syndicate, Ltd., was formed in 1892 to acquire three-fifths of the Buster copper mines in Arizona. The promoter, Frederick C. Beckwith, agreed to give the concern a ninety-nine-year lease immediately and full title "as soon as Arizona is admitted as a State"—all for the bargain price of $32,000.[99]

The ability to enter into such leasing agreements, plus the reluctance of the federal government to enforce the provisions of the law, undoubtedly did much to mitigate the possibly deleterious effect of the Alien Land Act. The fact remains that British mining companies continued to be formed and to enter into operations in the territories despite the bothersome statute.

Statistically there can be no doubt but that investments went on after 1887, although it is impossible to arrive at figures that are conclusive. But during the ten years that the Alien Land Law was in effect, a total of at least thirty British joint-stock companies, with an original nominal capitalization aggregating £7,319,000, were organized to operate mines in the territories (Table III).[100] Whether those figures would have been considerably larger had the law not been passed is, of course, impossible to say. Whereas the last nine months of 1887 and all of 1888 seems to have been poor, with few English companies registered for mines in western territories, the trend was not universal,[101] and where it did

[97] Skinner, *Mining Manual* (1894), 159; *Mem. & Art.*, 1, C.R.O. 39025.

[98] Memo. of Agreement (Sept. 7, 1888) between H. A. W. Tabor and Kaiser Gold Mines, cited in latter's *Prospectus* (Sept. 17, 1888).

[99] *Prospectus* (1892); Memo. of Agreement (April 8, 1892) between Frederick C. Beckwith and James Shearer, Stock Exchange Archives, London.

[100] These figures include only those concerns which went to allotment and actually commenced operations. Many registrations which were not completed to capitalization are omitted as they are reorganizations of old companies.

[101] Where three companies, nominally capitalized at £320,000, had been formed to operate in Montana in 1886, there were none in 1887 and only one, capitalized at £175,000, in 1888. Three were formed to work Idaho mines in 1886, with total capital of £700,000; only one was incorporated in 1887 (£200,000) but three were in 1888 (£1,070,000). In both Arizona and Dakota the number of companies increased in 1887 and 1888.

TABLE III

British Mining Investment under the Alien Land Law, 1887–1897 *

Territory	Years under alien law	Number of companies	Nominal capital
Arizona	10.00	17	£ 1,960,000
Dakota	2.66	1	3,000,000
Idaho	3.33	7	1,494,000
Montana	2.66	1	175,000
New Mexico	10.00	4	690,000
Utah	8.83	0	. . . .
Wyoming	3.33	0	. . . .
Total		30	£ 7,319,000

* Compiled from company files in the offices of the registrar of joint-stock companies, London, and the Queen's remembrancer, Edinburgh.

occur it would be folly to attribute it wholly to the uncertainty created by this particular piece of legislation without recognizing that dozens of other factors, foreign as well as domestic, may have contributed.

Nor is it possible to make any effective comparison between British concerns in the territories and those in the states during a corresponding period. A survey of five territories plus the states of Colorado and Nevada for the three and a fraction years immediately prior to the Alien Land Act and for the corresponding period immediately following shows a general increase in the number of companies formed in the years after the act was passed; but other than this no over-all pattern emerges clearly. Some individual territories dropped below their previous positions, while some climbed. The state of Colorado experienced an upsurge of British investment immediately after the Alien Law was enacted, but was this the result of this restrictive statute forcing capital from the territories or was it the natural impulse generated by a normal development of mineral resources within the state? Certainly the sister state of Nevada did not show the same trend.

Probably the only conclusion which may be drawn is that the Alien Land Law did not eliminate the entrance of British capital into the territories. If western complaints are believed, the effect of the act was to cut off every farthing of outside investment sharply and cleanly.

TABLE IV

English Mining Companies Registered for Western States and Territories, 1884–1890 *

	1884–1887		1887–1890	
	Territories			
	Number of companies	Nominal capital	Number of companies	Nominal capital
Arizona	0	£	7	£ 1,050,000
Idaho	3	700,000	7	1,494,000
New Mexico	2	400,000	2	390,000
Utah	0	....	0	....
Wyoming	1	50,001	0	....
Total	6	£ 1,150,001	16	£ 2,934,000
	States			
Colorado	12	£ 1,245,000	29	£ 3,803,960
Nevada	6	1,500,000	5	717,500
Total	18	£ 2,745,000	34	£ 4,521,460

* Compiled from company files in the offices of the registrar of joint-stock companies, London, and the Queen's remembrancer, Edinburgh. Neither Dakota nor Montana is included because they became states in 1889.

Actually the flow went on, retarded to some degree perhaps, but still significant. So long as the federal government did not enforce its provisions rigorously and so long as loopholes were available, capital never ceased to cross the Atlantic bound for western mines.

⁑ CHAPTER X ⁑

Total Investment and Profit

UNFORTUNATELY, materials covering the nineteenth century are far from complete—or even satisfactory—and the statistical approach often is doomed to fall short of its goal. Such is bound to be the fate of any attempt to measure the total amount of English capital investment in western mines between 1860 and 1901, or the profit or loss on that investment. In the first place, there is inevitable difficulty, omission, and error in identifying capital destined for American mines amidst all types of British investments in the four corners of the world. Many passing references throughout the period indicate that considerable English capital was invested in mining companies incorporated in the various states and territories; but specific information is lamentably lacking. Unlike Great Britain, the United States government has never maintained a central companies registration office, with specific requirements to be met for incorporation. Instead that task has been left to the states or territories, whose requirements have varied greatly and have seldom been comprehensive enough to include pertinent data on the nationality of shareholders.

Nor are federal documents always more instructive. A Senate investigation (1888) of alien ownership of mines in the territories lists many mines and American companies but employs with infuriating consistency only such hazy terms as "partly owned by aliens," "to some extent developed by foreign capital," and "purchased in 1884 by a wealthy foreign corporation." [1] Undoubtedly, were such references clarified, a

---

[1] Report of Committee on Mines and Mining on Mining Interests of Aliens in the Territories, *Senate Report* No. 2690, 50 Cong., 1 Sess. (1888–1889), 10, 13.

significant amount of English capital might be revealed. As it is, definite information is almost nonexistent in the Senate's report.

If it is virtually impossible to measure the amount of British capital in American-registered concerns, it is only slightly less difficult to ascertain the total amount in English companies. It is true that English company law required the registration of all limited-liability corporations, but such controls did not extend to partnerships, trusts, or associations with unlimited liability. Consequently the activity of these groups in western mines is most obscure, although scanty fragments of evidence imply that at least a minor portion of investment was made in this way.

Even where the registered joint-stock company is concerned, quantitative conclusions are hard to reach. Many factors must be evaluated and reservations made at almost every point. To begin with, there is no certainty that all pertinent joint-stock concerns have been unearthed. No individual could survey every file contained in the miles of subterranean corridors of the Companies Registration Office in London. Indexes are alphabetical and chronological without regard for continents or types of companies. Many concerns may be located by name, yet even this approach is far from infallible. Such names as the Central City (Colorado) Mining Company, Ltd., and the Montana Mining Company, Ltd., fix the territory of operation. Might it not be reasonable to expect, then, that the Central City Company, Ltd., and the Montana Diamond Company, Ltd., were incorporated to carry on business in Colorado and Montana respectively? Instead both conducted jewelry enterprises in London.[2] By the same token, the Colorado Nitrate Company, Ltd., and the Zeehan-Montana Mine, Ltd., should logically have represented investments in the West. Actually the former operated in Chile and the latter in Tasmania.[3]

Another complication stems from the fact that companies initially incorporated to invest in American mines, according to their *Memorandums of Association*, frequently turned to undertakings in other parts of the world. For example, the Cripple Creek Gold Fields, Ltd., was originally registered in 1895 to operate primarily in Colorado.[4] Subse-

[2] *Mem. & Art.*, 1–2, Central City Co., C.R.O. 44306; *ibid.*, 1–3, Montana Diamond Co., C.R.O. 65253.

[3] *Ibid.*, 1–2, Colorado Nitrate Co., C.R.O. 21265; Zeehan-Montana Mine, *Directors' Report*, April 24, 1894.

[4] *Mem. & Art.*, 1, C.R.O. 45243.

quently reorganized two years later under the same name, the firm abandoned all idea of mining in the Rockies and turned instead to the West African gold fields, carrying with it a name which certainly implies that it was an Anglo-Colorado concern.[5] In similar fashion the Idaho Exploring Company, Ltd., a reconstruction of an earlier firm with property in Boise County, Idaho, did almost nothing in the United States after its incorporation in 1893 but gave its attention almost entirely to new property in the Coolgardie fields of Western Australia, although it did retain its American interests.[6]

On the other hand, a number of British companies formed to work properties in other parts of the world eventually invested in the American West. The Stanley Gold Mines, Ltd., was incorporated in 1890 to operate in the Witwatersrand [7] but because of a dispute with the vendor the bargain was not consummated.[8] Instead the company acquired leases in Gilpin County, Colorado.[9] Likewise the Golden Valley Mines, Ltd., was formed in 1890 to work property in the Barberton de Kaap gold fields of South Africa [10] but it actually acquired interests in the Rockies.[11] These and numerous other instances of sudden or unannounced shifts from one part of the globe to another add a further impediment to identifying all British joint-stock companies with capital invested in the West.

Identification is part of the problem, but by no means all. To be sure, impressive figures might be presented from a survey of the registration of joint-stock companies organized to engage in western mining. It might be pointed out, for example, that between 1860 and 1901 there were at least 518 such companies registered with the Board of

[5] *Ibid.*, C.R.O. 55379; "Acquisition of a promising new Company Known as the Dominasi Gold Concessions, Upper Wassau District, Gold Coast, W. Africa," MS Memorandum (Dec. 22, 1897), records of Cripple Creek Gold Fields in possession of Miss Winifred Watt, 11 Pembridge Avenue, Twickenham, Middlesex. Some of its capital went into early Colorado efforts, but how much is difficult to say.

[6] *Mem. & Art.*, 2, C.R.O. B-40047; Idaho Exploring Company, *Annual Report*, year ending Dec. 1, 1895.

[7] *Mem. & Art.*, 5, C.R.O. 31235.   [8] Skinner, *Mining Manual* (1894), 357.

[9] Memo. of Agreement (Jan. 16, 1891) between Ingalls Gold Mining Co. and the Stanley Gold Mines; *ibid.*, (June 1, 1892) between Philip Milford, Edwin Reed, and the Stanley Gold Mines, Stanley Gold Mines, C.R.O, 31235.

[10] *Mem. & Art.*, 1, C.R.O. 30786.

[11] Memo. of Agreement (Dec. 31, 1890) between Ernest Percy Edelstein and the Golden Valley Mines, *ibid.*

Trade with a total nominal capitalization of not less than £77,706,751 or approximately $389,000,000.[12] Beneath the surface, however, these figures are far from meaningful. Too many adjustments must be made before they have validity; too many unknowns must be solved before adjustments can be completed.

The process of registration might be accomplished with comparative ease and lack of expense, but the task of raising capital to carry out the avowed purpose of a company frequently proved more arduous. Many concerns were incorporated but never "went to allotment" because insufficient shares were subscribed to warrant proceeding with business. Other companies may have allotted their shares but for various reasons—dishonesty, adverse reports, or superior opportunities elsewhere—did not go into operation in western America. Many of these instances are not clear-cut, but reasonable calculations indicate that of the 518 companies mentioned above probably 143 of them, with an aggregate registered capital of £17,000,000, never started work in the West.[13] Thus 22 per cent of the total nominal capital can be written off almost from the beginning.

Moreover, another 101 of these companies, with an aggregate nominal capitalization of £17,000,000, were reconstructions of older concerns. Reorganization was normally accomplished by issuing new shares which were from 80 to 100 per cent paid up in exchange for the shares of the old company. Consequently, under ordinary circumstances reconstruction seldom brought in more than 20 per cent of the nominal capital registered. One illustration will suffice to indicate why the registered capital of such concerns is often misleading. Total nominal capitalization in five reconstructions of the Flagstaff Silver Mining Company of Utah, Ltd., between 1881 and 1893 was listed as £1,115,000. Yet as Table V shows, only £108,360 was actually brought in by these arrangements.[14]

[12] See Appendix I. These figures are compiled from individual files in the offices of the registrar of companies, London, and the Queen's remembrancer, Edinburgh. Included are exploration and promoting companies and reorganizations of older concerns.

[13] From the Board of Trade files it is not always possible to be absolutely certain that a company did or did not operate. Concerns carried on the register for twenty or thirty years may not have actually functioned.

[14] Frequently records of these reconstructed companies give the number of shares issued and the total paid up, but this does not indicate what part was paid in cash and what part in old shares.

217

TABLE V

Reconstructions of the Flagstaff Silver Mining Company, 1881–1893 *

Name of reorganization	Year	Nominal capital	Due per share	Pounds paid
Flagstaff District				
Silver M. Co., Ltd.	1881	£ 160,000		£ 34,600
Flagstaff Mines, Ltd.	1885	175,000	2/6	19,760
New Flagstaff M. Co., Ltd.	1888	300,000	0/0	. . . . . .
"Flagstaff," Ltd.	1889	240,000	2/–	24,000
Flagstaff Co., Ltd.	1893	240,000	2/–	30,000
Total		£ 1,115,000		£ 108,360

* Chart compiled from the Summaries of Capital and Shares of these companies, filed in Registrar of Companies Office, London.

In the 1881 reorganization part of the new shares were to be allotted fully paid, part with 3s. due, and part with 5s. due on them.

The Flagstaff is probably a fair sample, and very likely about 90 per cent of the nominal capital of reconstructed companies existed on paper only. Thus nearly another £16,000,000, or roughly 20 per cent of the total nominal capital figure for the period, must be disregarded.

At least 274 companies, with total capital of not less than £43,000,-000, did operate for varying lengths of time in the West between 1860 and 1901. As pointed out elsewhere, however, nominal and actual capital frequently varied widely. The whole amount of capital might not be taken up; shares issued to vendors might not fall into English hands or if they did they might do so at subpar rates which cannot now be determined. Moreover, the issue of debenture bonds to raise additional capital was a relatively common phenomenon throughout the period, but until the latter part of the century official files gave no hint of the amount issued by an individual company. An estimate based on debentures known to have been issued by a number of concerns and applied to the broader whole would be that approximately 20 per cent of the total nominal capital of companies in operation was subscribed in debentures in addition to the registered share capital.[15]

[15] This is but an approximation and is based on partial evidence from about forty companies.

Another complication comes from the presence of non-English share-holders as investors in British-incorporated firms. Probably a majority of Anglo-American companies registered in London or Edinburgh listed at least some "foreign" shareholders on their rosters. Americans sometimes dominated British concerns, frequently by retaining vendor's shares given as part or all of the purchase price.[16] A few companies might boast cosmopolitan investors, including English, French, German, Dutch, Italian, Swiss, Portuguese, Corsican, and Turkish.[17] Others might be controlled by continental shareholders representing one particular country—Holland,[18] France,[19] Germany,[20] Belgium.[21]

Although domination of a company by American or continental investors was undoubtedly an exception rather than the general rule, the fact remains that an appreciable amount of capital subscribed to the British joint-stock companies was not British. How much is conjectural; probably 10 per cent would be a conservative estimate.

Considering all these factors, it is apparent that any estimate of the amount of British capital invested in western mines between 1860 and 1901 must be approached gingerly. When all adjustments are made, the total investments in limited-liability, joint-stock companies for mines in the West would probably run between £40,000,000 and £50,-000,000 for the period under consideration. But for want of complete evidence and because of the unreliability of estimating, such figures are inconclusive and must remain open.

It might also be informative to compare British investments with domestic investments in western mining. Again figures are wholly insufficient to substantiate any comprehensive or precise judgments, although the generalization that English capital made up only a small percentage of the total investment in trans-Mississippi mines would

[16] Summary of Capital and Shares to Dec. 5, 1892, "Maid of Erin" Silver Mines, C.R.O. B-34033; *ibid.*, July 6, 1903, Utah Consolidated Gold Mines, C.R.O. B-46526.

[17] *Ibid.*, Jan. 11, 1901, Morenci Copper Mines, C.R.O. B-62248.

[18] *Ibid.*, March 21, 1876, Winamuck Silver Mining Co. of Utah, C.R.O. 6744.

[19] *Ibid.*, Dec. 31, 1898, South Central and Christiania Syndicate, C.R.O. 52916.

[20] *Ibid.*, Feb. 28, 1901, Rocky Mountain Exploration Co., C.R.O. B-52760.

[21] *Ibid.*, Dec. 30, 1902, Carr Mine and Colorado Co., C.R.O. B-72337. It was rumored that King Leopold held an interest in this concern and in the Camp Bird (Colorado). *Anglo-American and Mexican Mining Guide and General Financier*, I (Dec. 30, 1905), 184; *Daily Express and Morning Herald* (London), Nov. 2, 1900. No real verification of this rumor has been found.

certainly be valid. Woefully inadequate compilations for the Tenth
Census covering 1,172 concerns engaged in deep-level mining conclude
that in 1880 Americans owned 98.55 per cent of the properties re-
porting.[22]

Though this fragmentary report is hardly indisputable, data from
other periods lend some support to it. According to the British vice-
consul in Denver during the early Cripple Creek boom, there were
632 mining companies registered or incorporated in Colorado in 1895
with a total capital of nearly £108,000,000.[23] But as Vice-Consul
Pearce noted: "These figures are of little value, except to show the
extent of the speculative fever which has started since the discoveries
in Cripple Creek."[24] During the same year (1895) at least twelve British
joint-stock companies, with a total nominal capitalization of £1,349,000,
were registered to exploit mineral resources in Colorado, mostly in the
new boom district. A comparison of the two—domestic and British—
indicate that only about 1.5 per cent of the capital registered for Colorado mines in 1895 was British. But again it must be pointed out that
nominal capitalization figures of English companies are studies in casual
deception and that those of American concerns are equally misleading.

A comparison of British investment in American mines with British
investment in minerals elsewhere in the world is also desirable but
difficult to obtain. Throughout the period British capital went out into
the mines of whatever boom momentarily held the public attention.
It flowed into Australia in the fifties and sixties, into Latin America,
Bavaria, and Russia in the seventies.[25] In the following decade the iron
mines of Spain and Scandinavia[26] and the gold fields of India and

[22] According to the census figures, 67.32 per cent were owned by Americans in
the state or territory in which the mines were located and 31.23 per cent by
Americans in outside states or territories; the remaining 1.45 per cent were of
foreign ownership. "Precious Metals," *Tenth Census Report*, XIII (1880), 112.

[23] Consular Reports on Trade and Finance, U.S. Report for the Year 1895 on the
Trade of the Consular District of Chicago, Foreign Office, *Annual Series* No. 1725
(1896), 30–31.

[24] *Ibid.*, 31.

[25] For British interest in Peruvian guano and in gold on the island of Aruba,
off the coast of Venezuela, see *Stock Exchange Review*, IV (March, 1874);
Mining Journal, Dec. 7, 1872. For interest in Bavarian lead and Russian copper
see *Mining World*, Aug. 4, 1871, 424, and *Mining Journal*, Feb. 15, 1879, 154.

[26] See Michael W. Flinn, "British Overseas Investments in Iron Ore Mining,
1870–1914," unpublished M.A. thesis, University of Manchester.

western Africa were spotlighted.[27] In the 1890's competition for capital was stepped up tremendously as some of the great names of the mineral empire became familiar jargon in London financial circles—Mysore, Coolgardie, Ashanti, the Rand, and the Klondike.

Statistics of 1890 and 1900 indicate that American mining was hard pressed to hold its own in obtaining British capital in the face of rivalry from other areas. As the following tabulation giving the proposed geographical distribution of the capital of all mining companies registered in England in 1890 shows, 17.1 per cent was supposedly destined to work mines in the United States:

Area	*Per cent of capital* [28]
United States	17.1
Australia	18.8
Mexico	19.2
South Africa	20.3
All others	24.6
Total	100.0

How much of this was designated for areas within the scope of this study is impossible to determine, although those regions drew at least 45 per cent of the total English capital registered for the United States between 1880 and 1904.[29]

For the year 1900 another survey of British capital invested in mines throughout the world (Table VI) shows investments in all of North America as totaling nearly £8,600,000 out of a total of more than £64,000,000 registered,[30] or roughly 13 per cent of the aggregate. Companies, including reorganizations, registered to acquire or work mines in western America during the same year showed a total capital of £2,236,000. Thus it would appear that these regions accounted for only about 3.5 per cent of the total for 1900.

It must be admitted, however, that since none of these figures are

[27] *Economist*, Dec. 6, 1890, 1536.

[28] Skinner, *Mining Manual* (1891–1892), xi.

[29] Of a total of £99,568,000 registered between those dates, £48,319,000 was earmarked for the West. However, £11,970,000 of the whole figure is not assigned to any particular area, but is labeled "not defined." Ashmead, *Twenty-Five Years of Mining*, 82.

[30] *Mining Journal*, Jan. 19, 1901, 71.

TABLE VI

Proposed Areas of Operation of British Mining Companies
Registered in 1900 *

Area	Number of companies	Nominal capital
South America	18	£ 1,979,000
Asia	18	3,696,000
Europe	44	6,679,000
North America	65	8,593,000
Africa	133	14,023,000
Australia-New Zealand	101	14,059,000
Great Britain	146	14,997,000
Total	525	£ 64,026,000

* *Mining Journal,* Jan. 19, 1901, 71.

complete or conclusive, they can be of significance only in indicating
that competition for capital was keen and that the American West
received only a fraction of that invested by Englishmen in general. The
entire quantitative picture is too evasive, too uncertain, to allow a
simple measurement of all investment during the period.

It might well be asked if any pattern of investment emerges during
these forty years. Is it possible to determine which regions received the
most attention and which years were the high- and low-water marks
for British investments? Can such variations be explained? Here the
task is somewhat easier than before, since it is more general in nature.

The sixties composed the preliminary period of British investments
in western mining and brought only a few experimental endeavors.
The obvious difficulties engendered by the Civil War, the Indian, poor
transportation facilities, and the panic of 1866 combined with the failure of a few bold ventures on the Pacific Coast to inhibit any substantial movement of capital.[31] Only in Nevada and Idaho did British
companies attempt to carry on operations.

But at the end of the sixties and in the early seventies there came a

[31] In this connection W. Fraser Rae mentions the unsuccessful "Imperial Silver
Quarries" venture of California and the "Washoe Mines" in Nevada. *Westward
by Rail* (2d ed., 1871), xx.

speculative flurry in England which focused attention sharply upon mining in Colorado, Nevada, and Utah. In spite of momentary scares emanating from the Franco-Prussian War, the year 1871 produced a bumper crop of Anglo-American mining companies. A total of thirty-four, nominally capitalized at £4,550,000, was registered, and of these, twenty, with a capital of £3,211,000, actually operated. So impressive was this boom that one British traveler in the West expressed his belief in 1872 that "Nevada and the whole neighbourhood of Mormon land has already absorbed so much British capital, that the mines are more British than American." [32] Undoubtedly such an observation showed investments much out of their true perspective at that time, although it must be admitted that the year 1871 was the greatest of all those in the four-decade span so far as the flow of English capital into Utah was concerned.

The boom leveled off in 1872 and 1873; then, with the depression of the latter year, investments fell off sharply. Tumbling silver prices, brought about in part by the discovery of large silver deposits in Nevada and in part by the fact that a number of European nations adopted the gold standard, thus throwing a large supply of silver bullion on the world market, discouraged investments in the West.[33] Only fifteen new companies came into active existence during the seven years from 1873 to 1880, and their total nominal capital was only £1,546,000—about 48 per cent of the total for the single year 1871.

Not only did the financial confusion and the depressed prices of metals following the 1873 debacle restrain the formation of new companies, but they also disturbed those British firms already in operation. The "fearful state of panic" crippled the Utah Silver-Lead Mining Company, Ltd., and brought that concern to the verge of ruin, according to the chairman.[34] Manager John Longmaid admitted that the poor quality of minerals must be in part blamed for the closing of the company's mine. But "the fall in the price of ore," he said, "has also deranged my calculations considerably." [35]

The same disruptions brought grief to Mammoth Copperopolis of

[32] James Bonwick, *The Mormons and the Silver Mines* (London, 1872), 324.
[33] A result of this—demonetization of silver—was to aggravate the situation in the United States in future years.
[34] Report of meeting of the Utah Silver-Lead Mining Co. (Feb. 17, 1874), *Mining World*, Feb. 21, 1874, 374.
[35] Report of John Longmaid (Sept. 4, 1874), *ibid.*, Sept. 26, 1874, 488.

Utah, Ltd., when a loss of $14,000 was sustained because of falling ore prices.[36] Subsequent efforts to raise additional capital on debentures were not successful, the miners struck for their back pay, and creditors attached all movable property.[37] In Colorado the depression proved a vital factor in the downhill motion of the Clifton Silver Mining Company, Ltd.[38] The Colorado Terrible Lode Mining Company, Ltd., was forced to meet the crisis by reducing wages at its mine—an action which precipitated discontent and a temporary work stoppage.[39] But once the initial shock was over, the company revived and paid a dividend in 1874.[40] Even in the most discouraging of days its red streamer emblazoned with the silver letters "Terrible" never failed to float over its Georgetown property.[41]

Coupled with the general business stagnation of the mid-seventies was the reaction in England to American mining that developed after exposures of such nefarious enterprises as the Emma Silver Mining Company, Ltd. Utah in particular had a bad name in 1873,[42] but London brokers dispensed liberal warnings against all American shares and mining ventures.[43] A combination of these elements—depression and distrust—caused Americans to admit in 1875 that "no American mine can now be sold on the London market." [44]

The dearth of investment continued throughout the remainder of the seventies, and stiff competition from the booming new Indian mines and a mild financial crisis in 1878 did nothing to help relieve the situation. Beginning with 1880, however, English capitalists began to show a renewed interest in the area beyond the Mississippi. Except for a

[36] Report of meeting of the Mammoth Copperopolis of Utah (Feb. 17, 1874), *ibid.*, Feb. 21, 1874, 376.

[37] *Salt Lake Daily Herald,* Jan. 15, 16, 1874.

[38] Report of meeting of the Clifton Silver Mining Co. (June 15, 1874), *Mining World,* June 20, 1874, 138–139.

[39] Georgetown *Miner,* Dec. 1, 5, 1873.

[40] *Stock Exchange Year-Book* (1875), 160.

[41] Georgetown *Miner,* Aug. 8, 1874.

[42] "Amongst the innumerable enterprises which have been palmed upon the British investing public, we know of none which have been so unsatisfactory, in their results as a whole, as American mines, more especially those in the Utah district." *Railway News,* July 19, 1873.

[43] For a typical example see William Bartlett, *The Investors' Directory to Marketable Stocks and Shares, With a Description of their Nature, Security, etc.* (London, 1876), 59.

[44] *Weekly Miner,* May 1, 1875.

sharp downward trend in 1884 and 1885, the eighties brought a general increase in the amount of capital moving into the West from British sources. The year 1886 was the best since 1871; 1887 and 1888 were the two peak years of the entire pre-1900 period. At least thirty companies with a total nominal capital of £7,582,500 were formed in those two years and commenced operations. Concentration was primarily on Colorado, with Nevada, Idaho, Dakota, and Montana trailing behind. Utah was no longer a contender.

Despite a near panic in 1890 when the Barings threatened to crash, the level of investment remained high until 1892; then another international depression and a fall in metal prices caused the flow of capital to ebb momentarily. The drop in prices, particularly silver, came first, then the general period of financial distress. Vice-Consul Pearce at Denver reported in 1892 that the low price of silver which prevailed throughout the year had retarded progress in mining and forced a number of low-grade silver mines to suspend operations.[45] British concerns in all parts of the West were hard hit and their spokesmen complained bitterly. Directors of Garfield, Ltd., reported lax times and debased silver prices in 1892 and preached the gospel of rigorous economy in the operation of the company's Nevada mines.[46] Low prices halted work at the mill of Cortez Mines, Ltd., by mid-February 1893,[47] and the depression soon forced the discontinuance of dividend payments.[48] Similarly the fall in the market price of antimony forced the Big Creek Mining Company, Ltd., another Anglo-Nevada concern, to suspend the distribution of profits and to take losses from which it never recovered.[49]

Officials of the New Colorado Silver Mining Company, Ltd., also pondered the problems of their corporation. The concern had incurred heavy expenses in deepening and repairing the Terrible shaft late in 1892 and early in 1893. In July of the latter year the price of silver dropped to sixty cents and this "heavy and unprecedented fall," according to the board of directors, "disorganized the whole country, and

---

[45] Consular Reports on Trade and Finance, U.S. Report for the Year 1892 on the Trade of the Consular District of Chicago, Foreign Office, *Annual Series* No. 1233. (1893), 43.

[46] *Annual Report*, year ending March 31, 1892.

[47] *Annual Report*, year ending Sept. 30, 1892. This was actually issued Feb. 13, 1893.

[48] *Ibid.*   [49] Annual reports for years ending March 31, 1893 and 1894.

mining operations in Georgetown collapsed; our Bank there, with many others, suspended payment; our staff became demoralized, and finally broke up; and we were left with debts that we had no immediate means of paying." [50] In August of the same year, the Colorado manager had written the London office: "After being in a state of seige for ten days, we were able to pay off the most pressing creditors. My position here lately has been both unpleasant and dangerous, from the riotous state of miners whose work had become suddenly stopped by the heavy drop in value of Silver ores." [51]

Although some concerns struggled on in the West after depreciated prices severely crippled their operations and a few even prospered,[52] a great many others sought greener pastures. Company after company liquidated its western interests or simply ignored them while it purchased property elsewhere in the world. The Dickens Custer Mines, Ltd., for example, disposed of its Idaho workings at what the directors estimated to be a loss of £365,335 17s. 5d. and acquired holdings in Australia,[53] only to move on to West Africa within a few years.[54] The venerable Flagstaff Company, Ltd.—the fifth reconstruction of the original—transferred its attention to the Star of Coolgardie mine in Western Australia and retained its Utah property only because no purchaser was available.[55] La Plata Mines, Ltd., leased its Colorado property to its former manager, Philip Argall, and acquired interests in Mozambique.[56] In Montana the Jay Hawk and Lone Pine Consolidated Mining Company, Ltd., held on grimly until 1896, when it suspended operations in America and reorganized to carry on in New Zealand.[57] The "migration of the Jay Hawk," as London periodicals

[50] *Directors' Report,* Nov. 15, 1892 to May 31, 1894. The Bland-Allison Act of 1878 and the Sherman Silver Purchase Act of 1890 apparently had little effect in sustaining silver prices.

[51] Quoted in *ibid.*

[52] The successful De Lamar Mining Co. estimated that in 1893 it lost £13,000 due to the drop in silver prices. But the concern continued to pay its dividends with regularity. Annual reports for years ending March 31, 1893 and 1894.

[53] *Directors' Report,* April 1, 1893 to Dec. 31, 1895.

[54] *Annual Report,* year ending June 30, 1901.

[55] *Directors' Report,* Nov. 13, 1893 to June 30, 1895.

[56] *Directors' Report,* Oct. 27, 1892 to March 31, 1894.

[57] *Circular to Shareholders,* Aug 25, 1896, Stock Exchange Archives, London; Memo. of Agreement (Aug. 25, 1896) between the Jay Hawk and Lone Pine Consolidated Mining Co., John Lavington, and the Ethel Reef Gold Mining Co., Ethel Reef Gold Mining Co., C.R.O. 49231.

dubbed the shift,[58] attracted considerable attention because the company took with it its twenty-five-stamp mill at an estimated cost of more than £10,000.[59]

Unlike the depression of 1873, the dislocation of 1893 did not bring in its wake half a dozen years of meager investments in the West. True, investment slumped badly in 1893 and 1894, but capital flowed again in 1895 with renewed vigor. Yet never throughout the remainder of the nineties was the general predepression peak reached. It appeared in 1895 and 1896 that the Cripple Creek gold fields of Colorado would attract extraordinary British attention and investments. The British vice-consul at Kansas City cautioned his fellow Englishmen against agencies being established in Europe to sell stock in Cripple Creek mines.[60] Others foresaw the possibility of professional operators in London supplementing the "Kaffir circus" by a "Colorado sideshow." [61] Although such efforts were made, no real boom in Cripple Creek mines materialized in England. Informed sources suggested that the anticipated British participation in the development of this new gold region had not materialized because of general dullness and the Venezuela boundary scare.[62] With regard to the latter, at least one American promoter was convinced that sales would lag until "the United States Government settles the much talked about Monroe Doctrine, and eliminates it root and branch off of our American Politics." [63]

Undoubtedly this was a contributing factor, but equally if not more important was the fact that increased competition from other mineral-producing areas tended to draw off capital that might otherwise have been attracted to western America. South Africa, the Yukon, and Australia-New Zealand were all foremost rivals on the money markets of the world in the last half of the nineties, and their successes indubitably helped weaken the movement of British capital into the West.

---

[58] *Mining Journal,* Aug. 8, 1896, 1019.

[59] Skinner, *Mining Manual* (1897), 1043; *Statist,* Aug. 8, 1896, 245.

[60] Consular Reports on Trade and Finance, U.S. Report for the Year 1895 on the Trade of the Consular District of Chicago, Foreign Office *Annual Series* No. 1725 (1896), 51.

[61] *Mining Journal,* Dec. 21, 1895, 1547.   [62] *Ibid.,* Feb. 13, 1897, 213.

[63] William Rogers to W. E. Tustin (Wolverhampton, Eng., Jan. 25, 1896), copy in James A. Beaver MSS, Pennsylvania State University Library, University Park.

British Investments and American Mines

As to which regions received the most English investments in the intermountain area, again conclusions must be confined to a survey of activity by joint-stock companies. Over the entire forty-year period Colorado stood head and shoulders above other western states and territories in the amount of corporate attention. Nevada was a poor second, with Arizona, Idaho, Montana, and Utah grouped closely behind. The bulk of British capital in Nevada, oddly enough, was not invested in the Comstock Lode, although there were English interests there, particularly in the Sutro Tunnel,[64] but rather in the newer mining districts of the state—White Pine, Reese River, and Humboldt. Noticeable, too, is the fact that during the decade of the seventies more than twice as much capital was put into Nevada mines by British companies than into Colorado mines. In the eighties and nineties the opposite was true: new companies incorporated to operate in Colorado were capitalized at more than twice those active in Nevada in the eighties and more than nine times as much during the following decade.[65]

Another general question to be answered, or at least considered, concerns the degree of success encountered by British investors in their western mining ventures. Obviously the Englishman consented to pour his hard-earned funds down an unpredictable hole in an unknown wilderness thousands of miles from home for but one reason: he believed profits would result. And all too frequently the English investor was interested only in immediate profits and lost no time in making known his sentiments to his fellow shareholders.

Hardly had the echo of the chairman's gavel died away at the first statutory meeting held four months after formation of the company than some eager investor would be on his feet inquiring about the first

[64] Adolph Sutro solicited funds for his gigantic undertaking in England and managed to get some $650,000 in bond subscriptions. Report of the Commissions and Evidence Taken by the Committee on Mines and Mining of the House of Representatives of the United States in Regard to the Sutro Tunnel, *Ho. Rpt.* No. 94, 42 Cong., 2 Sess. (1871–1872), 408. Adolph Sutro, *The Sutro Tunnel and Railway to the Comstock Lode in the State of Nevada* (London, 1873), gives the sales talk to potential investors.

[65] Nominal capitalization of companies registered in England and operating in Colorado were: 1870's, £996,000; 1880's, £6,102,000; 1890's, £8,082,660. The figures for Nevada were: 1870's, £2,672,000; 1880's, £2,522,500; 1890's, £850,000.

distribution of earnings.[66] In numerous instances directors catered to these early demands, and dividends were paid before the company was financially stable. The Battle Mountain Mining Company, Nevada, U.S., Ltd., for example, paid dividends of 10 per cent in 1872, but the chairman subsequently admitted that the money might have been better used as a reserve fund to pull the concern through lean times.[67] The Mountain Chief Mining Company of Utah, Ltd., paid premature dividends for two months in the same year, then slipped off into oblivion.[68] A Salt Lake City resident later confided to the world that he had examined the company's property in 1873 and found it "the most innocent of any ore or vein matter I ever met with." [69] Numerous other Anglo-American firms followed the same course in the quarter of a century which followed.[70]

Competent engineers consistently advised against a policy of "picking the eyes out" of a mine in order to satisfy the short-term demands of greedy shareholders,[71] and, to their credit, many boards endeavored to resist the pressure for quick dividends. But in too many instances directors were willing to concur and permit the distribution of early profits no matter how small or how precarious the company's position.

Occasionally, too, directors or large shareholders were interested in promoting the payment of easy dividends at a premature date in order to "bull" the market and share values. The role of unearned dividends in enabling the promoters of the Emma Silver Mining Company, Ltd.,

[66] Report of meeting of the Last Chance Silver Mining Co. of Utah, *Mining Journal*, Aug. 10, 1872, 743; Report of meeting of the Tecoma Silver Mining Co. (May 12, 1873), *Mining World*, May 17, 1873, 980.

[67] Report of meeting, (Nov. 24, 1873), *Mining World*, Nov. 29, 1873, 1080.

[68] *Mining Journal*, Dec. 21, 1872, 1219–1220; London *Times*, Dec. 20, 1875.

[69] "Connoisseur" to editor (Salt Lake City, June 1, 1874), *Mining Journal*, Aug. 1, 1874, 835.

[70] For examples see annual reports of the Mount McClellan Mining Co. for years ending Dec. 31, 1891 and 1893; American Belle Mines, *Directors' Report*, thirteen months ending Dec. 31, 1891; *Report of the 3rd Annual General Meeting of the American Belle Mines, Ltd. held July 15th, 1893*, Stock Exchange Archives, London.

[71] Where Stratton's Independence had paid £400,002 16s. in dividends during its first fourteen months of existence, John Hays Hammond urged that dividends be reduced to £98,000 a year and the balance of profits be spent on "vigorous development." *Financial Times*, Dec. 8, 1900; Stratton's Independence, *Circular to Shareholders*, June 30, 1900.

to dispose of their vendor's shares at advantageous rates has been treated elsewhere.[72] Likewise mention has been made of the manipulations of Erwin Davis to bolster Flagstaff shares [73] and the attempts of the managers of Crooke's Mining and Smelting Company, Ltd., to use the same methods.[74] On the other hand, one unhappy Irishman blamed the burning of the International Mill of the Eberhardt and Aurora Mining Company, Ltd., in 1872 on bear parties interested in seeing that no dividends were paid! [75]

Such dividends as those paid to raise the value of shares or to promote sales were not at all indicative of the actual wealth of the property involved, nor did they reflect adept management. They were simply promoters' and speculators' techniques—merely tools of a particular trade—much as the highly colored prospectus with its alluring promises was an aid to an end. When considered in this light, they contribute little to an understanding of bona fide profits by Anglo-American mining companies during the period.

When dividends were paid, companies lost no time in publicizing their success. Thus total dividends are much less elusive than total actual capital. At least fifty-seven companies registered between 1860 and 1901 ultimately paid dividends aggregating an estimated £11,-750,000 prior to 1915.[76] Numerically this would mean that one company in every nine incorporated eventually paid some kind of dividend. But many of these were but token payments of slight significance; sustained dividend payers are more difficult to locate. Probably no more than ten joint-stock concerns registered in London or Edinburgh for operation in the prescribed area ever returned the shareholders' full investment in dividends. Arizona Copper Company, Ltd., eventually paid more than £3,500,000 to 1914, and the De Lamar Mining Company, Ltd., and its reorganization returned 267.5 per cent between 1891 and 1905. One of the most consistently successful concerns, the Richmond Consolidated Mining Company, Ltd., paid dividends totaling £882,768, or a 324 per cent return on its capital from 1872 to 1895.[77]

If only one company in nine returned profits of any kind and if

---

[72] Above, 155.   [73] Above, 109–111.   [74] Above, 100–101.

[75] John J. Woodburn to editor (Dublin, n.d.), *Stock Exchange Review,* IV (March, 1874).

[76] See Appendix IV.   [77] *Ibid.*

almost incredible debts were sometimes incurred, the reason for much dissatisfaction is readily apparent. When British concerns showed debit balances of more than half a million pounds sterling after fifteen years of operation in western mines,[78] no wonder shareholders came to believe that the comparative declension of the word "mine" was "miner" and the superlative "minus." [79] No wonder company officials expressed themselves as being "sick & tired" of Rocky Mountain ventures which had been nursed along unsuccessfully for more than a quarter of a century.[80]

If dividends were not paid and if debts frequently piled up, wherein lay the blame? It was not merely that "salted" or worthless properties were passed off on the naïve British investor, although that often happened. In many instances a number of contributing factors combined to spell disaster. Poor property purchased at inordinately high prices by companies which were overcapitalized, yet which often lacked sufficient working capital, could hardly be expected to prove remunerative. Excessive speculation and manipulation of shares by company officials or promoters seldom benefited the majority of shareholders. Nor did direction by boards made up of men frequently chosen for their names rather than their abilities and the difficulties of control and co-ordination over thousands of miles of distance tend to make for unmitigated prosperity. Sometimes the failure to understand American mining law and its labyrinths proved to be a major cause of failure.

But the story of mining in general during the nineteenth century is basically the story of risk. The truth of the old miners' adage that predictions go no farther than the end of the individual's pick made mining an unusually speculative enterprise, particularly in the "unscientific" period prior to 1900. The average Englishman recognized that investment in this type of industry was a wager that might possibly be won, but he was not wholly prepared to admit that failure came as a result of the same element of chance. His attitude was summed up in a stanza of verse which appeared in the London press in 1903:

[78] Adelaide Star Mines, a Scottish-Nevada concern dominated by the Coats family of thread-manufacturing fame, built up a debit total of £ 560,295 13s. 3d. between April, 1897, and the end of October, 1912. Adelaide Star Mines, *Annual Report,* year ending Oct. 31, 1912.

[79] *Mining Journal,* Sept. 9, 1871, 800.

[80] W. J. Rodatz to registrar (Birkenhead, May 15, 1919), Whitehead Mining and Smelting Co., C.R.O. 15259.

British Investments and American Mines

In modern speculation
Your language you must choose.
It's an "investment" if you win
But "gambling" if you lose.[81]

When the whole period is considered, the Englishman who poured his surplus funds into American mines was indeed "gambling."

[81] *Anglo-Colorado Mining Guide,* VI (Nov. 28, 1903), 170.

: CHAPTER XI :

A Backward View

THE story of British investment in western mines is an intriguing one, with many facets which would bear further investigation. If some of its chapters are written in faded, almost indistinguishable, scrawl, others are written in bold script and lend themselves to clear-cut generalizations. Quantitative evaluations may fall short of hopeful expectations, but there can be no disputing the fact that between 1860 and 1901 English capital flowed into the mineral industry of the trans-Mississippi West in significant amounts. And that influx, following the movement of human resources, drifted from east to west into the regions where mining had become relatively stable and where transportation and defense problems had been minimized. Usually it followed closely the dips and swells of national or international economic trends in general and of the mineral industry in particular.

The export of capital from Britain was not entirely spontaneous, however. It was imperative that the proper conditions should be present on both sides of the Atlantic before the movement would commence, and it was necessary that interested parties should lend support and direction. The mining West was certainly receptive to the idea of British investment in mines, as the struggle to "sell" the English public would demonstrate. It is true, there were those in the mining camps who were apathetic or even hostile, and the enactment of the Alien Land Law of 1887 indicated that a fairly wide segment of the population at large shared these sentiments.[1] But from the mines came constant pleas and a sharply competitive race for capital.

[1] The general manager of the Centennial-Eureka mine, for example, testified

233

British Investments and American Mines

If the need for outside capital to develop the industry was evident and widely publicized, Victorian England provided an excellent working ground for the host of promoters who assiduously cultivated that particular species of flora known as the *investor imbecillus*. American and British agents alike, acting co-operatively or individually, resorted to almost every conceivable technique and device in efforts to convince the potential investor that an outcropping in the Rockies or a shaft in the Nevada desert was worthy of his attention and—more important—of his money.

And the British investor displayed at least his share of gullibility. At times it appeared that, dazzled by promotional literature, sensational promises, and the use of titled guinea pigs, he simply closed his eyes and poured his funds blindly into whatever scheme was placed before him. Whether he was actually seduced or whether he was waiting hopefully for the opportunity is sometimes difficult to ascertain, but in all too many instances the investor was shorn of his money and left to lament at leisure the folly of his ways.

Often the Englishman was the victim of his own greed and naïveté, but Brother Jonathan was by no means adverse to mulcting him for all he was worth. Valueless or exhausted mines were palmed off at outrageously high prices, an occasional concealed mortgage was included in more than one bargain, and even a few "engrafted" or "salted" ore bodies changed hands across the trans-Atlantic counter. At the least the property offered was overvalued. Outright fraud—or rather its proof—may have been comparatively rare, but misrepresentation in one form or another was relatively common. Paying mines in English hands were far outnumbered by poor risks, which, like the Sutro Tunnel, "drained the Comstock lode to a depth of 1,600 feet, and the pockets of the English investors to a much lower level." [2] And

---

in 1899 that he doubted the wisdom of allowing English, Dutch, or French capitalists to take profits out of western mines. Testimony of Clarence E. Allen (Salt Lake City, Aug. 2, 1899), Report of the Industrial Commission on the Relations and Conditions of Capital and Labor Employed in the Mining Industry, *Ho. Doc.* No. 181, 57 Cong., 1 Sess. (1901–1902), 572. For a general treatment of agrarian hostility toward British investment see Roger V. Clements, "The Farmers' Attitude toward British Investment in American Industry," *Journal of Economic History*, XV (1955), 151–159.

[2] *Sci. Press,* June 30, 1883, 434.

seldom did the Englishman find satisfactory recourse at home or in America.

In Great Britain laws relating to companies were not always strict enough to prevent questionable sales and promotional tactics. The ease with which joint-stock companies were formed and re-formed during the period is astonishing. W. S. Gilbert caught the spirit of the era in his little-remembered operetta, *Utopia, Limited,* written in 1893:

> If you come to grief, and creditors are craving
> (For nothing that is planned by mortal head
> Is certain in this Vale of Sorrow—saving
> That one's Liability is Limited),—
> Do you suppose that signifies perdition?
> If so you're but a monetary dunce—
> You merely file a Winding-Up Petition,
> And start another Company at once! [3]

Even after the Englishman had been induced to invest, he frequently found that formidable barriers lay across the path to success. If he decided to invest in an American mining firm, he had little or no control; if he channeled his capital through a concern registered in London or Edinburgh there were other disadvantages. Overcapitalization and a lack of adequate working capital might seriously impair the company's operation if the widespread practice of issuing founder's or vendor's shares weakened the organization. Manipulation of shares on the London market by British or American "operators" often worked to the investor's detriment and occasionally brought down a corporate structure around his ears. The Emma was an extreme case, but the "bulls" and the "bears" plied their trade in the securities of most other Anglo-American concerns as well. Too many promoters or vendors were associated with mine sales merely for speculative purposes, and their presence helps explain why the Flagstaff and other kindred concerns were by 1874 "flying not even the Stars and Stripes of Yankee-Doodledom, but something very like the skull and crossbones," so far as the English public was concerned. [4]

One of the British investor's biggest and most pulsating headaches

[3] Act I, in *The Complete Plays of Gilbert and Sullivan* (New York, 1936), 622.
[4] "S" to editor (London, Feb. 24, 1874), *Mining World*, Feb. 28, 1874, 419.

came from management. It was seldom in the best interests of a concern to be saddled with guinea-pig directors who "hardly knew the difference between a mine and a haystack." [5] Mine officials of mediocre caliber, plus delay in transmitting information and instructions, only pointed up the inherent difficulties of absentee ownership across an ocean and three-quarters of a continent. Inferior men or even those of independent temperament could not be relied upon to serve the best interests of the company at the mine, but there was no simple, foolproof method of dealing with the situation.

Nor could the British firm keep from being swept into the same litigious whirlpool that sucked down to oblivion so many American companies. Indeed, because of its susceptibility the English concern probably received more than its share of legal entanglements. Mining law was complex enough for the expert, but for the British official, often selected for his name or family connection, it frequently became a hopelessly involved example of Yankee "justice" which spelled the corporate end of more than one undertaking. This failure to understand all the technicalities of American mining law exposed the Anglo-American company to the efforts of clever, if sometimes unprincipled, Americans to levy legal blackmail and force the purchase of adjoining claims at exorbitant prices. This and other costly litigations were never confined to British concerns alone, but the English were probably most vulnerable.

Although the federal government occasionally played a part, its direct role was in general relatively small. United States laws might extend to the regulation of almost any aspect of mining in the territories but only to the initial disposition of mineral land on the public domain in the states, with aliens theoretically excluded from locating or obtaining patents on claims. Despite this, federal policy was in practice fairly liberal, and circumvention of the statutes was usually not difficult. If the passage of the Alien Land Law was on the surface inimical to British investment in territorial mining, the act remained largely a dead letter and investment went on in spite of its restrictive provisions.

Nor did the British government play any important role in the investment story. The Foreign Office received with polite boredom the few complaints from British subjects which stemmed from western mining ventures, but apart from a few minor commentaries there were

[5] *Ibid.*, 420.

no significant diplomatic discussions on such matters, even when the ticklish Emma imbroglio reached its height. Whitehall displayed a mild interest in the alien land laws of the 1880's, but only inquiries, not protests, were forthcoming as a result.

Just what did the flow of British capital mean to the mineral frontier and to the West in general? If those westerners interested in amending the Alien Land Act could be believed, English capital virtually sustained territorial mining and without it the entire industry would have collapsed. But since such an extreme view was obviously designed for public consumption and its propaganda effect, it must be taken with the appropriate grains of seasoning.

Nevertheless, both directly and indirectly English capital investment made substantial contributions to the development of the American mineral frontier. Directly, capital responded at a time when it was vitally needed, not only creating a few additional American millionaires,[6] but sometimes doing much to further local prosperity as well. Such successful concerns as the Richmond Consolidated Mining Company, Ltd., the Montana Mining Company, Ltd., and the De Lamar Mining Company, Ltd., operated over sustained periods of time and became the cornerstones of the mineral industry in their respective localities. Even when the companies themselves were distinguished by their lack of success, the capital they provided was still welcome.

Indirectly, apart from the import of large amounts of capital actually invested, British concerns made contributions by pointing the way for American capitalists. The English were willing to take risks—often too many for their own good—and any semblance of success served to instill confidence in potential American investors. After all, if a cumbersome inefficient English company could return profits, then certainly any American could do the same with half the effort! If a British firm fell by the wayside, the American could always attribute it to corruption or mismanagement.

[6] In an 1892 inventory of 4,047 American millionaires, Thomas Cruse, William M. Stewart, Jerome Chaffee, H. A. W. Tabor, D. H. Moffat, William Gilpin, William A. Bell, John P. Jones, Adolph Sutro, and J. R. De Lamar were included. All made at least part of their fortunes dealing in mines on the English market. A son of H. H. Baxter and a son and a daughter of Trenor Park inherited enough from their respective fathers to place them on the list. See *The Tribune Monthly* (June, 1892) in Sidney Ratner (ed.), *New Light on the History of Great American Fortunes* (New York, 1952).

British Investments and American Mines

Nor can the impact of the men who followed in the wake of English capital be discounted. Undoubtedly many of the English or Cornish "experts" sent out as engineers or mining captains were unfamiliar with western conditions; some were in addition incompetent or even dishonest. But capable personnel were included also—men who proved themselves to be able, intelligent, and industrious. Sometimes they clustered in little knots in the West, clinging momentarily to their cricket matches, christening their new furnaces with toasts of "God save the Queen," [7] but soon they tended to lose their English identity and to become absorbed in the land of their adoption.

But whether they immediately abandoned their British traditions or endeavored to retain them, these men brought with them the advanced techniques and improvements gained from years of experience in mines and smelters the world over. To be sure, many of the new processes and machines could not be transplanted to the trans-Mississippi West *in toto:* much was discarded and frequent modifications were necessary to fit the peculiar needs of western environment. Yet the import of basic ideas played its part in the development of this frontier, just as in Australia, South Africa, or the Yukon.

The story of British investment in western mines, then, is one of dark moments and bright, of trials and tribulations for the English investor, and of partial consolidation of the world of technological advancement. Fortunes were made and lost; the same was true of reputations. Yet when the final chapters are written, probably the whole will be viewed as having been neither better nor worse than the development and exploitation of America's natural resources in general.

Certainly British investment in the mines of the West can only be considered as part of the larger picture. The period from 1860 to 1901 saw the throwing open of natural resources in the United States to rapid and often ruthless exploitation by private and corporate interests to a degree not heretofore witnessed in America. From all sides in flocked hungry capitalists, all eager to drink deeply and to feast greedily, as what Vernon L. Parrington has called the "Great Barbecue" got

[7] When the first Swansea-type furnace constructed in Colorado was completed by the United States General Smelting and Mining Co., Ltd., in 1872, a formal christening was held by employees in honor of the occasion. Orations and serenades filled the air and generous amounts of "old English cheer" flowed freely. Georgetown *Miner,* Oct. 24, 1872.

under way. Probably never before in the nation's history had capital enjoyed such an untrammeled opportunity to work its will on the public domain and never were so many fortunes made with so much ease. The Federal government changed or relaxed its laws or simply stood idly by with folded hands while not only mineral, but agricultural, grazing, timber, and power resources passed out of its care and the exploitative process gathered momentum.

British capitalists and investors were as willing as the Americans to participate in the Great American Grab Bag, and English investments in the mines were to continue unabated until World War I, from which the United States emerged as a creditor nation no longer actively soliciting capital as in earlier periods, but now lending money and investing abroad. If the East-West flow of capital ebbed or was at least diverted after 1914, it was not until English pounds had made concrete contributions to the development of an American financial and industrial structure which largely eliminated the need for outside capital.

Appendixes

British Limited-Liability Joint-Stock Companies Registered to Engage in
Mining Activities in the American West, 1860–1901 [a]

Limited-liability companies	Year	Area	Active?	Nominal capital
*Adelaide Star Mines	1897	Nev.	Yes	£ 350,000
Agnes Mining Company	1883	Colo.	Yes	30,000
Ajax (Big Indian) Silver Mining Company	1871	Colo.	No	40,000
Alturas Gold	1886	Ida.	Yes	300,000
Elmore Gold Company	1889	Ida.	Yes	300,000
Ida Gold Company	1892	Ida.	Yes	75,000
Alvarez Silver Mining and Smelting Company	1871	Nev.	No	52,000
American Belle Mines	1890	Colo.	Yes	400,000
Anglo-Colorado Exploration Syndicate	1896	Colo.	Yes	100,000
Anglo-Montana Mining Company	1886	Mont.	Yes	120,000
Argenta Falls Silver Mining Company	1883	Colo.	Yes	150,000
*Argyle Mining Company	1900	Ariz.	No	100,000
Arivaca Mining Company	1869	Ariz.	No	200,000
Arizona Consolidated Copper Mines	1899	Ariz.	Yes	150,000
*Arizona Copper Company	1882	Ariz.	Yes	875,000
*Arizona Copper Company	1884	Ariz.	Yes	715,000
Arizona Mortgage Corporation	1899	Ariz.	No	10,000
Arizona Trust and Mortgage Company	1883	Ariz.	Yes	360,000

[a] Included are companies designed to carry on promotional, milling, or smelting operations as well as actual mining. The symbol * denotes companies incorporated in Edinburgh; all others were registered in London. Nominal capital figures include subsequent additions as noted in the official Board of Trade files. Reconstructions are indicated by indentation.

APPENDIX I (*continued*)

Limited-liability companies	Year	Area	Active?	Nominal capital
Astor Alliance Mines	1886	Colo.	Yes	285,000
New Astor Mining Company	1888	Colo.	No	30,000
Astor Consolidated Silver Mining Company	1882	Colo.	No	200,000
°Atchison Mining Company	1875	Colo.	Yes	25,000
Atlanta Gold and Silver Consolidated Mines	1888	Ida.	Yes	650,000
Atlanta Gold and Silver Consolidated Mines	1897	Ida.	Yes	150,000
Atlanta Silver Mining Company	1871	Ida.	No	250,000
Austin Consolidated Silver Mines Company	1865	Nev.	No	100,000
Aztec Gold Mines	1893	N. Mex.	Yes	100,000
Basin-Elkhorn Mining Company	1892	Mont.	Yes	161,000
Battle Mountain Mining Company, Nevada, U.S.	1869	Nev.	Yes	50,000
New Battle Mountain Mining Company of Nevada, U.S.	1878	Nev.	Yes	28,000
°Bear Creek Alluvial Gold Company	1894	Ida.	Yes	65,000
°Bear Creek Alluvial Gold Company	1896	Ida.	Yes	80,000
Bear Creek Gold	1890	Ida.	Yes	20,000
Beaver Silver Mining Company	1872	Utah	No	100,000
Belcher Mining Company ᵇ	1882	Colo.	No	25,000
Bertha Silver Mining Company	1886	Colo.	Yes	50,000
Big Creek Mining Company	1891	Nev.	Yes	50,000
Bon Accord Placers	1891	Mont.	Yes	10,000
Bon Accord Placers	1898	Mont.	Yes	150,000
Boston Consolidated Copper and Gold Mining Company	1898	Utah	Yes	500,000
Boulder Valley Collieries Company of Colorado	1874	Colo.	No	260,000
British-American Co-operative Mining Association	1882	Ida.	Yes	5,000
British and Colorado Smelting Works Company	1872	Colo.	No	100,000

ᵇ The Belcher Mining Company, Ltd., and the Green Mountain Mining Company (of Silverton), Ltd., were amalgamated in 1882 to form the London and Silverton Mining Company, Ltd.

APPENDIX I (*continued*)

Limited-liability companies	Year	Area	Active?	Nominal capital
British Mining and Milling Company	1874	Nev.	Yes	100,000
Connolly Mine	1879	Nev.	Yes	60,000
Broadway Gold Mining Company	1881	Mont.	Yes	120,000
Bullion Mining Company	1884	Ida.	No	220,000
Buster Mines Syndicate	1892	Ariz.	Yes	15,000
Caledonia (Cripple Creek) Gold Mine	1897	Colo.	Yes	125,000
Caledonia Gold Syndicate	1886	Colo.	Yes	25,000
"California" Gold Mine Company	1881	Colo.	Yes	130,000
New California	1886	Colo.	Yes	160,000
California Milling and Mining Company	1893	Colo.	Yes	75,000
Camp Bird	1900	Colo.	Yes	1,000,000
Camp Floyd Silver Mining Company	1871	Utah	Yes	120,000
Camp Floyd Milling and Mining Company	1874	Utah	No	12,000
Canada Del Oro Mines	1891	Ariz.	Yes	30,000
Tucson Mining and Smelting Company	1894	Ariz.	Yes	20,000
Candelaria Waterworks and Milling Company c	1885	Nev.	Yes	200,000
Carisa Gold Mines	1889	Wyo.	No	180,000
Carlisle Gold Mining Company d	1886	N. Mex.	Yes	200,000
Carr Mine and Colorado Company	1900	Colo.	Yes	150,000
Catalina Gold Mines	1893	Ariz.	Yes	25,000
Catoctin Silver Mining Company	1891	Ariz.	No	25,000
Central Aspen Silver Mining Company	1891	Colo.	Yes	100,000
New Aspen Silver Mines	1897	Colo.	Yes	125,000
Central City (Colorado) Mining Company	1873	Colo.	No	640
Central City Mining Company	1871	Colo.	No	100,000
Central Development Syndicate	1896	Colo.	Yes	5,000
Central Pacific Coal and Coke Company	1878	Utah	Yes	500,000

c The Candelaria Waterworks and Milling Company, Ltd., and the Princess Mining Company of London, Ltd., were in 1891 joined with other properties to form the Consolidated Candelaria Company, Ltd.

d The Carlisle Gold Mining Company, Ltd., and the Empire Mining Company, Ltd., were absorbed in 1889 by a new concern, Golden Leaf, Ltd.

Appendixes

Limited-liability companies	Year	Area	Active?	Nominal capital
Cerrillos Mining Company	1889	N. Mex.	Yes	40,000
Champion Gold and Silver Mines Company of Colorado	1871	Colo.	No	75,000
Champion Mining Company	1870	Nev.	No	60,000
Charles Dickens Mining Company	1886	Ida.	Yes	250,000
Dickens Custer Company	1887	Ida.	Yes	420,000
Dickens Custer Mines	1889	Ida.	Yes	420,000
Dickens Custer Mines	1898	Ida.	Yes	420,000
Charter Oak Copper Mines	1898	Wyo.	Yes	40,000
Chicago Silver Mining Company	1873	Utah	Yes	150,000
Cincinnati Company	1884	Colo.	Yes	60,000
Cinnamon Mountain Gold and Silver Mining Company	1886	Colo.	No	150,000
City Rock Silver Mining Company	1873	Utah	Yes	30,000
Clarissa Gold Mining Company	1888	Colo.	Yes	100,000
Clear Creek Mining Company	1883	Colo.	No	2,000
Clifton Arizona Copper Company	1900	Ariz.	Yes	10,000
Clifton Gold Mining Company	1894	Ariz.	No	2,000
Clifton Silver Mining Company	1871	Colo.	Yes	35,000
Clifton Utah Mining Company	1896	Utah	Yes	2,250
Clipper Mine Syndicate	1888	Colo.	Yes	25,000
Cochise Mill and Mining Company	1892	Ariz.	No	30,000
"Colorado Boy" Silver Mines	1891	Colo.	Yes	120,000
Colorado California Gold and Silver Mining Company	1871	Colo.	No	80,000
Colorado Central City Gold Mining Company	1881	Colo.	No	35,000
Colorado Copper Company	1867	Ariz.	No	150,000
Colorado Copper Syndicate	1899	Colo.	No	10,000
Colorado Gold and Silver Extraction Company	1888	Colo.	Yes	100,000
Colorado Gold-Fields Syndicate	1896	Colo.	No	26,250
British American Gold Fields	1899	Colo.	No	125,000
Colorado Gold Silver and Lead Recovery Syndicate	1888	Colo.	Yes	30,000
Colorado Highland Mining Company	1871	Colo.	Yes	6,000
Colorado Investment Company	1896	Colo.	No	2,500
Colorado Mines Development Company	1882	Colo.	No	21,000

APPENDIX I (*continued*)

Limited-liability companies	Year	Area	Active?	Nominal capital
Colorado Mining and Land Company	1870	Colo.	Yes	250,000
Colorado Mining Syndicate	1888	Colo.	No	30,000
Colorado Mining Syndicate	1894	Colo.	No	500
Colorado-Montana Development Syndicate	1895	Colo.-Mont.	No	150,000
Colorado Prospecting Company	1891	Colo.	Yes	3,000
Colorado Terrible Lode Mining Company [e]	1870	Colo.	Yes	125,000
Colorado Silver Mining Company	1887	Colo.	Yes	325,000
New Colorado Silver Mining Company	1892	Colo.	Yes	65,000
Colorado Deep Level Mining Company	1897	Colo.	Yes	50,000
Colorado United Gold and Silver Mining Company	1871	Colo.	No	120,000
Comstock Mining Company	1888	Utah	No	250,000
Consolidated Candelaria Company	1891	Nev.	Yes	100,000
Consolidated Esmeralda	1885	Nev.	Yes	500,000
Esmeralda	1889	Nev.	Yes	500,000
Durand Gold Mines	1893	Nev.	Yes	25,000
Copper Queen	1884	Ariz.	No	500,000
Copper Queen United	1885	Ariz.	No	350,000
Cora Belle Mining Company	1891	Colo.	No	15,000
Cortez Mines	1888	Nev.	Yes	300,000
Crescent and Nyanza Silver Mines Company	1871	Colo.	No	30,000
*Crestone Gold Mining Company	1889	Colo.	Yes	160,000
Cripple Creek Agency Syndicate	1895	Colo.	Yes	2,000
Cripple Creek Bonanza Gold Mines	1896	Colo.	Yes	120,000
Cripple Creek (Bull Hill) Finance and Development Company	1896	Colo.	No	160,000
Cripple Creek Consolidated Mines	1896	Colo.	No	250,000
Cripple Creek Development Syndicate	1895	Colo.	No	11,000
Cripple Creek Exploitation Syndicate	1895	Colo.	Yes	30,000
Cripple Creek Gold and Exploration	1896	Colo.	No	50,000
Cripple Creek Gold Fields	1895	Colo.	Yes	100,000

[e] This name was changed to the Colorado United Mining Company, Ltd., in May, 1877.

Appendixes

Limited-liability companies	Year	Area	Active?	Nominal capital
Cripple Creek Gold Fields	1897	Colo.	No	250,000
Cripple Creek Gold Mines Development	1896	Colo.	No	100,000
Cripple Creek Mines	1896	Colo.	No	50,000
Cripple Creek Pioneers	1896	Colo.	Yes	50,000
Cripple Creek Proprietary	1896	Colo.	Yes	150,000
Cripple Creek Prospectors	1896	Colo.	No	50,000
Cripple Creek Shakespear Gold Mines	1896	Colo.	Yes	100,000
Crisman Corporation	1898	Colo.	Yes	10,000
Crooke's Mining and Smelting Company	1882	Colo.	Yes	301,000
Lake City Mining Company	1886	Colo.	Yes	130,000
Ute and Ulay Mines	1889	Colo.	Yes	100,000
Crown Prince Mine Syndicate	1888	Colo.	No	7,500
Czar Silver and Galena Mine	1883	Colo.	No	75,000
Davenport Mining Company	1872	Utah	Yes	120,000
Decatur Mines Syndicate	1892	Colo.	Yes	45,000
London and Denver Mining Corporation	1896	Colo.	Yes	120,000
De Lamar Mining Company	1891	Ida.	Yes	400,000
Del Norte Gold Mining Company	1887	Colo.	No	660,000
Delano Milling and Mining Company	1898	Colo.	Yes	160,000
Denaro Gold Mining Company	1886	Colo.	Yes	60,000
Denver Coal Company	1890	Colo.	Yes	100,000
Dexter, Colorado, Gold Mining Company	1886	Colo.	No	75,000
*Diamond Hill Gold Mines	1896	Mont.	Yes	455,000
*Diamond Hill Gold Mines	1898	Mont.	Yes	225,000
*Diamond Hill Syndicate	1896	Mont.	Yes	3,000
Doric Gold Mines	1895	Colo.	Yes	125,000
Doric Gold Mines	1900	Colo.	Yes	125,000
Doris Syndicate	1888	Nev.	Yes	251,000
East Sheboygan Silver Mining Company	1871	Nev.	Yes	95,000
Eberhardt and Aurora Mining Company	1870	Nev.	Yes	500,000
Eberhardt Company	1881	Nev.	Yes	210,000

APPENDIX I (*continued*)

Limited-liability companies	Year	Area	Active?	Nominal capital
Eberhardt and Monitor Company	1885	Nev.	Yes	260,000
New Eberhardt Company	1888	Nev.	Yes	75,000
Elk Mountain Gold and Silver Mining Company	1888	Colo.	No	400,000
Elkhart Mining Corporation	1900	Ariz.	Yes	300,000
Elkhorn Mining Company	1890	Mont.	Yes	200,000
New Elkhorn Mining Company	1895	Mont.	Yes	315,000
Emma Silver Mining Company	1871	Utah	Yes	1,000,000
New Emma Silver Mining Company	1882	Utah	Yes	700,000
New Emma Silver Mining Company, 1886	1886	Utah	Yes	350,000
Emma Company	1890	Utah	Yes	125,000
Emma Company	1895	Utah	No	150,000
Emma Company (1900)	1900	Utah	No	75,000
Empire Gold Exploration	1896	Colo.	No	75,000
Empire Gold Mines Company	1865	Colo.	No	100,000
Empire Mining Company f	1886	Mont.	Yes	100,000
Empire Summit Gold Mining Company	1880	Colo.	Yes	250,000
Empress	1886	Nev.	No	100,000
Empress Mines	1888	Nev.	No	300,000
Etta Mining Company	1895	Mont.	Yes	7,000
Eureka (Nevada) Silver Mining Company	1880	Nev.	Yes	100,000
New Eureka Mining Company	1886	Nev.	Yes	60,000
Farrington Mines	1886	Nev.	No	300,000
Fisk Gold Mines	1893	Colo.	Yes	200,000
Flagstaff Silver Mining Company of Utah	1871	Utah	Yes	300,000
New Flagstaff Consolidated Silver Mining Company	1880	Utah	No	80,000
Flagstaff District Silver Mining Company	1881	Utah	Yes	160,000
Flagstaff Mines	1885	Utah	Yes	175,000

f See note d above.

APPENDIX I (*continued*)

Limited-liability companies	Year	Area	Active?	Nominal capital
New Flagstaff Mining Company	1888	Utah	Yes	300,000
"Flagstaff"	1889	Utah	Yes	240,000
Flagstaff Company	1893	Utah	Yes	240,000
Flagstaff Mines	1898	Utah	No	240,000
"Flora" Gold Mine Syndicate g	1884	Colo.	Yes	25,000
Garfield	1886	Nev.	Yes	100,000
Garfield	1889	Nev.	Yes	100,000
Georgetown Syndicate	1897	Colo.	Yes	5,000
Geronimo Gold and Silver Mining Syndicate of New Mexico	1899	N. Mex.	Yes	20,000
Gilpin County Consolidated Mining and Milling Company	1883	Colo.	No	50,000
Gilpin County Mining and Leasing Syndicate	1887	Colo.	Yes	10,000
Gilpin Gold	1895	Colo.	Yes	90,000
Gilpin Gold Placers	1886	Colo.	No	75,000
Gladstone Smelting and Mining Company	1883	Colo.	No	150,000
*Glasgow and Western Exploration Company	1896	Nev.	Yes	30,000
Globe Mineral Exploration Company	1898	Ariz.	Yes	50,000
Godbe Company	1873	Utah	No	50,000
Gold and Silver Crown of Nevada Mines Company	1895	Nev.	Yes	260,000
*Gold and Silver Extraction Company of America	1893	Colo.	Yes	110,000
Gold-Basin Mining Company	1896	Ariz.	No	150,000
Gold King	1888	Colo.	Yes	350,000
Gold Mining Company of Yuba	1869	Ida.	Yes	35,000
"Gold Queen"	1888	Colo.	Yes	180,000
Gold Syndicate	1897	Colo.	Yes	50,000
Golden Eagle Syndicate	1898	Wyo.	Yes	60,000
Golden Horn Consolidated Mining Company	1896	Colo.	Yes	50,000

g This name was changed to the "Flora" Gold Mining Company, Ltd., in December, 1884.

APPENDIX I (*continued*)

Limited-liability companies	Year	Area	Active?	Nominal capital
		N. Mex–		
Golden Leaf	1889	Mont.	Yes	350,000
Golden Reefs	1895	Ariz.	No	50,000
Golden State Mines	1897	Ariz.	Yes	100,000
Golden Valley Mines	1890	Colo.	Yes	60,000
Goulding Placers	1887	Colo.	No	150,000
Governor Group	1887	Colo.	No	100,000
Gower Mines Syndicate	1898	Colo.	Yes	15,000
Grand Canyon Mining Company of Arizona	1890	Ariz.	Yes	75,000
Grand Central Silver Mines	1891	N. Mex.	Yes	200,000
Granite Gold Exploration Syndicate	1895	Colo.	Yes	1,200
Great Bonanza Gold Mining Company	1891	Colo.	Yes	100,000
Great Bonanza Syndicate	1890	Colo.	Yes	2,500
Great Western Silver Mining Company	1871	Nev.	Yes	30,000
Green Mountain Mining Company (of Silverton) [h]	1881	Colo.	Yes	19,000
Groome Company	1875	Nev.	No	42,000
Guston Silver Mine Company	1886	Colo.	Yes	100,000
New Guston Company	1887	Colo.	Yes	110,000
Hall Valley Silver-Lead Mining and Smelting Company	1873	Colo.	Yes	115,000
Upper Platte Mining and Smelting Company	1878	Colo.	Yes	50,000
Hamilton Mining and Smelting Company	1870	Nev.	No	5,000
Hamilton Smelting Company	1871	Nev.	No	60,000
Harney Peak (Dakota) Tin Company [1]	1887	Dak.	Yes	3,000,000
Harquahala Gold Mining Company	1893	Ariz.	Yes	300,000
King of the Hills Gold Mining Company	1899	Ariz.	Yes	80,000

[h] See note b above.

[1] This name was changed to the Harney Peak Consolidated Tin Company, Ltd., in January, 1890.

Limited-liability companies	Year	Area	Active?	Nominal capital
Henriett Mining and Smelting Company	1882	Colo.	Yes	300,000
Henriett Silver Mining Company	1882	Colo.	No	250,000
Horse-Shoe Mining Company	1887	Colo.	No	210,000
Hubert Gold Mines	1887	Colo.	No	155,000
Humboldt Electric Power and Mining Company	1888	Nev.	Yes	82,500
Humboldt Silver Mining Company	1867	Nev.	No	60,000
Hunter Consolidated Mining Company	1877	Nev.	Yes	120,000
Idaho Gold and Silver Mines	1887	Ida.	Yes	200,000
Idaho Mining Company	1889	Ida.	Yes	250,000
Idaho Exploring Company	1893	Ida.	Yes	100,000
Idaho Gold Mining Company	1881	Ida.	No	150,000
Huron Consolidated Gold Mining Company	1882	Ida.	No	160,000
Idaho Smelting Company	1880	Ida.	No	20,000
Idaho Syndicate	1890	Ida.	Yes	4,000
Illinois Gold and Silver Mining Company	1871	Colo.	No	62,000
Ingalls Gold Mining Company	1889	Colo.	Yes	20,000
Ione (Nevada) Silver Mines	1888	Nev.	No	120,000
Iron Mask Gold and Silver Mining Company	1887	Colo.	No	600,000
Irwin's Peak Mining Company	1887	Colo.	Yes	10,000
Jay Hawk Mining Company	1888	Mont.	Yes	175,000
Jay Hawk Mining Company	1889	Mont.	Yes	150,000
Jay Hawk Mining Company	1890	Mont.	Yes	165,000
Jay Hawk and Lone Pine Consolidated Mining Company	1891	Mont.	Yes	285,000
Jay Hawk and Lone Pine Consolidated Mining Company	1895	Mont.	Yes	285,000
Ethel Reef Gold Mining Company	1896	Mont.	No	120,000
Jersey Lily Gold Mines	1895	Ariz.	Yes	150,000
Kaiser Gold Mines	1888	Ariz.	No	200,000

APPENDIX I (*continued*)

Limited-liability companies	Year	Area	Active?	Nominal capital
Kansas Mining Company	1871	Colo.	Yes	55,000
Kelly Gold Placer Company ʲ	1884	Mont.	No	. . . . . .
Kent County Gold Mine Company	1883	Colo.	Yes	120,000
King Alfred Silver Mining Company	1873	Nev.	Yes	40,000
Kohinoor Silver Mining Company ᵏ	1880	Colo.	Yes	80,000
Lady Franklin Mining Company	1886	N. Mex.	Yes	200,000
Lander City Silver Mining Company	1865	Nev.	No	100,000
La Plata Mining and Smelting Company	1883	Colo.	Yes	400,000
New La Plata Mining and Smelting Company	1886	Colo.	Yes	400,000
La Plata Mines	1890	Colo.	Yes	105,000
La Plata Mines	1892	Colo.	Yes	101,250
Imperial Gold Company	1897	Colo.	No	125,000
Last Chance Silver Mining Company of Utah	1872	Utah	Yes	105,000
New Chance Mining Company	1880	Utah	No	60,000
Last Chance Consolidated Silver Mining Company	1880	Utah	Yes	100,000
New Last Chance Silver Mining Company	1884	Utah	Yes	100,000
West Mountain Mining Company	1888	Utah	Yes	70,000
Leadville Mines	1888	Colo.	No	210,000
Legal Tender Milling and Mining Company	1887	Colo.	No	200,000
Leland Stanford Gold Mining Company	1895	Ariz.	Yes	60,000
Lemhi-Argenta Gold Placer Consols	1884	Ida.	No	225,000
Lillie (Cripple Creek) Gold Mining Company	1898	Colo.	Yes	225,000
Little Josephine (Colorado) Mining Company	1888	Colo.	Yes	25,000

ʲ The only reference to this is in the *Mining Journal's* annual listing of mining companies registered. The name is listed in the indexes of the Registrar of Companies Offices in London, but the file is missing.

ᵏ This name was changed to the Kohinoor and Donaldson Consolidated Mining Company, Ltd., in October, 1882.

Appendixes

Limited-liability companies	Year	Area	Active?	Nominal capital
Little Josephine (Colorado) Mining Company	1891	Colo.	Yes	50,000
Little Wonder Gold Mines	1900	N. Mex.	No	30,000
Logan Gold Mines	1886	Colo.	No	120,000
London and Central City (Colorado) Gold Mining Company	1873	Colo.	No	300,000
London and Cripple Creek Reduction Corporation	1895	Colo.	Yes	130,000
Cripple Creek Ore Reduction Works	1898	Colo.	Yes	150,000
London and New Mexico Company	1883	N. Mex.	No	1,000
London and Silverton Mining Company	1882	Colo.	Yes	60,000
Silverton Mines	1887	Colo.	Yes	60,000
Lord Byron and Valentine Mining Company	1881	Nev.	No	100,000
Lucky Guss Gold Mine	1896	Colo.	Yes	120,000
Lucky Guss	1898	Colo.	Yes	60,000
Lucy Phillips Gold and Silver Mining Company	1866	Ida.	Yes	120,000
Lynx Creek Gold and Land Company	1890	Ariz.	Yes	80,000
Lynx Creek Gold Mining Company	1896	Ariz.	Yes	50,000
McHenry Mining Company	1874	Utah	No	300,000
McCoy Hill Silver Mining Company	1872	Nev.	No	80,000
MacKay and Revolution Silver Mining Company	1883	Utah	Yes	150,000
Madison Gold Mining Company	1894	Mont.	Yes	85,000
"Maid of Erin" Silver Mines	1891	Colo.	Yes	600,000
Mammoth-Collins Gold Mines	1895	Ariz.	Yes	100,000
Mammoth Copperopolis of Utah	1871	Utah	Yes	170,000
British Tintic Mining Company	1877	Utah	Yes	75,000
Mammoth Gold Mines	1889	Ariz.	Yes	500,000
Manhattan Consolidated Gold and Silver Mines	1887	Nev.	No	165,000
Manhattan Freehold Gold and Silver Mining Company	1885	Nev.	Yes	100,000
*Meldrum Tunnel and Mining Syndicate	1897	Colo.	Yes	40,000

APPENDIX I (*continued*)

Limited-liability companies	Year	Area	Active?	Nominal capital
"Minah Consolidated" Mining Company	1889	Mont.	Yes	250,000
Mine Owners' Trust	1891	Colo.	Yes	30,000
Mineral Creek Mining Company	1896	Colo.	Yes	20,000
°Mineral Hill Copper Syndicate	1900	Ariz.	Yes	5,000
Mineral Hill New Company	1877	Nev.	Yes	12,000
Mineral Hill Silver Mines Company	1871	Nev.	Yes	300,000
Mineral Rights Association	1866	Nev.	Yes	150,000
Minerals Assets Company	1898	Colo.	Yes	32,500
Mines Intersection Syndicate	1897	Colo.	Yes	12,000
Mining Adventurers of Utah	1873	Utah	Yes	24,000
°Mining Development Syndicate (of Colorado)	1892	Colo.	Yes	20,000
Monarch and Chalk Creek Mining Company	1880	Colo.	No	200,000
Monarch Copper Company	1883	Wyo.	No	75,000
Monarch Syndicate	1895	Colo.	Yes	200,000
Montana Company	1883	Mont.	Yes	660,000
Montana Mining Company	1892	Mont.	Yes	660,000
Montana Gold Ring Mining Company	1899	Mont.	No	2,000
Monte Cristo Mining Company	1900	Ariz.	Yes	100,000
Moon-Anchor Consolidated Gold Mines	1898	Colo.	Yes	400,000
Morenci and General Trust	1900	Ariz.	Yes	50,000
Morenci Copper Mines	1899	Ariz.	Yes	100,000
Mount McClellan Mining Company	1890	Colo.	Yes	300,000
Mountain Chief Mining Company of Utah	1872	Utah	Yes	50,000
Mudsill Mining Company	1888	Colo.	Yes	75,000
Natrona Syndicate	1891	Wyo.	No	10,000
Nevada Company	1885	Nev.	No	320,000
Nevada Consolidated Mines and Smelting Company	1884	Nev.	No	100,000
Nevada Nickel and Cobalt Company	1886	Nev.	Yes	250,000
Nevada Nickel Syndicate	1894	Nev.	Yes	10,000
Nevada Silver Mining Company	1866	Nev.	Yes	50,000
Nevada Syndicate	1896	Nev.	No	2,500
New Atlanta Silver Mining Company	1871	Ida.	No	250,000

Appendixes

Limited-liability companies	Year	Area	Active?	Nominal capital
New Independence Mine	1898	Colo.	Yes	200,000
New Mexican Copper Company	1898	N. Mex.	No	100,000
Newhouse Tunnel Company	1893	Colo.	Yes	100,000
Argo Tunnel and Mining Company	1899	Colo.	Yes	350,000
Ni-Wot and Madeleine	1891	Colo.	No	200,000
Ni-Wot Gold Mines	1888	Colo.	Yes	200,000
North American Exploration Company	1895	Colo.	Yes	500,000
North Aspen Mines Syndicate	1893	Colo.	No	20,000
North-Eastern Stevens Mining Company	1878	Colo.	Yes	25,000
North Montana Company	1884	Mont.	No	150,000
Northern Belle Mining Company	1896	Nev.	Yes	50,000
Northern Syndicate	1887	Ariz.	Yes	25,000
Nouveau Monde Gold Mining Company [1]	1887	Colo.	Yes	200,000
Olathe Silver Mining Company	1881	Colo.	Yes	150,000
Fryer Hill Silver Mining Company	1885	Colo.	Yes	75,000
Old Guard Mining Company	1887	Ariz.	Yes	200,000
Old Lout Mining Company	1888	Colo.	Yes	105,000
"Old Reliable" Gold and Silver Mining Company	1885	Colo.	No	40,000
Orimon Gold Mining Company	1896	Colo.	Yes	3,000
Oro Fino Mines	1888	Ida.	Yes	300,000
Ouray Consolidated Silver Mining Company	1883	Colo.	Yes	250,000
Ouray Gold Mining Company	1887	Colo.	Yes	105,000
Pacific Mining Company	1869	Nev.	Yes	105,000
New Pacific Mining Company	1873	Nev.	Yes	7,500
Pacific Northwest Mining Corporation	1898	Mont.	No	200,000
Pay Rock Silver Mines	1890	Colo.	Yes	200,000
Payette Alluvial Gold Company	1897	Ida.	Yes	25,000
Phi Kappa Mining Company	1893	Ida.	Yes	6,000
Pinto Silver Mining Company	1871	Nev.	Yes	130,000
Basye Consolidated Silver Mining Company	1873	Nev.	Yes	200,000

[1] This name was changed to the Tarryall Creek Gold Company, Ltd., in July, 1889.

Limited-liability companies	Year	Area	Active?	Nominal capital
Pioche Mining Company	1888	Nev.	No	250,000
Pioneerville Gravel Gold	1894	Ida.	Yes	60,000
Pitkin (Colorado) Mining and Exploration Company	1888	Colo.	Yes	30,000
Pittsburgh Consolidated Gold Mines	1887	Nev.	Yes	80,000
Pittsburgh Consolidated Gold Mines	1890	Nev.	Yes	80,000
Planet Silver Mining Company	1874	Colo.	Yes	20,000
Poorman Gold Mines	1895	Ida.	Yes	250,000
Poorman Gold Mines	1896	Ida.	Yes	100,000
Poorman Gold Mines	1900	Ida.	Yes	80,000
*Poorman Silver Mines (of Colorado)	1891	Colo.	Yes	130,000
*Prescott Development Syndicate	1895	Ariz.	Yes	100,000
Princess Mining Company of London ᵐ	1887	Nev.	Yes	250,000
Prize Gold Mines	1896	Mont.	No	150,000
Puzzle Mine	1882	Colo.	No	200,000
Quartz Hill Consolidated Gold Mining Company	1881	Colo.	Yes	205,000
Denver Gold Company	1882	Colo.	Yes	80,000
Denver Gold Company	1888	Colo.	No	60,000
Quebrada Copper and Silver Mines	1888	Nev.	Yes	4,000
Queen of the Hills Silver Mines	1894	Ida.	Yes	250,000
Ray Copper Mines	1899	Ariz.	Yes	360,000
Red Mountain Mines	1881	Colo.	Yes	6,000
Red Mountain Silver Mines	1890	Colo.	Yes	50,000
Reese River Silver Mining Company	1865	Nev.	No	100,000
Renishaw Silver Mining Company	1871	Colo.	No	60,000
Republican Mountain Silver Mines	1880	Colo.	Yes	150,000
Revenue Mineral Company	1875	Colo.	Yes	75,000
Rich Hill Gold Mines	1892	Ariz.	No	80,000
Richmond Consolidated Mining Company	1871	Nev.	Yes	270,000
*Richardson Gold and Silver Mining Company	1884	Colo.	Yes	50,000
Rigi Group Gold Mining Company	1897	Colo.	Yes	130,000
Rocky Bar Wide West Gold	1888	Ida.	Yes	120,000

ᵐ See note c above.

Appendixes

Limited-liability companies	Year	Area	Active?	Nominal capital
Rocky Bar Wide West Gold	1889	Ida.	Yes	250,000
Rocky Mountain Exploration Company	1897	Colo.	Yes	10,000
Rocky Mountain Milling Company	1895	Colo.	Yes	10,000
Ruby Consolidated Mining Company	1872	Nev.	Yes	325,000
Ruby and Dunderberg Consolidated Mining Company	1881	Nev.	Yes	300,000
Ruby and Dunderberg Consolidated Mining Company, 1885	1885	Nev.	Yes	150,000
Ruby Mining Company	1890	Nev.	Yes	100,000
Ruby Nevada Mines	1895	Nev.	Yes	800
Russell Gold Mining Company [n]	1884	....	...	......
New Russell Gold and Exploration	1897	Colo.	Yes	50,000
St. Helen's Smelting and Sulphate of Copper Company	1890	Colo.	No	62,000
*St. Patrick Gold Mine Syndicate	1900	Colo.	Yes	80,000
San Bernardo Silver Mines	1890	Colo.	Yes	151,500
San Bernardo Mining Company	1892	Colo.	Yes	100,000
San Juan Reduction Company	1877	Colo.	No	12,000
San José Gold Mining Company	1889	Nev.	No	12,000
San Miguel Concession	1882	Colo.	No	6,000
Santa Catalina Gold and Silver Mining Company	1888	Ariz.	No	225,000
Sapphire and Ruby Company of Montana	1891	Mont.	Yes	450,400
"Sapphire" Gold and Silver Company	1886	Colo.	Yes	130,000
Saturn Silver Mining Company of Utah	1871	Utah	Yes	75,000
*Scottish Colorado Mining and Smelting Company	1884	Colo.	Yes	250,000
Searle Mining Company	1875	Colo.	Yes	10,000
Sevier Gold Mines °	1896	Utah	Yes	300,000

[n] This concern originally operated in North Carolina but its reconstruction, the New Russell Gold and Exploration, Ltd., acquired holdings in Colorado. It is not included in the total number of companies, however.

° This name was changed to Utah Consolidated Gold Mines, Ltd., in December, 1896.

APPENDIX I (*continued*)

Limited-liability companies	Year	Area	Active?	Nominal capital
Silver Bell Mining and Smelting Company	1890	Ariz.	Yes	170,000
Silver Chord Mining and Smelting Company	1882	Colo.	No	100,000
Silver City Reduction Company	1891	Ida.	Yes	10,000
Silver Ledge (1892)	1892	Colo.	No	15,000
Silver Peak Mining Company	1880	Colo.	Yes	250,000
Silver Plume Mining Company	1871	Colo.	Yes	30,000
Silver Star Mining Company	1871	Nev.	Yes	150,000
Silverledge Syndicate	1890	Colo.	No	15,000
Silverton Mining Company	1881	Colo.	No	102,500
Simmons Consolidated Gold Mining and Milling Company	1883	Colo.	No	100,000
Sleepy Hollow Gold Mine	1882	Colo.	No	50,000
Slide and Spur Gold Mines	1887	Colo.	Yes	400,000
Snowdrift Silver Mining and Reduction Company	1871	Colo.	Yes	75,000
South Aurora Silver Mining Company	1870	Nev.	Yes	300,000
South Aurora Consolidated Mining Company	1873	Nev.	Yes	300,000
Consolidated Mining Company	1878	Nev.	Yes	120,000
New Consolidated Mining Company	1886	Nev.	Yes	160,000
Consolidated Copper Company	1899	Nev.	No	100,000
South Central and Christiania Syndicate	1897	Ida.	Yes	8,000
Star Syndicate ᴾ	1889	Ariz.	Yes	. . . . . .
South Utah Mining Company	1871	Utah	No	60,000
Springdale Gold Mining Company	1897	Colo.	Yes	125,000
Springdale Gold Mines	1900	Colo.	Yes	70,000
Stanley Gold Mines	1890	Colo.	Yes	130,000
Star of Nevada Silver Mining Company	1871	Nev.	Yes	50,000
Sterling Gold Mines (Montana)	1886	Mont.	Yes	100,000
Storm Cloud Gold Mines	1888	Ariz.	No	100,000

ᴾ This company was registered with no set nominal capital.

Appendix I (*continued*)

Limited-liability companies	Year	Area	Active?	Nominal capital
Storm Cloud Syndicate	1893	Ariz.	No	50,000
Stratton's Independence	1899	Colo.	Yes	1,100,000
Summit Flat Gold Mines	1896	Ida.	Yes	150,000
Sunrise Mining Syndicate	1897	Mont.	Yes	30,000
New Sunrise Mining Syndicate	1898	Mont.	Yes	40,000
Swan-River Gold and Silver Mines	1888	Colo.	No	200,000
Swansea Smelting and Silver Mining Company	1871	Colo.	Yes	60,000
Sylvanite Gold Mines	1898	Colo.	No	12,000
Syndicate No. 1	1899	Ariz.	Yes	1,000
Tahoma Company	1885	Ida.	No	300,000
Tecoma Silver Mining Company	1873	Utah	Yes	300,000
Thunderer Gold Mining Company	1893	Dak.	Yes	300,000
Tinto Copper Mines [q]	1895	Ariz.	Yes	100,000
Toiyabe Silver Mining Company	1871	Nev.	No	100,000
Tomboy Gold Mines	1899	Colo.	Yes	300,000
Troy Silver Mining Company	1870	Nev.	Yes	200,000
Tubac Mining and Milling Company	1877	Ariz.	No	50,000
Tumacacori Mining and Land Company [r]	1870	Ariz.	Yes	......
Sonora Company	1874	Ariz.	No	1,000,000
Turquoise Mines (Calaite)	1900	N. Mex.	No	60,000
Turquoise Syndicate	1897	N. Mex.	Yes	10,000
Twin Lakes Hydraulic Gold Mining Syndicate	1883	Colo.	Yes	50,000
Twin Lakes Placers	1892	Colo.	Yes	30,000
Twin Lakes Placers	1899	Colo.	Yes	60,000
Tybo Consolidated Mining Company	1874	Nev.	No	250,000
Union Hill Silver Company	1866	Nev.	Yes	60,000
United Gold Placers	1886	Ida.-Mont.	No	100,000
United States Exploration Company	1896	Colo.	No	250,000
United States General Smelting and Mining Company	1872	Colo.	Yes	100,000
United States Gold Placers	1886	Colo.	Yes	150,000

[q] This name was changed to Clifton Tinto Copper Mines, Ltd., in March, 1897.
[r] Information regarding the registered capital of this concern is not available.

APPENDIX I (*continued*)

Limited-liability companies	Year	Area	Active?	Nominal capital
United States Gold Placers (New Company)	1889	Colo.	Yes	150,000
Utah	1884	Utah	No	150,000
*Utah Cotton Wood Mining and Smelting Company	1872	Utah	No	6,000
Utah Mining and Smelting Company ⁵	1871	Utah	Yes	120,000
Utah Silver Mining Company	1871	Utah	Yes	140,000
Utah Silver Lead Mining Company	1873	Utah	Yes	70,000
Vermont Mine Syndicate	1885	Colo.	Yes	60,000
Vesuvious Gold Mining Company	1883	Colo.	No	50,000
Victorian Mine Syndicate ᵗ	1890	Ariz.	No	. . . . . .
Victorine Gold Mining Company	1881	Nev.	Yes	305,000
Viola Company	1886	Ida.	Yes	150,000
New Viola Company	1889	Ida.	Yes	150,000
Viola Mining and Smelting Company	1886	Ida.	No	500,000
Vishnu Gold Company	1890	Ida.	Yes	200,000
Washoe United Consolidated Gold and Silver Mining Company	1864	Nev.	Yes	100,000
Nevada Land and Mining Company	1867	Nev.	Yes	45,000
Western States (U.S.A.) Finance Syndicate	1900	Colo.	Yes	1,000
Western Syndicate	1887	Ariz.	No	25,000
Whitehead Mining and Smelting Company	1881	Colo.	Yes	6,000
White Pine Water-Works Company	1872	Nev.	Yes	50,000
White River, Colorado, Coal Syndicate	1890	Colo.	Yes	24,960
White Star Consolidated Mining Company	1882	Colo.	Yes	50,000
Wide West Gold	1887	Ida.	No	25,000
Wilson Mining Company	1888	Ida.	No	350,000
Winamuck Silver Mining Company of Utah	1872	Utah	Yes	250,000

ˢ This name was changed to the Ophir Mining and Smelting Company of Utah, Ltd., in February, 1873.

ᵗ This company was registered with no set capital.

Appendixes

Limited-liability companies	Year	Area	Active?	Nominal capital
Wyoming Coal and Coke Company	1885	Wyo.	Yes	50,001
Wyoming Sweetwater Mining Company	1870	Wyo.	No	60,000
Yankee Girl Silver Mines	1890	Colo.	Yes	260,000
Yellow Mountain Gold Mining Syndicate	1898	Colo.	No	32,000
Total capital (518 companies)				£77,706,751

Appendix II

Anglo-American Mining Companies and Their Nominal Capital Registered with the Board of Trade, 1860–1901

Year	Active companies		Inactive companies		Reconstructions		Total	
	No.	Nominal capital	No.	Nominal capital	No.	Nominal capital	No.	Nominal capital
1864	1	£ 100,000	..	......	..	......	1	100,000
1865	..	......	4	400,000	..	......	4	400,000
1866	4	380,000	..	......	..	......	4	380,000
1867	..	......	2	210,000	1	45,000	3	255,000
1868	..	......	..	......	..	......	..	......
1869	3	190,000	1	200,000	..	......	4	390,000
1870	6	1,375,000	3	125,000	..	......	9	1,500,000
1871	20	3,211,000	14	1,339,000	..	......	34	4,550,000
1872	7	1,000,000	4	286,000	..	......	11	1,286,000
1873	6	659,000	3	350,640	4	577,500	13	1,587,140
1874	2	120,000	3	810,000	2	1,012,000	7	1,942,000
1875	3	110,000	1	42,000	..	......	4	152,000
1876	..	......	..	......	..	......	..	......
1877	2	132,000	2	62,000	1	75,000	5	269,000
1878	2	525,000	..	......	3	198,000	5	723,000
1879	..	......	..	......	1	60,000	1	60,000
1880	5	830,000	2	220,000	3	240,000	10	1,290,000
1881	8	941,000	4	387,500	3	670,000	15	1,998,500
1882	6	1,591,000	8	852,000	3	940,000	17	3,383,000
1883	9	2,170,000	8	503,000	..	......	17	2,673,000

APPENDIX II (*concluded*)

Year	Active companies		Inactive companies		Reconstructions		Total	
	No.	Nominal capital	No.	Nominal capital	No.	Nominal capital	No.	Nominal capital
1884	4	385,000	7	1,345,000	2	815,000	13	2,545,000
1885	5	910,001	4	1,010,000	4	660,000	13	2,580,001
1886	17	2,570,000	8	1,420,000	6	1,260,000	31	5,250,000
1887	11	4,480,000	10	2,290,000	4	915,000	25	7,685,000
1888	19	3,102,500	13	2,642,500	5	535,000	37	6,280,000
1889	7	1,320,000	2	192,000	11	2,610,000	20	4,122,000
1890	18	2,427,960	3	77,000	5	575,000	26	3,079,960
1891	15	2,333,400	4	250,000	2	335,000	21	2,918,400
1892	4	241,000	3	125,000	6	1,031,250	13	1,397,250
1893	8	1,141,000	2	70,000	4	440,000	14	1,651,000
1894	5	470,000	2	2,500	1	20,000	8	492,500
1895	18	2,215,200	3	211,000	4	750,800	25	3,177,000
1896	18	1,758,250	13	1,316,250	4	420,000	35	3,494,500
1897	14	1,020,000	..	......	6	750,000	20	1,770,000
1898	11	1,692,500	4	344,000	7	1,285,000	22	3,321,500
1899	7	2,031,000	3	22,000	5	715,000	15	2,768,000
1900	9	1,696,000	3	190,000	4	350,000	16	2,236,000
Total	274	£43,127,811	143	£17,294,390	101	£17,284,550	518	£77,706,751

Geographic Distribution of Anglo-American Mining Companies
Registered with the Board of Trade, 1860–1901

Area	Active companies		Inactive companies		Reconstructions		Total	
	No.	Nominal capital	No.	Nominal capital	No.	Nominal capital	No.	Nominal capital
Arizona	31	£ 4,441,000	19	2,297,000	4	1,815,000	54	8,553,000
Colorado	129	16,646,660	70	7,894,890	33	3,916,250	232	28,457,800
Dakota	2	3,300,000	..	....	..	....	2	3,300,000
Idaho	23	3,578,000	10	2,290,000	14	2,955,000	47	8,823,000
Montana	16	2,926,400	3	602,000	10	2,395,000	32	5,923,400
Nevada	42	6,559,500	23	2,778,500	21	2,881,300	86	12,219,300
New Mexico	8	1,120,000	4	191,000	..	....	12	1,311,000
Utah	20	4,406,250	7	916,000	19	3,322,000	46	8,644,250
Wyoming	3	150,001	4	325,000	..	....	7	475,001
Total	274	£43,127,811	143	£17,294,390	101	£17,284,550	518	£77,706,751

Dividends Paid by Anglo-American Mining Companies
Incorporated between 1860 and 1901

Name of company	Date paid	Total dividend paid	Percentage of capital issued *
Alturas Gold, Ltd.	1886–1891 £	48,357	17.2
American Belle Mines, Ltd.	1891	10,000	2.5
Arizona Copper Company, Ltd.	1892–1913	3,551,335	. . . .
Battle Mountain Mining Company, Nevada, U.S., Ltd.	1872	4,249	10.0
Bear Creek Gold, Ltd.	1891–1892	2,000	10.0
Big Creek Mining Company, Ltd.	1891	3,535	7.0
Camp Bird, Ltd.	1900–1911	1,505,000	177.0
Carlisle Gold Mining Company, Ltd.	1888	20,000	10.0
Central Development Syndicate, Ltd.	1898	415	10.0
Chicago Silver Mining Company, Ltd.	1874–1876	31,380	18.0
Colorado Terrible Lode Mining Company, Ltd.	1870–1875	14,175	13.5
Colorado United Mining Company, Ltd.	1883	3,081	1.0
Cortez Mines, Ltd.	1888–1892	147,000	49.0
De Lamar Company, Ltd.	1901–1905	570,000	142.5
De Lamar Mining Company, Ltd.	1891–1901	500,000	125.0

* Percentages are computed on the basis of total share capital issued, rather than on total nominal capital. No effort has been made, however, to take cognizance of capital invested in subsequent reorganizations of a concern or of earlier companies if the dividend payer was itself a reconstruction. Unfortunately, it is not always possible to determine exactly how much fresh capital was obtained by reorganization, however desirable that may be. Capital invested before or after reconstructions might alter very drastically a few of these percentages if computed. For example, records indicate that the Ruby Nevada Mines, Ltd., paid dividends totaling £1,120 or 130 per cent on its capital of £800 between 1896 and 1900. What is not indicated, however, is that this particular concern was the fourth reconstruction of the Ruby Consolidated Mining Company, Ltd., formed originally in 1872, and that a total of £345,955 had already been invested before the Ruby Nevada Mines, Ltd., raised its meager capital—all with no returns. Thus, dividends on the total investment between 1872 and 1900 aggregate .32 per cent rather than the impressive 130 per cent of first glance.

APPENDIX IV (*continued*)

Name of company	Date paid	Total dividend paid	Percentage of capital issued *
Eberhardt & Aurora Mining Company, Ltd.	1870–1877	38,539	7.7
Emma Silver Mining Company, Ltd.	1871–1872	195,000	19.5
Empire Mining Company, Ltd.	1886–1887	14,167	14.1
Elkhorn Mining Company, Ltd.	1890–1894	251,582	125.0
Fisk Gold Mine, Ltd.	1894	3,058	2.5
Flagstaff Silver Mining Company of Utah, Ltd.	1871–1873	123,000	41.0
Garfield, Ltd.	1886–1888	17,121	17.5
Harquahala Gold Mining Company, Ltd.	1893–1894	36,250	12.5
Henriett Mining & Smelting Company, Ltd.	1883	10,542	3.8
Idaho Exploring Company, Ltd.	1894–1896	7,411	13.3
Ingalls Gold Mining Company, Ltd.	1889–1890	107	5.0
Jay Hawk & Lone Pine Consol. Mining Co., Ltd.	1892	14,250	5.0
Kohinoor & Donaldson Consol. Mining Co., Ltd.	1881	250	2.5
Lady Franklin Mining Company, Ltd.	1887	18,002	10.0
Last Chance Silver Mining Company of Utah, Ltd.	1873	14,000	14.0
Lillie (Cripple Creek) Gold Mining Company, Ltd.	1898–1900	44,531	18.3
"Maid of Erin" Silver Mines, Ltd.	1891–1892	112,126	20.0
Mammoth Copperopolis of Utah, Ltd.	1872	375	2.5
Mineral Hill Silver Mines Company, Ltd.	1872	9,000	3.7
Montana Company, Ltd.	1884–1891	537,057	81.3
Montana Mining Company, Ltd.	1895–1899	90,355	13.7
Mount McClellan Mining Company, Ltd.	1890–1891	5,387	2.9
Mountain Chief Mining Company of Utah, Ltd.	1872	380	2.0
Nevada Land and Mining Company, Ltd.	1870	3,000	10.0
New California, Ltd.	1889	8,094	6.25

Appendixes

Name of company	Date paid	Total dividend paid	Percentage of capital issued *
New Elkhorn Mining Company, Ltd.	1896	4,375	1.1
New Guston Company, Ltd.	1888–1892	239,625	224.75
Ouray Gold Mining Company, Ltd.	1888	4,082	3.9
Pittsburgh Consolidated Gold Mines, Ltd.	1888	6,000	7.5
Poorman Mines, Ltd.	1891–1893	30,204	42.5
Richmond Consolidated Mining Company, Ltd.	1872–1895	882,768	324.0
Ruby Nevada Mines, Ltd.	1896–1900	1,120	130.0
South Aurora Silver Mining Company, Ltd.	1871	36,500	12.1
Sterling Gold Mines (Montana), Ltd.	1887	972	2.5
Stratton's Independence, Ltd.	1899–1908	949,798	86.3
Stratton's Independence, Ltd.	1908–1914	91,125	72.9
Tomboy Gold Mines Company, Ltd.	1899–1915	763,760	235.0
Twin Lakes Hydraulic Gold Mining Syndicate, Ltd.	1884–1887	9,885	19.7
Twin Lakes Placers, Ltd.	1894–1897	9,945	38.0
Utah Consolidated Gold Mines, Ltd.	1901–1904	600,000	200.0
Viola Company, Ltd.	1886–1888	52,500	35.0
Yankee Girl Silver Mines, Ltd.	1890–1891	104,000	40.0
Total		£ 11,750,770	

Bibliography

For the purposes of convenience the materials used in this study have been classified in the bibliography under the following major headings: Manuscripts; Special Corporate Records; Government Documents (British, Federal, State and Territorial); Court Testimony and Reports of Judicial Decisions (British, Federal, State and Territorial); Contemporary Newspapers and Periodicals; Contemporary Books and Pamphlets; Secondary Works, including both books and articles.

MANUSCRIPTS

a. *Miscellaneous*

Baldwin, Charles P. Bancroft personal interview statement of Oct. 15, 1885. Bancroft Library, University of California, Berkeley.

Beaver, James A. Papers and correspondence. Pennsylvania State University Libraries, University Park.

Bell, William A. Papers and correspondence. Colorado State Archives, Denver.

Byers, William N. Letterbook (1868–1871). University of Colorado Libraries, Boulder.

Colorado Territory. Records of Incorporation. Colorado State Archives, Denver.

Cripple Creek Gold Fields, Ltd. Books and correspondence of the registered office. In the possession of Miss Winifred Watt, 11 Pembridge Avenue, Twickenham, Middlesex.

Fish, Hamilton. Diaries and correspondence. Library of Congress, Washington.

Gladstone, William E. Papers and correspondence. British Museum, London.

Godbe, William Samuel. Bancroft personal interview statement of Sept. 2, 1884. Bancroft Library, University of California, Berkeley.

Great Britain, Foreign Office. Diplomatic and Consular Papers. Public Record Office, London.

Bibliography

John Taylor and Sons. MS index book of inspections (1883–1900). Located in the offices of John Taylor and Sons, 2 White Lion Court, London.

Johnson, Hiram André. Papers and correspondence. Bancroft Library, University of California, Berkeley.

Moran, Benjamin. Journals. 43 vols. 1851, 1857–1875. Library of Congress, Washington.

Old, Robert Orchard. Bancroft personal interview statement of May 21, 1886. Bancroft Library, University of California, Berkeley.

——. Diary (Feb. 6, 1866—Dec. 1, 1866). In the possession of Mr. George Old, Georgetown, Colorado.

Palmer, General William J. Papers and correspondence. Colorado State Archives, Denver.

Read, William Miles. Papers and correspondence. Bancroft Library, University of California, Berkeley.

Robertson, J. Barr. Letterbook (Aug. 21, 1874—May 28, 1877). Bancroft Library, University of California, Berkeley.

Sayr, Hal. Papers and correspondence. University of Colorado Libraries, Boulder.

Snowdrift Silver Mining and Reduction Company, Ltd. Account ledger (Dec. 27, 1871—March 31, 1873). University of Colorado Libraries, Boulder.

Teller, Henry Moore. Papers and correspondence. University of Colorado Libraries, Boulder.

Thomson, James. Diaries and correspondence. Bodleian Library, Oxford University, Oxford.

United States Department of State. Dispatches, Great Britain. National Archives, Washington.

Utah Territory. Territory papers. National Archives, Washington.

Wigfall, Louis T. Papers and correspondence. Library of Congress, Washington.

b. Theses and dissertations

Flinn, Michael W. "British Overseas Investment in Iron Ore Mining, 1870–1914." Unpublished M.A. thesis, University of Manchester.

Kokkinou, Epiphanie Clara. "The Political Career of Robert Cumming Schenck." Unpublished M.A. thesis, Miami University (Ohio).

Mack, Effie. "Life and Letters of William Morris Stewart, 1827–1909." Unpublished Ph.D. dissertation, University of California.

Bibliography

SPECIAL CORPORATE RECORDS

Companies Registration Office of the Board of Trade, Bush House, Strand, London. Here are housed the official corporate records of each joint-stock company registered in England and Wales since 1856. Files contain such documents as *Memorandums and Articles of Association,* resolutions concerning changes in capital or corporate structure or liquidation, either voluntary or involuntary. Copies of agreements and legal papers are frequently included, as well as an annual Summary of Capital and Shareholders for each company. In recent years many of the early files have been transferred to the Public Record Office. Offices of the Queen's Remembrancer, Parliament Square, Edinburgh, house similar materials on all joint-stock companies registered in Scotland.

The Stock Exchange, Share and Loan Department, Austin Friars, London. The department's reference library houses the prospectuses of all companies admitted to the Exchange since 1824. In addition, the Stock Exchange Archives contain a significant but little-used collection of materials pertaining to companies admitted from 1881 to the present. Included are many annual reports and accounts, circulars to shareholders, reports of meetings, resolutions, and other miscellaneous items of considerable historical worth which are generally unavailable elsewhere, either in England or in the United States.

GOVERNMENT DOCUMENTS

a. *British documents*

Hansard's Parliamentary Debates.

Foreign Office. Consular reports on trade and finance. United States Report for the Year 1892 [and 1895] on the Trade of the Consular District of Chicago. *Annual Series* No. 1233 (1893) [and No. 1725 (1896)].

——. United States Report for the Year 1892 [–1894, 1899] on the Trade of the Consular District of San Francisco. *Annual Series* No. 1251 (1893) [No. 1452 (1894), No. 1576 (1895), No. 2506 (1900)].

b. *United States government publications*

Census Reports. Eighth, Ninth, Tenth, and Eleventh (1860, 1870, 1880, 1890).

Congressional Globe.

Bibliography

Congressional Record.

Connection of Hon. Robert C. Schenck with the Emma Mine and Machado Claim, *House Report* No. 123, 44th Congress, 1st Sess., 1875–1876, serial 1708.

Decisions of the Department of the Interior and General Land Office in Cases Relating to the Public Lands.

Emma Mine Investigation, *House Report* No. 579, 44th Congress, 1st Sess., 1875–1876, serial 1711.

Report of the Commissions and Evidence Taken by the House of Representatives of the United States in Regard to the Sutro Tunnel, *House Report* No. 94, 42d Congress, 2d Sess., 1871–1872, serial 1543.

Report of the Committee on the Judiciary on Ownership of Real Estate in the Territories, *House Report* No. 954, 50th Congress, 1st Sess., 1887–1888, serial 2600.

Report of Committee on Mines and Mining to Amend the Alien Land Act, *House Report* No. 703, 50th Congress, 1st Sess., 1887–1888, serial 2600.

Report of the Committee on Mines and Mining to Amend Alien Land Act, *House Report* No. 1140, 51st Congress, 1st Sess., 1889–1890, serial 2810.

Report of Committee on Mines and Mining on Mining Interests of Aliens in the Territories, *Senate Report* No. 2690, 50th Congress, 2d Sess., 1888–1889, serial 2619.

Report of Committee on Mines and Mining concerning United States Suits Brought for Cutting Timber in Nevada, *Senate Report* No. 2, 50th Congress, Special Sess., 1889, serial 2619.

Report of Committee on the Public Lands on Land Titles to Aliens in the United States, *House Report* No. 2308, 48th Congress, 2d Sess., 1884–1885, serial 2328.

Report of Committee on Public Lands on Ownership of Real Estate in the Territories, *House Report* No. 3455, 49th Congress, 1st Sess., 1885–1886, serial 2445.

Report of Committee on Public Lands on Sale to Aliens of Certain Mineral Lands, *House Report* No. 3014, 50th Congress, 1st Sess., 1887–1888, serial 2605.

Report of the Director of the Mint upon the Statistics of the Production of the Precious Metals in the United States. 1882–1901. Published annually.

Report of the Industrial Commission on the Relations and Conditions of Capital and Labor Employed in the Mineral Industry, *House Document* No. 181, 57th Congress, 1st Sess., 1901–1902, serial 4342.

Bibliography

Report of James W. Taylor on the Mineral Resources of the United States East of the Rocky Mountains, *House Executive Document No. 273*, 40th Congress, 2d Sess., 1867–1868, serial 1343.

Statistics of Mines and Mining in the States and Territories West of the Rocky Mountains. 1867–1875. Published annually.

United States Statutes at Large.

c. *State and territorial documents*

Annual Report of the State Mineralogist of the State of Nevada for 1866. Carson City: Eckley, 1867.

Report of E. Le Neve Foster, State Geologist of Colorado. N.p., 1884.

Laws of the Territory of Arizona, 13th Sess., 1885.

General Laws of the Territory of Idaho Passed at the Fifteenth Session of the Territorial Legislature, 1888–1889.

General Laws of the State of Idaho, 1st Sess., 1890–1891.

Laws, Memorials, and Resolutions of the Territory of Montana, 7th Sess., 1871–1872; 8th Sess., 1874; 15th Extra. Sess., 1887; 16th Sess., 1889.

General Statutes of the State of Nevada, 1885.

Laws of New Mexico, 28th Sess., 1889.

Revised Code of North Dakota, 1895.

Laws of the Territory of Utah, 28th Sess., 1888.

COURT TESTIMONY AND REPORTS OF JUDICIAL DECISIONS

a. *British reports*

The Law Reports. 1865–   . These include Equity, Queen's Bench Division, Common Pleas, Chancery, and Chancery Appeals.

b. *Federal court testimony and reports*

Blatchford, *Reports*. . . . Circuit Court, 2d Circuit. 24 vols. 1845–1887.

The Emma Silver Mining Company, (Limited) of London, vs. Trenor W. Park, and H. Henry Baxter, Impleaded, &c. Complainants' Testimony and Defendants' Testimony. Circuit Court, 2d Circuit, 1877. Western Americana Collection, Yale University, New Haven.

The Federal Reporter, series I. 300 vols. 1880–1924.

The Pacific Reporter, 1883–   .

Sawyer, *Reports*. . . . Circuit and District Courts, 9th Circuit. 14 vols. 1870–1891.

United States Reports. 1875–   .

Bibliography

c. State and territorial reports

Colorado Reports. 1864–   .
Montana Reports. 1868–   .
Nevada Reports. 1865–   .
South Dakota Reports. 1890–   .
Utah Reports. 1855–   .

CONTEMPORARY NEWSPAPERS AND PERIODICALS

a. American newspapers and periodicals

Baltimore American and Commercial Advertiser. Dec. 31, 1875.
The Boulder [Colo.] *County News.* Oct. 12, 1869—Jan. 9, 1874.
Canon City [Colo.] *Times.* Feb. 16, 1861.
The Colorado Miner (Georgetown). June 6, 1867—Nov. 10, 1888. Weekly.
The Colorado Transcript (Golden). Jan. 1, 1868–1871.
Copp's Land Owner (Washington). April, 1874—March, 1890. Title is *Copp's Western Land Owner* until 1875.
Daily Central City [Colo.] *Register.* Jan. 1, 1868—Jan. 1, 1870; Jan. 1, 1872—Nov. 1, 1872. Title is *Daily Miner's Register* prior to July 25, 1868.
The Daily Colorado Herald (Central City). Jan. 8, 1868—Dec. 30, 1868.
Daily Colorado Miner (Georgetown). July 1, 1869—Aug. 19, 1869; Jan. 10, 1873—March 11, 1874.
The Daily Colorado Tribune (Denver). May 15, 1867—Dec. 30, 1871.
Daily Denver Times. June 24, 1872—June 30, 1874.
Denver Mirror. June 29, 1873.
The Denver Republican. Oct. 22, 1882; April 26, 1892.
The Engineering and Mining Journal (New York). 1866–1901. Title is *American Journal of Mining* until July, 1869.
Georgetown [Colo.] *Courier.* Aug. 27, 1898.
Great Falls [Mont.] *Tribune.* May 3, 1887.
Mining and Scientific Press (San Francisco). 1860–1901. Title from 1870 to 1872 is *Scientific Press.*
The Mining Industry and Tradesman (Denver). Dec. 3, 1891.
The Mining Review (Georgetown and Denver). Sept. 1872—May, 1876.
The Nation. 1865–1880.
New York Evening Post. April 30, 1877.
New York Tribune. 1874–1877.

Rocky Mountain News (Denver). Aug. 27, 1860—Aug. 28, 1862; March 3, 1863—Dec. 30, 1873.

St. Louis Democrat. Jan. 12, 1874.

The Salt Lake Daily Herald. July, 1872—July, 1874. Broken series.

San Francisco Chronicle. June 5, 1870.

San Francisco News Letter. June 8, 1872.

Utah Mining Gazette (Salt Lake City). Aug. 30, 1873—June 20, 1874.

Utah Mining Journal (Salt Lake City). March 13, 1873—May 21, 1873.

b. *London newspapers and periodicals*

Anglo-Colorado Mining and Milling Guide. Feb. 26, 1898—May 31, 1905. After May, 1905, the title becomes *The Anglo-American and Mexican Mining Guide and General Financier.*

Daily Express and Morning Herald. Nov. 2, 1900.

Daily Telegraph. Nov. 24, 1871.

The Economist, Weekly Commercial Times, Bankers' Gazette, and Railway Monitor: A Political, Literary, and General Newspaper. 1860–1902.

Financial & Mining News. Jan. 23, 1883—June 24, 1884.

The Financial Critic. March, 1885—Dec. 1886.

The Financial News. March 22, 1887.

Financial Observer and Mining Herald. Jan. 28, 1890—Dec. 27, 1890.

Financial Times. Dec. 8, 1900.

The Financial "Who's Who?" May 6, 1896—Dec. 30, 1896.

The Hour. Jan. 4, 1876—April 27, 1876.

Investors' Guardian. June 15, 1872.

Investors' Monthly Manual. Jan. 25, 1873.

Iron Times. Nov. 11, 1871.

The Journal of The Shareholders' Corporation, Limited. June 16, 1880—Nov. 17, 1880.

The Mining Journal, Railway and Commercial Gazette: Forming A Complete Record of the Proceedings of all Public Companies. 1860–1902.

The Mining Magazine and Review; A Monthly Record of Mining, Smelting, Quarrying & Engineering. Jan., 1872—June, 1872.

The Mining News. Jan. 5, 1889—May 11, 1889.

The Mining World, and Engineering & Commercial Record. April 8, 1871—Jan. 8, 1876.

The Monetary & Mining Gazette. Jan. 2, 1875—Dec. 25, 1875.

The Railway News and Joint Stock Journal. July 19, 1873; Aug. 23, 1873.

The Rialto. Dec. 11, 1897.

Bibliography

Standard. Feb. 1, 1872; April 29, 1875.

The Statist, a Weekly Journal for Economists and Men of Business. 1878–1902.

The Stock Exchange Review. Jan., 1871—Dec., 1874.

The Times. 1860–1902.

CONTEMPORARY BOOKS AND PAMPHLETS

Bartlett, William. *The Investors' Directory to Marketable Stocks and Shares, With a Description of Their Nature, Security, etc.* London: Clayton & Co., 1876.

Bonwick, James. *The Mormons and the Silver Mines.* London: Hodder & Stoughton, 1872.

Chittenden, L. E. *The Emma Mine.* New York: B. H. Tyrrel, 1876.

Colorado Territorial Board of Immigration. *Resources and Advantages of Colorado.* Denver: Rocky Mountain News, 1873.

Corbett, Thomas B. *The Colorado Directory of Mines.* Denver: Rocky Mountain News, 1879.

Corregan, Robert A., and David F. Lingane (eds. & comp.). *Colorado Mining Directory: Containing an Accurate Description of the Mines, Mining Properties and Mills, and the Mining, Milling, Smelting, Reducing and Refining Companies, and Corporations of Colorado.* Denver: Colorado Mining Directory Co., 1883.

The Cripple Creek Gold-Fields Syndicate, Limited (Prospectus, Sept. 19, 1896). Bodleian Library, Oxford University, Oxford.

Cushman, Samuel, and J. P. Waterman. *The Gold Mines of Gilpin County.* N.p., 1876.

Dilke, Charles Wentworth. *Greater Britain: A Record of Travel in English-speaking Countries during 1866 and 1867.* 2 vols. London: Macmillan, 1868.

Douglas, Charles. *Report on Certain Mines, Owned by the Pacific National Gold-Mining Company of Colorado, and Edward J. Jaques of New York, Situated Near Central City, Colorado.* New York: S. W. Green, 1877.

"An Edinburgh Lady." *A Rapid Run to the Wild West.* Edinburgh: R. & R. Clark, 1884.

Farrell, Ned E. *Colorado, the Rocky Mountain Gem, as It Is in 1868.* Chicago: Western News Co., 1868.

Fossett, Frank. *Colorado; Its Gold and Silver Mines.* New York: Crawford, 1879. 2d ed. New York: Crawford, 1880.

Gilpin, William. *Notes on Colorado; and Its Inscription in the Physical*

Geography of the North American Continent. London: Witherby & Co., 1871.

Hollister, Ovando J. *The Mines of Colorado.* Springfield, Mass.: Samuel Bowles & Co., 1867.

Ingham, G. Thomas. *Digging Gold among the Rockies.* Philadelphia: Hubbard Brothers, 1880.

James, Burton S. *An Analysis of Modern Mine Promotion.* London: Paternoster Printing Co., 1900.

"Jaycee." *Public Companies from the Cradle to the Grave; or, How Promoters Prey on the Public.* London: Wyman & Sons, 1883.

Kantner, H. W. B. *A Hand Book on the Mines, Miners, and Minerals of Utah.* Salt Lake City: R. W. Sloan, n.d.

Laing-Meason, Malcolm Ronald. *Sir William's Speculations; or, The Seamy Side of Finance.* London: Sampson Low *et al.*, 1886.

Lawrence, George Alfred. *Silverland.* London: Chapman & Hall, 1873.

Legard, Allayne Beaumont. *Colorado.* London: Chapman & Hall, 1872.

Lyon, James E. *Dedicated to William M. Stewart, My Attorney in the "Emma Mine" Controversy in 1871.* N.p., n.d.

Macdougall, Alexander W. *The Emma Mine.* N.p., 1874.

——. *Emma Mine.* London: Witherly & Co., 1876.

Marsh, John Roy. *Cripple Creek: The Richest Goldfields of the World.* London: Sheppard & St. John, 1896.

Mining Bureau of the Pacific Coast. San Francisco: Bacon & Co., 1872.

Murphy, John R. *The Mineral Resources of the Territory of Utah, with Mining Statistics and Maps.* London: Trubner & Co., 1872.

The New York Mining Directory. New York: Hollister & Goddard, 1880.

Old, Robert Orchard. *Colorado: United States, America.* London: British & Colorado Mining Bureau, 1869.

——. *Colorado: United States, America, Its Minerals and Other Resources.* London: British & Colorado Mining Bureau, 1872.

Paffard, Samuel Thomas. *The True History of the Emma Mine.* London: W. H. & L. Collingridge, 1873.

Prospectus of the American Bureau of Mines. New York: W. C. Bryant, 1866. New York Public Library.

Rae, William Fraser. *Westward by Rail: A Journey to San Francisco and Back and a Visit to the Mormons.* 2d ed. London: Longmans, Green & Co., 1871. 3d ed. London: W. Isbister & Co., 1874.

The Rocky Mountain Directory and Colorado Gazetteer, for 1871. Denver: S. S. Wallihan & Co., 1870.

A Selected List of Companies, Foreign Loans, and Miscellaneous Projects, Many of Which Were Issued under the Auspices of Albert Grant,

Bibliography

Shewing the Nominal Amount of Capital, and Price of Issue, As Taken from Each Prospectus, (Copies of Which Are Contained Herein), Also the Capital Paid Up, Market Value of Same, and Uncalled Capital. London: Grobecker, Son & Co., 1874.

Silliman, Benjamin. *Report of Professor B. Silliman on the Emma Silver Mine.* Salt Lake City: Oct. 16, 1871. Western Americana Collection, Yale University, New Haven.

——. *Supplemental Report of Prof. B. Silliman on the Emma Mine in Little Cottonwood Canyon, Utah Territory.* Salt Lake City: Feb. 29, 1872. Western Americana Collection, Yale University, New Haven.

Skinner, Thomas (ed.). *The Stock Exchange Year-Book and Diary for 1875.* London: Cassell, Petter & Galpin, n.d.

Skinner, Walter R. (ed.). *The Mining Manual.* London: W. R. Skinner, 1887–   . Published annually.

Smith, Matthew Hale. *Bulls and Bears of New York, with the Crisis of 1873, and the Cause.* Hartford & Chicago: J. B. Burr & Co., 1874.

Sutro, Adolph. *The Sutro Tunnel and Railway to the Comstock Lode in the State of Nevada.* London: Edward Stanford, 1873.

Taylor, Bayard. *Colorado: A Summer Trip.* New York: G. P. Putnam & Sons, 1867.

The Territory of Arizona; A Brief History and Summary of the Territory's Acquisition, Organization, and Mineral, Agricultural and Grazing Resources; Embracing a Review of Its Indian Tribes—Their Depredations and Subjugation; and Showing in Brief the Present Condition and Prospects of the Territory. Tucson: Citizen Publishing Co., 1874.

Townshend, Samuel Nugent. *Colorado: Its Agriculture, Stockfeeding, Scenery, and Shooting.* London: "The Field" Office, 1879.

——. *Our Indian Summer in the Far West.* London: G. Whittingham, 1880.

Vanderbilt, Lincoln. *The New and Wonderful Explorations of Professor Lincoln Vanderbilt, the Great American Traveller, in the Territories of Colorado, Arizona, & Utah, and the States of California, Nevada, & Texas, Adapted for the Emigrants, Settlers, Mine Speculators, Fortune Hunters, and Travellers.* London: J. W. Last, 1870.

Vivian, Henry Hussey. *Notes of a Tour in America.* London: Edward Stanford, 1878.

Weston, William. *Descriptive Pamphlet of Some of the Principal Mines and Prospects of Ouray County, Colorado.* Denver: Republican Publishing Co., 1883.

Bibliography

SECONDARY WORKS

Ashmead, Edward. *Twenty-Five Years of Mining, 1880–1904.* London: Mining Journal, 1909.

Athearn, Robert G. *Westward the Briton.* New York: Scribner's, 1953.

Bagehot, Walter. *Lombard Street.* 14th ed. London: John Murray, 1915.

Balfour, Jabez Spencer. *My Prison Life.* London: Chapman & Hall, 1907.

Bancroft, Hubert Howe. *History of Utah.* San Francisco: History Co., 1890.

Beeson, J. J. *Report on the Property of the Emma Silver Mines Company in Little Cottonwood Mining District, Alta, Utah.* N.p., 1919.

Brayer, Herbert O. *William Blackmore.* 2 vols. Denver: Bradford Robinson, 1949.

Byers, William N. *Encyclopedia of Biography of Colorado.* Chicago: Century Publishing Co., 1901.

Clapham, Sir John. *The Bank of England.* 2 vols. New York: Macmillan, 1945.

Clements, Roger V. "British Investment and American Legislative Restrictions in the Trans-Mississippi West, 1880–1900," *Mississippi Valley Historical Review,* XLII (Sept., 1955), 207–227.

———. "The Farmers' Attitude toward British Investment in American Industry," *Journal of Economic History,* XV (June, 1955), 151–159.

Davis, William W. *History of Whiteside County, Illinois.* 2 vols. Chicago: Pioneer Publishing Co., 1908.

Federal Writers' Project. *Utah.* New York. Hastings House, 1941.

Furniss, Harry. *Some Victorian Men.* New York & London: Dodd, Mead & Co., 1924.

Gilbert, W. S., and Arthur Sullivan. *The Complete Plays of Gilbert and Sullivan.* New York: Modern Library, 1936.

Hall, Frank. *History of the State of Colorado.* 4 vols. Chicago: Blakely Printing Co., 1891.

Hammond, John Hays. *The Autobiography of John Hays Hammond.* 2 vols. New York: Farrar & Rinehart, 1935.

Harpending, Asbury. *The Great Diamond Hoax and Other Stirring Incidents in the Life of Asbury Harpending.* Ed. by James H. Wilkins. San Francisco: Barry, 1913.

Hess, Henry (ed.). *The Critic Black Book.* 2 vols. London: British & Colonial Publications Co., 1901.

Hills, Fred. *The Official Manual of the Cripple Creek District Colorado, U. S. A.* Colorado Springs: Fred Hills, 1900.

Bibliography

History of Clear Creek and Boulder Valleys, Colorado. Chicago: O. L. Baskin & Co., 1880.

Hoover, Herbert. *The Memoirs of Herbert Hoover.* 3 vols. New York: Macmillan, 1951–1952.

Jackson, W. Turrentine. "The Infamous Emma Mine: A British Interest in the Little Cottonwood District, Utah Territory," *Utah Historical Quarterly,* XXIII (Oct., 1955), 339–362.

Jefferys, J. B. "The Denomination and Character of Shares, 1855–1885," *Economic History Review,* XVI (1946), 45–55.

Jenks, Leland H. *The Migration of British Capital to 1875.* New York: Knopf, 1927.

Johnson, Allen, and Dumas Malone (eds.), *Dictionary of American Biography.* 22 vols. New York: Scribner's, 1928–1944.

Jones, Olive M. "Bibliography of Colorado Geology & Mining," *Colorado State Geological Survey Bulletin* No. 7. Denver, 1914.

Joyner, Fred B. "Robert Cumming Schenck, First Citizen and Statesman of the Ohio Valley," *Ohio State Archaeological and Historical Quarterly,* LVIII (July, 1949), 286–297.

Lee, Sidney, *et al.* (eds.). *Dictionary of National Biography.* 54 vols. London: Smith, Elder & Co., 1901–1949.

Lewis, Cleona, and Karl T. Schlotterbeck. *America's Stake in International Investments.* Washington: Brookings Institution, 1938.

Lindley, Curtis H. *A Treatise on the American Law Relating to Mines and Mineral Lands within the Public Land States and Territories and Governing the Acquisition and Enjoyment of Mining Rights in Lands of the Public Domain.* 2 vols. San Francisco: Bancroft-Whitney Co., 1897.

Nevins, Allan. *Hamilton Fish.* New York: Dodd, Mead & Co., 1936.

Oberholtzer, Ellis Paxson. *Jay Cooke.* 2 vols. Philadelphia: George W. Jacobs, 1907.

Perrigo, Lynn. "The Cornish Miners of Early Gilpin County," *Colorado Magazine,* XIV (May, 1937), 92–101.

Portrait and Biographical Record of Denver and Vicinity, Colorado. Chicago: Chapman Publishing Co., 1898.

Ratner, Sidney (ed.). *New Light on the History of Great American Fortunes.* New York: Augustus M. Kelley, 1953.

Rickard, Thomas Arthur. *A History of American Mining.* New York & London: McGraw-Hill, 1932.

———. *Retrospect.* New York & London: McGraw-Hill, 1937.

Shannon, H. A. "The First Five Thousand Limited Companies and Their Duration," *Economic History,* II (Jan., 1932), 396–424.

———. "The Limited Companies of 1866–1883," *Economic History Review*, IV (Oct., 1933), 290–307.

Shinn, Charles Howard. *The Story of the Mine*. New York: D. Appleton, 1901.

Sprague, Marshall. *Money Mountain*. Boston: Little, Brown & Co., 1953.

Stewart, William Morris. *Reminiscences of Senator William M. Stewart of Nevada*. Ed. by George Rothwell Brown. New York: Neale, 1908.

Teetor, Henry Dudley. "Mines and Miners around Idaho Springs," *Magazine of Western History*, XII (Oct., 1890), 667–669.

———. "Some of the Mines and Miners of Georgetown, Colorado," *Magazine of Western History*, XII (Sept., 1890), 490–504.

Venn, J. A. (comp.). *Alumni Cantabrigienses*. 8 vols. Cambridge: University Press, 1947.

Waters, Frank. *Midas of the Rockies*. Denver: University of Denver Press, 1949.

Whitney, Orson F. *History of Utah*. 4 vols. Salt Lake City: George Q. Cannon & Sons. 1893.

Who's Who in America. Chicago: A. N. Marquis Co., 1899–   . Published biennially.

Who's Who in Mining and Metallurgy. London: Mining Journal, 1908–   .

Who Was Who (1897–1916). London: A. & C. Black, 1920.

Wold, Ansel (comp.). *Biographical Directory of the American Congresses*. Washington: Government Printing Office, 1928.

Young, Frank C. *Echoes from Arcadia*. Denver: privately printed, 1903.

Index

Index

Index

Lewis and Son, 141, 176

Limited liability, 12

Litigation: numerous examples of, 129-136; expenses of, 136-137; effects of on investment, 137-138; of the Emma Silver Mining Company, Ltd., 161, 171-172, 175, 176-177

London and Colorado Company, 45-46

Longmaid, John, 56, 71, 223

Lowe, Theodore H., 93-94

Lucy Phillips Gold and Silver Mining Company, Ltd., 84

Lyon, James E., 140, 153, 159

McCook, Edward M., 24

McCree, William, 97

McDermott, Walter, 130

Macdougall, Alexander, 174

McKean, Judge, 161

McLaughlin, Eugene, 37

Malet, Alexander, 109

Mammoth Copperopolis of Utah, Ltd., 223-224

Marks, Harry, 40

Maxwell, Nicholas, 71, 105-106, 109-110; criticism of, 112; salary of, 118

Memorandums and Articles of Association, 80

Middlemen, 39-41

Mine management: general problems of, 92-120, 236; distance factor in, 92-93; criticism of, 105-107, 111-112; joint arrangements for, 108-111

Mine managers: selection of, 94-95; inexperience of, 96-99; criticism of, 105ff, 111-112; rapid turnover of, 112-113; salaries of, 118-119

Mineral Assets Company, Ltd., 81

Mineral Hill Silver Mines Company, Ltd., 54

Mineral Mines Company, 79

Mining: speculative aspects, 12, 231-232; "experts" in, 69

Mining and Financial Trust Syndicate, Ltd., 48

Mining Bureau of the Pacific Coast, 46-47

Mining Journal, 8, 16, 141, 193

Mining law: complexity of, 121-122;

diverse interpretation of, 191-192; act of 1872, description of, 192-193; act of 1872, effect on British concerns, 193; act of 1872, interpretation of, 198-199; act of 1872, suggested changes in, 200-203

Mining World, 16, 35, 113, 114, 122, 123, 125, 150, 159, 167

Misrepresentation, 55-56, 58, 129-132

Moffat, David H., 75

Montana Company, Ltd., 60, 63, 116-117; versus the St. Louis Mining and Milling Company, Ltd., 123-124; expenses of litigation of, 137; and the Alien Land Law, 209

Montana Mining Company, Ltd., *see* Montana Company, Ltd.

Moon-Anchor Consolidated Gold Mines, Ltd., 28

Moran, Benjamin, 23, 67, 150, 152, 156

Morgan, Henry, 58

Mormons and mining, 11

Mortgages, hidden, 67-68

Mountain Chief Mining Company of Utah, Ltd., 229

Mudsill Mining Company, Ltd., *v.* Watrous, *et al.,* 129-131

Muir, Francis, 119

Murphy, John R., 106

Nancarrow, James, 72

Nation, 151, 157, 162, 169, 172

National Tunnel Company, 32

Nepotism in the appointment of mine officials, 94-95

Nevada Freehold Properties Trust, 52-53, 59, 65, 79

New Colorado Silver Mining Company, Ltd., 225-226

New Eberhardt Company, Ltd., 118, 119

New Emma Silver Mining Company, Ltd., 178-179

New Emma Silver Mining Company, 1886, Ltd., 179

Newberry, J. S., 54

Newhouse, Samuel, 23-24, 99

North American Exploration Company, Ltd., 48, 137-138

Index

O'Connor, William S., 62
Old, Robert O.: *Colorado, United States, America,* 18; promotional activities of, 34, 44-45, 79
Old Guard Mining Company, Ltd., 33, 63
Ophir Mining and Smelting Company, Ltd., 81-82
Options, 34-35
Ore: shipment of to England for smelting, 14-15, 44, 141; displayed abroad, 38-39, 44; "salting" of, 131
Orr-Ewing, Archibald, 165
Overcapitalization, 86
Overend and Gurney, 4
Oxenford, Alfred H., 119

Pacific Mining Company, Ltd., 99
Paffard, Samuel T., *True History of the Emma Mine,* 168-169
Panic: of 1864 and 1866, 4; of 1873, 223-224; of 1893, 225-227
"Parent" companies, 47-48
Park, Trenor W.: role of in promotion of the Emma Silver Mining Company, Ltd., 140ff; acquires shares of the Emma Silver Mining Company of New York, 154; "bulling" activities of, 155; disposes of his English shares, 155-156; ousted from directorate, 165; criticism of, 166-167; *see also* Emma Silver Mining Company, Ltd.
Parrington, Vernon L., 238
Patrick, J. N. H., 110-111
Pearce, Richard, 102, 220, 225
Pemberton, Edward Leigh, 146
Periodical advertising of mines, 36
Petitions: from the "honest miners of Utah," 174; on the Alien Land Law, 206-207
Phillips, John Arthur, 101
Phillpotts, Thomas, 95
Pittsburgh Consolidated Gold Mines, Ltd., 105
Power of attorney: need of, 35; abuse of, 114
Prices, 86-88
Probert, Edward, 98, 126

"Process mania," 6-7
Promoters: description of, 21-29; problems of, 30-31; techniques of, 34ff, 51-76
Promotion: techniques, 34ff, 51-76; via mail or cable, 36-37; role of English agents in, 39-41; co-operative, 43-50; expenses of, 148
Prospectuses: described, 58-67; omissions from, 67-68
Publicity: via newspapers and magazines, 16-17; via pamphlet, 18-19
Puleston, John J., 147
Purchase guarantees, 74-75
Pyramid Range Silver Mountain Company, Ltd., 57-58

Quartz Hill Consolidated Gold Mining Company, Ltd., 66, 134

Railroad development and mining investment, 8-10
Ray Copper Mines, Ltd., 105
Raymond, Rossiter W., 51, 200
Read, William M., 118
Reconstructions, 217-218; *see also* Joint-stock companies
Reed, Edward T., 56
Reed, Verner Z., 27-29
Reese River Silver Mining Company, Ltd., 53-54, 133-134
Republican Mountain Silver Mines, Ltd., 58-59, 93
Richardson, Charles S., 16, 198
Richmond Consolidated Mining Company, Ltd.: dividends of, 69, 230; criticism of management of, 98; litigation of, 125-126; timber suits of, 196-197
Rickard, Alfred, 109
Rickard, James, 102
Rickard, Thomas A., 71, 95, 103, 107-108, 116
Risk in mining, 12, 231-232
Robertson, J. Barr, 36-37, 86-87, 171
Robinson, William E., 203
Roche, Hugh H., 94
Rocky Mountain News, 16
Rodham, Thomas, 97
Rossetti, William M., 96

Index